HOTEL TRÓPICO

JERRY DÁVILA

Hotel Trópico

BRAZIL AND THE CHALLENGE OF AFRICAN DECOLONIZATION, 1950–1980

DUKE UNIVERSITY PRESS
DURHAM AND LONDON
2010

Printed in the United States of America on acid-free paper ∞
Designed by C. H. Westmoreland
Typeset in Quadraat by Achorn International, Inc.
Library of Congress Cataloging-in-Publication Data appear
on the last printed page of this book.

FOR ELLEN

Contents

Acknowledgments

THIS BOOK EXPLORES the swift and often tumultuous change that the Atlantic world underwent in the second half of the twentieth century, driven by the currents of decolonization, developmentalism, authoritarianism, and the cold war. The main focus is on the way a cohort of Brazilians perceived these currents of change, and particularly on what their perceptions reveal about Brazilian racial thought. In writing this book it was possible to cover various places and themes only because of the support of many friends and colleagues in Brazil and the United States, who shared materials, asked questions, opened doors, and granted me time for research. And as a book that relies heavily on oral histories, it is also the fruit of the generosity of many diplomats, intellectuals, artists, activists, and their relatives, who gave interviews about their experiences relating to Brazil and Africa.

My interest in Brazilian connections with Africa, and in Brazilian racial identity, developed in graduate school at Brown University through the encouragement of Thomas Skidmore and of Anani Dzidzienyo, whose interest in the African connection and the Afro-Brazilian condition nourished and guided this project from inception to publication.

Anani Dzidzienyo, Jeffrey Lesser, John David Smith, Mark Wilson, and two anonymous readers from Duke University Press read and commented on the entire manuscript. I am grateful to Valerie Millholland, my editor at Duke University Press, as well as Miriam Angress, associate editor, who have been consistent and thoughtful advocates. Paulina Alberto, George

Reid Andrews, Jürgen Buchenau, Greg Childs, Marshall Eakin, Lyman Johnson, Jeffrey Needell, and Thomas Rogers also read portions of the manuscript and offered advice and encouragement. Many others generously shared materials, offered opportunities to discuss questions, and provided support, among them Peter Beattie, Leslie Bethell, Amy Chazkel, Ralph Della Cava, Tom Cohen, Todd Diacon, James Green, Thomas Holloway, Hal Langfur, Bryan McCann, Zachary Morgan, Timothy Power, Uri Rosenheck, Wayne Selcher, Ken Serbin, Ariel Svarch, Luiz Valente, Daryle Williams, Erica Windler, Joel Wolfe, and James Woodard.

Many in Brazil offered advice, helped obtain access to sources, and provided introductions to interviewees. My thanks to Paulo Roberto de Almeida, Marcelo Bittencourt, Celso Castro, Vivaldo Costa Lima, Claudio DeNipotli, Peter Fry, Cristina Gouveia, Monica Grin, Keila Grinburg, Antonio Sergio Guimarães, Andre Joanilho, Angela Lühnig, Marcos Chor Maio, Beatriz Mamigonian, José Carlos Sebe Bom Meihy, Abdias and Elisa Larkin do Nascimento, Satiro Nunes, Paulo Sérgio Pinheiro, João José Reis, Cláudio Ribeiro, Heloisa Pimenta Rocha, Jocélio Teles dos Santos, Leila Santos, Lilia Moritz Schwarcz, Sandra Selles, Mariza Soares, Omar Thomaz, and Bruno Pessoa Villela. Sônia Oliveira transcribed many hours of interviews. Friends in Brazil, among them Andy Castonguay, Nando Duarte, Jürgen Heye, Beth Marino, Adilson Rachid, Gabi and Leo Rego, Luis Filipe Silveiro Lima, and Alina Skonieczny made my family and me feel at home during research trips.

In Lisbon, Maria Isabel Fevereiro, director of the Portuguese foreign ministry archive, offered access to one of the richest document troves this book draws upon, with unequaled openness and efficiency. The staff of the reading room of the Itamaraty Historical Archive in Brasília was also always welcoming and helpful.

Opportunities to present and discuss research provided a means for challenging and sharpening the analysis in this book. I am grateful to students and colleagues at UNC Charlotte, Georgetown University, the Manoel Oliveira Lima Library at the Catholic University of America, the University of Maryand, Columbia University, Denison University, Davidson College, Pontifícia Universidade Católica (PUC-Rio), the Federal University of Rio de Janeiro, the Federal University of Minas Gerais, the Getúlio Vargas Foundation/CPDOC, the Casa Rui Barboza, FIOCRUZ, Fluminense Federal University, the State University of Campinas, the University of São Paulo, the Sverdlin Institute of Latin American Studies at

Tel Aviv University, and the Brazil Centre at Oxford University. Students in the graduate seminar in Latin American history at Emory University engaged in a stimulating discussion of a full draft of the manuscript that benefited the book greatly.

This book was made possible by generous support from the National Endowment for the Humanities, Fulbright and Fulbright-Hays scholarships, and faculty research grants from the University of North Carolina, Charlotte. During my tenure on the Fulbright, Marco Antonio Pamplona, Angela Paiva, and Karl Erik Schollhammer, colleagues at the Pontifícia Universidade Católica (PUC-Rio), offered welcoming and stimulating dialogue. My thanks too to the Fulbright Brazil Commission director Luiz Loureiro, the Fulbright program officer Carol Robles, and the Fulbright staff for their consistent support.

My wife, Liv, encouraged, listened, challenged, and accompanied me at every page.

Finally, I am grateful to the diplomats, intellectuals, artists, activists, and relatives who generously gave interviews about their experiences with the history that follows. They gave their time (often on several occasions), shared photos and objects, and reflected in often very personal ways about their experiences. My thanks to Mário Gibson Barboza, José Clemente Baena Soares, Maria do Carmo Brito, Yedda Castro Pessoa, Alberto da Costa e Silva, Waldir Freitas de Oliveira, Antonio Gomes da Costa, José Manuel Gonçalves, Maria Yedda Linhares, José Osvaldo Meira Penna, Ivony de Andrade Melo, Ovídio de Andrade Melo, Candido Mendes de Almeida, Fernando Mourão, Antonio Olinto, Mário Osava, José Maria Nunes Pereira, Antonio Pitanga, Rubens Ricupero, Ramiro Saraiva Guerreiro, and Adyel Silva. Their willingness to share their reflections has been essential to this book.

Introduction

THIS BOOK BEGINS at the Hotel Trópico. There, as hundreds of thousands of Portuguese colonists fled Luanda during the months preceding Angola's independence in November 1975, the Brazilian diplomat Ovídio de Melo unpacked his bags. Sensing the tension and uncertainty, he asked the Brazilian foreign ministry (commonly known as Itamaraty) to let him buy a cistern, a power generator, and a car. Itamaraty only approved the car. In the months before independence, de Melo and his wife Ivony survived a city exploding in civil war and acted as brokers between a South American military dictatorship and a fragile African Marxist movement. During his months in Luanda the Hotel Trópico's Portuguese staff fled. Ovídio de Melo told me that the bartender was the last to leave, riding in the cockpit of a packed Varig DC-10 carrying one of the last loads of refugees to Rio de Janeiro: "Bartenders are generally patient. They deal with drunks. This guy stayed until he couldn't take it any more."[1] In an act of sabotage, someone had thrown onions into the hotel's elevator shafts. Their rot saturated the building. Ovídio and Ivony de Melo's presence was so quixotic that the hotel's staff thought they were ghosts.[2]

Ovídio and Ivony de Melo completed a circle of Brazilian encounters with Africa that began when the Brazilian writer Gilberto Freyre, who traveled to Angola in 1951 as a guest of Portuguese colonial officials, raised his glass in celebration of the "future Brazils" he believed Portuguese colonists were creating. This book is called *Hotel Trópico* because the hotel was the site of one of the most incongruous acts of Brazilian foreign policy, when Brazil's right-wing military dictatorship became the first government to recognize Angolan independence under the Popular Movement for the Liberation of Angola (MPLA). Hotels also connote transience, and this book analyzes the ways diplomats and intellectuals sojourning in African countries processed the meanings of Brazilian cultural and racial mixture. It explores a way of thinking that some of the Brazilians drawn to Africa embraced and others rejected: that there existed something called "lusotropicalism." The term, coined by Freyre, suggested that the Portuguese had a special way of being in the tropics characterized by race mixture and affinity for dark-skinned peoples, and that Brazil was the best example of the lusotropical ideal.[3]

The experiences and reflections of Brazilians who traveled to Africa in the 1960s and 1970s reveal mid-twentieth-century elements of Brazilian racial and ethnic identity. They illustrate ways by which the idea that Brazil was uniquely racially mixed and harmonious—that the country was a "racial democracy"—gave meaning to state policy, defined a global role for Brazil, and propelled a generation of diplomats, intellectuals, and artists across the Atlantic. The notion that Brazil might be a racial democracy has been rejected as a myth by scholars of race relations: all data indicate a deeply unequal distribution of economic, educational, and political resources, which remain overwhelmingly concentrated in the hands of Brazilians of European descent. The myth masks inequality and discrimination, in contrast to visible symbols of discrimination and segregation in societies like the United States and South Africa. In that sense the myth reinforces discrimination, both by helping to conceal it behind a positive national self-image and by making it more difficult for its victims to mobilize.

Did proponents of racial democracy conspire to suppress and subordinate Brazilians of color? Were they blind to the inequalities around them? How could Brazilian diplomats present their country as a racial democracy abroad even though citizens of color had no representatives among the professional diplomatic corps? The research presented here opens a window into these questions. Brazilians traveling to Africa commonly embraced the mythology of a racially democratic Brazil. They publicly represented and privately accepted it. They believed that all Brazilians had a common African heritage regardless of their color. These (almost exclusively white) diplomats and intellectuals believed that they, like all Brazilians, possessed African roots. At the same time, they recognized the deep racial inequalities of their society. They reconciled their belief in the myth with their recognition of discrimination and inequality because they believed that Brazil was different from (and better than) other countries in its degree of racial mixture and in the extent to which African influences permeated its culture.

Practically all these diplomats were white, reflecting the broader lack of integration of black Brazilians into senior roles in government and business during the twentieth century. Anani Dzidzienyo highlights this as one of the "glaring contradictions between Brazil's renewed interest in Africa and her failure to include Afro-Brazilians in the very operation of this interest. Upon closer examination, what we have called contradictory is, in fact, totally consistent with the general absence of Blacks in the process of decision making and policy implementation. It stands to reason that no exception would be made in the case of Brazil's officially declared Africa policy."[4]

The Brazilian policymakers and intellectuals who shaped relations with African countries were characterized by more than this racial homogeneity. The diplomatic corps had particular social and political characteristics that were aptly described by the United States ambassador to Brazil in 1971: "Brazilian diplomats have been drawn from a narrow, aristocratic base of European, Catholic background. Theirs is an ingrown group closely related by blood and marriage, competent in education and language ability which, however, is somewhat divorced from life in Brazil except as it had been known in Rio [de Janeiro] society. As a result, Brazilian diplomats have often lacked a thorough understanding of their own society and strong personal ties to their political leadership. Often, therefore, in order to defend their position in their society, the diplomats of Itamaraty have adopted more militantly nationalist positions than others who feel more secure in the country."[5] These diplomats and intellectuals are at the center of this book. They were often juxtaposed against competing political groups, and were often invested with a sense of mission that made them see connections with Africa as helping to realize Brazil's national destiny as a racially mixed world power.

The experiences of these Brazilians when they traveled to Africa inverted the identity question framed by the Martinican psychologist and philosopher Frantz Fanon in *Black Skin, White Masks* (1952). Fanon explored the anxiety and alienation produced by identities imposed upon blacks by whites. This book explores the opposite: the freedom that white Brazilians felt to assert their blackness and Africanness. In this world, where racial democracy flourished, white intellectuals, policymakers, and diplomats could imagine that they were African. They could just as easily imagine themselves to be Portuguese or Scottish or Japanese, indeed to have any other identity present in their family background or in Brazilian society. But African decolonization shifted the accent—it created an international context in which leveraging an African identity suddenly became especially meaningful. Though "Africa" had become an important element of Brazilian discussions of national identity in the early decades of the twentieth century, it was not until the African decolonization process that Brazilian intellectuals rushed to cross the Atlantic. Decolonization focused the attention of a generation of cultural and economic nationalists.

Decolonization changed the landscape of the broader world shaped by the African diaspora, and had a recognizable impact on Brazilian racial thought and its connections to the project of national development. In its broadest sense, it shaped the Brazilian state's responses to the cold war, creating room for Brazilian diplomats to propose an alternative to the logic of an "iron curtain" dividing East and West. As the former foreign minister Afonso Arinos de Mello Franco proposed in 1965, Brazil was on the moral side of a "racial curtain": it was a natural leader of the developing world because its racial democracy was a positive response to Jim Crow and colonialism.[6] Brazilian leaders used relations with Africa to assert autonomy from the United States and stake a claim as an emerging world power.

What Africa?

In 1972 the Brazilian foreign minister Mário Gibson Barboza traveled to eleven West African countries. Shortly after the trip, he dined privately with the United States national security advisor Henry Kissinger, who asked him: "What is your opinion about Africa?" Gibson Barboza recalled: "I replied in a Kissinger-esque fashion: 'Africa is an abstraction.' "[7] An abstraction of what? In 1975, just as Ovídio de Melo endured the worst combat in Luanda, the foreign minister Azeredo da Silveira offered an answer, declaring that "if Latin America is the essential environment of our foreign policy, Africa is the screen upon which we project it, demonstrating the shape that our foreign relations will assume in the future . . . it is practically virgin territory for our diplomatic action. What we do today on the African continent models our relations for the next twenty or thirty years. We are not planning a foreign policy for the 1970s, we are planning for the year 2000."[8]

For Brazilian diplomats and intellectuals traveling to Africa, their destination was usually an abstraction: an imaginary place that reflected on Brazilian culture, its past, its future, and its relationship with the world. On "Africa" they projected the meanings they gave to slavery and the presence of blacks within Brazilian culture and society. Brazilian sojourners looked at Africa and saw Brazil. Despite the symbolic importance of Africa to the constructions of Brazilian history and culture, there was scant information in Brazil about either African history or contemporary affairs. In part this lacuna resulted from European colonialism in Africa, which severed direct ties across the Atlantic. And in part it existed because "Africa" was a symbolic part of the imagination that viewed Brazil as a nation fusing three races (European, African, and Indigenous), which meant that interest in Africa always redounded to Brazil.

Brazil, alongside Cuba, was unique among Latin American nations in the pursuit of relations with African countries. As Piero Gleijeses and Carlos Moore illustrate, Africa was a space in which to assert Cuba's political influence and autonomy, and a place in which to project the meaning of the Revolution.[9] The Cuban experience was particularly dramatic: it culminated in the deployment of tens of thousands of troops to Angola and armed combat with the South African military. Though for much of the period of this study Brazil was governed by a right-wing military dictatorship, Brazilian policy in Africa, particularly in Angola, often dovetailed with revolutionary Cuba's.

When Brazil pursued new relations with Africa, diplomats and intellectuals looked back at five centuries of contact across the South Atlantic, which shaped Brazilian demography, culture, and social hierarchies. They looked at connections that began with Portuguese trading posts established in West Africa in the late fifteenth century and intensified by the slave trade. Over the next three centuries ships carrying slaves formed a connection through which goods, people, and information circulated. The connection between Brazil and Angola was particularly close. In the eighteenth century and the early nineteenth, Angola was governed by Portuguese colonial officials in Brazil. In 1822, when Brazil became independent, Portuguese colonists in Angola proposed uniting with Brazil. As a result, the first article of the treaty by which Portugal in 1825 recognized Brazil's independence prohibited Brazil from assuming possession of Portugal's African colonies.[10]

After Brazilian independence the slave trade continued to sustain broader exchanges across the Atlantic, including a current of former slaves and their descendants who migrated (or in some cases were exiled) to West Africa. In Nigeria the city of Lagos's early Muslim population was formed by former slaves and free Africans convicted of participating in the slave revolt in Bahia in 1835. The Catholic population of Lagos was similarly composed of Brazilian émigrés. Over the course of the nineteenth century perhaps three to eight thousand former Brazilian slaves settled across the West African coast, from Nigeria to Benin, Togo, Ghana, and the Ivory Coast.[11] They came to be called *agudás* (or, in Ghana, *ta-bom*). The first president of Togo, Sylvanus Olympio, was a descendant of Brazilians. Commercial exchanges meant the circulation of Brazilian goods to West Africa, and the flow of African goods, especially Afro-Brazilian religious ceremonial objects, to Brazil.

The consolidation of European colonialism from the late nineteenth century through the First World War gradually ended these connections. The merchant ships that circulated the South Atlantic disappeared. For the first time in four hundred years the flow of peoples and goods around the southern Atlantic world ceased, with the exception of passenger ships, and later aircraft stopping in Dakar, Senegal, as they crossed the Atlantic from Europe to South America. Though these passenger liner stops did not sustain much of a connection, they did allow a young Gilberto Freyre, en route to Europe in 1930, to spend two days in Dakar, where he believed that he "felt and saw Brazil vividly in its African origins."[12]

In 1960 sixteen newly independent African nations took seats in the United Nations. Brazilian diplomats there were struck by the new face of the UN General Assembly. While in 1958 one in twenty delegations to the UN represented a black African country (the four countries represented were Ethiopia, Ghana, Guinea, and Sudan), that proportion increased to one in five by 1960 and one in four by 1970. This change signaled the seemingly boundless possibilities of a world in transformation. New African nations experimented with a mix of free markets and socialist projects, seeking to find the key to erasing poverty, economic underdevelopment, and the lingering ties of colonialism. They also sought autonomy from the pressures of the cold war and collectively campaigned to end the last examples of colonial rule. These goals were most vehemently expressed at the Bandung Conference of Afro-Asian nations in 1955. In confronting these challenges, the experiences of new African nations echoed those of Brazil and other Latin American countries.

The sense of possibility unleashed by the end of colonialism crystallized into the early national experiences of Ghana, Senegal, and Nigeria. Ghana was the first sub-Saharan African country to free itself from colonial rule. Ghana's first national leader, Kwame Nkrumah, embraced socialist pan-Africanism as the future for Africa: for Nkrumah, pan-African unity would erode European influence and diminish ethnic rivalries. His political movement built a common cause between African and African American freedom struggles. African American militants like Richard Wright toured Ghana, and W. E. B. Du Bois spent his last years there.[13] Under Léopold Senghor, Senegal maintained close economic ties to France and shunned pan-African socialism, but Senghor embraced *négritude*, a cultural, intellectual, and political movement that challenged racism and celebrated a shared heritage in Africa and the Atlantic world. By contrast, the largest country, Nigeria, was less ideological. As it would be for his successors, the main challenge for Nnamdi Azikiwe was maintaining political unity across Nigeria's regional and ethnic divisions.

The seemingly limitless possibilities opened by independence were constrained by the legacies of colonialism. New leadership inherited colonial bureaucracies and borders. New economies remained bound to former metropolises. Domestic politics were riven by internal divisions and political consensus was elusive: only Senghor retired of his own volition, in 1980. Nkrumah and Azikiwe were both overthrown by military coups in 1966. Economic vulnerability and political instability prevented these new countries from gaining international projection beyond bilateral relations with their former colonizers. As Gilbert Khadiagala and Terrence Lyons explain, "African decisionmakers were constrained by the need to consolidate power and meet socioeconomic demands at home."[14]

There was one exception to the limits of African foreign policy: the shared effort to end Portuguese colonial rule and establish majority rule in Rhodesia, South Africa, and Namibia. When national leaders championed these causes they could unify domestic political support, find common cause with other African countries, and exert leadership in such international forums such as the United Nations, where African diplomats forged an influential voting bloc courted by other countries in exchange for support of majority rule. Often African countries built common cause with Asian and Middle Eastern countries, forming an Afro-Asian bloc. Yet clinging to a worldview defined by Freyre, the Brazilian government remained sentimentally bound to Portugal throughout its wars to preserve its African empire.

In the end Brazilian diplomats and policymakers saw Africa through what Dzidzienyo calls the "triangular mirror."[15] These Brazilians saw their actions with regard to Africa as reflecting upon Brazil's economic development and its system of race relations. But they continuously looked to Portugal too. For most of the period under study here, Brazilian policy toward African countries was subordinated to Brazilian policy toward Portugal. These ties to Portugal paralyzed Brazilian foreign policy over the very cause that unified African nations.

What Brazil?

"Will Brazil become the world power, or one of the world powers in the next century?"[16] The diplomat Adolpho Justo Bezerra de Menezes posed this question at the beginning of the book he published when he returned from the Bandung Conference, where he was the Brazilian observer. In *Brazil and the Afro-Asian World*, Bezerra de Menezes explained what would be necessary for Brazil to become a superpower: "We must, as the Americans say, 'think big,' to plan broadly . . . Our small-minded foreign policy that acts only in South America and passively follows the United States in the world no longer fits us. If we are to succeed today's giants, we must begin to implement policies that correct their errors."[17] Bezerra de Menezes believed that their main error was the "idea of superiority based on skin pigmentation, which is a purely Anglo-Saxon invention."[18] White supremacy would be the undoing of the United States: "the fear of miscegenation in the United States will only subside when the last black is extinct."[19] The intensity of racism in the southern United States was so great that "even if the citizens of the rest of the United States should suddenly consider themselves equal to other peoples and races; if through some miracle the rest of the country woke up one day with a 'luso-tropical' attitude toward miscegenation described by Gilberto Freyre, the 47 million Southerners would still deprive the United States of the moral force necessary to be the guide, the leader of humanity."[20]

Brazil's secret weapon was racial tolerance. Bezerra de Menezes proposed a strategy: in the short term Brazil should adhere to the anti-Soviet stance defined by the United States, but whenever the United States was aloof from the struggles of colonial peoples and racial minorities, or hostile toward them, Brazil should show solidarity. In the meantime Brazil should develop an "independent foreign policy," by which it "stealthily, discreetly engages in the extensive and long-term work of seducing the African and Asian masses, using our main political and diplomatic weapon—the almost perfect racial and social equality that exists in Brazil."[21]

In 1956 it was too early for Bezerra de Menezes to see a flaw in his argument, which would cripple Brazilian foreign policy toward the "Afro-Asian" world for the next two decades. The flaw was embracing the Freyrean notion that Portugal's African colonies "demonstrated the ways white men can live in peace and participate as equals with the natives," which meant accepting the premise that Portugal's form of colonialism was morally and substantively different from other forms of colonialism. By this reading, miscegenation, the catechism, and rudimentary education made the Portuguese colonies "islands of tranquility" in Africa. As a result, "there can be no doubt that the Portuguese colonial system is uniquely apt to be the bridge of friendship between Europe and the simmering African volcano."[22] Those Brazilian diplomats and politicians who accepted this view adopted foreign policies that sided with Portugal, against independent, majority-ruled African nations.

Bezerra de Menezes rewrote his book in 1961, just as his ideas were being put into practice by President Jânio Quadros. His revised version, *Afro-Asia and Brazil's Independent Policy*, lauded Quadros for implementing what was called the Independent Foreign Policy and described the "winds of renewal sweeping Itamaraty."[23] Bezerra de Menezes no longer saw anything laudable in Portuguese colonialism, dismissing Portugal as a "minor colonial power" that he expected would be especially tenacious in resisting the loss of its empire.[24] He compared Portuguese colonialism to apartheid, characterized by "men who are semi-slaves, in contrast to the elevated and free men" of other parts of Africa that had achieved independence.[25]

The two versions of Bezerra de Menezes's book frame the relationship between Brazil and Portugal, which in turn shaped relations with African countries. In the aftermath of the independence of much of Africa and the outbreak of wars for independence in Portuguese colonies, Portugal waged a fierce campaign to diminish foreign opposition to its colonial rule. The character and intensity of Portuguese resistance to decolonization posed a dilemma for Brazilians: Which side of their heritage should they support—the Portuguese or the African one? And what mattered more: the sentimental connection to Portugal, or the developmental aspiration to make Brazil an industrializing leader of the third world?

Brazil, the country of the future, sought to realize its potential in Africa. First it had to confront Portugal, the empire of the past. The former foreign minister Afonso Arinos de Mello Franco captured this challenge in 1965 when he invoked António Vieira, a seventeenth-century colonial Brazilian priest who defended indigenous rights, and Luis de Camões, whose sixteenth-century epic *The Lusiads* expressed the spirit of Portuguese imperial expansion in the Atlantic world. Arinos wrote: "our friendship with Portugal must not interfere with our interests or responsibilities. The Atlantic community of which President [Quadros] spoke can only be built within the spirit of liberty and democracy for all. It can only be directed at the future, no matter how beautiful the past was. Let us read Camões, but let us act like Antônio Vieira, who wrote a *History of the Future*."[26]

1 Brazil in the Lusotropical World

AS LUANDA SIMMERED in civil war, Ovídio de Melo wiled away the long, sleepless curfews by painting images of Angola's upheaval. One of his paintings captured a version of a common scene in the capital: a municipal crane made the rounds, lifting heroic statues of Portuguese explorers and colonial administrators off their pedestals and hauling them away. The painting, *Luis de Camões Goes to Municipal Storage*, shows a city square marred by bullet holes and revolutionary graffiti. Men with guns and other bystanders watch, one with his arms held triumphantly in the air, as a crane lifts away the statue of Camões, the sixteenth-century poet whose epics about Portuguese seafaring captured the Portuguese role in stitching together Africa and the Americas, his arm raised as if bidding farewell. Melo's choice to represent the removal of Camões from African soil, of all the statuary to choose from, was a meaningfully Brazilian one. Conventional imagination held that Brazil was the product of the fusion of Portuguese and African peoples, shaped by a supposed special proclivity of the Portuguese to extend civilization into the tropics and to soften racial lines through miscegenation. Yet the image that Ovídio de Melo captured shows this world being violently forced apart.

This image separates ingredients that Gilberto Freyre (1900–1987) drew together to make himself Brazil's most widely recognized intellectual. Freyre was the principal conduit of Brazilian national identity,

MPLA
UNITA
UNITA
Luis de Camões vai para o depósito da Prefeitura - Luanda Nov. 75

Luis de Camões Goes to Municipal Storage, Luanda, Nov. 75.
Image courtesy of Ovídio de Melo.

reappropriating ideas already in circulation but also sharpening and popularizing them. For example, the term "racial democracy," so tightly associated with Freyre, perhaps originated as the "social democratization" described by one of his intellectual mentors, Manoel Oliveira Lima, in 1922.[1] Freyre's name became a shorthand for several beliefs: Brazil was a "racial democracy"; Brazilian society was saturated with African culture; racial mixture was a national virtue; and Brazilian society was shaped by a special Portuguese proclivity for sexual and cultural mixing.

The imagination about Brazilian national identity that Freyre channeled was so powerful and influential in the middle years of the twentieth century that it pervaded the thinking of all Brazilians who shaped policy toward Africa or traveled there. Though Freyre was a partisan advocate for Portuguese colonialism, even those who disagreed with him relied upon his logic. Freyre's writing underpinned the Brazilian understanding of Africa and its significance to Brazil. By casting Brazil as the dialectical synthesis of Portuguese and African elements, Freyre created a framework within which both those who supported Portugal and those who pursued ties with Africa would operate.

This chapter explores how Freyre's influence, beginning in the 1950s, was felt among two different and increasingly incompatible constituencies. The first included Portuguese authorities seeking to preserve their overseas empire, as well as Portuguese ethnic communities in Rio de Janeiro and São Paulo. Together the Portuguese government and Portuguese ethnic groups in Brazil placed sufficient pressure on Brazilian national politics to command the support of Brazilian presidents, particularly Getúlio Vargas (1951–54), João Café Filho (1954–55), and Juscelino Kubischek (1956–61). For them Freyre's ideas synthesized the rationale for Brazilian support for Portugal and its effort to create "future Brazils" in Africa. The second constituency saw in Freyre's writing a justification for building ties with newly independent African countries and supporting decolonization. This group included younger diplomats, members of the intellectual left, and the organizers of Brazil's academic centers of African and Asian studies. Their opportunity came when President Jânio Quadros (1961) introduced what he called the Independent Foreign Policy, which pursued autonomy from traditional allies like the United States and Portugal and sought ties with the developing world.

Freyre was the intellectual protagonist of the nationalist cultural and economic transformation of Brazil that began in the 1920s and 1930s. Culturally this nationalism envisioned Brazil as different from and better than Europe and the United States. Economically it meant finding a path from an agrarian to an industrial society, be it through private enterprise and the free market, extensive intervention by the state, or both. This nationalism suffused Brazil's political life. It also guided Brazil's foreign relations and defined how Brazilians interpreted the opportunities and pitfalls of African decolonization.

The cultural awakening merged European modernist aesthetics with a project to "discover" what was authentically Brazilian. Freyre drew a seductive landscape in which the nation was an extended colonial plantation characterized by intimate and cordial interactions between blacks and whites (notwithstanding the reality that the blacks were enslaved by the whites). He not only cast the presence of blacks and of race mixture as a virtue, but also reimagined Brazil's Portuguese colonizers positively: though Britain had the Industrial Revolution and produced the United States, Portugal alone had the aptitude for creating civilization in the tropics, through harmonious mixture with nonwhite peoples. White Brazilians, like Freyre and his readers, romanticized plantation life because it started to seem remote. With abolition a half-century in the past, the number of surviving former slaves dwindled. And as in other industrializing and urbanizing societies, the embrace of modernity brought nostalgia for an idyllic, pastoral past. Freyre exploited similar sentiments to those popularized by *Ivanhoe* and *Gone With the Wind* in Britain and the United States, distilling the traditions that defined modernity.

Freyre's signature work, *The Masters and the Slaves* (1933), explored the mixture of cultures and customs, suggesting that a Portuguese proclivity for "interpenetration" enabled colonizers to settle in and adapt to Brazil's tropical environment by absorbing African and indigenous customs. Gradually Freyre extended this reading of Brazil to apply to all of the Portuguese empire. He defended Portuguese colonialism in Africa, even amid wars for independence. Freyre suggested that Africa was effectively present in Brazil through the influence of slaves and the prevalence of slave culture. What is more, Freyre claimed, Africa was present in Brazilians' homes, brought there by slave servants, cooks, and and wet nurses. And even more intimately, Africa was present in the family through sexual commingling.

Sexual and cultural "interpenetration," in Freyre's terms, infused all Brazilians with Africanness: "All Brazilians, even the fair skinned and blond ones, bear in their soul if not in their body the shadow or at least the hint of indigenous or black . . . The direct or remote influence of the African. . . . It shows in their tenderness, the excessive imitation, in the type of Catholicism that stimulates the senses, in the music, the way of walking, of speaking, in the children's lullabies. In everything that is a true expression of life, practically all of us bear the mark of black influence. From the slave or the nanny who raised us. Who nursed us. Who fed us . . . the mulatta . . . who initiated us into physical love and gave us, on a coarse cot, the first sensation of being a man."[2] This passage shows a common element of Freyre's writing: when he spoke of Brazilians, Jeffrey Needell argues, he "implicitly meant Brazilians who were white elite males, as driven by their libidos and the sensual ambiance of the tropics to a predatory, unceasing search for penetration."[3]

Freyre's work was as controversial as it was influential. After the 1940s Freyre associated with the Brazilian political right, as the authoritarian leanings evident in *The Masters and the Slaves* evolved into advocacy of dictatorship in Brazil and support for Salazar's regime in Portugal. Scholarship on Freyre has tended to separate his early work from the "shameless opportunism" of his "lusotropical years," focusing instead on the earlier work's rejection of dominant thought about the racial inferiority of blacks and mulattoes in favor of a rich analysis of cultural difference and patterns of cultural mixture.[4] Yet in his later years, Freyre used the intellectual prominence he had achieved through this earlier work to advocate in favor of Portuguese colonialism.

Freyre's ideas were a Gordian knot for Brazilian policymakers interested in relations with Africa. Freyre helped to popularize the view that African contributions to Brazilian culture and society were positive, thus making the case for developing relations across the Atlantic. But by hierarchically privileging the Portuguese as the catalyst for these relations, Freyre helped to draw the Brazilian government into costly support for Portugal's colonial wars. Supporters of Portugal in Brazil invoked Freyre. Opponents of Portugal did too. And even the small number of black Brazilian militants and exiled radicals who went to African countries would engage in a dialogue with Freyre's ideas. Freyre was so omnipresent that in 1973, when Foreign Minister Mário Gibson Barboza (a research assistant of Freyre in the 1930s) worked to unravel Brazil's association with Portugal and strengthen ties with African countries, his strategy included inviting Freyre to a luncheon at Itamaraty (the foreign ministry) at which the main dish was Apipucos Steak, named after Freyre's home, a restored plantation manor, and the dessert was Casa Grande Quindim, a palm-oil merengue named after Freyre's classic book.[5]

Freyre, Portugal, and Lusotropicalism

On the heels of the success of *The Masters and the Slaves* and its succeeding volume, *The Mansions and the Shanties* (1938), the Portuguese government latched onto Gilberto Freyre as a figure who could offer a compelling modern rationale—antiracist and gilded in the language of social science—for its ancient colonial project. In turn, Freyre found a patron in the Portuguese government, and seized upon what he saw in the Portuguese African colonies as a present-day laboratory demonstrating the processes of cultural and racial mixture that he described in colonial Brazil. The relationship would define Freyre's work and his increasingly conservative politics, and it would shape the character of the final decades of Portuguese colonialism.

Portugal had the longest colonial experience in Africa, beginning with a fifteenth-century "seaborne Empire" of trading posts which sent slaves to Brazil and other parts of the Americas.[6] After Brazil's independence in 1822 Portugal's colonial project in Africa languished until the end of the nineteenth century. Few Portuguese settled in the colonies, and when they did they intermixed with local populations because of their small numbers. After European empires demarcated dominions over Africa through the Treaty of Berlin in 1885, Portugal changed its colonial practices and promoted immigration to prevent encroachment by Britain and Belgium.

Portugal stagnated politically and economically through the nineteenth century after Brazilian independence. One of its main exports was people, and these emigrants favored Brazil over the African colonies. Nearly half a million Portuguese settled in Brazil in the nineteenth century, and over a million emigrated there in the twentieth.[7] Political and economic crises in the 1920s triggered a coup that brought António de Oliveira Salazar to power. In 1932 he consolidated his rule into a corporatist dictatorship called the Estado Novo, modeled on Italian fascism. It was similar to Brazil's own Estado Novo, the regime led by Getúlio Vargas: both Estados Novos banished political parties, stifled dissent, and governed through a centralized authoritarian bureaucracy. Brazil's only lasted from 1937 to 1945. Getúlio Vargas, the central political figure in twentieth-century Brazil, was president from 1930 to 1945 and again from 1951 until his suicide in 1954. During this time Vargas reinvented himself and his political style, from liberal reformer to corporatist dictator and finally nationalist populist. By contrast, António Salazar in Portugal ruled over an increasingly sclerotic dictatorship, and Portugal's Estado Novo endured until 1974.

After the Second World War Salazar modified the constitution to classify the colonies as "overseas provinces" of a unified nation, therefore making them not subject to decolonization. Facing growing nationalist militancy and international pressure against its colonial system and its abuses, the government abolished compulsory labor levies among the African populations, while continuing to promote white settlement. As the Portuguese colonial minister Sarmento Rodrigues wrote to Freyre in 1954, "worrying symptoms are arising, not of racism, but of a certain ecclesiastical nativism. We have to strengthen the European element and then peace will be assured."[8] The repressive political environment of Salazarist Portugal did not permit the types of debates over decolonization that took place in other European societies. António Costa Pinto suggests: "Had some of the elements of democratization been present, these would surely have led to a quicker negotiated settlement to the colonial problem."[9]

By the middle of the twentieth century Portugal's wealthiest colony, Angola, exported coffee, diamonds, and oil. It also had the largest white population. The Portuguese census of 1950 showed a population of 4,145,266 in Angola. It was divided between 4,036,687 "indigenous" inhabitants who did not speak Portuguese and were levied to provide forced labor on plantations, in the mines, and in public works; 30,080 "assimilated" inhabitants who spoke Portuguese and held rights generally equivalent to those of colonists; and 78,499 Europeans.[10] By the 1960s, after a decade of intense settlement policies by the Portuguese government, Angola had a white population nearing 500,000 out of a total of 5 million.

The census of 1950 still used the terms "civilized" and "not civilized" to distinguish among its colonial populations.[11] This semantic detail speaks not only to the Portuguese colonial mentality but to the entire logic of Salazar's Estado Novo, which immersed itself in the imagery of the country's golden age of seafaring colonial expansion in all of its Christian, crusading zeal. To outside observers Portugal seemed lost in time. Undersecretary of State George Ball recalled his meeting with Salazar in 1963 to encourage decolonization: "During our talks, history constantly intruded . . . Salazar was absorbed by a time dimension quite different from ours; it seemed as though he and his whole country were living in more than one century, and the heroes of the past were still shaping Portuguese policy. That impression was so acute that, after our second day of conversation, my reporting telegram to President Kennedy observed, among other things, that we had been wrong to think of Portugal as under the control of a dictator. It was instead ruled by a triumvirate consisting of Vasco da Gama, Prince Henry the Navigator, and Salazar."[12] Just as Salazar's regime relied on cold war ideology and crusading imagery, it also employed Gilberto Freyre's ideas about race relations to justify colonialism. Salazar's government embraced Freyre's idea that Brazilian racial harmony was a legacy of the Portuguese, using it as evidence that Portugal did not have colonies but rather "overseas provinces," and that these were part of a unified "pluriracial" and "pluricontinental" nation.

Freyre lent intellectual credibility to Salazar's regime, and in turn found in Salazar a symbol of the traditionalist authoritarianism that was central to his worldview.[13] As Needell explains, "Even though Freyre had creatively harnessed recent American social science to a project of creating a vision of traditional society, there is no doubt about his own prejudices. While profoundly 'modern' in his training and his experience of personal and social antitheses, he could not truly sustain a balance and he hungered for the security of the past . . . His critical distance is overpowered in his work by his embrace of patriarchy."[14] This relationship began when Freyre was invited to give a series of lectures which he published in 1940 as *The World the Portuguese Created*. His lectures stressed a dimension of his analysis that would resonate across the Atlantic in coming decades, amounting to an ethnically nationalist political manifesto about the heroic virtues of Portugal. Freyre even remarked that "after Jesus Christ, no one has done more for the spirit of human brotherhood than the Portuguese."[15]

Freyre generalized what he saw in Brazil as applicable to Portuguese colonialism in Africa and Asia, and holding true not just for the sixteenth century but for the colonialism of the mid-twentieth century. As a result, "for us, Portuguese and descendants of Portuguese, [there is a] shared sentimental and cultural climate that practically doesn't vary from Portuguese Asia to Brazil, nor from Portuguese Africa to Cape Verde."[16] Though Freyre did not yet use the term "racial democracy," he argued that this "unity of culture" spanning the Portuguese world was defined by "the good understanding among men shaped by the same traditions and guided by the same democratic aspirations. I mean to say human, essential, social democracy; political democracy little concerns me."[17] By "social democracy" he meant social mobility "spurred by miscegenation," and asserted the "ethical superiority of that process."[18] Freyre provided the central intellectual rationale for the preservation of Portugal's colonial empire.

In 1950 the Portuguese colonial minister Manoel Sarmento Rodrigues invited Freyre to tour Portugal's colonies in Africa and India for six months at the government's expense. Freyre agreed, replying that he was someone who "each day knows less how to separate Brazilian from Portuguese. And rejoices about the good that Portugal continues to achieve."[19] As Freyre was shuttled from colony to colony, he was received by colonial governors who scripted his interactions with their colonies, though Sarmento Rodrigues wrote to Salazar that he "didn't want . . . for him to see Timor," notorious for the violence with which the Portuguese ruled.[20]

During the tour Freyre celebrated the virtues of Portuguese colonialism, declaring to the press as he disembarked in Recife at the end of his journey: "The vivid impression I carry is that the Portuguese continue to be a creative people. To the achievements of the past—some of them monumental—they are adding a vast modern body of work in the tropics: in the Orient and in Africa. This body of work does not cut a bad figure alongside what Brazilians, as the descendants and continuers of the Portuguese, have achieved in America. And these two efforts . . . are animated by a common spirit characterized mainly by the feeling and by the practice of an—I wouldn't say perfect—but substantially advanced social and ethnic democracy."[21] Freyre was hosted by colonial governors, gave lectures at colonial research institutions, and was regaled in the colonial press. He produced two books out of these travels, *Adventure and Routine* (1952) and *A Brazilian in Portuguese Lands* (1953). *Adventure and Routine* was a travelogue in which he registered his impressions of Portugal (which he characterized as "routine" or familiar) and its colonies (which were "adventure," both in the exotic sense and in the sense of a dynamic colonial project under way). *A Brazilian in Portuguese Lands* synthesized lectures he had given and reprinted adulatory notices that had appeared in censored colonial newspapers. In his texts and his interviews, Freyre defended his trip as apolitical. He asked himself: if he lived in Portugal, would he support the government? "I don't know. Simple political democracy interests me less each passing day," he wrote, and went on to describe the "superiority of the Portuguese regime" over the Brazilian one.[22]

Freyre saw and spoke of "overseas provinces" rather than colonies, embracing the semantic trick that Portuguese officials used to skirt global pressures for decolonization. The idea that Portugal was really a "transnational" and "intercontinental" but unified nation of peoples of different colors and cultures, bound by their Portugueseness, perfectly matched the historical process that Freyre imagined had produced Brazil. The 2001 edition of *Adventure and Routine* cited here opens with a preface by Alberto da Costa e Silva, a diplomat who became one of Brazil's most prolific authors on African culture and history. Costa e Silva characterized Freyre as a "prisoner of his dream," seeing idealized Portuguese colonialism rather than modern colonialism: "he praised what for a long time was ceasing, or had ceased, to exist in the Portuguese empire."[23] Where Freyre saw evidence that contradicted his preconceptions about the Portuguese, he dismissed it. For instance, the diamond mining companies that were the base of the Angolan economy relied on slave-like labor in segregated mine towns. For Freyre, there was "something Belgian" about them: exceptions that proved his arguments.[24]

In Portuguese Africa Freyre discovered limitless possibilities for expanding upon his theses about Brazil's formation in lands where colonialism had created "a perfect African Portugal."[25] He imagined what he saw in twentieth-century Africa to be identical to what he believed had occurred in seventeenth-century Brazil. Costa e Silva suggests that Freyre did not see the true nature of miscegenation in Africa, a process that barely related to the Portuguese and was the result of centuries of encounters of Africans with Arabs, Persians, and Indians along an Indian Ocean of intense commercial and cultural exchange.[26]

Beyond being a "prisoner of his dream," Freyre also found the Portuguese government to be a generous patron. The colonial ministry sponsored many of his trips, published his lectures in several languages, and arranged credit for him in Portuguese bookstores.[27] In turn, Freyre took pains to protect the image of Portuguese colonialism in Brazil, Portugal, and even the United States.[28] Freyre developed a relationship with Sarmento Rodrigues that continued through the collapse of the Portuguese regime and its empire. As Sarmento Rodrigues wrote to Freyre in 1954, "it is enough to know that we defend the same cause."[29]

In contrast to Freyre's relationship with Portuguese colonial authorities, when the Angolan nationalist Mário de Andrade criticized Freyre's writing on the colonies in 1955, he had to do so under a pseudonym and in exile. Andrade was an intellectual who was one of the founders of the Movimento Popular de Libertação de Angola (MPLA). Writing in the Francophone nationalist journal *Présence Africaine*, Andrade argued that lusotropicalism was "a method of colonization" and condemned Freyre's "religious belief in the exclusive Portuguese hereditary aptitude to live under the tropical sun and arrange for himself a woman of color. Influenced by this belief, we understand that the essential nature of the colonial situation escapes him." For Andrade, Freyre's emphasis on the supposed influence of Portuguese male sexual preferences led to a neglect of the economic and political aspects of Portuguese colonialism. Far from a paradise of racial and sexual freedom, Andrade saw a violent process which eliminated agency and the free participation of native peoples in the lusotropical ideal. He asked: "What harmonious and cordial participation in this cultural ideal could exist in Africa under Portuguese domination, where native cultures are systematically destroyed by a fierce policy of assimilation? Men are detribalized and whole populations are reduced to forced labor."[30]

Seeing Africa through Portugal

Freyre offered a sweeping vision of "Lusitanian" culture that stretched from the colonial sugar plantations of Pernambuco to the "future Brazils" of Portuguese Africa. He defined Brazil as composed of African ingredients processed through Portuguese culture. This set of beliefs was so powerful that it formed the conceptual framework not only of those Brazilians who supported Portuguese colonialism but even of those who shunned Portugal, favored decolonization, and sought ties with independent African nations.

Much of the research presented in this book comes from documentary diplomatic sources, drawn particularly from the archives of the Brazilian foreign ministry and the Getúlio Vargas Foundation. This documentary research is complemented by memoirs, photographs, and other first-person sources. Beyond these, this book relies on the analysis of interviews with diplomats, artists, and intellectuals about their experiences in Africa. I often began interviews by asking: "How did you become interested in Africa?" The responses plotted into a tight pattern: interviewees commonly referred directly to Freyre's writing as the source of their interest, and if they did not, they usually accepted Freyre's triangulation of Brazil, Portugal, and Africa. For instance, I interviewed a Brazilian militant for Angolan independence who surprised me when he plainly stated: "Of course I committed incest with my half-sister when I was eight. She taught me. Even that. Even sex."[31] She was the mulatta daughter his father had borne with his black maid. This was uncannily true to the spirit of Freyre, who wrote in *The Masters and the Slaves:* "It is even possible that in some cases, the white son and mulatta daughter of the same father would love each other."[32] From this formative experience, the interviewee would, like others, develop an intellectual fascination with race that would take him inevitably first to Portugal, then to Africa.

I conducted twenty-one interviews between 2003 and 2008, with participants in events that had taken place thirty to fifty years earlier. Meaning is unavoidably modulated by past and present in ways that are impossible to separate. Whenever possible, I would bring to our session an archival document (often originally created by the interviewee) to help the interviewee recall the context in which the source was produced. But these interviews are still a product of the moment in which they were recorded. Recognizing this, I make clear when I am drawing from an interview, and I often recall the circumstances in which the interview was conducted. Many of the interviewees committed their lives to developing the relationship between Brazil and Africa, others to championing independence or revolutionary liberation, and the settings where we conducted the interviews reflect those commitments. They are also a reminder that the interviews were conducted in a particular moment and rely on memories processed in an early-twenty-first-century context within which Brazilian racial politics were changing and relations with Africa were being revived.

Several of the people whom I interviewed were the founders of Brazil's African and Asian studies centers. Their reflections on the context within which they worked capture the weight of Portugal on thinking about Africa and the influence that Freyre's ways of seeing had on both supporters of Portugal and advocates of decolonization. There are three centers for African studies in Brazil: the Center for Afro-Oriental Studies (CEAO; 1959) at the Federal University of Bahia; the Center for African Studies (CEA) at the University of São Paulo; and the Center for Afro-Asian Studies (CEAA; 1973) at Candido Mendes University. The CEAA was a continuation of the federal Brazilian Institute for Afro-Asian Studies (IBEAA), created by Candido Mendes de Almeida, a political advisor to Jânio Quadros. IBEAA was extinguished by the military after 1964. The CEAO in Bahia was created by the Portuguese exile George Agostinho da Silva. CEA in São Paulo and CEAA in Rio de Janeiro were organized by Fernando Albuquerque Mourão and José Maria Nunes Pereira (assistant director of CEAA under Candido Mendes), two Brazilians whose interest in Africa was rooted in their experiences as university students in Portugal. All opposed Portuguese colonialism and Salazar's dictatorship. While Agostinho da Silva followed a spiritual movement called Sebastianism, Mourão and Pereira became secular foes of colonialism and collaborated with the Marxist liberation movements of Portuguese Africa.

What drew them to Africa? Their encounters with Portugal. Agostinho da Silva was a millenarian who imagined the creation of a new kingdom of God on earth that would bring universal freedom and social justice, delivered through the return of Portugal's King Sebastian, killed in a 1578 crusade. Persecuted by Salazar's regime for these beliefs, Agostinho da Silva went to Brazil in exile in 1944. Mourão and Pereira developed their interest in Africa and their anticolonial militancy when they were students at Coimbra and Porto universities during the 1950s. Though both of Portuguese descent, they felt that as Brazilians they identified more with the African students, both white and black. Mourão recalled: "I had nothing to do with the Portuguese students . . . culturally, we lived in different worlds. I met some African students and we formed ties . . . it was just a closer way of being."[33] As Brazilians, both Mourão and Pereira could belong to the Casa dos Estudantes do Império, a colonial students' association which became a hotbed of nationalist and independence sentiment.[34] After Mourão entered the Casa in 1955 he became involved in the politics of decolonization and in the creation of the MPLA, carrying the texts of poets and writers to France, where they could be published by *Presénce Africaine*.[35]

Pereira's trajectory was similar. The son of a Portuguese immigrant, Pereira was sent to study in Porto and Coimbra, where he intended to become a Catholic missionary. Initially he had wanted to join the conservative Catholic organization Opus Dei, but as he later recalled, "I was the son of immigrants. I didn't come from the right social class for that."[36] But since he was close to the African students, the leaders of Opus Dei asked him to become an informant. In the process Pereira became a convert to the movement, going "from missionary to revolutionary."[37] Committed to Angolan independence, Pereira and Mourão returned to Rio de Janeiro and São Paulo, which were centers of support for Portugal, with organized immigrant communities, influential lusophiles, and Portugal's efficient diplomatic corps.

Militants like Mourão and Pereira also had allies who challenged Portugal's influence in Brazil. Foremost among them was José Honório Rodrigues, author of the canonical text *Brazil and Africa* (1961), which presented a history of Brazil's rich connections with West Africa that had been severed in the nineteenth century and the early twentieth and called for renewed connections. At Itamaraty's training institute Rodrigues taught many of the diplomats who challenged Portuguese colonialism and effected the political opening to Africa, including Ovídio de Melo. Each of these champions of African decolonization and opponents of Salazar emphasized beliefs similar to Freyre's: Mourão and Pereira connected to Africa through Portugal; Agostinho da Silva supported decolonization through a mixture of beliefs harkening to the Portuguese crusades; José Honório Rodrigues saw Brazil's connection to Africa as rooted in its racial democracy.

Brazilian Presidents and the Affinity for Portugal

From the 1930s to the 1970s Brazilian presidents courted the support of ethnic Portuguese communities in Rio de Janeiro and São Paulo. This was a means of cultivating political support among a particularly well organized and influential constituency. The relationship between Portuguese ethnic communities and national politics weighed decisively over Brazilian foreign policymaking from the 1950s onward. Portuguese ethnic organizations in Brazil were tightly bound to Salazar's regime and successfully tethered Brazilian foreign relations to Portuguese interests. Particularly with regard to Portuguese colonialism, the pressure from Portuguese ethnic communities constrained Brazilian foreign policy toward Africa by binding the Brazilian government to international support for Portugal's colonial struggles, positioning Brazil in opposition to uniformly shared foreign policy goals of African governments. The lusotropical ideal advanced by Gilberto Freyre was woven through the relationship between national politics, Portuguese ethnic militancy, and the challenges of African decolonization.

Over a million Portuguese immigrants settled in Brazil between 1900 and 1980, mostly in São Paulo and Rio de Janeiro.[38] This community controlled newspapers and financed political campaigns, forming a "Portuguese lobby" that was especially effective when Rio was the capital, and even while it remained the de facto capital through the 1960s. When I interviewed José Maria Pereira, he emphasized his sense of Rio de Janeiro as a Portuguese space. He quoted José Honório Rodrigues as saying that "Rio de Janeiro is the largest Portuguese city in the world," and Fernando Mourão as saying that "if the capital had not moved to Brasília, we would still be supporting [Portuguese] colonialism."[39] The Portuguese community in Rio and São Paulo (the "colony," as it called itself) organized institutions including sports and social clubs, schools and literary circles, political groups and newspapers. The colony employed the strategies used by other immigrant ethnic groups, which Jeffrey Lesser suggests were based on mutually reinforcing practices: building cohesion based on perceived difference, and asserting that Portuguese ethnicity was intrinsic to Brazilianness (even that Portuguese ethnic characteristics *were* Brazilianness). As the essayist Clodomir Vianna Moog stated, "those who are born here become Brazilian when they embrace Portuguese culture."[40]

There was a difference between the experiences of Portuguese immigrants and those of other minority groups: the great majority of the most affluent and influential Brazilians, including political, commercial, literary, and artistic figures, traced Portuguese ancestry. While minority groups have struggled to define themselves as the epitome of Brazilianness, the Portuguese did not even have to write themselves into myths of national origin, elements of dominant culture such as language, or the major artifacts of national identity such as the idea of racial democracy.

In Rio de Janeiro much of this community's organizing took place on a single stage: the Real Gabinete Português de Leitura, a lavish library built in the early modern Portuguese Manueline style. Though in the nineteenth century the Real Gabinete projected an image of the Portuguese in Brazil as a cultured élite, in the twentieth century it played a political role as the center of activity for the main Portuguese ethnic organization, the Federation of Portuguese Associations (FAP). It was the federation, using the Real Gabinete as its stage, which forged the relationship between the Portuguese "colony" and the Brazilian presidency. In 1937 and 1941 the federation invited the Brazilian foreign ministers Macedo Soares and Oswaldo Aranha to be guests of honor at its "Day of the Race" ceremonies on 10 June, and presented them with portraits of themselves rendered by Portuguese artists. Getúlio Vargas in 1939 received the same treatment, along with a portrait by the same artist who had painted Salazar's. In 1944 the Portuguese news agency Lusitania founded an ethnic community newspaper in Rio de Janeiro named *Brasil-Portugal* and appointed Getúlio Vargas's brother Lútero as its editor.[41]

I interviewed Antônio Gomes da Costa, president of the Federation of Portuguese Associations, in 2006. We sat in a paneled conference room at the Real Gabinete and talked beneath a portrait of Salazar. This was the physical center of the mid-century Portuguese "colony," and it still showed its Salazarist orientation. Gomes da Costa, who had been active in the federation since the early 1970s, remarked that "the Portuguese colony here had suffered because of the political disorder in Portugal, the lack of national credibility, the worthless currency, bad economy, and so on. So when the [Portuguese] Estado Novo came to power, there was a considerable approximation by the colony to the leaders of the Estado Novo, especially Oliveira Salazar, who embodied the new regime . . . The mainstream of the colony was always highly Salazarist."[42]

The mainstream press in Rio was also predominantly pro-Portugal. Assis Chateaubriand, owner of the largest newspaper chain in Brazil, Diários Associados, was an outspoken supporter of Salazar's regime. In gratitude for his support for the regime, Salazar named a street in Lisbon after Chateaubriand.[43] But beyond his chain, almost all the major dailies of the 1950s and 1960s in Rio—*Correio da Manhã*, *O Globo*, *O Jornal*, *Tribuna da Imprensa*, *Diário da Noite*, and *Jornal do Brasil*—were pro-Portugal.[44] Gomes da Costa recalled the political influence of the Portuguese community: "The colony had a certain political weight to it . . . the government, the political class of Brazil, always romanced the colony because the colony was a 'force' in electoral terms. This was in terms of its economic and commercial influence."[45] Together Salazar's regime, Portuguese ethnic groups in Brazil, and their allies like Gilberto Freyre kept constant pressure on Brazilian presidents. When Freyre returned from his trip to Portugal and its colonies in 1950, he traveled to Rio on a mission from the Portuguese government, which orchestrated his return for political effect. He bore a copy of Camões's *The Lusiads*, bound in silver and gems, to present to President Vargas, generating press coverage in both Brazil and Portugal and consolidating Freyre's status as a mediator between Salazar and Vargas and as the interpreter of the Portuguese character. Freyre embraced the role, declaring that Portugal did not have colonies but rather "overseas provinces" and that these were the fruits of a Portuguese "feat of social engineering unlike anything achieved by other Europeans."[46]

Freyre's relationship with Vargas had long been strained, but it seemingly found new life in his role as a mediator for the Portuguese government. Just after President Getúlio Vargas's suicide in 1954, for instance, Freyre related to Sarmento Rodrigues: "Shortly before his tragic end, my friend Getúlio Vargas insisted that I accept the presidency, with *carte blanche*, of a new National Department of Immigration and Colonization . . . He told me himself that it would be a super-ministry, almost another Presidency of the Republic. He told me: 'Now you can put into practice your ideas about colonization and bring your Portuguese to Brazil at will. That is, if Salazar lets you.' I told him that Prof. Salazar would agree: his ideas coincide with our own. I wrote back turning down the idea, but he insisted. His tragic end really moved me."[47] Freyre's remarks are curious, given that he had long been critical of Vargas. But what they show is that Freyre relished being an intermediary between the Portuguese and Brazilian heads of state.

Through the 1950s the combined Portuguese ethnic and diplomatic pressure redounded in a succession of government actions intended to align Brazil more closely to its former "mother country." Vargas and Salazar negotiated the Friendship and Consultation Treaty of 1953, by which both governments agreed to consult on international matters. The treaty was an umbrella for a series of smaller agreements over the next twenty years that extended economic and political privileges to Portuguese immigrants in Brazil and reduced barriers to the tiny amount of commerce between the two countries. It specifically excluded any connection between Brazil and the Portuguese colonies. José Honório Rodrigues condemned the treaty as "a victory by Portugal that pulls Brazil into its orbit . . . we obligate ourselves to consult with Portugal and its colonial dependencies on international matters . . . Imagine the United States consulting Great Britain on what it must or must not do."[48]

President João Café Filho, who took office after Vargas's suicide, continued the rapprochement with Portugal initiated by his predecessor. When the Bandung Afro-Asian conference took place, Café Filho sent an unofficial diplomatic observer, Bezerra de Menezes, while he conducted a state visit to Portugal.[49] Where Brazil stood with regard to looming challenges to Portuguese colonialism was made clear by President Café Filho and later by Juscelino Kubitschek, as the Indian government demanded that Portugal relinquish control over a collection of small enclaves on its coast, particularly Goa, Daman, and Diu. Café Filho responded to the Indian pressure on Portugal by declaring: "We stand alongside Portugal anywhere in the world."[50] At the same time, the Brazilian government sponsored Portugal's admission to the UN.

During Kubitschek's presidency (1956–61) the Brazilian identification with Portugal grew even more intense. In 1957 Kubitschek received Portugal's honorary president, Craveiro Lopes (Salazar never left the country, even to visit the colonies). During the visit the former foreign minister João Neves da Fontoura, who had been the chief negotiator of the Treaty of Friendship and Consultation, declared: "Our policy with Portugal is not really a policy. It is a family affair. No one plays politics with his parents and brothers. He lives with them in the intimacy created by bonds of blood and sentiment."[51] Kubitschek projected a genuine love of Portugal and admiration for Salazar, but he also appreciated the political weight of the Portuguese "colony." In his public dealings with the Portuguese colony and with Portugal itself he emphasized his second surname, d'Oliveira, which was typically Portuguese. When his term in office ended he was already looking ahead to a new presidential campaign in 1965, so he never missed an opportunity to court Brazilian lusophiles. Not only did Kubitschek appear at protests after Goa was annexed by India, but he also warned Prime Minister Nehru that "seventy million Brazilians could never understand nor accept an act of violence against Goa."[52]

Kubitschek found an unbeatably romantic way of pairing Brazil and Portugal, and tradition with modernity. While traveling to Portugal in 1960 he proposed the creation of a Luso-Brazilian Institute of Astronautics. Together Brazil and Portugal would explore outer space the same way the

Portuguese had explored the seas, using as their rocket base the Sagres promontory from which their caravels had left Europe centuries before.[53] Kubitschek did not specify how two countries with illiteracy rates over 30 percent and whose principal exports included cork and coffee might reach outer space. Nor did he note the irony of reprising past colonizing glory at the very moment when Africa was reaching independence. To the contrary, the fantasy of conquering space with Portugal rather than with the United States (an ally with an actual space program) reflected the depth of Brazilian sentimentality toward Portugal.

Challenging Portugal

Through the 1950s the mainstream of the Portuguese community, the major press, national political leaders, and foreign policymakers were all supportive of Salazar and the perpetuation of Portugal's colonies. But there was a constant countercurrent of opposition that reached from presidential aides to members of the major Portuguese ethnic institutions. Dissenters saw Portuguese colonialism as inconsistent with Brazilian racial values and advocated the democratization of Portugal. They maintained a constant pressure that sustained an atmosphere of controversy around Brazilian support for Salazar's regime. These criticisms echoed through the two major daily newspapers hostile to Salazar, *O Estado de S. Paulo* and *Diário de Notícias* (Rio de Janeiro), and their reporting reverberated through the rest of the press.[54] These challenges to Brazilian support for Salazar culminated in the decision in 1959 of Álvaro Lins, a former aide to President Kubitschek who was serving as the Brazilian ambassador to Portugal, to grant asylum to the major Portuguese opposition figure, Humberto Delgado.

An incident in 1956 involving the Vasco da Gama soccer team, named after the Portuguese explorer and directed by prominent members of the Portuguese colony in Rio de Janeiro, exemplified both ethnic Salazarism and the current of dissent. The Vasco club had received an invitation from a Portuguese sports promoter to play a series of games in Angola. The promoter "imposed the condition that the team not send players of color because of the racial prejudice in our overseas possessions."[55] Someone disclosed the racist terms of the invitation to the press. Portugal's ambassador denied "the existence of racial prejudice in Portuguese Africa," but wrote to his foreign minister "confessing" his "ignorance of soccer conditions in the overseas possessions . . . if these allegations are true, we should avoid letting them be publicized."[56] The Vasco board declined the invitation, since its members were "categorically against the team playing under terms that contradict Vasco's democratic and anti-racist traditions."[57] After the Portuguese embassy made the promoter "explain himself," he revised his story, and exported the racism: it was a misunderstanding that arose from the possibility that the team might also play in South Africa.[58] He cautiously explained: "being Portuguese . . . I know the laws and the customs of my country, and it would not be for me to say that there is racial prejudice in our Colonies, because if I did so, I would be lying."[59]

In later years, as African nations pushed for an end to Portuguese colonialism, directors of the Vasco club would ask Portuguese authorities to vet invitations to play in countries that might be hostile. In 1963 Vasco was invited to play exhibition games in Algeria, Ghana, and the Ivory Coast. The team's president consulted the Portuguese ambassador, who described these countries as among the most "aggressive" against Portugal. Though the team president agreed to decline the invitations, "affirming above all else the strong Lusitanian roots of the organization," his decision did not prevail. Vasco toured Ghana, the Ivory Coast, and Nigeria three months later.[60] Just before the team departed for Africa (and perhaps because of its tour), one of the members of Vasco's board of directors traveled to Portugal and its colonies. He met privately with Salazar. When he returned to Brazil he held a press conference at which he declared: "The weapons that are in Cuba today are the same ones that are besieging Portuguese territory in Africa." He also commented on his meeting with Salazar, whom he described as "the man of the 20th Century."[61]

On both occasions, though the directors of Vasco tended to support Salazar and colonialism, members of its board were willing to challenge the appearance of colonial racism in the press, or reverse a decision to avoid playing exhibition games in African countries that challenged colonialism. This kind of dissent was present too among presidential aides and within Itamaraty, and erupted after President Kubitschek appointed Álvaro Lins ambassador to Portugal in 1957. Lins was Kubitschek's chief of staff and a key ally in his presidential campaign, though he would create an intense diplomatic crisis between the two countries. Lins's experience shows the power of lusophilia in shaping Brazilian politics and policy. He recounted the crises of his ambassadorship in a six-hundred-page memoir called *Mission in Portugal*, and his experience was also recalled by João Clemente Baena Soares, whom I interviewed in 2006. Baena Soares was a third secretary at the Brazilian embassy in Lisbon (a junior diplomatic appointment), and his recollections reflect a sense of the degree to which Lins, a writer rather than a professional diplomat, relied on his secretaries, as well as the general climate of the embassy staff in Lisbon, echoed by Lins, which was cool to Salazarism and colonialism.

Lins arrived in Portugal believing that the Treaty of Friendship and Consultation subordinated Brazil to Portugal with no benefit in return. In Lisbon his embassy staff was composed of junior diplomats who typically favored decolonization and who believed, like Lins, that Brazilian policy was too submissive toward Portugal. Baena Soares recalled: "We were in a colonial situation . . . [Portugal] had a colonial relationship with Angola and also one with Brazil . . . We did not have autonomy in our diplomacy. Our foreign policy was shaped from outside by Portuguese diplomacy and shaped from within by the force of businessmen . . . who financed presidential campaigns. This influence was not only over the executive branch but also the legislative, which had emphatic defenders of Portugal."[62]

Baena Soares recalled that Lins, like the younger staff of the embassy, resented that Brazil treated Portugal as its "dear grandfather."[63] This attitude coincided with growing unrest in Portugal against Salazar's regime. In 1958 token elections were held. Portuguese elections produced an honorary president, while real power resided in the hands of Salazar, whose position was "President of the Council of Ministers." During this election, however, General Humberto Delgado of the Air Force ran on a platform of redemocratization. Censorship had been partially lifted during the campaign: when a journalist asked Delgado, "If you are elected president, what will you do with the President of the Council [Salazar]?," Delgado responded, "Fire him."[64] After Delgado lost the election he was stripped of his rank, which removed his partial immunity from prosecution as a military officer and led him to fear being imprisoned. He went to the Brazilian embassy, declaring: "I am General Delgado. Here are my pistols. I ask for asylum."[65]

The Portuguese government refused to allow Delgado to leave, so he lived at the embassy for the next three months. The Brazilian embassy abutted the headquarters of the Portuguese secret police (the PIDE). Baena Soares recounted that each morning Delgado would go to a room that had a window facing the PIDE headquarters, make a display of his daily calisthenics, and then open the window and yell insults at the PIDE agents until the PIDE asked Lins to tone down the general.[66] Lins defended Delgado's asylum over opposition from the Brazilian foreign minister, Francisco Negrão de Lima, and other lusophiles. Assis Chateaubriand, owner of the Diários Associados newspapers and at the time Brazil's ambassador to Britain, traveled on his own account to Lisbon to pressure Lins. Baena Soares recalled Chateaubriand asking, "What is this? You're against Portugal? You have to be colonial and submissive . . . He said it. I am telling you. I was there!"[67] After more Portuguese opposition figures sought asylum in other embassies, Salazar relented.[68] Delgado was whisked to Brazil, where he plotted against Salazar, eventually getting killed, along with his Brazilian wife, while clandestinely reentering Portugal along a remote part of the Spanish border in 1965.

The asylum standoff illustrated the weakness of presidential and ministerial authority in Brazil. Lins felt free to autonomously grant asylum to Delgado, and even to plot a course increasingly incompatible with Kubitschek's aims toward Portugal. At the same time, Assis Chateaubriand showed himself to be larger than his ambassadorship in London, carrying out his own foreign policy by traveling to Portugal to speak with Lins and then waging a campaign against him in his newspapers. This was characteristic of Brazilian politics in the 1950s and 1960s: it was a chaotic culture of confrontation that contributed to Vargas's suicide, Quadros's resignation, the military opposition to João Goulart's assumption of the presidency, and the military coup of 1964. This chaos was heightened when Portugal was involved because of the intensity of support for Portugal among parts of the Brazilian élite and the press.[69]

As the asylum case ended, the Portuguese Ministry of Foreign Affairs sent a delegation to meet personally with Kubitschek and invite him to the Comemorações Henriquianas, a commemoration of the five hundredth anniversary of the death of Prince Henry the Navigator, made into an extravaganza celebrating the endurance of the Portuguese overseas empire. Baena Soares recalled: "The Portuguese were great hands at stagecraft. They sent a mission to invite Juscelino to be co-president of the commemorations. You know, he wanted nothing more than this kind of display, and this made us instead of Portugal into the problem to be dealt with. Portuguese diplomacy was incredibly able. He went, co-presided, was given ovations. Great Portuguese hero Juscelino."[70]

Kubitschek replaced Lins with Negrão de Lima in order to repair relations with Portugal. Baena Soares questioned the appointment: "They sent Negrão de Lima. Even a third secretary like me was perplexed: how could they send the foreign minister who had been handling the previous crisis to Portugal's benefit, over the resistance of Itamaraty?" His unease increased when he watched Negrão de Lima speak to reporters as he stepped ashore in Lisbon. When asked what his policy would be, the new ambassador declared: "I have no policy. I came here to love Portugal." Baena Soares said to his wife, "We have to go somewhere else because I can't stay here with this man." Other diplomats at the embassy asked to be replaced as well.[71] Negrão de Lima's mission was to repair the damage that he and Kubitschek perceived Lins had caused. In the speech he gave as he disembarked, Negrão de Lima began the task of casting the Portuguese and Brazilians as a single people: "With this name—Negrão de Lima—it is not possible to consider me an outsider . . . [Portugal] has been a living presence in my spirit and in my blood. I am a Lusiad, as are all Brazilians who consider it not only a duty but a privilege to faithfully defend the sacred and immutable roots of their country."[72]

Soon after arriving Negrão de Lima learned that Kubitschek might not attend the Comemorações Henriquianas, and he was riven by anxiety because the new foreign minister heading the Brazilian delegation was Jewish. He confided to a friend: "This will be another disaster for our relations with Portugal . . . Horácio Lafer is a Jew from Krakow. This is not generally a defect. But to represent Brazil in Portugal for the quincentenary of the Grand Master of the Order of Christ makes very little sense. Doesn't Brazil have someone of the Portuguese race that can represent it at a historic event that speaks directly to the Christian faith? Dr. Juscelino's advisors don't do a very good job as you know. Perhaps you could head the delegation—you are characteristic of the Portuguese of Brazil and could speak of caravels bearing the Maltese Cross without reservations or without looking back on the Holy Inquisition. At any rate, sending Horácio Lafer repeats the Álvaro Lins disaster."[73] In fact Lafer was born in São Paulo, and his father had emigrated from Lithuania, not Poland. Still, Negrão de Lima's preoccupation illustrates the extent to which he identified with Portugal. Following the Salazar regime's crusading logic, Negrão de Lima could feel emboldened enough to complain to one of his president's advisors that his boss, the foreign minister, was an inappropriate representative of the nation because he was Jewish.

While Kubitschek cultivated political support for Portugal in Brazil, an undercurrent of opposition was strengthened by Lins and the Delgado affair. Two months after Delgado's exile in April 1959, when the former colonial minister Sarmento Rodrigues (who had hosted Freyre's voyage) traveled to Rio de Janeiro, opponents organized a protest at the docking of his ocean liner. An organization called the Catholic Front for Portuguese Liberation distributed flyers in downtown Rio, calling for the protest and proclaiming: "The man who arrives today, on his swine and subservient mission, calls himself Sarmento Rodrigues. The only human thing about him is his shape, because his character is dubious and perverse. His visit affronts the dignity of this Free and Democratic People. He bears the medals that Salazar awarded him for whipping the Blacks of Angola and Mozambique. He is a filthy racist fanatic, yet he dares to speak of a Land where there is no racial prejudice, where men are truly free and equal before the Law. If our compatriots of color were under his orders, they would suffer the same fortune as our brothers of Angola and Mozambique. This man spits in the face of men of color and sees blacks as an inferior race."[74] The ship's first mate reported to the PIDE that when the ship reached port, it was met by "a hostile demonstration, predominantly of Brazilians of color, along with some Portuguese, bearing rotten eggs, thousands of flyers, and picket signs critical of the Gentleman."[75]

The rest of Sarmento Rodrigues's visit was guarded. He spoke at the Higher War College and the Naval Academy and was presented with a medal from the Brazilian Navy. The director of the Higher War College did not allow questions after Rodrigues's talk because he feared that some of the officers intended to question him about Salazar's regime.[76] Sarmento Rodrigues also gave the traditional Portuguese National Day lecture at the Real Gabinete. The *Diário de Notícias* condemned the choice of Sarmento Rodrigues as a speaker, calling him an agent of the "fascist system of Lisbon . . . which denies the progress implicit in Portugal's great discoveries by confusing the masts of the caravels with the torture pillories of the PIDE."[77]

The Independent Foreign Policy

Jânio Quadros's presidency (1961) began with a repudiation of many of Juscelino Kubitschek's policies and the announcement of a new "Independent Foreign Policy" that questioned relations with Portugal and supported decolonization. The change was greeted enthusiastically by foes of Salazar and colonialism like José Honório Rodrigues and Álvaro Lins. Their enthusiasm seemed vindicated as Quadros dealt with his first international crisis after taking office. On 22 January 1961 the former Portuguese colonial officer Henrique Galvão, who had sought asylum at the Argentine embassy in Lisbon during the Delgado affair, hijacked the Portuguese liner *Santa Maria* off the coast of South America. He intended to take the ship to Angola to incite a rebellion against Portugal. The first uprising in Angola took place a month later, as suspected MPLA militants were jailed in the aftermath of the hijacking. Chased by Portuguese and United States warships, the *Santa Maria* docked in Recife. Quadros granted Galvão and his fellow conspirators asylum, against protests from Portugal. Though Quadros had planned on distancing Brazilian policy from Portugal, the hijacking set his administration on a path of confrontation with Portugal from the outset.

Quadros's Independent Foreign Policy distanced Brazil from its automatic alignment with the United States and Portugal. It defined Brazil as a leader of the developing world rather than a follower of the United States, indulging Brazilian aspirations to become a world power. It also involved pursuing markets for Brazilian manufactures in places like China. Quadros's Independent Foreign Policy was similar to other expressions of mid-century developmentalist nationalism advanced by Jawaharlal Nehru in India, Gamal Abdel Nasser in Egypt, Josef Tito in Yugoslavia, and Juan Perón in Argentina. The political scientist Wayne Selcher notes the change implied in Quadros's new policy: during the presidential campaign of 1960 Quadros visited Cuba, and in the months before his inauguration he traveled to the Soviet Union, the United Arab Republic, Yugoslavia, India, and Japan. Selcher contrasted this tour with that taken by Kubitschek after his election: the United States, Britain, the Netherlands, Belgium, Luxembourg, France, Germany, Italy, Spain, and Portugal.[78] Candido Mendes,Quadros's advisor for international affairs, recalled that Quadros was "fascinated by Nehru and Tito," the nationalist leaders of India and Yugoslavia. He kept portraits of them on the walls of his office.[79]

Quadros's Independent Foreign Policy repeatedly invoked Brazil's identity as a racial democracy. For Quadros this meant supporting decolonization, even of Portugal's colonies. And it meant building connections with the new countries across the Atlantic. In 1961 Quadros submitted an article explaining the Independent Foreign Policy to *Foreign Affairs*, which appeared after his resignation. He introduced Brazil as "a nation of continental proportions . . . relatively close to Africa and, ethnically having indigenous, European and African roots. Within the next decade our population will amount to close to 100,000,000 inhabitants, and the rapid industrialization of some regions of our country heralds our development into an economic power."[80] He added: "Our democracy is greater than that of other nations of our same cultural sphere. We have thus become the most successful example of racial coexistence and integration known to history."[81]

That the Independent Foreign Policy diminished Brazil's historic deference to the United States was signaled by Quadros when he established diplomatic relations with Cuba, China, and Eastern Europe, and when he bestowed the Order of the Southern Cross upon Che Guevara. He also rejected his country's sentimental deference to Portugal by supporting anticolonial resolutions in the United Nations. Quadros explained: "For many years, Brazil made the mistake of supporting European colonialism in the United Nations . . . Misinformed circles, overly impressed with European patterns of behavior, contributed to a mistake which must be attributed more to a disregard of the deeper commitments of our country than to political malice. Our fraternal relationship with Portugal played its part in the complacency shown by the Ministry of Foreign Affairs of Brazil in this matter. Therefore, everything points to a necessary change of position with regard to colonialism . . . which from now on will meet the determined opposition of Brazil. This is our policy, not merely in the interests of Africa, nor for the sake of platonic solidarity, but because it is in keeping with Brazilian national interests."[82]

Quadros conveyed an image of Brazil as an emerging world power. Africa would be the setting for the expansion of Brazil's influence: "I believe that it is precisely in Africa that Brazil can render its best service to the concepts of Western life and political methods. Our country should become the link, the bridge, between Africa and the west, since we are so intimately bound to both peoples . . . we can give the nations of the Black continent an example of the complete absence of racial prejudice, together with successful proof of progress without undermining the principles of freedom."[83] Brazil would be the bridge between a white, developed West and a black, undeveloped Africa, because of its status as a developing and racially mixed nation.

The architect of Quadros's policy was Afonso Arinos. Son of the prominent politician and foreign minister Afrânio de Mello Franco, Afonso Arinos's intellectual and political trajectory carried him from anti-Semitic writings about the threat of "Jewish internationalists" in the 1930s to becoming the author of the law that barred racial discrimination, commonly known as the Afonso Arinos Law (1954).[84] Arinos's vision of Brazil's role in the world and its character as a beacon of racial tolerance echoed Quadros. As Arinos wrote in 1965, "the fact that we are, to a degree, immune to the racial question does not mean that Brazil should be disengaged from the steps necessary to resolve it . . . no country today has Brazil's standing to become the center of negotiations toward the eradication of racism as a threat to peace and international security."[85]

Arinos's and Quadros's vision of Brazil's race relations and its place in the world was commonplace in the early 1960s, and was often framed by comparison with the United States. The Freyrean vision of racial harmony contrasted viscerally with the images of confrontation, violence, and degradation in the segregated South of the United States. In fact, when cases of racism within Brazil were reported, they were often reports of racist acts by foreigners upon Brazilians, or acts of racism by Brazilians upon African Americans. The Afonso Arinos Law was passed in reaction to the experience of the dancer Katherine Dunham, who was denied a hotel room in São Paulo.[86] The law was seldom used, except as proof of Brazil's racial democracy. Now Quadros and Arinos mobilized the image of racial harmony to cast an image of Brazil's international leadership as an alternative to the lines drawn by the cold war.

Looking Ahead

Contemporary Brazilian relations with Africa began with the administration of Jânio Quadros. Though he was only president for eight months in 1961, his Independent Foreign Policy defined an alternative to the support of Portugal advocated by his predecessors, and did so at the very moment when violent uprisings for independence erupted in Portugal's African colonies. Quadros opened embassies in Ghana, Nigeria, and Senegal. Quadros's successor, João Goulart, continued his policies until he was deposed by the military in 1964. The military installed General Castelo Branco as president of a dictatorship that lasted until 1985. The military reversed the direction of Brazilian foreign policy and jailed supporters of Portuguese African independence movements. Relations with the United States and Portugal were restored. Castelo Branco's foreign minister, Juracy Magalhães, declared "what is good for the United States is good for Brazil." Interviewed by a Portuguese journalist, Magalhães expanded on this sentiment: "What's good for Portugal is received with great joy in Brazil."[87]

During Emilio Medici's presidency, from 1969 to 1974, Brazil's economy grew at an annual average rate of over 11 percent. This "economic miracle" created a new rationale for relations with Africa, and Foreign Minister Mário Gibson Barboza rekindled policy toward African countries that had languished since 1964 in order to develop export markets. He intensified diplomacy with West Africa, attempting to broker negotiations with Portugal. He embarked on a tour of eight West African countries in October 1972, hoping that personal diplomacy would overcome African resentments and open the door to Brazilian exports.

Portugal rejected Gibson Barboza's proposed negotiations. In the meantime, when the United States airlifted military supplies to Israel during the Yom Kippur war of 1973, Arab countries responded by imposing an oil embargo. African countries joined the embargo, which expanded to include countries associated with Portugal. Brazil, which imported over half of its oil, narrowly escaped the embargo, but its economy was destabilized by a tenfold increase in world oil prices. For Gibson Barboza relations with Portugal were a "mortgage" that Brazil could not afford.[88] Médici's successor, Ernesto Geisel, agreed. He had been president of Petrobras during the oil embargo and understood the brutal economic costs of the sentimental connection with Portugal. Geisel did not have an opportunity to change Brazil's policy toward Portugal before his regime was overthrown in the Carnation Revolution of April 1974.

Eager to restore Brazil's credibility in Africa, Geisel made Brazil the first country to recognize the independent government of Angola, even though it was a Marxist regime. That decision was part of a new foreign policy that the regime named "Responsible Pragmatism." The government distanced itself from the United States, believing that the Brazil of the economic miracle was ascendant and the United States was in decline. Ironically, even as it embraced Marxist Angola, the Brazilian government distanced itself from newly socialist Portugal. Brazilian policy, coupled with revolution in Portugal and the liberation of Angola, shaped new currents of migration. Portugal gave asylum to leftist Brazilian exiles as tens of thousands of Portuguese fled to Brazil from the colonies, along with thousands of others from Portugal.

For the rest of the 1970s the Brazilian government worked to realize the potential of its relationships with African countries. It experienced limited success, particularly in Nigeria, which was flush with oil revenue and able to purchase quantities of Brazilian meat, automobiles, and domestic appliances. By 1984 Africa consumed 7.9 percent of Brazil's exports. In the 1980s Brazil's debt crisis limited its foreign policy options and compelled a return to political and economic subordination to the United States. Trade with Africa withered, in part because of Brazil's deteriorating economic conditions, and in part because of the political and economic decline of its African partners like Nigeria. Riven by civil war, Angola did not become the economic and political partner long imagined by Brazilians.

By situating Brazilian racial thought within an Atlantic world context, this book illustrates two things. First, patterns of Brazilian racial thought have been conditioned by international events, such as decolonization in Africa, the Portuguese conflict, and the civil rights struggles of the United States. Second, these experiences among countries shaped by the African diaspora are linked by shared influences, with events in each country unfolding simultaneously. In 1961 and 1975, for instance, Brazil, the United States, Portugal, and Angola were bound by events occurring in each county that were driven by the beginning and culmination of the movement for Angolan independence. This narrative focuses on Brazilian experiences with events in the Atlantic world shaped by decolonization, development, the cold war, and shifting patterns of race relations. Gilberto Freyre provided its dialectical logic: Portugal would be the filter through which Brazilian diplomats and intellectuals would face Africa, and Africa was an abstraction through which Brazilians negotiated the challenges of development and inclusion.

2 Africa and the Independent Foreign Policy

IN 2006, AT A USED BOOKSTORE in Rio de Janeiro, a friend handed me a tattered photo album with photos taken in Africa.[1] There were several dozen prints loosely folded into the album. They had been taken in West Africa in the early 1960s, and they showed Raymundo Souza Dantas, Brazil's first ambassador to an African country and also Brazil's first, and only, black ambassador. The photo album had belonged to the journalist and writer Gasparino Damata, who had served as press attaché at the Brazilian embassy in Ghana.[2] Damata, who later gained renown as the author of queer fiction about bohemian nightlife in Rio de Janeiro, captured a landscape of connections between West Africa and Brazil. The subjects of the photographs ranged from a Portuguese slave fort, to communities of descendants of freed Brazilian slaves who retraced their ancestors' journey and resettled in West Africa (known as *Ta Bom* in Ghana and *agudá* in Nigeria), to members of the first generation of Brazilian intellectuals, artists, and diplomats to travel to newly independent West African countries. Finally there were photos of African independence leaders, like President Nnamdi Azikiwe of Nigeria, as well as street scenes juxtaposing traditional and modern images.

The photographs convey the idealism with which Brazilian diplomats and intellectuals turned toward West Africa in the wake of its decolonization, moved by cultural connections on both sides of the Atlantic: Afro-Brazilian Candomblé in Brazil's northeast, derived from West African

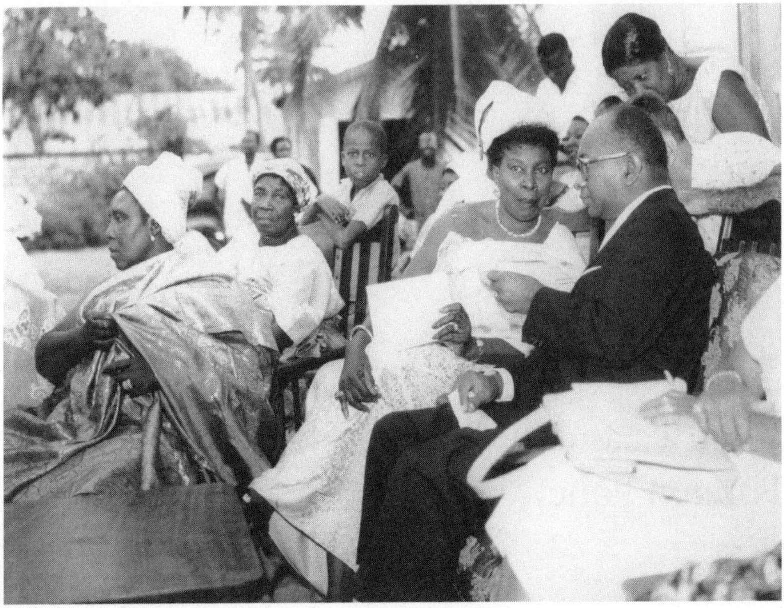

Ambassador Raymundo Souza Dantas with the Ta Bom community in Accra. Author's collection.

spiritism, and the Brazilian identity of agudá communities in West Africa. They were also moved by the sense that African decolonization was transforming the world in a way that would propel Brazil into a global leadership role based on benign race relations. Yet the photos also capture events that belied this romantic optimism. Sending a black ambassador to Ghana did not mean that Brazil was a racial democracy: to the contrary, Souza Dantas had a painful experience. The development of relations with African countries also exposed long-lived rifts between intellectual circles in different regions in Brazil. Finally, the first experiences in developing a foreign policy toward Africa revealed the conflicts faced by Brazilians encountering an Africa based almost entirely on imagination.

These experiences were the fruit of the Independent Foreign Policy carried out by President Jânio Quadros (1961) and continued by his successor, João Goulart (1961–64). Through the Independent Foreign Policy the Brazilian government opened a first embassy in Accra, Ghana, in 1961. A year later embassies in Dakar, Senegal, and Lagos, Nigeria, followed. This chapter looks at Quadros's Independent Foreign Policy, the opening

Vivaldo Costa Lima and Gasparino Damata.
Auhor's collection.

Zola Seljan at a gathering of agudás.
Author's collection.

IFP "Independent Foreign Policy" → Quadros 1961

Agudás at a Bonfim Festival. Author's collection.

Gathering of Ta-Bom and Ambassador Souza Dantas.
Author's collection.

toward Africa, its resonance within Brazil, particularly with regard to the regional competition that it spurred.

Quadros opened Brazil's first sub-Saharan embassy in Ghana because it was the first West African nation to gain independence, and because Kwame Nkrumah's pan-Africanism seemed to make him a natural leader of the continent. The excitement about Nkrumah was captured seven years later by a Brazilian ambassador, Mário Vieira de Mello: "More than anything, Nkrumah was the man who brought independence to Ghana . . . it was easy for the public to embark on his dream of African unity, with all of its consequences. In Nkrumah's personal image, the fate of Ghana seemed at one with the fate of the entire African continent. It was a question not of emancipating a country from the yoke of imperialism, but of liberating all of Africa and making it a continent capable of addressing, on an equal footing, the world that had exploited and terrorized it."[3] Ghana seemed to lead the way for Africa, and it was there that Quadros chose to begin Brazil's diplomatic presence.

Brazil in Africa: The Condemned Mission

Jânio Quadros's decision to send his press aide, Raymundo Souza Dantas, to Ghana epitomized his brief, quixotic presidency in its desire to break with the past, its dismissiveness toward the professional bureaucracy, and its reliance on a close personal associate to fill an important position. Quadros did this with other newly created embassies in North Africa, sending the writer Rubem Braga to Morocco and the painter Cícero Dias to Tunisia.[4] But naming Souza Dantas ambassador to Ghana held particular significance: his color generated resistance among Brazilian diplomats and intellectuals, and provoked existential reflection by the ambassador about the relationship between being black and representing Brazil.

Souza Dantas's nomination as ambassador was practically ignored by Itamaraty. In Ghana he complained to the foreign ministry about the long delays in receiving responses to his telegrams—in one case a response took more than five months.[5] He faced what he saw as racist criticism over the choice to name him ambassador, which left him feeling wounded and isolated. His appointment was condemned in the press.[6] Even José Honório Rodrigues publicly criticized Souza Dantas's appointment as "reverse racism." Rodrigues wrote: "In this Republic, no one should be chosen because of his color, but rather for his moral and intellectual qualifications. It makes especially little sense to choose a person of color to contend with African affairs."[7]

By all accounts and especially his own, Souza Dantas's ambassadorship was a disaster. By the time he arrived in Accra, Quadros had resigned, so Souza Dantas found himself without political support and rejected by his foreign ministry. Itamaraty's disdain for him was exemplified by the behavior of the chargé d'affaires in Accra, Sérgio Corrêa do Lago. Sent to open the embassy in Accra, Corrêa do Lago became the first Brazilian posted to an independent African country. As he organized the embassy, he sent long reflections to Itamaraty about he nature of being a diplomat in Africa, where "after the workday is over, the silence descends, the noisy and nostalgic silence of the African nights, permeated by the natural murmuring of the barren surroundings and the hum of mosquitoes."[8] Corrêa do Lago had previously served in Egypt, had attended summits of African nationalist leaders in the years leading up to independence, and believed that "Brazil could play an important role as natural intermediary between the African continent and the Western world . . . above all, because we are the only true multi-racial democracy in the world."[9] The "easy" way of building these relations would be "drawing on the enormous reserves of folklore that we share with West Africa," by sending musical groups to perform.

Despite Corrêa do Lago's reading of Brazil's racial democracy, when Souza Dantas was named ambassador he felt snubbed and complained to Itamaraty. Once Souza Dantas arrived, Corrêa do Lago refused to move out of the ambassador's residence and Souza Dantas was compelled to spend his first months living in a series of hotels. His presence as a black ambassador representing Brazil in an African country was riddled with contradictions which Souza Dantas explored in a memoir aptly named *Difficult Africa: Diary of a Condemned Mission.*

In the opening pages of his memoir Souza Dantas recounts buying a copy of Frantz Fanon's *The Wretched of the Earth* at a bookstore in Dakar. While Souza Dantas eschewed Fanon's philosophy as "violent," the sentiments in his memoir resemble the anxiety and alienation that Fanon expressed in his work. He struggled with the meaning of being black and Brazilian in Africa, echoing the alienation felt by African American intellectuals like Richard Wright.[10] He reflected that "for obvious reasons, it would not be hard for me to pass for a native, but there were other factors having nothing to do with color but rather with my way of being and of seeing things, that, being a man from another world, was a boundary to the intimacy that I desired."[11] This was the basic challenge that Souza Dantas repeatedly confronted: the difference between being black and being African. The challenge was compounded by being a black man resented for representing Brazil.

Two questions faced Souza Dantas. The first was initially posed by Martin Appiah, an aide to Nkrumah: "You must feel right at home, right?" Did Appiah believe that Souza Dantas should feel at home in Ghana? Or did he ask because feeling "at home" was what a growing number of African Americans traveling to Ghana wanted?[12] Souza Dantas's answer was: "There was no way that I could feel at home, even for being black and the descendant of Africans. My world, my civilization, is a different one, despite all the things that we share and despite my interest for what goes on here." He would return to this point again and again in the memoir, declaring, "I repeat that I belong to another universe, I am a black man of a different civilization."[13]

The second question was equally alienating: "Is there no racial discrimination in Brazil?" Souza Dantas related that when it was posed by a student at the University of Ghana, he had hesitated in responding. He described the student as "waiting for the answer as if something that was really important to him depended on my response." Souza Dantas weighed his answer, noting later that "in different conditions, without the responsibility that was invested in me, the answer would be easy. Whatever I said, as a simple citizen, would represent the opinion of one man, among seventy seven million Brazilians. The student broke the silence, saying 'you don't need to respond' to my raised brow."[14]

Much of Souza Dantas's memoir is dedicated to the burden that this question placed on him. Like all of Brazil's ambassadors, he was charged with presenting the country's race relations in the positive light of racial democracy. Yet this public role contrasted with the discrimination to which he was subjected by Itamaraty, his critics in Brazil, and even his subordinates. He captured the irony of his position when he described drafting the text that he would read when presenting his credentials to President Nkrumah: "I prepared to talk about the ethnic and cultural roots the two countries shared, and to reaffirm our stance of blunt opposition to colonialism and our fight against racial discrimination. I wrote this in the Ambassador Hotel, where I lived for a month waiting for Secretary Corrêa do Lago to vacate the house intended for the chief of mission."[15]

This experience disturbed Souza Dantas. He felt betrayed by his country's response to his color. The ambassador was an outcast, rejected by Itamaraty and challenged by his subordinates:

> I continue to feel let down . . . [but] I do not want to get into that. My purpose is only to register that though everyone considers my becoming ambassador a conquest, for me it has been nothing but a drama. Just as I have decided not to deal with the problems I have had with the embassy in these pages, I also do not want to dwell on being let down by those who, because I am ambassador, strive to put every imaginable obstacle in my way, adding to the difficulties that are naturally part of this job . . . I know that I can't count on anyone in Brazil, be that in Itamaraty, where I have no support, be it in the office of the President, which does not even remember it has embassies in Africa. No one sees us as significant. In the face of that, why stay?
>
> Happily, not everything is cause for bitterness. I received a letter from Brazil with news of my son, Roberto's studies. It was comforting on this depressing morning. May God help him and also get out of his head the idea of going into a diplomatic career. I know what he will suffer for being black.[16]

Souza Dantas understood that though white Brazilians celebrated Africanness and blackness as positive national characteristics, they did not recognize black Brazilians as their peers, nor were they accustomed to sharing positions of authority in their institutions with Brazilians of color. His ambassadorship was an ordeal.

The question of Brazilian race relations and Souza Dantas's ambassadorship generated a quote often repeated and often attributed to Nkrumah. João Clemente Baena Soares, who headed the Africa Division of Itamaraty in 1962 and 1963, recalled: "President Nkrumah took three months to agree to receive his credentials. He declared that Brazil was racist for sending a black person to Africa. He should send a black ambassador to Sweden—that would not be racism. He had a point to a degree. It was simplistic. Why does the first black Brazilian ambassador get sent to Africa? Why not to Europe?"[17] Candido Mendes, head of the IBEAA and one of Quadros's close advisors, recalled hearing the same line directly from Nkrumah during a visit to Ghana. When I interviewed him, Candido Mendes repeated what he recalled as Nkrumah's words: "What the hell has your President done, to send a black ambassador to Ghana. Please send him to Sweden." Mendes explained that Nkrumah "was really irritated with what he saw as reverse racism, sending a black ambassador to

Ghana . . . Raymundo did not have much success because of that . . . it was an error in our Ghana policy."[18] Yet there is no mention of this in Souza Dantas's account.

Why did Souza Dantas not recount the widely repeated exchange? His memoir was structured around two distinct forms of alienation: one was the result of humiliation by Itamaraty, the other of feeling different from Africans. Souza Dantas generally related feeling welcomed and well treated by Ghanaians. He wrote of Ghanaian authorities referring to him as "my brother."[19] He contrasted this with the disrespect he received from Brazilians. It is possible that Souza Dantas did not recount Nkrumah's rebuff because it was embarrassing to be dressed down by the president of the country to which he was posted, and because of his sense that he was a legitimate representative of Brazil regardless of his color. As he made clear, being black did not make him feel like an African, and he resisted the discrimination he faced for being black and being named ambassador. He stressed this challenge when he prefaced his narration of his meeting with Nkrumah with a reference to the hotel where he was still compelled by Corrêa do Lago to live. Nkrumah's remarks undermined the very legitimacy of the ambassadorship that he struggled to assert before Brazilians. It cut against Souza Dantas's identity struggle and illustrated the gulf that separated Africa and Brazil.

But would Nkrumah criticize a black Brazilian to a white Brazilian? Nkrumah had always been receptive when interacting with African Americans ranging from Richard Wright to W. E. B. Du Bois. But whether or not the exchange occurred, this was the most frequently repeated anecdote I heard in the course of my research. Its telling reinforces a dominant Brazilian narrative about race relations: proof of Brazil's racial democracy lay in the fact that a Brazilian of any color could appropriately represent the country before Africans, and that the choice of a black Brazilian as ambassador could be a form of reverse racism, as José Honório Rodrigues had suggested.

Souza Dantas's credentialing ceremony illustrated the distance between Brazil and Ghana in another way as well. Souza Dantas recalled that Nkrumah told him, "I met your new President . . . I met him in Beijing, when he was Vice-President," referring to João Goulart.[20] Goulart traveled on a trade mission to China at Quadros's request, and Quadros resigned during the trip. The timing was inopportune because Goulart's presence in Beijing symbolized the supposed leftist extremism that was grounds for military officers and conservative politicians to oppose his presidency. From the perspective of domestic Brazilian politics, Goulart's trip to China was unfortunate. Yet from the perspective of Brazilian relations with Africa, it was propitious. In the end Goulart's visit to China showed a path not taken, but one that would have aligned Brazilian policy much closer to African leaders like Nkrumah.

While in Ghana, Souza Dantas confronted the potential futility of the Brazilian diplomatic opening toward Africa. Moving between Ghana and Brazil, he came to appreciate how unknown each was to the other: "In Brazil, as is to be expected, I faced all sorts of questions about Africa in general and Ghana in particular. Many irritated me because they were based on either complete bad faith or ignorance. The truth is that little is known about Africa in my country. On the other hand, the same is true for Africans about us."[21] He found himself as an intermediary between two societies that were ignorant of each other, accentuating his feeling that he was "a black man of a different civilization."[22]

This ignorance was accompanied by the absence of a Brazilian political or economic strategy with regard to Africa, beyond simply opening embassies. Quadros's resignation and the ensuing political turbulence left a vacuum. He wondered, "What is the point of having an ambassador here? Just to show up at cocktail parties and receptions," and he concluded: "I am planning to return to Brazil within the month. I already have the terms of the resignation letter I will send to President Goulart. I intend to stress that not much has been done here . . . It is my duty to report that this embassy never had the resources it needed to function effectively. Nothing, really, was done to increase our commercial exchange . . . I don't intend to make excuses for myself over what has not been done, even with the lack of resources. But I have to make clear what our actions in Ghana could have been, if we had had the resources to do what was planned. The truth is I will never send a letter like that. It will be a simple resignation letter that will only mention the need to attend to my health. The truth is that all this was never more than a drama."[23] Souza Dantas returned to Brazil in 1963, frustrated about the limits of Brazilian relations with Ghana, though his personal struggles with race and identity loomed larger. Meanwhile, the embassy in Ghana stagnated further after his departure. It was not part of any of the foreign ministry's truncated priorities in 1963 and 1964. And it was even less so after the coup of 1964. Nkrumah was overthrown in a military coup in 1966, which further diminished Ghana's international exposure as the new regime turned away from Nkrumah's pan-Africanism. But for Souza Dantas, it was "a mission condemned from the outset."[24]

The Brazilians traveling to Ghana were confronted by difficult realities about their own country. Quadros's Africa policy spurred competition and resentment between the intellectual circles in Rio de Janeiro and Salvador most interested in Africa. Meanwhile, Corrêa do Lago was petulant about serving under an ambassador not like himself, white and a career diplomat. For his part, Souza Dantas had built a career in government as a public affairs officer, and although by no means a militant on questions of race, he found himself demeaned and undermined for being black. If Brazil was a racial democracy, it was not one in which Souza Dantas could be ambassador and Corrêa do Lago his subordinate.

After Souza Dantas returned to Brazil in 1963, Itamaraty did not send another ambassador to Ghana until 1968. The embassy was staffed by a chargé d'affaires, and its communications with Itamaraty dwindled to sparse telegrams about basic administrative matters like the scheduling of vacations and the updating of ciphers for decoding classified communications. Souza Dantas had suggested to Itamaraty that the most important forum for relations with Ghana was the UN, where Nkrumah sought Brazilian support for Portuguese African decolonization. The Brazilian military regime's ties with Portugal after 1964 shredded this means of connecting. Corrêa do Lago saw an additional problem: "As a rule, in West Africa, Brazil is nothing more than the legendary land to which people's forefathers were taken or from which their forefathers came . . . it is not surprising our ties have not developed more fully for two reasons: 1) we do not yet have an Africa policy; 2) Africans do not yet know what Brazil is."[25]

These difficulties were illustrated by an exchange between Souza Dantas and Itamaraty in 1962 about the delivery of coffee for the embassy. In a typical gesture, Quadros issued a decree in 1961 that the governmental Brazilian Coffee Institute (IBC) send bags of coffee to Brazilian embassies, to promote the country's main export.[26] Six months after the embassy in Ghana was notified that it would be receiving the shipments, no coffee had arrived. Souza Dantas cabled Itamaraty to ask where the coffee was, and five months later he received his reply: "Until now, our effort to deliver coffee to the embassies has not been crowned with anything but incomplete success. On the one hand, the steamers of Lloide Brasileiro are willing to transport the sacks of coffee free of charge. But on the other, this means that the shipments only go to their destinations in Europe and North Africa, which nowhere near satisfies the commitment to serve every embassy, let alone do so regularly. I believe that in the future this situation will improve and your embassy will receive its regular supply of coffee."[27] If Itamaraty and the merchant marine, acting under presidential order, could not deliver a bag of coffee to the embassy in Accra, it is little surprise that not much else flowed between the two countries.

When a new ambassador, Mário Vieira de Mello, finally arrived in March 1968, what he encountered must have seemed like the last Brazilian embassy on earth. The telegram he sent on his first day there described the embassy as "totally undignified . . . there is no country so badly set up as Brazil." Lacking air conditioning, the embassy was "absolutely uninhabitable."[28] Remaining in Accra for four years, Vieira de Mello brought momentum and continuity to the embassy, even though relations with Ghana were a low priority and trade was negligible.

A year into his tenure in Accra Vieira de Mello reported to the foreign ministry on the difficulty in getting trade going. His analysis was "not intended to stimulate new trade efforts . . . everything that could be said about that already has . . . the difficulties [to trade] persist purely because by their nature they are not simple to solve."[29] Vieira de Mello analyzed these problems on both sides of the Atlantic. In Ghana he pointed to foreign debt, neocolonial ties to Britain, and a weak consumer market as barriers, and suggested that West Africa was disadvantaged by the Atlantic world trade system still dominated by Europeans. While in his view Nkrumah had tried to contend with Ghana's lack of economic dynamism, Vieira de Mello believed that Ghana's development plan had foundered and led to a "re-colonization" of the country.

Vieira de Mello saw Brazil's economic potential for trade with Africa in similarly pessimistic terms. Brazil's export sector was still immature, capable only of selling to two types of clients: wealthy countries that had reserves of hard currency to spend on imports, and countries with complementary economies that allowed basic exchanges of goods. The capacity that Brazil did not have, according to Vieira de Mello, was that of stimulating trade by exporting capital. Those countries that did well in Africa, he explained, were those that could finance private and public sector development, and build foreign markets for goods through that capital flow. In the end neither Brazil nor Ghana had reached a stage of development at which trade currents could be sustained. This meant that there was little sense in trying to resolve the obvious barriers, like the lack of shipping between the two sides of the Atlantic. Eight years after Souza Dantas began the condemned mission, Brazil still had really no mission in Ghana.

"What Africa? Why Africa?"

These questions, posed by Maria Yedda Linhares, trace the limits of the diplomatic opening toward Africa initiated by Jânio Quadros as a core of his Independent Foreign Policy. To her questions we can add, "What Brazil?" Under Quadros and Goulart the Brazilian foreign ministry expanded its diplomatic reach and its bureaucratic capacity, opening embassies in Ghana, Senegal, and Nigeria, as well as consulates in Angola and Mozambique. These legations, and the Brazilians who staffed them, were an expression of the Brazilian imagination, synthesized by Quadros. This imagination held that Brazil was an emerging world power, Africa was its natural sphere of influence, and racial democracy was its calling card. In turn, Africa would help propel Brazil industrially and bring autonomy from the cold war powers.

At ninety-four, looking back on her role in the effort to establish ties with African countries in the 1960s, Maria Yedda Linhares recalled, "At the time Africa was really important for us intellectuals, and people who imagined ourselves to be on the left. We believed we had to change Brazilian policy and turn it towards Africa, that Brazil had its roots in Africa." With hindsight, though, Linhares felt, "Today it is hard to take it seriously. It was all done by very honest, very serious people," but it was "totally ingenuous."[30] Linhares taught African history at the University of Brazil and participated in the Brazilian Institute for Afro-Asian Studies (IBEAA), and through IBEAA worked closely with Cândido Mendes and others involved in developing policies toward Africa.

Maria Yedda Linhares's recollections about her involvement in IBEAA convey the enthusiasm that Brazilian intellectuals, particularly on the left, felt about African decolonization and its potential for harnessing Brazil to the dynamics of world change. Looking back in 2008, she criticized what she saw as the naïveté of members of her intellectual generation. As she saw it, they knew little about Africa and the changes it was experiencing, and their interest was inspired by idealism rather than practical

Maria Yedda Linhares, Cândido Mendes, and their spouses with Kwame Nkruma. Photo courtesy of Maria Yedda Linhares.

experience. But it was exactly her criticisms which highlighted the mentality of the period and the sense of potential that she and others perceived.

Linhares was one of Brazil's first women to hold a university faculty position as a historian, and she faced limits on research and teaching. Her field was defined by what her male peers at the University of Brazil already covered: she could not teach the history of Brazil, the Americas, or Europe. Hiring was conducted through the presentation of a succession of theses. Her first was on the Suez crisis of 1956, when Britain and France invaded Egypt in a failed attempt to halt Gamal Nasser's nationalization of the canal. Her second was on British colonialism in Sudan.[31] She achieved promotion with a thesis on French colonial expansion in Africa, becoming one of the few professors teaching the history of Africa in Brazil.[32]

In the early 1960s her university became a hotbed of support for African liberation, and Linhares found herself at the center of it.[33] She recalled the prevailing view: "We have to go to Africa, to bring Africa to Brazil. Instead of building relations with France and England and all those decadent countries, we have to do it with Africa [she laughs] . . . it was all of that craziness that people used to go on about."[34] As for the environment in which these ideas resonated, "It comprised important Brazilian intellectual circles, well known figures. 'We have to go back to Africa.' 'Africa is our origin.' Such a romantic idea . . . Suddenly, being mulatto was an honor, a dignifying thing. 'I am mulatto. I am African.' It was silliness, really. But Africa really became an inspiration, and it drove people to want to go. I had a huge interest in going to Africa . . . 'So, let's all go to Africa!' 'We are going to be Africans, we are going to be Africans!' It's going to be great! 'We are all Africans, all Africans.' In the end it was foolishness. I don't know. It was fashionable, but ingenuous."[35] Progressive intellectuals found inspiration in the landscape that Maria Yedda Linhares described. It meant something about Brazil, and it meant something about themselves: "These were intellectuals who thought of themselves as being 'the left,' but we didn't have a truly militant left. What were we fighting for? How? By what means? So we went along building up these things about Africa. We spoke of 'Brazilian policy toward Africa,' as though Brazil was going to suddenly save Africa!"[36]

Africa was a symbol of change within an intellectual milieu which was committed to development measures ranging from industrialization to land reform, and which defined success as Brazil's ability to step out from under the shadow of the United States and become a world leader in its own right. Jânio Quadros's foreign policy matched these aspirations. His new policy direction meant allocating new resources and reallocating existing resources. The opening toward Africa created opportunities, competition for resources, and resentments. One example was the presidential order creating scholarships to bring African university students to Brazil. Quadros financed the scholarships by cutting the pay of the diplomatic corps. The scholarships typified Quadros's vision of governance: distrusting bureaucracy, he shifted authority and resources away from the foreign ministry and used his own entity, IBEAA, to coordinate the program and assign students to Brazilian universities based on their areas of interest.

Race, Region, and Africa

Beyond Souza Dantas, relations with Africa almost completely excluded black Brazilians from senior policy positions, the diplomatic corps, or universities. Thus the debate to define policies unfolded among white political and intellectual élites against a backdrop of regional rivalries. This process unfolded primarily between Rio de Janeiro, Brasília, and Salvador, though São Paulo also played a role once industrial goods and engineering services began to be exported to African countries in the 1970s. Rio de Janeiro concentrated political power, while national development was symbolized by Brasília and Brazil's connection to Africa by Salvador.

While the capital had formally moved to Brasília, the foreign ministry, Itamaraty, remained in Rio until the end of 1970. In addition, through the 1960s Brazilian presidents maintained governing offices and staff in both Brasília and Rio de Janeiro. As a result, politicians, intellectuals, journalists, ethnic groups, and others in Rio de Janeiro continued both to wield disproportionate influence over presidential politics and to cull disproportionate rewards. The Portuguese lobby was an example of this influence. The result was that politicians and intellectuals in Rio de Janeiro continued to think of themselves as a national élite. The sense that Rio was the center of the nation is conveyed by the names of the department and university where Linhares worked: the *National* Faculty of Philosophy of the University of *Brazil*.

Since Rio remained a de facto capital, the major figures developing Africa policy were based there, even though many were originally from other parts of the country. Linhares had been born in Ceará. Candido Mendes was a professor at the Catholic University in Rio. Other artists and intellectuals interested in Africa, such as the Bahian writer Jorge Amado, the literary critic Antonio Olinto (originally from Minas Gerais), and the writers Zora Seljan and Rubem Braga, formed an intellectual circle in Rio de Janeiro that succeeded in connecting itself to Quadros's Independent Foreign Policy. Quadros's penchant for trusting friends and associates over members of the professional bureaucracy magnified the influence of this group.

Through the 1960s Brasília had limited influence in Brazilian relations with Africa, though it had a rhetorical and symbolic role. The national congress functioned in Brasília. The Chamber of Deputies, with many members elected from centers of Portuguese immigration like Rio de Janeiro and São Paulo, became a forum for advocating support for Portugal. The Senate, on the other hand, was a center for support of Quadros's policies in Africa. Foreign Minister Arinos, one of the leaders of the president's National Democratic Union (UDN) party, still held a seat there, as did his successor San Tiago Dantas. The Senate ratified ambassadors, and its Foreign Relations Commission was a forum for discussing the opening toward Africa.

Inaugurated in 1960, the capital was as new as the emerging African countries. Brasília's modern architecture and urban planning, and its function as a hub of transportation and communications intended to open and develop Brazil's interior, represented strategies for state-sponsored development that were compatible with the goals of new African governments. Brasília attracted the attention of Senegalese and Nigerian officials in particular. The concepts employed in Brasília to evoke progress and modernity were reference points that resonated with Africans and others in the developing world as well. One of Brasília's architectural centerpieces was a television tower. It was such a geographic and technological landmark that it had a tourist restaurant in its base. While a television tower was no longer a milestone in the United States or Europe, most African countries lacked television systems when they became independent. Brazilian authorities held up Brasília's architectural and urban plan as an example to African nations. In 1963 Itamaraty organized a photo exposition entitled "Brasília and Other Brazilian Cities," which it circulated among Brazilian missions in Africa.[37] In the 1970s, when Nigeria used oil profits to move its capital from Lagos to Abuja, a planned city in the center of the country, Brazilian urban planners participated in the project.

Salvador, on the other hand, symbolized Brazil's past connections to Africa. It was a traditional center of commerce with Africa and of the slave trade, and was the capital of Bahia, a distinctive region which retained remnants of West African languages and cultural practices. In Salvador politicians, intellectuals, and businesses worked to preserve historical neighborhoods and practices defined as "Afro-Brazilian," such as *candomblé* and *capoeira*, that presented Salvador as the cultural heart of Brazil. As Jocélio Teles dos Santos explains, beginning in the late 1950s Bahia was reimagined as a space that crystallized black culture into "the raw material of a new program of development and of foreign affairs."[38]

In tandem with the political and economic goal of scripting Salvador as the center of Brazilian national identity and making it into a tourist destination, a community of intellectuals and artists worked to mine and interpret "African" cultural practices in Bahia. They traced the history of contacts between Salvador and West Africa and explored the cultural expressions that these contacts sustained. These scholars and artists formed a community interested in the Brazilian political opening toward Africa. It cooperated and competed with the intellectual circle in Rio de Janeiro for access to the channels opened by Quadros's foreign policy. They competed at a disadvantage because they were further from the political center in Rio de Janeiro, but they successfully leveraged Salvador into an indispensable link in the Brazilian connection to West Africa.

The two key Bahians involved in forging this presence were the French photojournalist Pierre Verger and the Portuguese exile George Agostinho da Silva. Agostinho da Silva gained the support of the state governor and the rector of the University of Bahia to establish a Center for Afro-Oriental Studies (CEAO)—an endeavor that was compatible with promoting Bahia as the African heart of Brazil. Teles dos Santos cites Agostinho's son, who explained that the creation of CEAO was "less because of academic interests than for creating a political instrument that would act locally (it taught a course on Yoruba for members of local *candomblés* . . .), nationally (fostering student and faculty exchange between Brazil and Africa), and internationally (as a center for promoting a policy of relations with the Third World)."[39]

Because of his connections in West Africa, Verger became an intermediary for the Brazilian foreign ministry and for Brazilian diplomats traveling to Africa. Verger settled in Salvador in the late 1940s and began photographing street scenes of Afro-Bahian culture. His ethnographic photography mapped religious and cultural connections between West Africa and Brazil, and as the title of a documentary on his work suggests, Verger became a "messenger between two worlds."[40] The connections that Verger studied were rooted in cultural and commercial ties between West Africa (particularly Lagos) and Bahia through the nineteenth century and the early twentieth. These connections nourished the Afro-Brazilian religion of Candomblé, whose adherents presented it as an "authentic" African space in Brazil. The leaders of one Candomblé terreiro (ceremonial site), Ilê Axé Opô Afonjá, employed these connections with particular adroitness, crafting the site into the "headquarters of Bahian African purism."[41]

That Opô Afonjá Candomblé became a central site for artists and intellectuals interested in Afro-Brazilian culture and its African roots was one result of efforts by its *mãe de santo* (head priest), Mãe Aninha, to recast her Candomblé rituals as "authentically" African, by modeling them on an emerging Nigerian Yoruba cultural identity developed in resistance to British rule.[42] Mãe Aninha and her successor, Mãe Senhora, cultivated contacts with anthropologists, artists, and intellectuals, whose quest for "authentic" cultural practices fit with Opô Afonjá's project. Fry described this connection with regard to Roger Bastide, who made the transition from a scholar of Candomblé to an initiate: "initiation in nagô Candomblé confers African *status* . . . there is a selective affinity between nagô Candomblé and intellectuals, between Africa and disenchanted professionals in the humanities."[43] The "authenticity" and "purity" of this Candomblé made it increasingly sought out by white intellectuals and artists like Bastide.[44] Verger became a *babalaô* (diviner of cowrie shells) at Opô Afonjá, a role that facilitated his movements between Bahia and West Africa. Verger also introduced Opô Afonjá to white artists and intellectuals like Zora Seljan and Antonio Olinto.

Connections to the Opô Afonjá terreiro spurred a rivalry between intellectuals in Salvador and Rio de Janeiro that was still visible during interviews conducted in 2006. The Salvador group coalesced around Agostinho da Silva and the University of Bahia and included Waldir Freitas, a geographer who directed the CEAO in the 1960s; Verger; the anthropologist Vivaldo Costa Lima, who studied Candomblé; and the linguist Yedda Pessoa Castro. Competition was uneven, since the Rio group wielded its proximity to political power effectively. Freitas recalled that "the Rio group had intellectuals of serious influence. Among them, Jorge Amado [originally from Bahia but living in Rio]. Alongside Jorge Amado, there was Antonio Olinto. Alongside Antonio Olinto, there was Raymundo Souza Dantas . . . What this group really wanted was for Brazil to create embassies in African countries and then choose them as the ambassadors."[45] While the Rio group was more successful in shaping policy and in gaining diplomatic postings, members of the Bahia group developed a relationship with the Itamaraty Cultural Affairs Department, which supported their travel to West Africa as visiting lecturers and financed a monthly CEAO newspaper, published in English as *Brazil Report* and in Portuguese as *África e Ásia*, that was mailed to university libraries across Africa.[46] Itamaraty also sent visiting African politicians and diplomats to Salvador to see Brazil's "African roots."

It was this quest for Brazil's "African roots" that drew artists and intellectuals from Rio to Salvador as well. The modernist playwright Zora Seljan Braga became interested in Candomblé when she traveled as a tourist to Salvador in the early 1950s. Verger took her to Opô Afonjá, and she "became enraptured by Mãe Senhora," Antonio Olinto recalled.[47] She returned to Rio de Janeiro convinced that Candomblé reflected Brazil's roots, and committed to incorporating West African mythology into construction of a national Brazilian theater. Based on her studies of Candomblé and her travel in Nigeria, Seljan declared that "Yoruba is the greatest of the African cultural influences in Brazil, because its legends and traditions still inspire literature, the arts, and the mystical unconscious of our people."[48] She became an initiate in Opô Afonjá and used the history and stories that Mãe Senhora shared to craft novels and plays on Afro-Brazilian religious themes. Seljan's experience exemplified the fascination that Candomblé held for Brazil's affluent cultural avant-garde, particularly in Rio, as well as the resentment of outsiders like her felt by some devotees of Candomblé in Bahia.

In 1955, when Mãe Senhora traveled to Rio, Zora Seljan organized receptions in her honor. Writing to Verger, Seljan captured the fascination that Afro-Brazilian religion held for high-society artists and intellectuals. The first reception was at the home of an art magazine editor and was attended by artists and musicians. Seljan recounted: "The popular musician Jorge Fernandes sang several folkloric tunes and Léa Abdias [García] recited black poems. It was in a beautiful apartment in Urca, with views of the Sugarloaf and the bay."[49] Another reception, "more for leftist writers," was held at "one of the most sumptuous mansions [in the city . . . the owner], grandson of Mayor Passos, has dedicated himself wholeheartedly to popular causes, so this palace is today playing the true role of palaces." The third was in "a luxurious [Copacabana] apartment, with an enormous terrace suitable to a good party." At the party, with "too many guests to list," a thirty-person folkloric ensemble danced traditional sambas.[50]

This was all part of Seljan's cultural and artistic plan to "influence the creation of a Brazilian style of theater." She explained to Verger: "We have all of this rich material from the African, Indigenous and Iberian traditions. It is an embryonic theater that we must develop in order to popularize our own myths. It is not fair, for example, that our northeastern troubadours speak of Jupiter and not Xangô [hail!] . . . We can create, here in Brazil, a totally new theater with a clear national character."[51] West African spiritism and its Brazilian derivatives would replace European classics as Brazil's mythology and literary canon. She began to write to Verger in Yoruba, and when she signed her name she would punctuate it with a double axe, symbol of Xangô.

In 1955 Zora Seljan married the writer and literary critic Antonio Olinto. I interviewed Antonio Olinto in May 2006, in the study of the art deco apartment building in Copacabana where he and Zora Seljan had lived since 1960. He was still mourning her death a month earlier, and our conversations were steeped by a sense of loss that drew him into a recollection of the journey into Afro-Brazilian and African culture on which Zora Seljan had taken him. Before we began to talk about their experience in Lagos, he showed me room after room of African masks, carvings, and textiles that he had collected in West Africa, including a staff for divining cowrie shells, the task that Verger performed in Mãe Senhora's terreiro.

When I asked Olinto how he became interested in Africa, he replied, "because of Zora. She was interested in Yoruba culture, in Candomblé culture. She brought me into that medium. I had never thought about Candomblé in my life."[52] He too became an initiate of Opô Afonjá, and Candomblé and Africa shaped his writing. He published a trilogy celebrating the connections between Brazil and Africa. Olinto explained to me: "we have to be very faithful to the [African] tradition. That tradition helped create us. We are not Europeans. We are Brazilians mixed with Africa."[53] The first book of the trilogy, *The Water House* (1969), was the story of freed Brazilian slaves migrating to West Africa. It was published in nineteen languages, and Olinto showed me a photo of himself handing a copy to Pope John Paul II. In the text the freed slaves originate in the town in Minas Gerais where Olinto was born, and he wrote himself into one of the black Brazilian characters, Antonio. I asked him if this was intentional. He smiled and replied, "Yes, there is an Antonio there."[54]

Antonio Olinto told me on two occasions how he and Seljan had gained the opportunity to go to Nigeria, first at his apartment and again three weeks later at the library of the Brazilian Academy of Letters, where he was a member. As he told the story, the opportunity to travel to Africa was a result of the national political crisis that followed the sudden resignation of President Jânio Quadros in 1961. The Brazilian Congress resolved the crisis by crafting a compromise according to which João Goulart became president but his cabinet was appointed by Congress and headed by a prime minister. The compromise lasted until the beginning of 1963, when Goulart regained full presidential powers.

Through 1962 the Minas Gerais congressman Tancredo Neves was prime minister. At a reception Neves offered his fellow *mineiro* Olinto a diplomatic posting as cultural attaché and asked him where he wanted to go. Olinto replied that he wanted to go to Nigeria. Neves was surprised by the response and asked why. Olinto recalled: "He thought it was strange that I asked to go to Nigeria. 'Why didn't you ask for France?' "[55] Olinto responded that he had several reasons: "I asked for Nigeria for cultural reasons, because Zora and I are in that environment here, that black environment here, inside of black culture. Nigeria was the Rome of Yoruba culture, it was Rome—the base. Nigeria and Dahomey. For her it was great. She developed her literature. For me too."[56] While Neves did not understand why Olinto would choose Lagos over any other city in the world, he arranged the appointment.

At the time Pierre Verger gave a different account of the circumstances that allowed Olinto and Seljan to go to Nigeria. His impression, shared by others in Salvador, was that Olinto campaigned to become ambassador rather than cultural attaché. In November 1961 Vivaldo Costa Lima wrote to Verger from Accra and asked: "Is your friend Olinto still going to be ambassador?"[57] Verger replied that he spoke about this with the director of Itamaraty's Cultural Division, and that in spite of the "waves" Zora Seljan had made, "mobilizing all of Brazil's intellectual circles" to have Olinto named as ambassador to Nigeria, Itamaraty would name a career diplomat for the post.[58]

The difference between these accounts highlights Olinto's construction of a narrative situating himself within Afro-Brazilian culture, alongside Africa, and at the center of a national political crisis, navigating its opportunities through regional personal connections. Olinto's account accentuated Tancredo Neves's surprise. This surprise, based on the presumption that Africa should be a distant choice, helps position Olinto and Seljan "inside" Afro-Brazilian culture. By calling Nigeria Brazil's "Rome," Olinto drew into his personal narrative Zora Seljan's belief that African religion and culture should become the foundations of a truly national Brazilian culture. Olinto's account positioned him to describe Nigeria as the birthplace of his identity as a writer: "In Africa, I gained a topic—Africa itself."[59]

The difference between Olinto's narrative and Verger's also signals the deep division between intellectual circles in Salvador and Rio de Janeiro over access to Africa through the new channels being opened by Itamaraty. At the bottom of the rivalry, beyond professional competition and diplomatic posts, lay the question of whose connections to Opô Afonjá were legitimate. All but Freitas were initiates in Opô Afonjá. Verger, Costa Lima, and Freitas all conducted ethnographic research there. Despite Seljan's florid letters in Yoruba to Verger and her dedication to Afro-Brazilian culture, she and Olinto were perceived as interlopers. Expressing the rivalry in blunt terms, Costa Lima wrote to Verger, "Your friend Zora has announced that she is writing a biography of [Mãe] Senhora that will naturally lie and deceive as Zora does . . . These people are vultures, and they exploit Senhora even in death."[60] When Pierre Verger and Vivaldo Costa Lima corresponded, they both referred ironically to Zora Seljan as "your friend Zora," and at other times Verger referred to Seljan only as "Olinto's interesting wife."[61]

These tensions were not just regional. A photograph in Gasparino Damatta's photo album was folded to exclude Zora Seljan, revealing a rift also present in Souza Dantas's memoir. After traveling with Damatta to visit Togo, Souza Dantas commented that "if his health were better," Damatta would be the best person to write about the communities of descendants of Brazilian slaves on the coast of West Africa, "better than the famous Verger . . . or the pretentious and the ambitious [Olinto and Seljan] . . . I have better things to do than worry myself with those people."[62] Still, these personal conflicts reflected competition over resources, and over who was best qualified to interpret the significance that Africa held for Brazil.

Final Thoughts

Some of the first Atlantic crossings of the 1960s were made by African students receiving scholarships from Itamaraty. The first cohort of African students arrived in the second half of 1961. There were fifteen students from Ghana, Senegal, Nigeria, Cameroon, Cabo Verde, and Guiné-Bissau. IBEAA assigned them to universities around Brazil, but it sent them first to Salvador, where they would take three months of classes on Portuguese and "Brazilian Civilization" at the CEAO at the University of Bahia. In Bahia, not surprisingly, one of their first stops was Mãe Senhora's terreiro. They also visited an oil refinery. Together the trips marked the cornerstones of Brazilian self-representation: African roots and industrial development.[63]

One Nigerian student's experience captured the contradictions between Brazilian imagination about Africa and African visions of Brazil. The student was housed in a women's dorm at the University of Bahia. According to Freitas, her dormmates complained that she kept them awake all night, hysterically singing evangelical hymns. Freitas visited her and recalled her trying to keep him away, saying, "No, you are Xangô!"

Back row, third from left, Maria Yedda Linhares at the World without the Bomb Conference, Accra. Photo courtesy of Maria Yedda Linhares.

(meaning a devotee of the god of war and thunder). She would not allow anyone from the university near her. Finally George Alakija, a psychiatrist with family ties to Nigeria, interned her in a mental hospital. What had happened? "She had been educated at a rigid Anglican school. Arriving in Bahia, everything she had been taught was the work of the devil—the orixás, candomblé—surrounded her here. The hotel she was first housed in was called the Oxumaré. Afterward she was moved to the Oxalá. She began to lose herself . . . it was as if she were in hell. So she began to keep everyone awake at night while she sang evangelical hymns trying to keep the demons away." For Freitas, in Bahia she "discovered the Africa she did not know."[64]

The student was a victim of what Yedda Linhares later saw as impractical idealism. Yet her critique frames that idealism:

> The idea was to bring Brazil out of its shell and open it to the world. Brazil would be the natural heir of Africa and its natural mentor, since in turn it was Africa that made Brazil. So Africans here in Brazil came to be esteemed

and celebrated because they had come from Africa. Our intellectual world was really naïve and immature. It saw Brazil's fate as tied to the future of Africa and Asia. So we were full of idealism, but it was all talk. In terms of concrete policies, there was nothing. They convinced themselves that because they were Brazilians, they would have a policy toward Africa. Alright. But what in Africa? How in Africa? What are the goals, the objectives? "Ah, but it's Africa . . ." My impression is that it was a left that was unprepared. Honest, extremely honest, extremely idealistic. It wanted things to be different, but it did not have the means to change them. So what to do? How to get into government? Because these things aren't achieved by, say, twenty people. They are historical changes that take a long time, that are really difficult, etc.[65]

Linhares saw her own role in the push toward Africa as representing a kind of access point and a source of information within an environment in which everyone was African and wanted to connect to Africa but no one had any knowledge or information about it: "Say it's the anniversary of Nigeria's independence, 'what are we going to do?' No one even knows where Nigeria is. 'Yedda, come here, tell us about Nigeria.'"[66] Like the African exchange students arriving in Bahia, the Brazilians traveling to West Africa were strained by imagined connections and the contradictions they revealed.

Gasparino Damata's photographs retain a trace of the initial idealism and enthusiasm with which the first Brazilian diplomats turned towards Ghana. His photographs captured the fascination with which Brazilians beheld agudá communities, were drawn to Portuguese slave-trade relics, and soaked up the sense of change that permeated the liberation of former colonies. At the height of this enthusiasm Candido Mendes, Maria Yedda Linhares, and their spouses traveled to Ghana as Brazilian delegates to the "World without the Bomb Conference" organized by Nkrumah. They posed for a photograph with Nkrumah, a photograph which Linhares shared with me. The moment was a high point for their conviction that Brazil, with Africa, would change the world.

3 "The Lovers of the African Race"

Brazilian Diplomats in Nigeria

ANTONIO CARLOS TAVARES WAS DEAD. Perhaps it was the Orixás' revenge for the slave trade. The messengers of the Brazilian embassy in Lagos, employed because of the unreliability of the Nigerian telephone system, cleaned the blood-spattered floor of the stairwell after the chief of the Brazilian mission fell from the embassy's third-floor offices. He died in September 1963, a year after he had arrived as the chargé d'affaires to open the new Brazilian embassy in Lagos. A "Tribute to Carlos Tavares" in the *Nigerian Monday Post* eulogized: "Mr. Tavares, popularly known in Brazil as the 'lover of the African race' being enthusiastic about Africa requested to be transferred to Nigeria."[1] He had just married and his wife was pregnant. At thirty-two, Tavares was the youngest chief of mission in Lagos. He was not the first to die.

Seven months earlier Brazil's first ambassador designated to Nigeria, Luiz de Souza Bandeira, had died of a heart attack. He had been in Nigeria for only two weeks. With Souza Bandeira's arrival, Tavares requested his transfer back to Brazil.[2] Instead Tavares found himself with the grim task of finding a coffin for the ambassador's body. Souza Bandeira was a heavyset man, and there were simply no coffins large enough to be found in funeral homes in Lagos; Tavares despaired of removing the body from the morgue, which he likened to Dante's Inferno. Luckily the United States embassy gave Tavares an extra-large coffin from its supply.[3]

Was the mission cursed? The first Brazilian ambassador to survive his posting to Lagos raised this question in his final report. José Osvaldo Meira Penna (1963–65) related the embassy's misfortunes to the foreign minister: "In fewer than three years, we have had three deaths, a child run over, a cook poisoned to death, a grave illness, embezzlement of funds, four fights and the violation of a minor."[4] Meira Penna mused that perhaps the old adage held true, and West Africa really was the "white man's grave."[5]

I asked Meira Penna about the curse when I interviewed him in 2006 in Brasília. He responded: "We were surrounded by bad luck, there was a whole series of things and it wasn't something you could just blame on the climate."[6] Meira Penna was more specific in his report in 1965 about the nature of that luck, suggesting that it was "a malediction of the Yoruban *orixás* that are avenging the sad fate of their bygone devotees, carried by the millions to Bahia in the holds of slave ships, casting over this office what is called *jújú*. What we call *urucubaca* [cursed fortune]."[7]

Meira Penna's interpretations of the misadventures of Brazil's first diplomats in Nigeria are rooted in two distinct ways of relating to Africa. First, when he described it as a "white man's grave," he employed European colonial discourse. Writing at nearly the same time as Meira Penna, Philip Curtin explained, "there is a 'black legend' about the climate of tropical countries, that lives on . . . it is usually elaborated with such elements as 'primitive tribes,' burning heat, fever-laden swamps . . . Above all, West Africa is thought of as a place where white men cannot work. Only Africans can work there, and Europeans 'go out' for brief periods at considerable risk to their lives."[8] In his reports and recollections, Meira Penna frequently invoked climatological interpretations of Nigeria and Brazil. But in his report of 1965, Meira Penna pivoted from a European reading of these misadventures to an Afro-Brazilian one, and did so again when I interviewed him forty years later, emphasizing that the difficulties could not be attributed to climate. Alongside the reference to the "white man's grave," on the same pages Meira Penna could characterize the curse in the language of Afro-Brazilian spiritism and even assert his mastery of it by accentuating African ethnic semantics about the origins of the word *urucubaca*, debating in his report whether the term belonged to the Bantu or the Yoruba language family.

Meira Penna captured a basic element of Brazilian national identity: that ethnicity and race are imagined to be collectively shared characteristics. This pluralism means that racial and ethnic identities were interchangeable. Meira Penna could simultaneously interpret Tavares's death through the European lens of the "white man's burden" and the Afro-Brazilian lens of "jújú." The Brazilians who traveled to Nigeria in the years immediately following its independence were predominantly white, and they often embraced Afro-Brazilian culture to a much greater extent than Meira Penna did. And to varying degrees, they all shared a sense that they too were African, regardless of the color of their skin, because they were Brazilian.

This chapter explores early Brazilian encounters with independent Nigeria, focusing on the experiences of Zora Seljan, Antonio Olinto, Alberto da Costa e Silva, Osvaldo Meira Penna, and Adhemar Ferreira da Silva, all posted to Lagos between 1961 and 1983. It draws on Itamaraty records, Nigerian newspapers, memoirs, and interviews. The job of these Brazilians in Lagos was to present Brazil as a racial democracy that was partially African and culturally similar to Nigeria. The documentation they generated while representing Brazil, their interpretations of the connection between Brazil and West Africa, and their narratives about going to Nigeria characterize the state project to represent Brazil as a racial democracy. The sources also reveal a web of personal beliefs about Brazilian racial identity: the diplomats' observations show an embrace of racial democracy as well as a recognition of Brazil's racial inequalities.

These diplomats reconciled the seeming contradiction between their racial values and their understanding of the structures of inequality because they believed that all Brazilians, regardless of their background, shared an African heritage. In other words, without ignoring the reality of discrimination in Brazil, they believed that a black African presence saturated Brazilian culture. They were part of a broad intellectual movement in mid-twentieth-century Brazil. Writing of their intellectual generation, the anthropologist Roger Bastide observed, "it was as if Brazil, in the grips of the 'modernist' literary movements that had sought to discover Brazil's originality and cut the European umbilical cord, suddenly gained a consciousness of the value of cultural traits that had come from Africa."[9]

The remarks on identity by Brazilian diplomats in Lagos were reflected perfectly by a piece of Brazilian propaganda published in a newspaper in Ivory Coast in 1972, which declared that Brazil was "a country of Africans of every color."[10] The exception to this discourse in Nigeria was provided by Adhemar Ferreira, the only black Brazilian posted to Lagos (just as the exception to this discourse in Ghana was provided by the black Brazilian ambassador Raymundo Souza Dantas). An Olympic medalist, Ferreira was greeted as a hero and a model for Nigerians. As it did for Souza Dantas in Ghana, being in Nigeria made Ferreira feel like a Brazilian, not an African. The notion that Brazilians were all Africans was not just a construction tied to Brazil and Africa. Brazilians made similar arguments about being Portuguese or, as Jeffrey Lesser shows, being Japanese: constructions of sameness have been applied at different times and in different places.[11] It is not surprising that aspects of Brazilian identity linked to Africa should have been employed by Brazilian diplomats and intellectuals traveling to Nigeria. But this construction in this setting offers an insight into the values born of the idea that Brazil was a racial democracy.

Balancing Racial Democracy and Inequality

When Nigeria became independent in October 1960, Alberto da Costa e Silva was present at the ceremonies. He was an aide to the ambassador in Lisbon, Francisco Negrão de Lima, who was sent by the foreign ministry to represent Brazil. Knowing of Costa e Silva's interest in Africa, Negrão de Lima invited him along. Costa e Silva returned to Nigeria as ambassador from 1979 to 1983 and was ambassador to Portugal from 1986 to 1990. Brazil's most prolific historian of Africa, Costa e Silva explains in *A River Called the Atlantic: Africa in Brazil and Brazil in Africa* that "the history of Africa is important to us Brazilians because it helps explain us."[12] When I interviewed Costa e Silva in 2004, I asked him how he had developed his interest. He replied that it began when he was sixteen and read Gilberto Freyre's *The Masters and the Slaves* and Nina Rodrigues's *Africans in Brazil*. During the interview he stressed emphatically, "We are the blacks!"[13] He described himself as Freyrean because Freyre helped Brazilians to understand that "blacks are not something external to the nation, not a problem, the blacks were us! The blacks were within us, not just through miscegenation if you will, but as [Freyre] reveals . . . also through the civilizing influence blacks had on Brazil . . . We are descendants of thc Portuguese, indians and blacks: blacks in a much greater proportion to the other two."[14]

Freyre's impact, Costa e Silva explained, was that "his book and the discussions it sparked showed that Brazil was not a racial democracy. Though it wasn't, from then on it wanted to be. Being a racial democracy became one of the great national aspirations."[15] Still, Costa e Silva stressed the existence of a legacy of inequality rooted in slavery, "which accustomed whites to not dialogue with blacks and to disrespect the work they performed . . . The greatest error, whose consequences we still bear today, was the economic and social marginalization of the blacks."[16] Costa e Silva argued that Brazil bore a debt for slavery and its aftermath. That debt is not with Africa but "with its descendants brought forcibly to Brazil and during a perverse and humiliating exile, painfully made into Brazilians. Our debt is with a part of ourselves."[17]

Antonio Olinto wrote sentiments similar to Costa e Silva's when he returned from Nigeria and published *Brazilians in Africa* (1964), an account of the descendants of Brazilian slaves and of the experiences that he and his wife Zora Seljan had during their two years at the Brazilian embassy in Lagos. Olinto, who described himself as being "inside of black culture," ended the book with an appendix entitled "Racial Prejudice" in which he wrote: "When I speak of racial prejudice in this book, I assert that no such thing exists in Brazil. It is essential to precisely explain what this means. Brazilians know no racial prejudice and do not allow segregation." Olinto leaps from this seemingly unambiguous declaration into a nuanced discussion of racial inequality:

> Is this true? Generally, yes. But having inherited the Portuguese spirit of paternalism which is an asset in interacting with people of any race we also bear that fatherly or superior attitude that regards those who are lower on the social ladder that is a disadvantage when it comes to accepting that everyone is truly and effectively equal. This is particularly the case among Brazil's middle class, which comes from the old rural world. If we aren't racially prejudiced, per se, we do display a social conscience that does not always accept colored men. The truth is that black Brazilians started with nothing. May 13, 1888 brought emancipation. Great. Anything else? No . . . blacks went on being marginalized, to the point of reaching positions of prominence in our twentieth century society only as exceptions. This is a mistake that excludes more than twenty million people from the broader endeavors of Brazil. Among the many reforms that the 1960s herald, we must also change the way we confront the problem of Brazilians of color. The Afonso Arinos Law [barring discrimination] is good, but it is not enough. We must eliminate the causes that make it necessary.[18]

Olinto's discussion of racial prejudice relied on an assumption that Brazil was implicitly different from the United States: Brazilian racial inequality was simply a lag that would be overcome through time, whereas segregation seemed part of the essence of the United States.

Zora Seljan too wrote a book about her experiences in Lagos that captured the contradiction between the values of racial democracy and her experience with the lack of socioeconomic racial integration in Brazil. The book, *Are There Still People of My Color in Brazil?*, drew its title from a question asked by Romana da Conceição, a Brazilian-born black woman whose family had resettled in Lagos. According to Olinto, Conceição asked this question because the Brazilian embassy "only had whites" on its staff. Yet in the book Seljan expressed pride in what she called "our anti-racist policies, and of our capacity for commingling and solidarity."[19]

I have not seen a direct explanation of why Antonio Carlos Tavares would be described in a Nigerian newspaper as "the lover of the African race," though he had worked under the anticolonialist ambassador Álvaro Lins in Portugal. But the title characterized Brazil's diplomatic approach to Africa and the attitude of many of the white Brazilian diplomats who took posts in the growing number of Brazilian embassies in West Africa. Nigeria was a place where Brazilians went temporarily and gained a new perspective on Brazil, and specifically on Brazilian race mixture, the idea of racial democracy, and the sense of an African heritage shared by all Brazilians. What is more, in the presence of ethnically Brazilian communities in Nigeria and other parts of West Africa, these Brazilians found evidence that Brazil was African and Africa was Brazilian.

Brazilians in Nigeria: "At Home"

Antonio Olinto and Zora Seljan disembarked in Lagos in June 1962, carrying diplomatic passports and sixteen crates of books and paintings by Brazilian artists.[20] The first members of the new diplomatic mission to arrive, Olinto and Seljan checked into the Federal Palace Hotel, which would house the Brazilian embassy for its first six months, and dialed a telephone number given them by Pierre Verger. Romana da Conceição answered. Born in Pernambuco in 1892, she was the granddaughter of a Yoruba woman sold into slavery by her uncle and sent to Brazil. Conceição moved to Nigeria in 1900 with her mother and grandmother on a ship famously described by Raymundo Nina Rodrigues in *Os africanos no Brasil* (1935). She still spoke Portuguese, and Verger had told Olinto and Seljan that she was an "enthusiast for all things Brazilian. She's who you will deal with."[21]

The night they arrived, Olinto and Seljan heard a commotion outside their hotel. A member of the hotel staff at the reception desk called them down to the lobby. Romana da Conceição was in front of the hotel with a group of agudás from the Brazilian neighborhood in Lagos. They had come to celebrate Olinto's and Seljan's arrival by performing a dance that was familiar to them: the *Bumba-meu-boi*, an allegorical dance performed during northeastern Brazilian Christmas festivities by people who often no longer knew the meaning of the Portuguese words or had translated them into other languages. Descendants of Brazilians across West Africa performed the Bumba-meu-boi for visiting Brazilian diplomats as a means of making them feel at home. Antonio Olinto and Zora Seljan had traveled to Africa and were greeted by Brazil. What is more, they were greeted by the folkloric Brazil that they, like other modernist intellectuals and artists, celebrated as the authentic essence of Brazil.

Romana da Conceição became the matron of the Brazilian diplomatic mission and was the living symbol of the ties binding the two countries, a role that she embraced enthusiastically.[22] She brought members of the agudá community to embassy functions and made sure that Brazilian diplomats attended the agudás' Catholic mass. It was Conceição who gave meaning to Antonio Carlos Tavares's death, describing it as *consumição*, an archaic Brazilian word meaning "consumption": Tavares had been consumed by Nigeria. Seventy years old, Conceição also received a small pension that Zora Seljan gave her from her salary as a lecturer. Once Seljan left, Ambassador Meira Penna continued to pay the stipend, while complaining to Itamaraty that the Brazilian government should not be paying pensions in Nigeria.[23]

Antonio Carlos Tavares arrived soon after Olinto and Seljan and began organizing the new embassy and preparing for the arrival of Brazil's first ambassador, Luiz de Souza Bandeira. Establishing a diplomatic mission in newly independent Nigeria was difficult. There was insufficient housing and office space for the new foreign legations and other foreign and domestic workers drawn to the new capital. The ambassadors' residence was a hotel room at the Federal Palace Hotel until Souza Bandeira's death, after which the hotel managers asked the Brazilians to leave.[24] As the mission got organized during the second half of 1962, the embassy carried out few diplomatic or cultural initiatives. In September, Tavares met with the Nigerian foreign minister, Jaja Wachuku, telling him that Brazil and Nigeria "share innumerable problems common to underdeveloped tropical countries, and are bound together by ethnic and cultural ties."[25]

With their preparations done and with the arrival of Ambassador Souza Bandeira, the Brazilian embassy was ready to mark its presence in 1963. For Seljan and Olinto, the new year brought evidence of Brazil's potential in Nigeria right to the entrance of the apartment building where they and diplomats from several other countries lived. Romana da Conceição organized a group of agudás to perform the Bumba-meu-boi in front of the building, drawing its residents to the street. Seljan recalled: "Our diplomat neighbors were really impressed with Brazil's prestige. Such a new embassy, and still without an ambassador, but already drawing such crowds. No other country's embassy has accomplished anything like this yet. Hearing these comments, I smiled and thought: this is the result of our antiracist policies, and of our capacity for commingling and solidarity."[26]

The embassy's agenda covered a broad spectrum of commercial, political, and cultural activities. Souza Bandeira's only official act before his death was to meet with the Nigerian foreign minister to suggest the creation of an international association of exporters of cacao, a commodity produced in both countries. And even though Olinto's passion was culture, he understood the political and economic circumstances of postindependence West Africa, and the first chapters of *Brazilians in Africa* gave the most detailed survey of African current events published in Brazil at the time. He explained, "For Brazil, with its tropical-Atlantic orientation, a precise understanding of what is happening in Africa is of the greatest importance. No other country can better understand the challenges and opportunities of the new Africa."[27] But Souza Bandeira's death at the beginning of the year, followed by Tavares's suicide, derailed this agenda. There was practically no trade between Nigeria and Brazil. The main Brazilian export was propane tanks that had to first be shipped to Germany for transshipment to Lagos.[28] From 1962 to 1972 Brazil exported only $221,000 in goods to Nigeria.[29]

What remained was Seljan's and Olinto's interest in cultural ties, as well as the official effort to present Brazil as a racial democracy, which the embassy began by seizing an opportunity to compare Brazilian race relations favorably to those of the United States. In January 1963 a newspaper in Lagos reported on the decision of James Meredith, the first black student to enroll at the University of Mississippi, to leave school because of the racist pressure he faced. The newspaper's editorial picked up a

Brazilian press release, announcing that "the neighboring Brazilians were so inspired they offered Good Jim a scholarship to study in a more friendly and conducive atmosphere."[30] In the end James Meredith, who did not speak Portuguese, returned to the university, but the editorial presented an early opportunity to paint Brazil "in a particularly sympathetic light before the Nigerian public."[31]

At the same time, Seljan and Olinto combined their interest in discovering Brazilian cultural traces in West Africa with their task of promoting Brazil based on shared ethnic ties. In January, on Verger's recommendation, they traveled to Porto Novo, Benin, to witness the religious festival of Nosso Senhor do Bonfim, derived from a Catholic religious festival in the city of Salvador in Bahia. Olinto reported to Itamaraty on his trip, marveling at the number of people with Brazilian surnames, including the president's wife (Rego). He described the festival as beginning with an "authentically Brazilian 'Bumba-meu-boi,' with hundreds of people singing songs in Portuguese . . . The figures of the ox, the horse, the rhea and of the giant, traditional to these processions in the Brazilian northeast, are all preserved."[32] In Porto Novo, Olinto found that "Brazil continues to exist in Africa, through the miracle of a culture that refused to die."[33]

Over their year and a half in Lagos, Olinto and Seljan traveled frequently in western Nigeria and Benin, seeking centers of Brazilian settlement and sources of African influence over Brazil. For Olinto this landscape felt familiar. In *Brazilians in Africa* he declares: "In time, the Brazilian presence in Africa could be felt more and more strongly. The peoples and landscapes of that coast became, for me, familiar. It became easy for me to get into the Africanness of things . . . Nothing African seemed alien because traces of Brazilian influence appeared in the smallest details. I was always shocked that I was not in Rio, because the truth is I was at home. This certainty about belonging in this environment confronted me . . . all along the territory divided today between Dahomey and Nigeria. Old Brazilian colonial architecture accompanied me down the roads."[34] In both his diplomatic correspondence and his later writing Olinto repeated the theme that as a Brazilian he felt perfectly at home in West Africa. He recounted riding in a car with Romana da Conceição when a Nigerian boy yelled "oyimbô" (white man) at him. Conceição replied, "not oyimbô, agudá, like me." This encounter prompted Olinto to reflect: "It is natural that Europeans would be received reservedly in more exclusively Nigerian settings. Understanding different customs is not a trait of the common 'European

Man.' But the Brazilian case is completely different . . . the agudá, or Brazilian, whatever his color, is closer to the Nigerian in general and the African descended from Brazilians in particular."[35]

Seljan's and Olinto's work promoting a shared identity between Brazil and Nigeria culminated with an exposition, "Contemporary Brazilian Art," organized by Seljan in Lagos in May 1963, based on the collection that the two had brought with them in their baggage. The exposition, held over two weeks at the Nigerian Museum in Lagos, included 104 paintings and engravings by Brazilian artists.[36] The exhibit demonstrated Brazil's ties to Nigeria and projected an image of the "humane treatment received by Africans in Brazil."[37] The motif of racial democracy was implicit in the work, which Seljan described as demonstrating the "ethnical formation of Brazil and its spiritual democracy."[38] The Nigerian labor minister J. M. Johnson, an agudá, inaugurated the exposition, drawing on the same themes, describing "the tremendous goodwill Nigeria has towards Brazil" as "the result of the kind treatment received by Nigerians during their service in Brazil . . . In spite of the unkindness of the slave trade age, Nigerians affected still returned home without any feeling of bitterness toward Brazilians." Rather, he continued, they considered Brazil their first home and would do everything to defend her.[39] Seljan and Johnson used the idea of racial democracy based on benign slavery as a discursive space for promoting connections between Brazil and Nigeria.

Seljan returned to the ideas which she expressed almost a decade earlier and which Olinto still referred to after her death. In interviews and articles Seljan explained: "As in the past Roman artists and poets who followed the Greek tradition showed the strength of Jupiter, the grace of Venus, or the wisdom of Pallas Atheneia, Brazilian artists today, inspired by Nigerian traditions, sing the worth of Shango and express on canvass the majesty of his figure with the double axe."[40] While Olinto characterized Nigeria as Brazil's Rome, Seljan went further, suggesting that Brazil was the new Rome, and Nigeria its Greek inspiration.

The exhibit drew positive press coverage, particularly stressing Johnson's remarks, but a dissenting note was struck by a columnist for the Lagos *Sunday Times* who questioned Johnson's characterization of Brazilian slavery as benign. In his commentary "Culture Brazilians Took This from Us," the columnist analyzed the "interesting character" Olinto: "His office and home are decorated with carvings and our locally woven cloths are conspicuously paraded. His window and door blinds are made of

Yoruba printed (adire) cloths. The floors of both his office and his house are covered with our raffia mats. Well, how did Nigerian culture penetrate into Brazil? It all happened during the slave trade which depopulated Africa."[41]

If the idea of a shared Brazilian-Nigerian culture could stir resentment, there was still one type of Brazilian presence that could be seen uncritically in Nigeria: soccer. The Vasco da Gama soccer team from Rio de Janeiro arrived in Lagos on the day of the opening of the exhibition, which the team attended. The team was on a tour of West Africa, playing exhibition games in Ghana, Nigeria, and the Ivory Coast. Antonio Carlos Tavares reported to Itamaraty that the team's diverse racial composition made a great impression and gave a sharp demonstration of the harmony between the different ethnic groups that make up Brazil's population.[42] After a dinner hosted by the Brazilian Descendants' Association, two newspapers in Lagos published photographs of the Vasco team playing percussion instruments. One ran over the headline "At Home," with the caption "Vasco da Gama footballers are no stranger to bongo drums and African music. They were 'at home' at a party in their honour given by the Brazilian community in Lagos."[43]

Vasco's presence in Lagos was big news. After Vasco defeated the Nigerian national team 6–0, one newspaper wrote of the "Soccer Massacre": "these Brazilian artists won the hearts of every fan at the stadium yesterday and showed our players how football should be played." Another columnist wrote, "Send me to England. I will wish to come back. Send me to Sweden, I will still love to come home, but send me to Brazil and I will stay there indefinitely. Not because I will forget my home but because I will love to see more those soccer displays akin to the Brazilian footballers and the type displayed by the Vasco da Gama team."[44]

The newspaper coverage in Lagos of Vasco da Gama's trip to West Africa was more extensive than any other coverage of Brazil, including that of the carefully promoted art exhibit. And despite a single reference to the team's feeling "at home" in Lagos, Nigerian newspapers were much more interested in the sporting angle of Vasco's visit than in its ethnic and racial implications. Enthusiasm for Brazilian soccer had led the Nigerian Soccer Federation to contract with the Brazilian Jorge Penna on the eve of Vasco's visit to coach the Nigerian national team, just as the Ghanaian National Sports Council in 1967 had contracted with Carlos Alberto Parreira (who in 2006 coached the Brazilian national team at the World Cup).[45]

In Vasco's visit Antonio Olinto saw "a field with black and white players, which in Africa in general, is something praiseworthy."[46] Nigerians saw soccer.

The months of promoting Brazil had begun to pay dividends, though. On 7 September, Brazilian independence day, several newspapers carried profiles of Brazil. An article by Ebenezer Curtis, published in both the *Morning Post* and the *West African Pilot*, was seemingly drawn from Itamaraty promotional materials. It was Curtis who referred to Tavares as the "lover of the African race."[47] In language reminiscent of Freyre, Curtis wrote: "Brazil is a sound example of a modern civilization successfully established in the heart of the tropics, with a democratic system of government where people and races of the most varied ethnical origins live and work peacefully to build up a great nation."[48] Another article, "Brazil's Links with Nigeria," showed Olinto's and Seljan's hand: "Brazilian-Nigerian friendship is an old and strong feeling . . . The mythologies taken from Nigeria helped the formation of Brazilian mentality and Brazilian artists, authors and scholars think Nigerian-Brazilian traditions are the most serious and the most original source of inspiration to their work and researches."[49]

This reporting was punctuated by news of Tavares's death a week later. What happened to Tavares? Itamaraty's investigator concluded that Tavares had killed himself when he realized that he would not have time to conceal his embezzlement of funds before the arrival of the new ambassador. Traumatized by Ambassador Souza Bandeira's death, he married a Swissair employee living in Lagos. He spent lavishly to give her a sense of status as the wife of a head of mission, spending from embassy accounts. He believed, wrongly, that he had ample time to replenish the accounts, since he doubted that Itamaraty would be able to quickly find a replacement for the deceased ambassador, or that the Nigerian foreign ministry would act quickly once a new ambassador was named. When these presumptions proved untrue, he despaired. Tavares bet his life on the prospect that relations between Brazil and Nigeria were stalled.[50]

When Tavares died, Olinto and Seljan were on vacation in Brazil and the embassy was left practically inactive. After the deaths of the ambassador in February and the chargé d'affaires in September, administration fell to a succession of diplomats sent on short assignments from Brazil. One Brazilian, Vera Sauer, went briefly to be the first woman head of a diplomatic mission in Africa.[51] Another, Paulo Rio Branco Nabuco de Gouvêa, a descendant of the abolitionist statesman Joaquim Nabuco and the Baron of Rio Branco, the turn-of-the-century foreign minister who was considered the father of modern Brazilian diplomacy, was sent at the end of the year, and remained chargé d’affaires until he was hospitalized in Portugal with bleeding ulcers.[52] He returned as ambassador to Nigeria in 1971.[53]

Tavares’s death generated further favorable press coverage of Brazil. Most newspapers published obituaries casting Tavares as a “friend” or even “lover” of Africans and Afro-Brazilians.[54] An obituary by Arthur Omorodion declared: “Already at home, he had been the champion of the cause of Afro-Brazilians . . . including the remarkable Yoruba community in the state of Bahia.”[55] Six weeks later another article by Omorodion, on the “Afro-Brazilian relationship,” described Brazil as “the most successful European civilization in the Tropics . . . as much a home of the descendants of the Portuguese and Spanish conquistadors . . . as it is of the Afro-American Negro whose origin can be traced to the slave labour of the sugar and coffee plantations of 15th and 16th century Brazil. They form a distinct element in this peaceful multi-racial Society, a classic example of peaceful coexistence.”[56]

Omorodion suggested that Afro-Brazilians wished to return to, or at least visit, Africa, as the agudá had done. As evidence of this desire Omorodion stated that “the popular West Indian calypso song ‘I want to come back home Africa’ is as much heard in the streets of Rio de Janeiro, Bahia . . . and São Paulo as in Trinidad and the Bahamas. Herein lies the romance of an age: the African age.” The source of Omorodion’s information is unclear. Almost all of the reporting on Brazilian race relations or in the obituaries of Tavares drew on similar details that would seemingly have been provided by embassy staff. The calypso reference was an exception. It is hard to imagine Lord Kitchener’s calypso “Africa, My Home” echoing through the streets of Brazilian cities, capturing Afro-Brazilian desires in English. The musicologist Ray Funk explains that calypsos like this one were commonly broadcast by the BBC in West Africa, “where they were proving immensely popular,” particularly because of their messages about decolonization.[57] The statement about Brazil was actually true about Lagos, where calypso was popular and there was a community of descendants of Brazilians who had indeed “come home.”

If Brazilians used Africa to imagine Brazil, Omorodion used Brazil to imagine Nigeria. He characterized Brazil through music popular in West Africa, and his discussion, like popular calypsos of the era, was about independence. He attributed to Tavares the idea that "Africans, whether in Brazil, West Indies, America or Africa, must project the African personality and spirit of brotherhood." Omorodion explained that the agudás were an example of that brotherhood and its importance to the independence process, since "it was the early descendants of these Yorubas that kindled the flame of nationalism in the early twenties and thirties." As Africa served as a guide for understanding Brazil, Brazil in this case was a means for discussing African independence.[58]

Brazilian like Me: Meira Penna and Adhemar

At the time of Tavares's death Zora Seljan and Antonio Olinto were on vacation in Rio de Janeiro, and they decided that it was time to leave Nigeria. In the course of their year in Lagos they had staged the Brazilian Contemporary Artists exhibition. They had traveled to the religious sites that Verger had indicated to them, seeking the African roots of Candomblé. And they had explored the phenomenon of communities of descendants of Brazilian slaves who resettled in West Africa. They had gathered material for a lifetime of writing on Brazil's connections to Africa. They had also witnessed the crises that destabilized the embassy, and had come to appreciate the irony of the Brazilian diplomatic presence in Africa: though the embassy and its staff sought every opportunity to characterize Brazil as a racial democracy whose culture and population were deeply shaped by African (and particularly Yoruba) peoples, everyone at the embassy was white, bringing to mind the question that Seljan used as the title of her book: "In Brazil, are there still people of my color?"

Olinto recalled that he and Zora Seljan had struggled over this question, to the point of suggesting the name of Olinto's possible replacement as cultural attaché. Olinto recounted that he and Seljan made a case for sending black Brazilians as diplomats: "We didn't want to fight, but we wanted them to take advantage of our blacks . . . not just in Africa, but also in Europe. To send them as cultural attachés or as embassy staff. Isn't Brazil full of black intellectuals? . . . This was a struggle, and in the end, they haven't done it. Even Jânio Quadros, who was crazy, sent Raymundo [Souza Dantas], you know? . . . And [Souza Dantas] was humiliated by Itamaraty. Imagine, if they condescend to whites who are subordinate to them, imagine what they do to an ambassador who is black. They humiliate."[59] Olinto explained that Seljan's book was intended to provoke the

Brazilian government to change: "We need a black person in the embassy. Its ridiculous that there isn't even one."[60]

Olinto related a meeting with Goulart in which he recommended his successor as cultural attaché in Lagos. He reasoned that Goulart was "an intelligent and progressive man" and decided to tell him that he needed to replace him with a black Brazilian. Whom would Olinto recommend?

> It came to me. Adhemar Ferreira da Silva, three-time Olympic champion, lawyer. He held a law degree, intelligent, black. So here was a black who could be cultural attaché. It was within his abilities. I went to Brasília and tracked down a friend who worked in the presidential press office and told him: "If I make this suggestion to Itamaraty, it is going to be tough. They are just going to ask a lot of questions. This can only get done with a presidential order. I want to speak to the president" . . . I spent three days going to the palace and waiting. On the third day . . . he was going down the hall and I approached him. I said Mr. President, you can do something wonderful: name the first black Brazilian diplomat. He asked, "How?" I am a cultural attaché named by Tancredo Neves, and I am leaving my position after three years. I suggest that you name a black and I already have the name. Adhemar Ferreira da Silva. And he says "OK, but . . . excellent idea." Not just three-time champion but also a lawyer. He speaks English, I have spoken with him in English. He says "It's a good idea." And he nominated him.[61]

That Olinto had been in the post a single year rather than three, that he was asking the president to name the second black diplomat, not the first, and that Adhemar Ferreira did earn a law degree, but in 1968, after returning from Nigeria, are mischaracterizations which underscore the constructed nature of memory. They add emphasis to Olinto's telling. And the emphases shape Olinto's reconstruction of the episode to stress the foreign ministry's bureaucratic hostility to racial integration, as well as the importance of an individual act that in this case followed the traditional Brazilian script for petitioning authorities in their antechambers.

Olinto had already approached Ferreira with the idea, and Ferreira suggested that the authorities "won't accept." In his telling Olinto accentuated these words, giving them a fatalistic and resigned tone. He remembered replying: "I agree with you. If it were you telling me, I would also say they are not going to accept. But I am going to talk to the president. When you want something done, you just do it. Would you agree? 'Of course,' he said."[62] Olinto and Seljan returned to Lagos for another three months, where they prepared for Ferreira's arrival in February 1964. They would stay for a week after his arrival and introduce him to their contacts in Lagos, especially among the agudá community.

Adhemar Ferreira da Silva won the triple jump in the Olympics in Helsinki and Melbourne in 1952 and 1956, becoming the first Brazilian to earn multiple Olympic medals. He set long-standing records and was reputedly the first athlete to do a victory lap. A proficient language learner, he taught himself phrases in Finnish before competing in Helsinki, endearing himself to fans who cheered his events. He played the role of Death in Vinicius de Morais's play *Orfeu da Conceição* and the film *Black Orpheus*. With two Olympic gold medals and a role in an Oscar-winning film, Adhemar Ferreira was by far the most decorated Brazilian. He went to Lagos with his wife and two children. His daughter, Adyel Silva, was six at the time. She recalled that her father saw their sojourn in Lagos as an opportunity to teach his children about the world, and to give them opportunities they would not have in Brazil.[63]

Adhemar Ferreira was acclaimed in the Nigerian press as an example of what Nigerian athletes should aspire to. Newspapers ran over a dozen articles about his athletic achievements, with headlines like "Olympic Champ Turns Diplomat."[64] He attended athletic competitions and sometimes performed, making him the center of attraction.[65] He reported to Itamaraty that when he attended the national police athletics championship, after the arrival of President Azikiwe was announced over the public-address system, Ferreira's presence was announced next. He recounted that Azikiwe, "also an athlete in his youth," motioned him to his side and told him: "Mr. da Silva, welcome. I was also present that afternoon at the Helsinki stadium, when you stunned the crowds with your jumps. I hope that through your presence among us, Nigeria will also come to have its own da Silva."[66]

After Olinto left, Adhemar Ferreira faced difficult adjustments with the position of cultural attaché. Elderly Brazilian-born agudás began to approach him, seeking continuation of the pensions that Seljan had given them out of her own pocket. He had no knowledge of the pensions and no budget to pay them. He also learned that despite Olinto's and Seljan's passion for the roots of Candomblé, the Brazilian descendants in Lagos were averse to spiritism. Romana da Conceição told him, "I don't know and don't want to know about those things. That's for backward people. People from the bush."[67] In fact da Silva soon realized that his main job

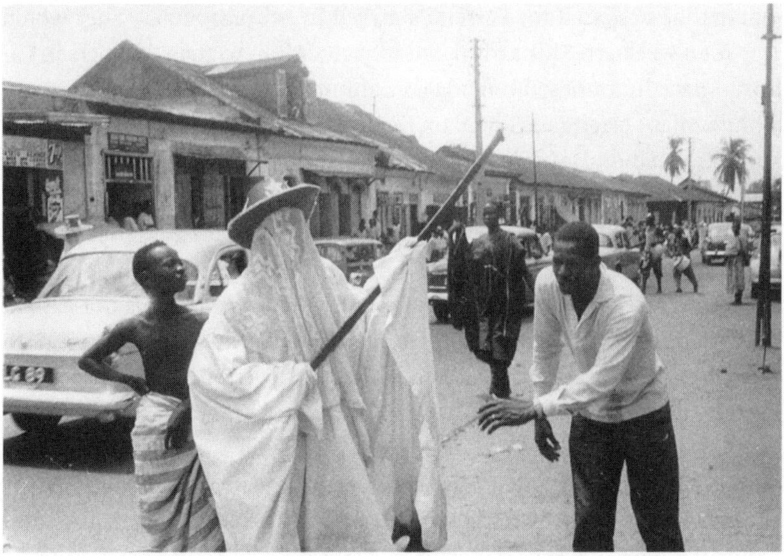

Adhemar Ferreira and Lagos Eyo Masquerade. Photo courtesy of Adyel Silva.

Adhemar Ferreira, center, in Nigeria. Photo courtesy of Adyel Silva.

needed to be educational. The students, journalists, and others who contacted him showed "complete ignorance of Brazil." Among the points he stressed, da Silva made clear that "though in Brazil, like Nigeria, there is syncretism, 95 percent of the population is Catholic."[68] Ferreira's approach to his role as cultural attaché differed fundamentally from Olinto's, and it meant that he found a very different Nigeria from the one Olinto saw. He did not emphasize cultural similarities between the two sides of the Atlantic. Instead he sought to educate the public about Brazil, giving lectures and press conferences, speaking on geography, culture, music, commerce, and industry. He played Brazilian music on his guitar, carried records of popular Brazilian music with him to events, and arranged for a local radio station to include segments with Brazilian music.[69]

Two months before Adhemar Ferreira reached Lagos at the end of February 1964, the new Brazilian ambassador, José Osvaldo Meira Penna, arrived. In his first days Meira Penna held a ceremony at the embassy at which the Catholic bishop of Lagos came to bless a black Madonna figure. A newspaper in Lagos ran a photograph of the bishop and Meira Penna standing alongside the figure of the Madonna, with the caption "Our Lady of Brazil, the only coloured Madonna in the world who is an official patron-saint of a country, has had her image brought to Nigeria and enshrined at the Brazilian Embassy in Lagos."[70] Soon after, Meira Penna traveled with Olinto and Seljan to Benin, meeting Verger to witness a last Bonfim festival and Bumba-meu-boi before Olinto and Seljan returned to Brazil.

During Meira Penna's credential ceremony before President Azikiwe, the ambassador and the president engaged in a scripted public ritual of discussing the similarities between the two countries, noting Nigeria's cultural influence over Brazil and Brazil's cultural influence over Nigeria. Meira Penna's remarks followed Itamaraty's instructions about the proper way to describe Brazil: a developing power and a racial democracy. As he stood next to President Azikiwe, Meira Penna proclaimed that thanks to African labor, "Brazil is an experiment in the successful establishment of a modern industrial civilization in the tropics." He noted that Brazil had become the country with the second-largest population of African descent outside Nigeria, and "but for the sweat and toil of the Africans, surely the early colonists of Brazil could never have faced the appalling conditions of a hostile environment." He never mentioned slavery, instead transferring the suffering of Africans in the slave system to a shared struggle to

Adhemar Ferreira with Ambassador José Osvaldo Meira Penna and Dorothy Meira Penna. Photo courtesy of Adyel Silva.

"surmount geographical determinisms." This task was undertaken in a "patriarchal society" where "bonds between the two races were not based upon servitude but upon respect and affection. This indeed was the source of the racial democracy of which we are rightfully so proud."[71] The president echoed Meira Penna, praising Brazil's "sane attitude to the race problem." The *West African Pilot* dedicated its lead story to the ceremony, and its banner headline quoted President Azikiwe, proclaiming "Brazil, a laboratory of inter-racial cooperation."[72]

For Meira Penna and Ferreira, the embassy itself was a laboratory of interracial cooperation. Ferreira was the first black Brazilian the ambassador had ever worked with closely. When I interviewed him, Meira Penna recalled a road trip that he and Ferreira had taken through western Nigeria: "I had never had the experience of interacting so intimately with a black person, you know. In Brazil there was a big difference still [between the races] . . . But after three, four, five days, I suddenly realized the following: that the reactions we had, that he and I had, were exactly the same . . . In other words, I felt Brazilian like him, with a Brazilian reaction. And he had nothing in common with the Africans, other than the fact that he was black, his race . . . His skin was black, but our reactions were the reactions of Brazilians. We commented to each other about things and found them funny . . . From then on I really became what you could call culturalist. I think the real factor in shaping the identity of a people is culture, not race . . . We were Brazilian, I felt Brazilian, it was not like being with an African."[73]

Meira Penna reported to Itamaraty about the trip, emphasizing that Adhemar Ferreira had been "good company" and stressing the symbolic benefit of Ferreira's presence in promoting Brazil's racial democracy: "Aside from representing a living example of the importance of the African element in Brazilian ethnicity, Mr. Ferreira da Silva generated great sympathy among our hosts with his personal 'charm' and his guitar, thanks to which we could immediately demonstrate through music the reality of intimate cultural relations between Brazil and Yorubaland that we had just spoken of."[74] Adhemar Ferreira was a token. Though Meira Penna noted his "great help in the job of public relations and disseminating information about Brazil," he emphasized Ferreira's musical skills and skin color as his principal contributions to the representation of Brazil in Nigeria.

There was a difference between what Meira Penna proclaimed officially and what he believed personally. In his communications with Itamaraty he made clear that it was only as a responsibility of his job that he repeated the rhetoric about a natural Brazilian role in West Africa based on cultural affinities. A supporter of the coup of 1964, Meira Penna rejected the more radical readings of race and of politics expressed by liberation movements in Africa and in Itamaraty's promotion of Brazil in Africa. Meira Penna argued with Itamaraty when he felt that the tools he was given to represent Brazil's racial democracy were inconsistent or contradictory.

The contradictory message was personified by the arrival of the black Brazilian actor Antônio Pitanga. Pitanga traveled to West Africa in 1964 on a tour arranged by the Itamaraty Cultural Division, bringing prints of the film *Ganga Zumba*, in which he played Zumbi dos Palmares, the leader of a runaway slave community fighting the Portuguese. When I interviewed Pitanga about his trip to West Africa, he arrived at my apartment in a driving rainstorm, sat down, and with unusual directness declared, "I am a person committed to the Brazilian racial problem. I bring it to cinema. I participated in some Cinema Novo films that were a way of developing black themes."[75] After the coup in 1964 Pitanga said that he worried about being imprisoned because of his films. He met with the head of the Cultural Affairs Division, a fan of Cinema Novo who had promoted Pitanga's films abroad. Pitanga asked for help in leaving the country, and the division chief arranged for him to present some of his films at a festival in Beirut and go on a tour of West Africa. Pitanga's tour was a form of exile, but it was sponsored by allies in the government. What is more, it was sponsored by the Itamaraty cultural division, which understood, Pitanga recalled, that he "didn't go to sell the myth of racial democracy. I went as a person from the black movement, presenting my, our vision of the black question, which was different than Itamaraty's."[76]

Pitanga traveled across West Africa, carrying reels of *Ganga Zumba*, which he showed both to the public and to leaders who had emerged from African independence movements to convey a vision of the struggle that black Brazilians shared. He explained: "My films were a register of information about another black country called Brazil . . . since this was an Itamaraty cultural mission, the Brazilian embassies in the countries I visited made arrangements for me to show them to the authorities of those countries." *Ganga Zumba* explored the seventeenth-century struggle of the leader of the runaway slave community of Palmares in northeastern Brazil. In the film Ganga Zumba fights and is eventually defeated by the Portuguese, and in one of its climactic scenes, a traitor to Palmares is killed. Pitanga recalled screening the film in Ghana to an audience that included Kwame Nkrumah, who according to Pitanga "jumped out of his seat and yelled 'That's it! The black man who betrays [his brothers] must die!'"[77]

When Pitanga arrived with his film in Lagos, he met with opposition from Meira Penna. Unlike the diplomats at other embassies, who helped Pitanga arrange screenings, conduct interviews with the press, and promote the films, Meira Penna tried to block the films and complained about them to Itamaraty. He telegrammed the foreign ministry, stating that he had screened *Ganga Zumba* privately with the Lebanese owner of the largest chain of movie theaters in Nigeria, and they had concluded that the film should not be shown. Meira Penna reported the concern of the owner of the theater chain that the film would likely not be allowed by the state censors, "not only because of its scenes of violence but for its ideological content." And Meira Penna himself believed that the film did not present an image of Brazil "consistent" with its "interests in this part of the world."[78]

Meira Penna wrote to the foreign minister, complaining that the film contradicted what he understood to be the official discourse about Brazilian society. His exposition began with a history of the study of race in

Brazil, explaining that "all of the scholars of the African problem in Brazil, from Nina Rodrigues through Arthur Ramos, [Arthur] Hehl Neiva and Gilberto Freyre, have insisted in constructing Brazil as the world's most admirable example of coexistence and harmony between the races."[79] These scholars took pains to stress that even colonial slavery was far more benign in Brazil than in other parts of the Americas, and was the basis for promoting Brazil's image. "Rightly or wrongly, true or illusory," Meira Penna continued, the idea that Brazil was free of racial prejudices represented "an essential principle" of Brazilian propaganda abroad, extensively employed by the Itamaraty Cultural Division.[80] "That Brazil is a 'racial democracy' is always repeated, at any opportunity, by our representatives abroad."[81] Meira Penna was following Itamaraty's instructions to stress the point when he presented his credentials to the president of Nigeria.

Meira Penna professed himself perplexed that the "first expression of our cinematic art to be shown in Nigeria would seem deliberately designed to deny those principles [of racial democracy]."[82] He found the scenes of violence particularly objectionable and wondered how a Nigerian public of "generally low cultural level" could dissociate the resistance to Portuguese slavery in Palmares from the wars of liberation in Africa: "The motive of the film is obscure: it's as though we were watching the rebellion in Angola, the civil war in the Congo. The film seems intended to train Zulu guerillas in South Africa, or to have been tailor-made for Misters Nkrumah or Ben-Bella. The decapitated heads rolling on the ground, the prisoners beaten to death, hearts cut out by knife, rapes and ambushes, war without quarter between whites and blacks. I don't know if these things even happen in Africa (except in the ghastly world of Chinese communist propaganda). In any case, it is anachronistic and has nothing to do with Brazil. As propaganda for Brazil, I frankly cannot agree with it."[83]

Ganga Zumba was a film about black resistance to white domination. Despite Meira Penna's objections, those sentiments might have resonated particularly well with an African audience and reflected Brazilian solidarity with struggles for liberation. This was the impact that Pitanga perceived: "People who saw these films had their first chance to see something different. These were films that weren't colonized by Hollywood, like Sidney Poitier's films, or Harry Belafonte. Less Belafonte because he had a political position, unlike Sidney Poitier . . . The enthusiasm and acceptance my films generated was because it was cinema of struggle, it was ideological . . . It had to do with their struggle. I wasn't teaching them anything. But something shone in their eyes when they saw them. They appreciated seeing a Brazilian-Bahian brother be at the forefront of a project like this and showing it to them. As Nkrumah had said, each of us has to wage our own struggle for independence. I was showing our black history and our struggle."[84] Pitanga declared: "Meira Penna was totally racist." He opposed Pitanga's trip and his message, and prevented the public presentation of *Ganga Zumba*. But Adhemar Ferreira discreetly worked to circumvent Meira Penna's opposition. Pitanga recalled that when he arrived in Lagos, Ferreira took him aside and told him that he was going to have difficulties with the ambassador. He encouraged Pitanga not to react to Meira Penna's hostility, while he worked "within the black world" to arrange for "strategic people, important people in the government" to meet with him and see his films.[85] Ferreira quietly arranged screenings for Nigerian political authorities and interviews with the press. Pitanga made several public appearances. The Nigerian *Sunday Post* described him as "storming" Lagos and told the story of a "product of a humble birth who has been able to stumble on a career and make a huge success of it," adding that he would inspire others to "similar fits of unexpected, world-acclaimed achievements."[86] The *Morning Post* described *Ganga Zumba* as "striking . . . [telling] with much human touch the story of slaves taken from some Negro countries and how they were treated by their white masters (the Europeans) in the sugar cane plantations. The brutality meted out to the slaves by the whites and how they were deprived of their rights and their freedom of association are keenly portrayed in the film." The report was illustrated by a still from *Ganga Zumba* showing Pitanga, clutching a large knife, struggling with a white man. Pitanga recalled that his experience in Lagos was different from that with the other Brazilian embassies. Elsewhere, Brazilian diplomats collaborated with his project. Here he faced both the opposition of the ambassador and the support of a "brother."

Meira Penna's opposition illustrated both the changing political climate in Brazil between the nationalist-populist impulse toward Africa of 1961–64 and the post-1964 military regime, as well as the gap separating the Brazilian military regime from African political culture. Showing his political sympathies, Meira Penna declared that "among the objectives of the revolutionary movement that took place in Brazil last April [the military coup] is bringing good sense back to public administration."[87] In

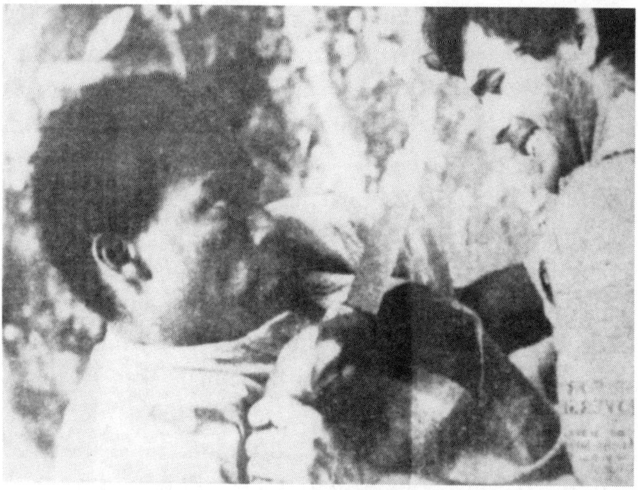

Film still of Antônio Pitanga as Ganga Zumba.
Source: Arquivo Histórico do Itamaraty.

this vein he recommended withdrawing the film from Africa and scaling back Antônio Pitanga's tour, on the grounds that Pitanga did not speak English or French and that he "already faces financial difficulties." These financial difficulties were worsened by Meira Penna, who delayed issuing the payment of $500 for expenses that Pitanga was to receive at each of the embassies.[88] He concluded that "it is hard under these circumstances to see which is more disastrous: the success or the failure of the 'tour.'"[89]

At the end of his tenure in Nigeria, Meira Penna submitted a report that outlined the difficulties the Brazilian embassy had experienced and questioned the purpose of diplomatic relations in Africa, specifying that a sense of national grandeur and historical affinity was no grounds for the sacrifices he and his ministry had made. Was its "bureaucratic existence" justified? The cost of running the embassy was $125,000 for 1964, and Meira Penna suggested that this money was misspent. His report was entitled "Parkinson's Law and the Embassy in Lagos," referring to the concept that "work expands so as to fill the time available for its completion." In other words, he said, 90 percent of the work of the embassy consisted of such routine administrative matters as arranging funerals; tracing lost luggage; solving electrical, telephone, and mechanical problems; resolving the chaos of the filing system; keeping the telex functional; dealing with miscommunication caused by "pidgin English" and "français petit-nègre"; and battling obstinacy, impertinence, lethargy, usury, and corrupt practices.[90] He asked, "Why do we have a shredder when documents already arrive shredded by the dirty hands of those who brought them from the post or the stationer?"[91]

Why was Brazil in Africa? Meira Penna suggested that embassies in Lagos, Dakar, and Accra were created out of the "demagogic enthusiasm" of the Quadros era. His instructions had been to solidify the Brazilian presence in West Africa because of "historical and anthropological ties as old as our colonial life. It is a fact that, in the seventeenth and eighteenth century, the South Atlantic was almost a Lusitanian lake." He noted the trading posts that the Portuguese had created centuries earlier, from which "departed the ancestors of one of the most important elements of our population, or our 'cosmic' race." He noted as well the existence of the agudás who sustained strong affective ties with Brazil.[92]

If Meira Penna expected Itamaraty to provide better conditions for diplomats working in Lagos, the reality would be the opposite. The coup in 1964 ended the Independent Foreign Policy. The military regime turned away from Africa and tightened relations with Portugal just as the wars against Portuguese rule in Angola, Mozambique, and Guiné-Bissau became one of the unifying concerns of independent African countries. The last thing that seemed appropriate in Africa of the 1960s was the idea that the Atlantic was a "Lusitanian lake."

After the coup students in Lagos protested the detention of Chinese journalists in Brazil. The Lagos *Daily Times* condemned the detention of Portuguese African nationalists who had opened an office in Rio de Janeiro.[93] Meira Penna replied with a letter to the editor declaring that "no African national in Brazil . . . [has] been subject to any kind of action from the Brazilian authorities . . . May I bring to your notice that the present Brazilian Government was legally elected by the Brazilian Congress after a popular uprising which freed the country from a totalitarian ideology."[94] Angolan and Mozambican nationalists had in fact been arrested in Rio de Janeiro and questioned by both naval intelligence and members of the Portuguese secret police.[95]

Meira Penna left Lagos in 1965. Adhemar Ferreira da Silva left in 1967. The embassy in Lagos was without an ambassador or a cultural attaché for years. Meira Penna would only be replaced in 1971. Ten years after the embassy opened, the connections between Brazil and Nigeria had actually lessened. The last Brazilian-born agudás had died. The Brazilian embassy was nearly dormant. By 1968 the chargé d'affaires in Lagos wrote that the embassy "has for some time now lacked Brazilian staff."[96] He also suggested that diplomats had "without malice or premeditation, created an erroneous perception of our country . . . emphasizing only folkloric similarities between the countries . . . Forgetting altogether the considerable culture Brazil inherited from Europe. We now face the task of breaking this perception that Brazil is only of African descent."[97]

Brazilians carried to Nigeria the image of a racially mixed society in which the benign treatment of blacks by whites signaled Brazilian goodwill toward Nigeria. Some messengers, like Olinto and Seljan, held a deep conviction that Brazil and Nigeria were bound by a shared culture, and that an understanding of Nigeria was a precondition for understanding Brazil. Others, like Meira Penna, made clear that this image was a professional obligation. In one case, a Brazilian attaché designated to deliver a Christmas message on Nigerian radio brought the connections between Brazil and Africa to a ridiculous extreme. He began his address with the appropriate message about Brazilian racial harmony, proclaiming, "Many of us are of Portuguese descent, others of African or German or Italian or Japanese blood, etc., while millions of still other Brazilians are the product of the intermarriage and happy coexistence—thank God we have it—of people of different stocks." He continued, describing regional Christmas traditions in Brazil: "The people of Bahia . . . pride themselves in their acarajé [a shrimp and palm oil fritter], which is our form of saying *jè akara*, the good old Yoruba dish. And in my own province of Pernambuco . . . a Christmas table is not acceptable if it does not include a cake called *pé de moleque*, which means *foot of negro*. It is simply delicious."[98]

The connections between Brazil and Nigeria were presented in more sophisticated ways by others. But these messages did not resonate beyond the immediate environments where Brazilians made them. Nigerians repeated them to Brazilians in scripted settings like Meira Penna's presentation of credentials and the inauguration of the Brazilian art exhibit. Two Nigerian journalists, Ebenezer Curtis and Arthur Omorodion, carried the messages a little further. But looking only at Brazilian sources distorts the picture of Brazil's influence. Nigerian newspapers refocus the image: Brazil was almost wholly absent from Nigerians' views of the world. Reading the Nigerian newspapers as a whole creates an understanding that Brazil's system of race relations, whatever it may be, held basically no significance for Nigerians, who were concerned with national questions, relations with neighboring countries, Britain, and the process of decolonization. That Brazil did not fit in this equation was clear to Ferreira. Playing his guitar and records and lecturing across Nigeria for three years, he sought to generate a rudimentary understanding of Brazil in an environment where "needless to say, our country is entirely unknown."[99] During the first decade of diplomatic ties between Brazil and West African nations, the two margins of the Atlantic may have seemed tantalizingly close, but they remained almost impossibly distant.

4 War in Angola, Crisis in Brazil

IN MARCH 1961 Ciro Freitas Vale, the venerable face of Brazil before the United Nations, wrote to Foreign Minister Afonso Arinos to express his frustration with his government's decision to abstain from a forthcoming vote to condemn Portuguese colonialism as war broke out in Angola. Freitas Vale had headed the Brazilian delegation to the meetings to organize the United Nations in 1945 and the Brazilian delegations to the UN five times since. Now he complained that in defending Portugal, the Brazilian government was reneging on its commitment to decolonization:

> Everyone at the United Nations knows that Portugal uses forced labor in Angola, divides Angolans into first and second class citizens ("assimilated" and "not assimilated") and practices racial discrimination against the blacks who are 97 per cent of its population. Everyone also knows that after five centuries of Portuguese rule, 99 per cent of the black population of Angola is illiterate. Finally, everyone knows that in Angola there are violations of human rights and individual liberties. Portugal denies this, but it refuses to admit any kind of international observers . . . To invoke a bilateral agreement with Portugal to justify Brazil's vote means admitting that Brazil has specifically committed itself to supporting Portugal's policies in Angola, which would be disastrous for our standing at the United Nations . . . In the end, Brazil's abstention in the vote would be a needless sacrifice of our prestige, both because the proposed resolution is going to be approved overwhelmingly, and because the dismantling of the Portuguese empire in Africa is inevitable and will probably happen in short order.[1]

Freitas Vale rejected the argument that Portugal's territories were not colonies: "the Portuguese theory that their colonies are 'overseas provinces' is a legal fiction. These are typical colonies, in terms of the physical and cultural character and their social order."[2] Freitas's appeal failed. Brazil became one of the few public defenders of Portuguese colonialism at the United Nations, undermining its own relations with newly independent African countries.

This was a striking reversal of Jânio Quadros's Independent Foreign Policy. At the outset of his presidency Quadros sought to end Brazil's support for Portuguese colonialism, but he backed away from this goal under pressure from Portugal. Between 1961 and 1964 his successor, João Goulart, also sought to break with Portugal, but in the end his administration capitulated to Portuguese pressure as well. This chapter looks at the Brazilian response to the outbreak of wars of independence in Portuguese Africa in 1961, particularly Angola, and explores the political conflict over Brazil's response. This story has three ingredients: Gilberto Freyre's way of interpreting Brazil and its racial mixture as a legacy of the Portuguese; the influence of the Portuguese ethnic and immigrant community; and the steely effectiveness of Portugal's diplomatic corps, which succeeded in paralyzing opposition not only from Brazil but from the United States. The conflict unfolded both in the turbulent landscape of Brazilian politics, culminating in the coup of 1964, and within the United Nations, where Brazilian diplomats like Freitas Vale watched their country's credibility with new African and Asian nations erode as Brazil capitulated to Portugal. Like Afonso Arinos, Freitas Vale had departed from his earlier anti-Semitism (as ambassador to Germany in the late 1930s, he blocked Jewish immigration to Brazil), and now saw Brazilian racial democracy as the characteristic that defined its international role—a characteristic being undermined by support for Portugal.[3]

The Brazilian UN delegation represented its country as a racially mixed democracy bearing the responsibility to support decolonization, but it was unable to act in accordance with this principle on the only subject that mattered: Portugal. This incapacity demonstrates the lopsided influence over national affairs that Brazilians who assumed a Portuguese ethnicity possessed, compared to those who traced their origins to Africa. The resolutions introduced at the UN by African countries left no room for ambiguity, and Brazil's response to them laid bare contradictions and divisions in Brazilian society. Those Brazilians who wanted to build ties to Africa, like Afonso Arinos and José Honório Rodrigues, recognized the need to stop supporting Portugal and were frustrated by the power of Brazil's Portuguese ethnic community to block opposition as well as the effectiveness of the Portuguese government in mobilizing the ethnic community in Brazil to shape Brazilian policy.

The United Nations and the War in Angola

When clandestine movements for the independence of Portugal's colonies formed in the 1950s, Fernando Mourão and José Maria Pereira had been present at their inception, as students at the Casa dos Estudantes do Império. In 1961 these movements became armed uprisings. The first revolt took place in Luanda, on 4 February 1961. After a wave of arrests of nationalists and radicals in Angola, the Popular Movement for the Liberation of Angola (MPLA) raided the jail to release the political prisoners. This raid was followed on 15 March by a series of attacks on Portuguese settlements and administrative posts on the northern Angolan border with Zaire, carried out by the Union of Angolan Peoples (UPA). Portuguese colonists responded with vigilante attacks on Angolan settlements and against perceived supporters of independence. Each side accused the other of indiscriminate massacre.[4] The attacks were not coordinated: the MPLA and UPA (which would become the Frente Nacional de Libertação de Angola, or FNLA) were rivals through independence, and fought a civil war against each other after independence. The outcome of that struggle is reflected in the name of the Luanda airport, 4 de Fevereiro.

For the next fourteen years the MPLA, the FNLA, and the National Union for the Total Independence of Angola (UNITA) fought against Portuguese rule and often against each other. The MPLA became a Marxist movement headed by Agostinho Neto. It had the largest and most interracial base of support, which ranged from urban slum dwellers to intellectuals and included many of the colony's native-born administrators, both black and white. The FNLA, led by Holden Roberto, was a predominantly Bakongo ethnic movement concentrated in northern Angola along the border with Zaire, from which it received support. UNITA, led by Jonas Savimbi, was a predominantly Ovimbundo ethnic movement that split from the FNLA in the mid-1960s and had its base of support in the central Angolan plateau.

Angola was Portugal's largest colony, with the most significant white colonial settlement and economy, so war there dominated the international reaction. But soon after the uprising in Angola, wars of independence began in Portugal's other African colonies. Under the leadership of Amílcar Cabral, the African Party for the Independence of Cabo Verde and Guinea-Bissau (PAIGC) began its armed uprising in 1962, while the Front for the Liberation of Mozambique (FRELIMO) began its uprising in 1964.[5] Salazar's government responded by widening conscription and committing the armed forces to fight simultaneously on multiple fronts in Guiné-Bissau, Angola, and Mozambique.

The nationalists fighting Portuguese rule had the universal support of independent African nations (except South Africa and Rhodesia, whose white minority governments sided with Portugal). From 1961 until the Portuguese dictatorship was overthrown in 1974, African countries campaigned constantly at the UN against Portuguese colonialism. Their campaign was based on the United Nations Charter's defense of the right of self-determination and on resolutions in favor of decolonization, particularly UN Resolution 1514, approved in 1960. African delegates to the United Nations submitted motions to condemn Portugal, create commissions to ascertain facts about Portugal's colonial wars, and impose economic sanctions. These resolutions received the support of newly independent African and Asian nations, most of Latin America, and the Soviet bloc. In turn, Portugal was able to block negative votes by the United States and often garnered the support of other European colonial powers, particularly Spain, France, and Britain.

These resolutions were a minefield for the Brazilian government. There was no better way to build relations with African countries than for Brazil to lend its diplomatic and moral influence to their single unifying international cause. Still, though Brazilian diplomats and political leaders wasted no opportunity to issue general calls for decolonization, they were immobilized by the debate on Portugal. With the single exception of a vote in favor of UN Resolution 1742 in January 1962, which "reaffirmed the right of the Angolan people to self-determination and independence [and] disapproved of repressive measures and the denial of human rights and fundamental liberties to the Angolan people," Brazil abstained from, or voted against, the resolutions against Portuguese colonialism.[6]

The explanation for Brazil's single vote in favor of Angolan independence, like the explanation for its long record of abstentions with regard to Portuguese colonialism, does not lie in the debate at the United Nations. Instead it lay in domestic Brazilian politics and the depths of the ethnic attachment that influential Brazilians felt toward Portugal. In the years after his experience as foreign minister, Arinos recalled that "Salazarist diplomacy was shrewder, and firmer—it did not vacillate like ours. It dragged Brazil along, exploiting the sentimentalism of some of our elites, drawing in politicians and intellectuals through paid trips and conferring honorary titles; manipulating the press through its economic influence, especially in Rio de Janeiro."[7]

The United States, Brazil, and Portugal's Struggle to Remain in Africa

Between 1961 and 1964 the Quadros and Goulart governments buckled under pressure from Portugal. The creativity and intensity that the Portuguese regime applied to Brazil can also be seen in the regime's equally effective handling of United States support for decolonization. In the early 1960s the United States held an ambiguous position in the eyes of emerging African leaders. President Eisenhower's administration had been uninterested in decolonization, abstaining on resolutions at the UN. African diplomats came in direct contact with segregation when they went to Washington. African newspapers like Nkrumah's *The Spark* reported on the struggle for rights in the United States. Still, in some ways the United States held a favorable position relative to newly independent African countries. It was not complicit with colonialism, and was politically, economically, and technologically ascendant over the western world. Like Langston Hughes and Thurgood Marshall, Ghana's Nkrumah and Nigeria's Azikiwe were graduates of Lincoln University in Philadelphia. If segregation was reminiscent of colonialism, the civil rights struggle evoked African struggles for independence.

President Kennedy cultivated relations with African countries and supported UN motions in favor of decolonization. In the aftermath of the uprising in Angola, the United States delegation at the United Nations voted in favor of Resolution 1603, condemning Portuguese colonialism and calling for an investigation into the uprising.[8] The United States supported other resolutions over the course of 1961 that pressed Portugal to free its colonies (table 1). Salazar's regime neutralized pressure from the United States government by threatening to revoke its lease on an airfield in the Azores. The airfield had been used by the United States military during the Berlin Wall crisis of August 1961. Thereafter the Portuguese government moved to annual renewal of the lease based on United States policy. Undersecretary of State Chester Bowles declared that "it would be unthinkable to modify an effective policy in a key continent to fit the 18th Century views of the Lisbon Government."[9] He was wrong. The airbase was deemed essential to United States military strategy; Salazar silenced a potentially decisive voice against its colonies. John Kenneth Galbraith, United States ambassador to India during the annexation of Goa, rued that American foreign policy turned on "a few kilometers of asphalt in the Atlantic."[10]

In January 1962 the United States delegation at the UN voted in favor of Resolution 1742, which reaffirmed "the inalienable right of the Angolan people to self-determination and independence" and condemned "the repressive measures and armed action against the people of Angola."[11] It was the last time the United States government would vote against Portuguese colonialism at the UN. Still, leaders of the civil rights movement saw African decolonization as an analogue to their struggle, and organized to press Kennedy to again support decolonization. This was the agenda of the Harriman Conference in November 1962: to create a unified voice among civil rights leaders to lobby Kennedy on decolonization. The conference included the most visible leaders of the United States civil rights movement: Martin Luther King Jr., A. Philip Randolph, Whitney Young, Dorothy Height, James Farmer, and Roy Wilkins.

The Portuguese foreign and colonial ministries watched the "fiercely anti-Portuguese" civil rights movement and worked to neutralize its influence on United States government policy.[12] They concluded that African American leaders were communists who wanted only black supremacy in Africa. Otherwise, shouldn't they be sympathetic to the Portuguese civilizing mission and culture of racial harmony? Portuguese officials thought the African American position illogical but explainable: it was "transference" of suffering into resentment of other "white" countries. A Portuguese diplomat wrote: "They ask for the 'liberation' of Angola and Mozambique when what they really want is that the Portuguese 'turn over' these areas to black leaders (their 'colleagues' of color)—when it is more than evident that there are no leaders in those areas who are capable and the masses do not possess the competence and capacity to govern themselves." African Americans supported black supremacy, "even if it results in a step backwards in civilization."[13]

Table 1. General Assembly Votes by Brazil and the United States on Portuguese Colonialism

	Brazil	U.S.	Yes	No	Abstain
Resolution No. (Session No.), Subject, Date					
1514 (XV), Self-Determination, 14 Dec 1960	Y	A	89	0	9
1542 (XV), Information from Portugal, 15 Dec 1960	N	A	68	6	16
1603 (XV), Angola, 20 April 1961	A	Y	73	2	9
1699 (XVI), Information from Portugal, 19 Dec 1961	Y	Y	90	3	2
1742 (XVI), Angola Self-Determination, 30 Jan 1962	Y	Y	99	2	1
1807 (XVII), Portuguese Territories, 30 Jan 1962	A	N	82	7	13
1819 (XVII), Portuguese Suppression, 18 Dec 1962	A	N	57	14	18
1913 (XVIII), Self-Determination Portuguese Terr., 3 Dec 1963	A	A	91	2	11
2107 (XX), Portuguese Territories, 21 Dec 1965	N	N	66	26	15
2184 (XXI), Portuguese Territories, 12 Dec 1966	N	N	70	13	22
2270 (XXII), Portuguese Territories, 17 Nov 1967	A	N	82	7	21
2395 (XXIII), Portuguese Territories, 29 Nov 1968	N	A	86	3	15
2507 (XXIV), Portuguese Territories, 21 Nov 1969	A	N	97	2	18
2707 (XXV), Portuguese Territories, 14 Dec 1970	N	N	96	6	16
2784 (XXVI), Portuguese Territories, 6 Dec 1971	N	N	92	6	6
2795 (XXVI), Portuguese Territories, 10 Dec 1971	absent	N	105	8	5
2918 (XXVII), Portuguese Territories, 14 Nov 1972	N	N	103	6	8
3061 (XXVIII), Guinea-Bissau, 2 Nov 1973	A	N	94	7	30
3113 (XXVIII), Portuguese Territories, 12 Dec 1973	N	N	105	8	16

Lynn Schopen, Hanna Newcombe, Chris Young, and James Wert, eds., *Nations on Record: United Nations General Assembly Roll-Call Votes (1946–1973)*. Oakville-Dundas: Canadian Peace Research Institute, 1975.

Portuguese officials responded to this threat by paying $100,000 to a public relations firm in Richmond, Virginia, to develop a pro-Portugal propaganda campaign. The campaign included making payments to influence newspaper coverage, so as to shape perceptions in the "American media with regard to the possible effects on American foreign policy of the conference of black American leaders last month in Harriman, N.Y."[14] The officials also contracted with an African American public relations firm in New York that "paid for visits to Angola by writers, editors and publishers of a number of black publications . . . [and] special supplements in black newspapers and even provided employment for the relatives of some black editors in its New York office."[15]

Portuguese authorities exploited the logic of the cold war and white resistance to racial integration to deal with pressure from African Americans. As part of the propaganda campaign, the Shreveport (La.) *Journal* published an editorial entitled "U.S. Backing Red Plot in Africa." The *Journal* suggested that the United States government promoted "racial equality on the home front while encouraging Negro domination in Africa . . . the overthrow of the Portuguese government in Angola and elsewhere in Africa is the primary aim of Soviet Russia and Red China. Their propagandists attack the Portuguese without cessation. The reason behind Communist hatred is plain. The government of Premier Salazar in Portugal is strongly anti-Communist. Moreover, Portugal is a member of NATO and has long been friendly to the United States and the West."[16]

Another editorial appeared in the Charleston (S.C.) *News and Courier*. Under the headline "The Pan-African Peril," it warned that the Harriman meeting "threatens U.S. security on the Dark Continent."[17] It questioned the patriotism of civil rights leaders: their meeting was "a gauge of American Negro opinion with regard to the left-wing Pan-African movement. Careful readers of the Negro press know that links with African peoples are currently being emphasized at the expense of the responsibilities of U.S. citizenship." The editorial suggested that King and others had ties to socialist countries like Algeria and Cuba, and called for an investigation of foreign contributions to the "Africa lobby," an ironic demand given that the editorial was paid foreign propaganda. The editorial equated civil rights leaders with savages, declaring that the Harriman meeting was "shaping up as a spear to be thrown at U.S. security interests in Africa."[18]

One Portuguese diplomat found it ironic that his country simultaneously represented itself as a champion of equal rights for the blacks in its colonies while building an alliance with segregationists in the southern United States. In his view the "black masses" in the United States were responsible for creating this paradox because they had become "agitated" by the sight of new delegates from Africa participating in the UN, "as equals—if not even superior to—the great white race powers." For the same reasons southern segregationists had embraced Portugal as a natural ally, "multiplying the paradoxes" with regard to the politics of Portugal in the United States. Consequently the diplomat warned that the Portuguese press should be cautious in its reporting of the United States civil rights struggle, because "anti-(white) American sentiments would only antagonize politically influential allies, and yet they would not be appreciated by black Americans who feel no sympathy toward Portugal."[19]

The conflict over American policy with regard to Angola and the Azores illustrates the constraints and opportunities created by the mix of American racial politics and cold war concerns. Not subject to independent public opinion and rejecting the voices of African nationalists as "foreign," Portuguese officials were not bound by the constraints of ideological consistency and could move across the surreal landscape of racial values in the Atlantic world, borrowing the rhetoric of racial democracy even as they built alliances with racist extremists in the United States.

Portuguese authorities were agile at manipulating the foreign policies of both the United States and Brazil, and tailored their campaigns to reflect the domestic politics of each country. While Salazar's regime targeted African American leaders, Brazil did not have an organized black movement in the early 1960s that could challenge and influence foreign policy toward Africa. In fact, Foreign Minister Afonso Arinos explained that one of his aims in developing relations with African countries was to "awaken the interest and support of the great Brazilian masses of mestizo blood" in relation to his government's foreign policy. Instead, the Portuguese mobilized a large, organized, and loyal immigrant community concentrated in Rio and São Paulo, and appealed to Brazilians' sense of Portuguese ancestry.

The Independent Foreign Policy and Portugal

Could the Brazilian government strike a different course than that imposed by Portugal on the United States and advocated by Gilberto Freyre? Quadros tried. When he appointed Arinos as foreign minister, his initial instructions were that "Brazil will not tie itself to Portugal's colonial policies."[20] When war erupted in the first months of 1961, Quadros asked Arinos to meet with Salazar and explain that Brazil would not support Portugal at the UN, reasoning that the meeting satisfied the expectations of the Treaty of Friendship and Consultation. Arinos traveled to Lisbon from Dakar, where he had attended the Senegalese independence ceremonies.

At the meeting Arinos encouraged Salazar to accept decolonization and Salazar pressed Arinos to support Portugal. Two memoirs describe their meeting. Arinos published his in 1968, shortly after leaving politics in frustration over the authoritarian tone of the Constitution of 1967 promulgated by the military regime. In recalling his meeting with Salazar, Arinos described himself as an observer, trying to gauge the dictator: "I watched him like a writer—curious, even though I felt diametrically opposite to his political opinions. As I watched him hold forth moderately and with clarity about so many international issues, I couldn't help but ask myself whether this lucid composed old man approved of the brutalities of the PIDE, the miseries of Tarrafal [Portugal's prison island]. Or was he just another cog in the monstrous machinery of twentieth century dictatorships, a machine that escapes the control of its engineers and runs on its own momentum, obeying an obscure design. Or worse yet, running without any design at all?"[21] For Arinos there was no way for the two to agree, since Salazar "defended the Portugal of the past and I the Brazil of the future."[22]

Vasco Leitão da Cunha, the first foreign minister of the Brazilian military regime, related Salazar's supposed response to the meeting in an oral history. According to Leitão da Cunha, Salazar later commented: "This boy came here, he was very bright and talked a lot, trying to convince me that Brazil's policy was correct. But in the end, he left me thinking that what Brazil really needs is to be ruled from [the Portuguese governing palace]."[23] Arinos and Salazar attributed their mutual disdain to age: the old dictator, who was seventy-one, versus the clever boy, who was fifty-six. And both recollections come through the filter of Brazil's dictatorship: Arinos writing against the military regime in power and Leitão da Cunha condemning the pre-dictatorship foreign policy as immature.

After returning from the meeting in Lisbon, Arinos and Quadros drafted a presidential statement: "Brazil reserves the right to follow the development of the African situation with the freedom of action that corresponds to its firm policy of anticolonialism, antidiscrimination, and frank support for the self-determination of all peoples aspiring to independence."[24] Arinos instructed Freitas Vale that he was "authorized to vote in favor of the Afro-Asian proposals on Angola."[25] The Brazilian ambassador in Lisbon, Negrão de Lima, learned of the decision from the Portuguese foreign minister, Marcelo Mathias. He sent a telegram to Quadros in which he related Mathias's plea that Brazil abstain, since "Portugal's resistance has no other purpose but to safeguard those sacred interests, based on history, of establishing a Luso-African civilization in Angola that permits the co-existence of everyone and not exclusion with the total sacrifice of the Portuguese part of the Angolan population."[26]

Mário Gibson Barboza recalled the ensuing conversation between the Portuguese ambassador Rocheta and Afonso Arinos in Rio de Janeiro after the ambassador returned from a meeting with Quadros in Brasília. Rocheta told Arinos that Quadros changed his mind and Brazil would vote in favor of Portugal. According to Barboza's memoir, Arinos responded: "I cannot accept that you would say something like that. I am the Minister, and the President would not change his mind about a decision like that without notifying me directly." Rocheta suggested that Arinos call Quadros, who confirmed the change of vote and said he had even cried when Rocheta described the difficult position Brazil was creating for Portugal.[27]

Finding Facts in Angola

Salazar ignored the UN request to send observers to Angola. Instead, in a sign of his confidence in Ambassador Negrão de Lima, he invited him to tour the colony. Negrão de Lima went to Angola in May 1961, accompanied by Alberto Costa e Silva and the Brazilian lecturer at the University of Coimbra, Thiers Martins Moreira (Antonio Carlos Tavares's uncle).[28] Negrão de Lima realized that he would be shown a sanitized version of the colony. Colonial authorities wanted him to stay in Luanda and its surroundings. Though he insisted that he be allowed to see other parts of the country, including the combat areas of the north, they did not allow him to visit the diamond mining areas, renowned for their harsh labor conditions. Costa e Silva recalled how the ambassador divided his entourage. So that the newly arrived Brazilian consul, Frederico Carlos Carnaúba, would not antagonize colonial authorities, Negrão de Lima would keep him at his side, participating in the scripted events. But he told Costa e Silva and Martins Moreira: "I am not going to see anything because wherever I go, there will be children waving Brazilian and Portuguese flags at me. Get by on your own and see what you can find."[29]

Negrão de Lima and the other Brazilians stepped into an environment in which they were constantly watched by the PIDE and where almost every event was scripted. The PIDE, which spied extensively on anyone perceived to threaten Salazar's regime and its dominions, was extinguished by the revolution of 1974, and its records are now open to the public. Among them is the folder of reports monitoring Negrão de Lima's delegation. These reports cover rumors circulating in Luanda, events that the Brazilian delegation participated in, stakeouts at hotels, and various information gathered from the network of informants who surrounded the Brazilians.

The delegation flew to Nova Lisboa, a city near Luanda that Portuguese officials had planned as a new capital. It was a natural stop, since its architecture and master plan cast the colonial regime as modern and progressive. On stepping out of the plane Negrão de Lima was "enthusiastically greeted by close to 4,000 Europeans and over 1,500 natives."[30] After lunch at the provincial governor's palace, the governor took the delegation to a nearby village. The PIDE report of the visit illustrates the choreography that Portuguese officials enforced on African populations. The visitors were greeted by "5,000 natives that formed two wings, holding Portuguese and Brazilian flags, cheering Portugal and Brazil. There were four speakers, two white and two black. Each . . . affirmed that Angola is also a Portuguese land where there is no distinction between races or colors." Negrão de Lima replied: "I feel as if I haven't left Brazil, because what I see here are a people and not races." The event ended with "the national anthem being sung by all of the blacks and whites. Before this, there was a cocktail reception in the town commissioner's home, where blacks were seen mingling with whites."[31]

The next day the Brazilians visited an iron mine, where Negrão de Lima was greeted by a Portuguese engineer and "1,500 workers, forming two lines, each holding their tools. They cheered Brazil and Portugal, greeted the visitor and sang the national anthem." During lunch the "private choral group of the mines, consisting only of blacks, performed music" including the national anthem, which the delegation must have grown weary of hearing. At the end of his dinner that evening at the governor's palace,

Negrão de Lima was called to the veranda, where a multitude of students greeted him, placed a cap on his head, hoisted him on their shoulders, and "triumphantly" carried him around the palace gardens. Negrão de Lima thanked them and declared that they "reminded him of his Brazil, where there were no distinctions made by race nor color."

At a reception in the governor's palace on their first day, Negrão de Lima was approached by the white Angolan journalist and poet Ernesto Lara Filho, who entered "without having been invited."[32] Before being expelled Lara approached Negrão de Lima and handed him some newspapers. He became the conduit between the Brazilians and members of the opposition in Angola. The PIDE spotted him at a number of meetings with Costa e Silva and Martins, and recorded a conversation in which Lara declared to Martins that "he fought for a free, better and greater Angola," and Martins said of Portugal, "this tree does not deserve the fruit it produces." PIDE agents also reported that Costa e Silva "seemed aloof to everything and everyone," and that "he should be watched because he is anti-Portuguese. In fact, in his few conversations he declared himself a supporter of Jânio Quadros and revealed his socialist leanings." Any contact with the delegation aroused the PIDE's suspicion. After a lawyer spent two hours speaking with Costa e Silva alone in a room during a reception, the PIDE described him as "a highly regarded member of the community who until now was not politically suspect."

From Nova Lisboa the delegation traveled to Sá Bandeira, in southwestern Angola, and from there proceeded up the coast to Lobito. In Sá Bandeira, Negrão de Lima met with "opposition figures" in the presence of the provincial governor. They claimed to be members of the opposition who had become loyal to the government because they rejected "the acts of terrorism in the north." Negrão de Lima sat through scripted confessions of support for Portugal in order to free Costa e Silva and Martins to seek out real members of the opposition. These opposition figures turned out to be a ruse as well: a PIDE agent reported that "these contacts were scripted in order to keep the gentlemen from contacting dangerous opposition figures, which would have been the intention of Costa e Silva, who showed himself to be a dangerous element who is very knowledgeable about African challenges and made clear he supports the total independence of Angola."[33] Oddly, the PIDE agent reported that Negrão de Lima himself had warned the provincial governor "of the need to control his delegation, especially Costa e Silva."

In Benguela, though the city commissioner and police chief aimed to "control possible contacts with the opposition," this control was less effective than in Sá Bandeira.[34] At an exposition of modern Brazilian architecture, Martins Moreira met a civil engineer and spoke loudly enough to make sure his handlers heard him: "I understand you are developing some buildings, which I would like to visit, since I am also interested in architecture." Martins and the engineer left and walked through the city for an hour together, talking, being followed, but not being heard. From there they followed to the official luncheon, and were taken to the airport back to Luanda.

One of the leaders of the independence movement in Benguela recalled his encounter with the Brazilian delegation in his memoirs. Sócrates Dáskalos described a lessening of the military and police presence of the Portuguese authorities on the eve of Negrão de Lima's visit, since "it was not convenient to demonstrate the typical repression." Still, it was impossible to get near the delegation without being "surrounded by paunchy plainclothes agents." Dáskalos arranged a meeting with Costa e Silva, whom he remembered as "a young man, but very knowledgeable about African independence movements." Dáskalos wrote that Costa e Silva encouraged him to have his organization join the MPLA, and to leave Angola ahead of the repression, which he failed to do in time. Dáskalos's meetings were observed and recorded by the PIDE from beginning to end.[35] When the Brazilians departed, Dáskalos accompanied the delegation to the airport, and recalled seeing an unknown stranger in dark glasses: it was the "PIDE detective who was about to arrest all of us."[36]

At the end of the trip, as the Brazilian delegation boarded the plane back to Lisbon, someone whispered that all the people whom they had informally spoken with had been arrested. As Costa e Silva recalled, "in totalitarian regimes, there is an underground message system that works incredibly efficiently," so everyone knew this.[37] On his return to Portugal, Negrão de Lima appealed personally to Salazar to secure freedom for those who had been arrested. According to Costa e Silva all were released, though almost all were removed from Angola and sent to Lisbon. Dáskalos was among them. He spent three months in prison, mostly in solitary confinement, before he was given conditional release in Lisbon.[38]

While the Brazilian consul Carnaúba stayed away from opposition figures during Negrão de Lima's visit, the PIDE in Angola deemed him an enemy of Portugal and placed him under surveillance. His PIDE file described him as "cautious, but when he is in the presence of partisans for Angolan emancipation, he reveals his clear animosity toward the current Portuguese regime."[39] One of the files on Carnaúba struck the paranoid tone common to PIDE records, declaring him to be a "democrat-socialist" who was sent to Angola as part of a conspiracy to wrest it away. As evidence of this, the author of the record offered a rhetorical question: "What actions has Dr. Carnaúba taken in defense of the colonial policy of Portugal? None." The PIDE agent elaborated by describing his reaction as he watched a mob of white youths push the car of the United States consul into Luanda bay, presumably in protest of a vote at the UN. Carnaúba reportedly commented: "And these jerks want to be considered civilizers, when the truth is that they should be governed by the blacks, who should school them. This is truly savagery and it could only come from the Portuguese."[40]

Portuguese authorities had Carnaúba removed from his post. He was replaced by Sérgio Corrêa do Lago, the diplomat who had refused to move out of the ambassadors' residence in Ghana for Souza Dantas. The PIDE conducted surveillance of him as well, chronicling his increasingly erratic behavior, fueled by heavy drinking. Corrêa do Lago's tenure abruptly ended after the Portuguese foreign minister informed his Brazilian counterpart that Corrêa do Lago had been interned in a cardiac clinic for what was publicly described as a medical condition. Drunk, he fought with and shot at his wife, and then ran down a street in Luanda, firing wildly into the air.[41]

In the end, what did Negrão de Lima's mission find? They learned firsthand the lengths to which the Portuguese would defend their colonies. And Negrão de Lima's report on the mission stressed the economic toll that the war had already taken on Portugal and the colony. He predicted, though, that "this will likely be a lengthy struggle." He hoped that the Portuguese would come to realize the futility of the struggle, and cede autonomy to the white, mestizo, and assimilated black population, which he called the "non-racial" part of Angola, to prevent a takeover by the majority black population that had no linguistic or cultural connection to the Portuguese. Negrão de Lima concluded that Brazil's best course of action was to "maintain friendly dialogue with Portugal," in the hope that this would give its leaders time to embrace change, and that the future Angola would "be built into a country like Brazil, with a black majority, it's true, but in which reigns the same harmony between peoples of different origins, and where the word race does not mean anything depressing or dangerous."[42]

A Deal with Portugal?

As it did with the United States, the Portuguese regime paralyzed Brazilian opposition. Quadros vacillated between support for decolonization and cautious abstentions at the United Nations, frustrating both proponents of decolonization, like Arinos and Freitas Vale, and supporters of Portugal, like Negrão de Lima. Meanwhile tension at the embassy in Lisbon remained, not only because of Brazilian policy but also because of the steady stream of dissidents seeking asylum. Portuguese authorities stalled their release. There were asylum seekers living in the embassy continuously from 1961 to 1963, with at one point over a dozen people living there and waiting to depart. After living in the embassy for up to two years, some grew weary and simply abandoned the attempted asylum.[43]

In July 1961 Negrão de Lima offered his resignation to Quadros in a disagreement over Portuguese policy.[44] Quadros rejected the resignation. Instead it was Quadros who resigned a month later. The new government organized in September 1961, with Goulart as president and his powers transferred to a parliamentary cabinet headed by Prime Minister Tancredo Neves, attempted to continue the foreign policies that had been inconsistently implemented under Quadros. The new government replaced Afonso Arinos with Francisco Clementino San Tiago Dantas in the process of parliamentary deal making that created the new government. Dantas was foreign minister for less than a year (September 1961 to June 1962), and over the remaining two years of Goulart's presidency four others would hold the post, including Arinos again for four months. The successive ministers continued the foreign policy introduced by Quadros in 1961, but Brazil's political instability prevented consistent policymaking. The turnover created a leadership vacuum within Itamaraty which emboldened both lusophiles and supporters of decolonization, who increasingly acted on their own.

Among the succession of foreign ministers San Tiago Dantas had the clearest policy vision and was the only one who faced a stable environment for implementing policies. As the Sixteenth Session of the United Nations General Assembly neared, Dantas met with the Portuguese ambassador, Ramos, to tell him that "frankly the Brazilian position with regard to

Angola could not continue to be 'abstention' . . . Brazil favors the African peoples' grand movement toward independence." Ramos responded that "the Portuguese case is unique . . . based on the consent of peoples who happily coexist in typically Portuguese multiracialism, just like Brazil. We consider ourselves to be the solution between black racism and white racism. In our territories there was no discrimination, exploitation or coercion. Until Angola started to be invaded by foreign men, weapons and ideas, it was a place of Portuguese peace of the luso-tropical type described by Freyre." Dantas replied that Brazil had to meet the expectations of new countries, and "abstaining on the Portuguese case would let these countries down."[45]

Why did Dantas want to meet these expectations? Ramos believed that the new Brazilian government "aspired to international leadership that could not be reached without the support of the Afro-Asiatic group," and that "newspapers were already reporting on a Brazilian candidacy for the position of Secretary General of the United Nations." Still, Ramos reported Dantas's "position in the new government to be weak."[46] In truth, the whole government was too weak to consistently defy Portugal, with the exception of its vote in favor of UN Resolution 1742 in 1962. The resolution, supported by both Brazil and the United States, called for Portugal to prepare Angola for independence. Dispirited, Negrão de Lima requested to be transferred to a different country, because he "felt uneasy in Portugal, in the face of Brazilian policy against the Portuguese colonial regime."[47] He also pursued the opportunity to attempt to negotiate an understanding between Brazil and Portugal, and in doing so developed a lasting, but also a failed, Brazilian framework for trying to solve the colonial impasse.

In August 1962 Negrão de Lima attempted to negotiate a shared position between Brazil and Portugal. He met with Goulart, Prime Minister Neves, and Foreign Minister Dantas. They conceded that it was "in Brazil's interest that Angola and Mozambique remain Portuguese." Negrão de Lima brought this gesture of support to the Portuguese foreign minister, Franco Nogueira. He asked Nogueira how long Portugal could bear the military and political costs of its wars in Africa, and suggested that the Brazilian gesture could help form the basis of a Luso-Brazilian community that would keep the colonies effectively tied to Portugal. Negrão de Lima's idea was to get the Portuguese government to agree to a lengthy timetable for granting autonomy to its African territories. If the Portuguese regime agreed, the Brazilian government would vote with Portugal at the UN. What is more, Negrão de Lima implied that Brazil could bring the government of the United States along with the arrangement, which would guarantee Portugal "a long period of rest, blocking or attenuating the Afro-Asian attacks."[48]

Franco Nogueira rejected the idea of a timetable and dismissed the offer of support from the United States. When Negrão de Lima suggested that the Brazilian government had to respond to public support for decolonization, Nogueira retorted that it was the responsibility of Brazil's leadership to guide public opinion and "vacate" that sentiment. For another decade Brazilian diplomats would continue to try to negotiate with the Portuguese government for a timetable for independence, always receiving the same truculent rejections from the Portuguese. In this first instance, Nogueira's negotiations were eased by Negrão de Lima's lusophilia. The conversation ended with his promise to "defend our common cause with total vigor."[49]

Defending Portugal in Brazil

Rallying to defend the Portuguese empire, Gilberto Freyre addressed the celebrations for the Portuguese community in Rio de Janeiro on 10 June 1962. At different times this Portuguese national day was called "Day of the Race," "Day of Portugal," or at this moment, to invoke its colonial grandeur in an age of crisis, "Camões Day." The Salazarist mainstream of the Portuguese ethnic "colony," gathered through its main ethnic organization, the Federation of Portuguese Associations, invited Freyre to speak at the Real Gabinete. His speech was widely reprinted; the source cited here is a journal at the colonial ministry archive. In 1968, as the wars in Africa raged, the colonial ministry reprinted the address in a scholarly journal that it published called *Portugal in Africa: Journal of Missionary Culture*, which featured on its cover a Portuguese caravel with bright red Maltese crosses on its sails, a coastline (presumably African) along the horizon. The journal illustrated the crusading fictions of golden age grandeur that sustained the dictatorship and its ailing empire.

Though speaking in a hallowed library, Freyre stepped beyond the scholarly tone he had struck in Portugal and gave a sharply political address. He lamented the annexation of Goa by India, proclaiming that "a Portuguese wound is Brazilian pain."[50] He repeated the refrains he often used when talking about Portugal in which he described himself as an objective observer: "I don't look at the question from a political standpoint, but from a sociological standpoint." Freyre argued that attacks on the Portuguese presence in Africa were motivated by the Soviet Union. This was an easier case to make once Portugal had succeeded in silencing American pressures for decolonization. Through this device Freyre argued that supporters of Angolan independence were unwittingly supporting the spread of communism, and that Angolan nationalists were in reality foreign. He characterized Angola as an "adolescent little sister" to be protected from predators like the Soviet Union.

Gilberto Freyre used the term "racial democracy" for the first time, declaring, "My thanks go to those who participated by being present at the commemorations of Camões Day in Rio de Janeiro this year, and came to hear the words of someone who, as a disciple of Camões . . . is as opposed to the mystique of 'negritude' as to 'whiteness': two sectarian extremes that are contrary to the very Brazilian practice of racial democracy through *mestiçagem*: a practice that imposes special duties of solidarity with other mixed-race peoples . . . Especially with those of black and *mestiço* Africans marked by the Portuguese presence."[51] Until then Freyre had always used the terms "ethnic democracy" and "social democracy," which meant the same thing but were more compatible with a culturalist interpretation of peoples. Since Freyre cast himself as a pioneer of that approach, he shunned the use of the word "race." But when he spoke passionately about Portugal in Africa he used more direct and political language.

Since the early 1950s scholarship on Brazilian race relations had moved away from Freyre's theses and increasingly recognized racial inequality. Similarly, scholarship on the Portuguese empire had increasingly focused on its nature as a system of exploitation. Charles Boxer, the best-known scholar working on the history of Portugal's overseas expansion, published a series of lectures in 1963 to refute Salazarist propaganda that the Portuguese "have never involved the slightest idea of superiority or racial discrimination."[52] Boxer stressed that the Portuguese legitimated slavery based on the belief that Africans were "indisputably an inferior being to the white man."[53] Referring to Freyre, Boxer declared: "[It is] sufficiently clear that racial prejudice and racial tension existed in colonial Brazil to a much greater extent than some modern authorities . . . are willing to allow. In Brazil, as in Portuguese Asia and Portuguese Africa . . . the free Negro and the dark-hued Mulatto had little or no hope of ascending in the social scale, whatever their aptitudes and qualifications. One or two exceptions merely confirm this general rule."[54] Boxer did not imply that the Portuguese were especially racist. Instead he gently suggested that "the Portuguese were neither angels nor devils; they were human beings and they acted as such; their conduct varying greatly according to time, place and circumstances."[55]

Freyre reacted in his newspaper column. As a British intelligence officer in Asia and later a Japanese prisoner during the Second World War, Boxer learned Portuguese and Dutch, languages that served him later for conducting archival research into the history of Portuguese expansion.[56] Freyre suggested that Boxer "perhaps confuses eruptions among the Portuguese in the Orient and Africa with racial prejudice—eruptions that no one who knows the history of Portuguese expansion in the tropics would deny—with the prevalence of prejudice." Writing of Boxer and Basil Davidson, also British and a prominent critic of Portuguese colonialism, Freyre suggested that their criticism of the Portuguese was born of their "bitter experience of witnessing the crumbling of the mighty British Empire." Freyre suggested that they wrote out of envy and a desire to see the Portuguese empire undone as well.[57]

Gilberto Freyre's speeches and newspaper columns were part of a larger political campaign on behalf of Portuguese colonialism. The Portuguese community's organization and allies bore down on Quadros's and Goulart's governments. Their influence was magnified by the willingness of politicians from Kubitschek to members of state assemblies to cultivate their political support. Kubitschek, for example, remarked in Lisbon: "When I was president, I never differentiated between Brazilian and Portuguese foreign policy . . . The distinctions between Brazil and Portugal will eventually be wiped out." Back in Brazil, when Kubitschek was questioned about what seemed like a foreign policy capitulation to Portugal, he replied that when he spoke, he had "felt more Oliveira than Kubitschek," invoking his second surname as he often did to assert Portuguese ethnicity, but added, "We are not Portuguese through choice, but because we are the product of the creative genius of Portugal."[58]

After his presidency Kubitschek became even more of an advocate for Portugal, as he worked to build the political base for a campaign to be elected president again in 1965. That meant cultivating the Portuguese ethnic colony in Rio as well as maintaining relations with Portuguese officials. In 1963 he met in Paris with the Portuguese foreign minister Mathias, for instance, and told him that he would "try through his personal and political friends to keep Brazil from taking a position against [Portugal]" at the United Nations. Mathias appreciated Kubitschek's sentiments, but replied ominously that "the day Brazil ceases to recognize that in Angola we are carrying out the traditional Portuguese practice of non-discrimination that forged Brazil, it will expose itself to the same international communist campaign to spur racial hatreds in Brazil." He warned that it would "not be hard to allege that political power in Brazil is concentrated in the hands of a white or pseudo-white minority, without real equity for the black, indigenous or mixed population that constitutes the great demographic mass of Brazil."[59]

Portugal's pull over members of Congress was even more powerful. The Portuguese government could offer trips and honors. The Portuguese ethnic colony could deliver votes. In the atomized political environment of Brazil in the late 1950s and early 1960s, it was easy for Portuguese diplomats to find and court supportive politicians. They were treated to trips to Portugal and the colonies and in return defended Portuguese colonialism in Brazil. The strategy resembled the one that the journalist Elio Gaspari discusses in his history of the Brazilian military dictatorship. He cited Abbie Hoffman's *Steal This Book*, which taught readers that they could get free trips: "Some counties have special deals for inviting writers, journalists and artists to travel for free. Brazil and Argentina for sure. Write or call the embassy of the country you want to visit. It is best if you can get your hands on letterhead from some publication or press."[60]

It was an easy deal for a Brazilian legislator to score a trip to Portugal and to the beaches of Mozambique. The congressional leader Ranieri Mazzili (who briefly held the presidency after the coup of 1964) thanked Ambassador Ramos for "Portugal's initiative in inviting Brazilian legislators to its territories."[61] José Honório Rodrigues commented on the members of the Brazilian Congress who "visited Dictator Salazar in Lisbon to express solidarity on the Angolan question and support for the Luso-Brazilian community. Indiscreet, with always the same old story of our 'being descended from Portuguese,' they censured the Brazilian government abroad."[62]

While some politicians of the political right, like Arinos, supported Portuguese decolonization, many cast independence movements in Portuguese Africa as leftist subversion and a threat to the Luso-Brazilian way of life, turning Portugal's problems into a domestic political issue. Foes of Goulart charged that his government was infiltrated by communists, evidenced by "Itamaraty's anti-colonialism against Portugal, forgetting the colonialism that comes from Moscow and Peking."[63] Plínio Salgado, who had headed the fascist Integralist Party in Brazil in the 1930s and was exiled to Portugal after a failed coup attempt against Vargas, was a federal deputy in Brazil in the late 1950s and 1960s and part of the coalition of supporters of Portugal. He declared: "The information about Angola that reaches Brazil is untrue: Angola is a province where blacks and whites coexist with equal rights."[64]

The main advocate for Portuguese colonialism in the Brazilian Congress, Eurípides Cardoso de Meneses, delivered long speeches in Congress defending Portugal that Portuguese officials reprinted as they did Freyre's lectures. The Portuguese embassy fed evidence and anecdotes to Meneses to mount his defenses.[65] Meneses's rhetoric was a guidepost for supporters of Portugal. He argued that "there is no slavery nor racial discrimination in the colonies, and evidence to the contrary is Bolshevist propaganda,"[66] and that Portugal had "a truly Christian racial equality," unlike independent African countries like Ghana and Senegal, which were based on "black racism."[67] Meneses stressed that blacks were fortunate to be part of the Portuguese world: "Both the Brazilian black and the Angolan black are proud of the Portuguese culture that assimilated them and that they assimilated . . . It is with us, the Lusiads of Brazil, of Europe, of Asia, Africa and the Atlantic Islands, that the world will have to learn the great lesson of brotherhood, racial democracy, and respect of the human being . . . While in the United States, racial hatred mounts."[68] Portuguese authorities rewarded their "great friend" by sending him on a monthlong trip to Macau, Goa, Angola, and Mozambique.[69]

In Rio de Janeiro and São Paulo, Portugal's political pull was even stronger because of the organized political and financial weight of the Portuguese colony. State elections in 1962 brought evidence of this, since they mobilized an ethnic community that was already on a war footing over the challenges to Portugal's empire. In the State of Guanabara (comprising the old Federal District of Rio de Janeiro), the journalist Carlos Lacerda won election for governor. Lacerda's clash with Getúlio Vargas in the 1950s culminated in Vargas's suicide. His position on Portugal had been vague until he sought the support of the Portuguese colony. His stance quickly evolved, as did the editorial tone of his newspaper, *Tribuna da Imprensa*, which took up vitriolic support for Portugal. José Maria Pereira

José Maria Pereira and Afonso Arinos de Melo Franco.
Photo courtesy of José Maria Pereira.

recalled that "Lacerda was a lusophile because of his campaign . . . He tested the electoral efficiency of the Portuguese community's political and financial organization. They moved millions."[70] Similarly, the São Paulo gubernatorial candidate Adhemar de Barros criticized Brazilian support for decolonization measures at the United Nations, calling it "interference in [Portugal's] internal affairs."[71] Both politicians were household names and aspired to the presidency in 1965, so support for Portugal was not only good for getting votes in their state elections, it was a challenge to Quadros and Goulart that helped sustain their national stature.

Just as there was a mass of politicians and diplomats who were "friends of Portugal," there was a less vocal and perhaps smaller number of politicians and diplomats who saw the Portuguese empire as archaic and on its last legs. For instance, when the economist Roberto Campos was named ambassador to the United States by João Goulart in 1961, he remarked, "If our Portuguese friends focused on a calendar for decolonization rather than a lost fight on quicksand, they might be able to make possible a transition that involves less bloodshed and less hatred."[72] Portuguese diplomats took note of these criticisms, just as they noted the speeches by their allies. In 1961 the Portuguese ambassador in Athens met with the Brazilian ambassador to Greece and Mário Guimarães, the new Brazilian ambassador designated to India, en route to his new post. The Portuguese ambassador probed Guimarães about the Indian seizure of Goa. Guimarães "exploded" and declared that it was "necessary for the Portuguese to comprehend that the age of colonialism is over." The Portuguese ambassador replied that Portuguese colonialism was based on miscegenation and the "creation of multi-racial societies like Brazil." Guimarães retorted that this was "not enough of a reason to prevent independence."[73]

Portugal and Brazil's Political Crisis

João Goulart never enjoyed a strong enough political base to sustain a coherent foreign policy with regard to Portuguese decolonization, particularly given the organized support for Portugal in Brazil that stretched from the Portuguese embassy through ethnic organizations, a large pro-Portugal congressional block, and lusophiles within Itamaraty. Goulart's weakness was fully displayed in March 1963, when early copies of his annual presidential message to Congress included a sentence that read: "We have recognized, and continue to recognize the right of all colonial peoples to independence . . . including Angola and the other overseas territories of Portugal, as well as that of Southwest Africa [Namibia]."[74] The first printing of several dozen copies of the message contained this language, which was immediately disavowed by the government. The second printing of thirty thousand omitted the portion that began with "including Angola . . ."[75]

José Honório Rodrigues believed that the original statement of support for Angolan independence was written by presidential aides, and attributed the retraction to vacillation by the "weak" foreign minister Hermes Lima acting under the influence of Ambassador Negrão de Lima, who was in Brazil at the time.[76] In fact Negrão de Lima sought out the Portuguese ambassador, Ramos, to explain that "he was aggravated by the question of the presidential message. He said he was in Brasília at a presidential reception when he was told what had happened and became very irritated. He immediately met with Hermes Lima, who was similarly irritated . . . Negrão de Lima suggested that [the message] be corrected, which the minister later accomplished."[77] Negrão de Lima blamed the language on a "maneuver by leftist extremists acting within Itamaraty," and the pro-Portugal newspaper *O Jornal* reported that Negrão de Lima refused to return to his post as ambassador in Lisbon "until there is a formal disavowal by the Brazilian government."[78]

Itamaraty did publicly disavow the language, and privately reassured Ambassador Ramos that it was an error. The Itamaraty chief of staff Henrique Vale told Ramos, "The draft of the message submitted to the President did contain that language, but the President crossed it out himself. Both the president and Foreign Minister Hermes Lima were aggravated about the lapse that kept the text in place in the final version sent to Congress." Ramos told Vale that the mistake was "offensive" and demanded a public explanation. Vale gave his consent that the Portuguese government "could publicize his disavowal as much as it liked."[79]

The episode illustrated the ability of the Portuguese government to shut down Brazilian policy and to exact contrition even from senior Brazilian government officials. It also shows the influence of lusophiles within the Brazilian government, as well as Goulart's weakness. But this episode had wider consequences: the disavowals by Brazilian officials like Negrão de Lima were based on the suggestion that the language was the malicious act of leftist saboteurs. This was seized upon by opponents of Goulart, who saw it as proof of the charge by the United States ambassador Lincoln Gordon that his government was "infiltrated by communists."[80] Soon after, Negrão de Lima resigned as ambassador to organize Kubitschek's presidential campaign in 1965, and one of the final legacies of his tenure was to demonstrate that Goulart no longer had the political authority to challenge Portuguese colonialism. His remaining year as president saw no action by Brazilian authorities on Portugal other than two abstentions in UN votes.

When the military seized power in April 1964, Brazil's new leaders reaffirmed their alignment with the United States and Portugal in a "western" front against communism. Given the paralysis of Brazilian foreign policy in the preceding years, their embrace of Portugal reflected little real change. But the military regime abandoned the African diplomatic project that had germinated during the preceding years. The ideology of the new regime was captured by remarks by Manuel Pio Correia, Itamaraty's chief of staff in the early years after the coup. Pio Correia told the Portuguese ambassador that the Portuguese could "count on him." He was a supporter of the white Rhodesian government, which had recently declared its independence from Britain in order to preserve white minority rule, remarking, "I have a certain understanding for the independence movement in Rhodesia, which is identical to Brazil's independence."[81]

In his memoir Pio Correia nostalgically recalled traveling to colonial Mozambique, which he contrasted with what he perceived as its failures after independence: "According to the newspapers, there was a 'war of national liberation' there. Crossing the country from north to south, I saw no sign of that; just well-tended fields, and black and white people smiling affably. In Lourenço Marques, today dishonored with that vile epithet *Maputo*, and transformed into a squalid sub-favela, I found a happy, prosperous and clean city with thriving commerce and a lively night life, all in the process of intelligent and advanced racial integration."[82] In the years following the coup, Brazil's political leaders and diplomats would revel vicariously in Portuguese colonial fantasies.

5 Latinité or Fraternité?

Senegal, Portugal, and the Brazilian Military Regime

IN SEPTEMBER 1964, six months after Brazil's military coup, President Léopold Senghor of Senegal stepped onto the tarmac of the Galeão Air Force Base in Rio de Janeiro. Senghor was the first head of state to visit Brazil since the military seized power, and over the next week he would visit Rio, Brasília, São Paulo, and Salvador, on a mission to challenge Brazil's support for Portuguese colonialism. With the domestic political opposition routed or exiled, and the alliances with Portugal and the United States renewed, the Brazilian military regime seemed likely to face no opposition to an alignment with Portugal that could go as far as the creation of an anticommunist "South Atlantic Defensive Pact" binding Portugal, South Africa, Argentina, and Brazil. Senghor posed an unanticipated challenge.

Senghor sought to compel Brazil to become a mediator between Portugal and the independence movements in its colonies, using its potential influence over Portugal to achieve what the United Nations and African countries could not and spur the negotiated autonomy of the territories under Portuguese rule. The Senegalese government had a direct interest in ending Portuguese rule because Senegal shared a border with Portuguese Guinea, one of the colonies with the most intense fighting. Senegal received thousands of refugees and suffered repeated border incursions and bombings of border towns by the Portuguese armed forces.

Léopold Senghor, arriving at Congonhas Airport in São Paulo, September 24, 1964. Última Hora/Folhapress.

The Senegalese government determined that its best option for challenging a European regime with armies equipped with NATO equipment was to leverage Brazil's influence, promoting the idea of an "Afro-Luso-Brazilian Community" akin to the British Commonwealth or the relationship between France and its former African colonies.

The Brazilian military regime embraced "fraternity" with Portugal, and when Senghor arrived in Rio de Janeiro he was ready to propose an alternative, "Latinité," a universal spirit of Latin values that he suggested French Africa shared with Brazil, Portugal, and Portuguese Africa. Latinité was an adaptation of Senghor's *négritude*, the movement of black cultural and political affirmation that Senghor developed specifically as a means of moral suasion over Brazilians, whom he hoped to coax away from Portuguese colonialism. Instead, in the spirit of Latinity, he suggested, Brazil could create the conditions by which it would become the natural leader of a Portuguese-speaking world of independent nations awash in Lusitanian values.

Senghor's government worked to turn around the rhetoric of racial democracy and lusotropicalism. This chapter traces the Senegalese project, which ranged beyond Senghor's moral and sentimental appeals to constant political pressure. It included taking advantage of Brazilian policies toward Africa, like the student exchange program, to train cadres for Guiné-Bissau's eventual independence, and providing logistical support for Portuguese African nationalists in Rio, both when they operated openly before 1964 and once they were rounded up after the coup. Senegalese policy combined praise of Brazil and its system of race relations with criticism of the same, displaying a keen appreciation of the ways to exploit Brazilian insecurities. Senghor worked with the Freyrean way of looking at Brazil and the world. Senghor earned Freyre's praise even as Freyre condemned *négritude* as un-Brazilian.

Senegalese policy toward Brazil began to take shape in 1963 when Léopold Senghor named his nephew, Henri Senghor, as ambassador to Brazil. Henri Senghor mobilized political support in Brazil for Portuguese decolonization and stimulated political consciousness and mobilization among black Brazilians. Anani Dzidzienyo suggests that "the arrival of African diplomats in Brazil, whether or not from a conscious effort on their part, has had a significant impact upon the framework of traditional Brazilian race relations and the position of Afro-Brazilians therein."[1] Certainly for Ambassador Senghor this was a conscious effort.

José Maria Pereira and the Angolan exile José Manuel Gonçalves recalled the activism of the Senegalese embassy in Rio de Janeiro under Ambassador Henri Senghor. For Gonçalves, Ghana had asserted early leadership in favor of the total decolonization of Africa, and Brazil's first African embassy was opened there, but "Ghana never took advantage of that to pressure Brazil." Instead it was Senghor who "took on a leadership role, speaking on behalf of the Portuguese-speaking territories."[2] Pereira recalled the logistical support that Ambassador Senghor brought to the circle of activists for Portuguese decolonization in Rio, which included allowing them to use the embassy to hold meetings and make international phone calls, as well as organizing physical protection from assaults by Portuguese defenders of colonialism.[3]

Senegalese authorities arranged for students from Portuguese colonies to travel with Senegalese passports to Brazil, filling the quota established for scholarships from Senegal. Among them, the Portuguese Guinea law student Fidelis Cabral became the PAIGC representative in Rio. His studies made him one of the few trained lawyers in the country after independence from Portugal, so he became its first minister of justice and helped draft the Guiné-Bissau constitution. Another student became minister of education of Cabo Verde.[4] Candido Mendes, who helped develop the exchange program under Quadros, recalled realizing that the students from Portuguese Africa who came to Brazil to study were overwhelmingly activists for independence, so the exchange program meant "bringing a subversive seed to Brazil."[5] They were under Portuguese surveillance, which reported on their militancy.[6] But just as they were watched by the Portuguese, they were watched over by the Senegalese.[7]

African Activism in Brazil

Two Brazilian students, Fernando Mourão and José Maria Pereira, returned from Portugal having become activists committed to Portuguese African liberation. In São Paulo, Mourão helped create the Afro-Brazilian Movement for the Liberation of Angola (MABLA) while working as a reporter for *O Estado de S. Paulo*, one of the most outspoken newspapers against Portuguese colonialism. In Rio, José Maria Pereira became a full-time activist for Portuguese decolonization. He organized students and pressed the already anti-Salazarist National Student Union (UNE) to embrace Portuguese decolonization.

Soon Pereira's apartment became the Brazil bureau of the MPLA and PAIGC, as Portuguese African nationalists began arriving in Rio. In 1962 José Lima de Azevedo, an MPLA member exiled in Ghana, arrived to organize an MPLA presence and moved in with Pereira. José Manuel Gonçalves and Fidelis Cabral joined Pereira too.[8] Their group included a PIDE informant who had been one of the asylum seekers at the Brazilian embassy in Lisbon. (Unlike other asylees, who spent up to a year living at the embassy waiting for permission to leave the country, the informant was given immediate permission from the PIDE and the Portuguese foreign ministry to depart, a fact that failed to raise the suspicion of Brazilian authorities.)[9] Pereira recalled that they all knew who the informant was: "He passed himself off as a member of the opposition, but the way he talked plus our conspiratorial paranoia led us to consider him PIDE."[10] Pereira was right, and the PIDE archive in Lisbon holds the informant's reports on the nationalist activists in Rio. The informant kept track of activists arriving in Rio, and he chronicled the support from allies like the former ambassador Álvaro Lins, who gave legal advice.[11] On the other hand, the Senegalese embassy provided logistical support, and it housed Fidelis

Cabral. According to Pereira, this aid went as far as arranging physical protection against Salazarist Portuguese immigrants by mobilizing supporters of Palestine among Rio de Janeiro's Middle Eastern community (the Senegalese embassy served as a conduit for this community to the Palestinian al-Fatah movement's office in Dakar). Pereira recalled that "the MPLA people had a problem with getting beaten up."[12]

Meanwhile in São Paulo, MABLA formed broad alliances among anti-Salazarist Portuguese immigrants and exiles (who published a newspaper called *Portugal Democrático*), university students, and trade unionists, but it also sought ties outside the left. As Mourão recalled, "What we needed was *Brazil's* support for Angola's independence, not the support of the left or the right, but the support of anyone and everyone." He contrasted this approach with "the Rio group . . . [which] approximated itself to the Brazilian left."[13] Still, MABLA members engaged in direct clashes with Salazarists that were reported by the anti-Salazar Portuguese community newspaper *Portugal Democrático*, as well as being watched by the Portuguese embassy and PIDE informants. For instance, in November 1961 the Angolan ice hockey team visited São Paulo and played an exhibition game at the city's largest indoor arena, the Ginásio Ibirapuera. The sparse public (ice hockey is not popular in Brazil) included several dozen university students connected to MABLA, who unfurled banners reading "Down with Colonialism" and "Independence for Angola." A fight between MABLA members and Salazar supporters ensued. The *Portugal Democrático* gave its story the headline "Fascism on Ice."[14]

MABLA was not infiltrated to the extent that the Rio group was, though a PIDE informant attended their public meetings and reported on discussions about the future of Portugal and its colonies. The informant always noted whether speakers were Brazilian, Portuguese, or Angolan, and white or black. On one occasion the informant reported on a trip from Rio by José Manuel Gonçalves, who presciently declared that after decolonization, "Portugal will have only two possible paths: to fall off the map, since it won't have anyone to steal from anymore, or become a Socialist republic." (After 1974 Portugal did become socialist.) The informant went on to describe "the black Paulo Matoso's declaration of surprise at Brazil's neutral stance on the Angola question at the United Nations." The informant noted that when he was asked what he thought of race relations in Brazil, he responded that "he was happy there was not racial discrimination, at least among progressives." Two parts of this report stand out. First,

Matoso offered a qualified statement about Brazilian race relations. I asked José Manuel Gonçalves about this, and he explained that among Angolan militants in Brazil there was an understanding that their fight was about Angola and not about Brazil, and that they should avoid criticizing Brazilian race relations. Second, it shows the informant's preoccupation with the potentially racialized mobilization of opposition to Portugal in Brazil, akin to that taking place in the United States. The informant reported that "of the close to 30 participants at the meeting, two were black."[15]

In addition to its network of informants, the PIDE maintained a more direct presence in Brazil, particularly in Rio. Its presence was first alleged in an editorial in *O Estado de S. Paulo* supporting the hijacking in January 1961 of the ocean liner *Santa Maria*.[16] In Brazil the PIDE relied on what Mourão characterized as "corrupt police." He continued: "We later learned that the Brazilian authorities did not know of their presence. Brazilian police working with the PIDE formed a parallel network that the Brazilian government could not control."[17] There is evidence of this network as early as 1960, before the outbreak of war in Angola, when PIDE directors in Lisbon corresponded about the visit to Portugal of a detective from the Brazilian Departamento de Ordem Política e Social (DOPS) as a guest of the Portuguese embassy in Rio. The detective was described as an "active collaborator . . . neutralizing or fighting the difficulties that have been caused by ex-General Delgado."[18] After the coup of 1964 the collaboration became more formal, with DOPS and PIDE agents exchanging documents. In the case of a batch of letters to *Portugal Democrático* in 1973 intercepted by the DOPS and sent to the PIDE, a PIDE agent acknowledged the materials with a warm note reiterating "the spirit of friendship and collaboration that joins us, count unconditionally on your friend, who sends you an embrace and awaits your visit to the 'Old Continent.'"[19]

In the aftermath of the military coup the shadowy presence of PIDE agents came into focus as the DOPS and military intelligence services cast a dragnet to detain suspected radicals. José Maria Pereira was detained twice. The first time, he reasoned, was because of his connections to the National Student Union (UNE), and he was released after three days. A short time later Pereira was arrested again in a sweep that apprehended all the African nationalist activists in Rio de Janeiro. This time the DOPS handed them off to CENIMAR, the Naval Intelligence Service. José Maria Pereira recalled that he was interviewed by both CENIMAR agents and Portuguese PIDE agents, and that the African nationalists were threatened with deportation to Portugal.

During Pereira's detention two agents searched his apartment in the presence of his Angolan wife, Filomena Pereira. He recalled that one was a Brazilian naval officer who introduced his companion as a PIDE agent. Filomena Pereira went to the press, and *Última Hora* published an account of her husband's arrest and the search of their apartment under the headline "PIDE Detains Angolans in Brazil." Ambassador Henri Senghor pressed Brazilian authorities and President Senghor sent a letter to the Brazilian ambassador in Dakar, Francisco Chermont Lisboa, calling for the nationalists to be freed and mentioning Fidelis Cabral by name. Senghor called on the Brazilian government to "join the popular struggle for freedom" from colonial rule.[20] Cabral was released after two days of detention and took exile in Senegal. Others were held for another month, during which the Senegalese government maintained continued pressure.

Beyond direct diplomatic pressure, Senegalese diplomats and Portuguese exiles mounted a press campaign in support of detained nationalists, including an article that appeared in *Le Monde*. Though the report was sourced to the MPLA office in Paris, its placement in a French newspaper and its tone were both consistent with the Senegalese government's campaign for their release. The article, which cast the detentions as part of Brazil's renewed support for Portuguese colonialism, threatened the new regime's image in Europe. After Ambassador Chermont Lisboa reported to Itamaraty on the account in *Le Monde*, the Brazilian foreign minister Leitão da Cunha contacted the DOPS political police in Rio and São Paulo to seek the release of the remaining nationalists to Senegal. A few days after the article was published, Leitão da Cunha telegrammed Chermont Lisboa that the Angolans had just been released to Senegal, and explained that "they were arrested for subversive activity in accordance with Brazilian national security laws . . . There was no intention to turn them over to Portuguese authorities because the affair was under the sole jurisdiction of the Brazilian government."[21]

The detainees were freed, and the Angolan and Guineans exiled. Released from detention, Pereira felt like "a fish in water," acting as an activist under dictatorship: he recalled that his experience evading the PIDE in Portugal prepared him to work at the margins of a police state, and he "became a pamphleteer for the UNE."[22] José Manuel Gonçalves was one of the Angolans arrested. He recalled that after he was released, Ambassador Henri Senghor gave him a letter asking the authorities to grant him safe passage to Chile, where he would await papers with which to travel to Senegal. Gonçalves described the letter as "a document that was really worthless. It didn't have a photograph on it or anything, but it was the safe-conduct that I had. [Henri Senghor] told me that he had personally gotten in contact with his uncle, the president of the republic, in order to arrange for me a visa to go to Senegal." He traveled through Bolivia and into Chile, where he "got a call from the French embassy, which represented Senegal there, saying that documents had come for me from the office of the Senegalese president. When I got to Senegal, I met with Senghor to thank him personally, and I saw how carefully everything was arranged: I was given a job at a university institute so that I could continue my studies."[23]

Gonçalves saw the detentions as a tactical error by the military regime that were the turning point in Senegal's relationship with Brazil: "The military regime soon realized it had made a mistake. What caused the mistake? The Portuguese lobby, which was behind Lacerda. There was no reason to arrest the Angolans—the police didn't even know what to do with us. It was Lacerda paying back the support he had received from the Portuguese. Probably even Lacerda and even the DOPS believed that holding the Angolans for a couple of months was enough to pay back the Portuguese, and then they let everyone go. It was a problem for everybody . . . it resulted in an international campaign against Brazil that sullied the image of the military regime."[24] The detentions gave the Senegalese government the upper hand, allowing it to pressure the new Brazilian regime and compelling it to engage with Senegal on the question of Portuguese Africa. For Gonçalves, "Senegal assumed the leading role in the Brazil-Africa dialogue. And the Brazilian military regime, realizing its mistake in jailing the Africans, would work to correct their error . . . Senghor in turn would work the question of Portugal's colonies."[25] If Brazilian foreign policy was malleable to Portuguese influence, it also proved malleable to Senegalese influence.

After the Coup: "Brazil Stands with Portugal"

The Brazilian dictatorship's first foreign minister, the career diplomat Vasco Leitão da Cunha, held conservative beliefs compatible with the new regime, and believed that the previous policy toward Portugal was wrong: "It was exaggerated. It was a very hostile act toward people who considered themselves our friends."[26] Though Leitão da Cunha worked to shield the diplomatic corps from the waves of military and police inquiries into the infiltration of subversives in the government, he assented to a military police inquiry into potential subversion among opponents of Portuguese colonialism. Four diplomats were purged, including Antônio Houaiss, who was removed for making remarks hostile to Portugal when he was posted at the United Nations in 1961. During a committee hearing Houaiss had said that Brazil "vehemently condemned" Portugal's failure to provide information about its colonies as required by Resolution 1514.[27] Houaiss was no stranger to controversy. His protest against the principal of his vocational school in 1935 contributed to the firing of Anísio Teixeira, progressive director of the Rio de Janeiro school system.[28] After Houaiss was expelled from the diplomatic corps he compiled the standard reference dictionary for Brazilian Portuguese.

José Clemente Baena Soares recalled that Houaiss had been part of a core of diplomats at Itamaraty who were oriented toward African relations and favored Portuguese decolonization.[29] Vasco Leitão da Cunha saw them as "a bunch of lunatics."[30] Leitão da Cunha declared that he could not understand why Brazilian diplomats with Portuguese last names would do that: "It's impossible to understand that thing with Portugal. Houaiss I understand. He was not Portuguese, he has an Oriental [Middle Eastern] name. But Otávio Dias Carneiro is a Portuguese name!"[31] Houaiss was convicted of subversion. Leitão da Cunha wrote, with a certain relish, that at the end of the sentencing the colonel overseeing the hearing told Houaiss and the other three diplomats, "'Now give a cheer for Brazil!' And they did."[32]

Meanwhile President Castelo Branco sent Governor Carlos Lacerda of Guanabara on a trip to France and Portugal to explain the meaning of the "1964 Revolution" for Brazil's foreign relations. At the time Lacerda was seen as the military's presumptive candidate for the presidential elections in 1965, which the military had not yet canceled. This expectation was so widespread that the records of his visit to Lisbon were catalogued under "Presidential Visits" in the archive of the colonial ministry. The main newspaper in Lisbon, *Diário de Notícias*, interviewed Lacerda in Paris on the eve of his arrival in Portugal. The banner headline quoted Lacerda as saying, "We are for Portugal." Beneath it was a photograph of President Américo Thomaz of Portugal placing medals on the chests of veterans of the African wars for their "epic heroism" in the fight against "terrorist subversion." Alongside the photograph and article, the interview with

Lacerda read: "More important than my opinion is the position of the Government of Brazil. We are for Portugal. For its rights, its dignity, its presence in the world which the Portuguese expanded and civilized."[33]

On arriving at the airport in Lisbon, Lacerda received a hero's welcome. Passengers and workers at the airport parted, forming a corridor for Lacerda. As he passed through it, "a group of gentle maidens, vivaciously dressed in folkloric style," cast rose petals over Lacerda.[34] Lacerda stepped to the microphones and told the press and the crowds, "I come this time not only bearing the constant and loyal friendship of a Brazilian. I come bearing a message from President Castelo Branco, who wishes to convey to your government and your people, our feelings of understanding, of fraternal loyalty, and shared identity." The cheering crowd chanted "Viva Lacerda" and "Lacerda '65."[35]

Lacerda met for two hours with Salazar, a duration that the Portuguese press attributed to the importance of the meeting, and the two gave a press conference afterward at which they commemorated the "resurrection" of Brazil by the revolution of 1964, as a result of which Brazil could "again fulfill its duty to Portugal."[36] Lacerda gave a television and radio address simulcast across Portugal and Brazil in which he condemned Quadros and Goulart for "disgoverning Brazil" and "reneging on Brazil's role alongside Portugal in the face of the threats it confronts." He proclaimed: "I am in favor of anything that keeps the Portuguese nation whole," and condemned the United Nations, which he said had a "dictate" of making "Asia for the yellow man, Africa for the blacks, Europe for the Whites." To which he asked: "What about us, the mestizos?" He declared, "Brazil is proud of its miscegenation and its total freedom from racial prejudice—one of the most noble legacies of the Portuguese."[37] The cancellation of the elections in 1965 made Lacerda into an opponent of the military regime. But in the early days after the "1964 Revolution" he was its defender, its messenger, and its presumed heir.

The regime's approach to Portugal and its colonies was exemplified in the classified instructions that Carlos Silvestre de Ouro Preto received from Foreign Minister Juracy Magalhães when he was appointed ambassador to Portugal in 1966. Magalhães commended him for having "served the cause of Luso-Brazilian approximation, a cause we must defend not only as a diplomatic imperative, but also as a traditional part of the collective historical consciousness of our country."[38] It was Brazilian policy to "publicly recognize what we owe our Portuguese elders: as the President of the Republic has stressed, the conviction held in the soul of our public that we are a nation integrated in the Lusitanian consciousness, and western, Latin culture of the Portuguese is a doctrine serenely embraced today by the most impartial names of Brazilian history and sociology," meaning Freyre.

With regard to the colonies Ouro Preto's instructions were clear: "Despite certain differences of time, place and other less relevant specifics, any criticism that we make of Portugal's role in its overseas territories would be the equivalent of condemning the Portuguese role in creating Brazil."[39] Acting on these instructions, Ouro Preto visited Angola and reported that "the moment could not be better for accelerating Brazil's commercial and cultural penetration of the Portuguese overseas territories." Ouro Preto reasoned that the security situation was under control, aided by the tightening relations between Portugal, South Africa, and Rhodesia, and that the native population remained "elemental" and not sufficiently developed to challenge Portuguese rule. The restoration of Portuguese hegemony was clearing the way for "new and vast opportunities" for Brazilian commerce.[40]

Senghor in Brazil

Senghor had sought an invitation to Brazil in early 1962, when Goulart was president and the Brazilian government nominally supported decolonization.[41] The trip was delayed as Goulart focused on domestic crises. Finally, at the insistence of the Senegalese government, Senghor's visit was set for September 1964.[42] In June, after the question of the jailed nationalists was resolved, the military regime confirmed the dates of Senghor's state visit. Over six days beginning on 19 September 1964, Senghor traveled to the Brazilian cities of Recife, Rio de Janeiro, Salvador, Brasília, and São Paulo. He met with Castelo Branco and Lacerda. He sat through long speeches about the virtues of Brazil's system of race relations, and gave addresses intended to nudge Brazilian thinking about Portuguese Africa. Brazil's leaders signaled their solidarity with Portugal. Senghor intended to keep Brazil's position ambiguous.

On the day Senghor arrived he was greeted at Galeão Air Force Base in Rio de Janeiro by Foreign Minister Leitão da Cunha and an honor guard of air force servicemen. That the honor guard was all black spurred criticism in the press and compelled the base commander to issue a statement that "here at Galeão, as in the entire FAB [Air Force], there are no racial problems . . . Everyone is treated equally and the same honor guard received President Castelo Branco that same afternoon when he arrived by helicopter from Petrópolis en route to Brasília. Our discrimination is only directed at agents of subversion, who are doing all they can to undermine our constitutional authorities."[43] The statement was a warning against public criticism of the armed forces.

The black honor guard was one of many gestures intended by Senghor's hosts to present an image of benign race relations. These speeches and gestures often devolved into patronizing statements like the address delivered by the chief justice of the Supreme Court, who proudly proclaimed that "the intense labor of the African racial elements, following the guiding hand and the initiative of the old barons, plantation masters and rural bosses, spurred the development of vast agrarian regions . . . This was realized through the constant, humble and steady labor of the colored elements. We are their brothers from the cradle, nurtured by their protective and loyal aid. We are honored by your visit to our country at the moment that colonial ties in the African continent are broken, and are certain you will gather from us evidence of the fraternity, equal treatment and absence of racial discrimination that characterize our entire nation. Work liberates the negro, who entertains with . . . his songs, with the rhythm and flavor of the dances that characterize the mystical spirit of solidarity that eliminates unemployment and vagrancy from Africa."[44] These remarks were a common refrain during Senghor's visit. Since black leaders were utterly unimaginable in Brazil, Senghor was regaled not as an ordinary leader but as an exceptional one.

For his part, Senghor pursued both private and public opportunities to make the case for decolonization. He met repeatedly with President Castelo Branco and Carlos Lacerda, testing the potential for steering Brazil toward a more neutral position, or better yet into a mediating role between nationalist movements and the Portuguese government. He followed this private pressure with public diplomacy, projecting the vision of Brazil as a leader of an "Afro-Luso-Brazilian Community" of independent nations. His first public opportunity came during the banquet held by Lacerda in his honor on his first day in Brazil. Lacerda spoke first, warning that "Brazil must not confuse the emergence of new African nations with the imposition from the outside of a forced rupture between Angola and Mozambique and the necessary and indispensable multiracial culture that

Léopold Senghor meeting with Humberto Castelo Branco, Brasília, September 23, 1964. Última Hora/Folhapress.

is Afro-Luso-Brazilian." In response, Senghor proposed an "Afro-Luso-Brazilian Community" and called on Brazilians to "help suppress the remaining anachronism in Africa." Countering Portugal's argument that it remained in Africa to defend lusotropical culture, Senghor suggested that Brazil was an example of a colony that gained its independence without losing its culture. Senghor called out Lacerda, asking him to "help solve the problem by reminding Portugal, of which he is such a friend, that Brazil's success is an example of how Portugal should finish the task other European powers had already done."[45]

At the reception held by President Castelo Branco, Senghor built on the theme of an Afro-Luso-Brazilian community by offering Senegal as an example of what lay ahead for Portuguese Africa. Senghor praised Brazil as an example of racial integration and argued that "what binds us is our Latin culture . . . which spurs your politics of racial integration." Senegal was a relevant example of what lay ahead for Senghor's proposed community: "[Like Brazil] in its Latinity, we advance the spirit of multiracialism and religious coexistence, that is our modest contribution to universal civilization." In response, Castelo Branco declared that Brazil sought a peaceful solution to colonialism, but warned against "swapping forms of domination" and implied that the independence movements in Portuguese Africa were inspired by communism.[46]

While Senghor prodded Brazil's leaders directly, his visit also provided space for advocates of Portuguese decolonization. *O Estado de S. Paulo*, the most outspoken opponent of Portuguese colonialism in the Brazilian press, published an editorial entitled "Carrying the World's Hopes," in which it defined the meaning of Senghor's visit: "His confidence in Brazil's mission should inspire the revolutionary leaders of Brazil, that is, the old Brazil, the true Brazil, to proceed on the path of framing an active foreign policy . . . Because Brazil, in Senghor's words, 'carries on its broad shoulders the hopes of this world, especially of Africa.' And with the 'grace' that is such a part of his spirit, and which he admires about Brazil, the president of Senegal has proposed that the Brazilian missionary spirit be applied to mediating an end to the difficult problem of Portuguese colonialism."[47] As he toured Brazil, Senghor was received by black leaders who expressed support for decolonization. In Rio de Janeiro he attended the mass of the black religious brotherhood Rosário, whose leaders praised Senghor as "a representative of the African peoples who struggle for self-determination, because no form of colonialism, no matter how paternalistic, can be democratic or part of the free world."[48] He met with members of the Portuguese community who favored decolonization. And on his last night in Brazil he held a literary and political discussion long into the night in the apartment of Antonio Olinto and Zora Seljan, hours after attending the inauguration of the "Senghor School" in a working-class neighborhood in Rio.[49]

Senghor's visit counterbalanced the military regime's turn toward Portugal. One visit alone could not change Brazilian policy, but it did hearten advocates of decolonization. His nephew continued the pressure. But since the Portuguese African nationalists had all been expelled from Brazil over the course of 1964, Henri Senghor shifted his focus to mobilize black Brazilians. José Maria Pereira recalled that the ambassador "was oriented toward négritude," and in early 1966 Ambassador Senghor began holding meetings at the embassy with black professionals, artists, and activists, as well as some whites interested in Africa like Antonio Olinto. Through the meetings Senghor aimed to create a Brazilian Society for African Culture akin to the black organization of the same name headquartered in Paris which edited *Présence Africaine*. As Pereira remembered, after a few months the organization failed to coalesce.[50] Still, Senghor the president and Senghor the ambassador continued to find ways to pressure Brazil.

The Festival of Black Arts

In June 1966 the government of Senegal held the first Pan-African Festival of Arts and Culture (FESTAC), a weeklong event celebrating black culture in Africa and the Americas. Invited to send a delegation, Itamaraty formed a commission to carefully choose artists and works to represent Brazil. The commission chose artists and themes intended to demonstrate Brazil's African cultural roots and the integration of African culture and of blacks into mainstream society. The Brazilian delegation, numbering forty-three persons, included singers, painters, sculptors, capoeira performers, an Afro-Bahian chef, and part of the Mangueira Samba School from Rio de Janeiro. The delegation was rounded out by Candido Mendes, Raymundo Souza Dantas, Waldir Freitas, the sociologist Edison Carneiro, the mayor of Salvador, and Clarival do Prado Valladares, a museum curator who was then organizing Salvador's Afro-Brazilian Museum. A sculpture by Agnaldo dos Santos won the festival's plastic arts award.[51]

Henri Senghor saw Brazil's participation in the festival as an opportunity to stimulate black activism in Brazil. The Brazilian organizing committee included Freitas, Souza Dantas, Carneiro, and Valladares, as well as Ambassador Senghor. Senghor clashed with the committee over its composition, demanding that it only include blacks (the only black member was Souza Dantas). Freitas recalled that he and the other Brazilians were opposed, including Souza Dantas, prompting a dispute in which Senghor "turned to Raymundo Souza Dantas . . . [and] told him: 'you are a degenerate black.' Souza Dantas stood and put his finger in [Senghor's] face and said 'you will respect me. I am not a Brazilian black. I am a black Brazilian," indicating that his Brazilian identity was more significant than his color, and defending the view that the commission should be composed of Brazilians of any color.[52]

Senghor remained defiant, prompting Itamaraty to send a telegram to the Brazilian ambassador in Dakar, Francisco Chermont Lisboa, complaining of his antagonism and warning that Senghor could attempt to block parts of the Brazilian delegation from performing. The telegram sent to Lisboa struck a tone characteristically used to reproach children, stating that Senghor "has behaved indiscreetly at the various meetings of the National Commission for the Festival in Dakar, trying to force the inclusion of names on the list of participants that have been rejected by all of the other members of the commission. His Excellency, acting with aggressiveness and presumption that can only be forgiven because of his relative youth and inexperience . . . has vigorously opposed the selection of . . . artists who represent the integration of African values in Brazilian culture."[53]

The clash between Itamaraty and Senghor illustrates the breach between negritude and the idea of racial democracy. In Brazil it was inadmissible to suggest that African peoples and cultures were less than indissolubly mixed with the rest of Brazilian society. There could be no such thing as a "Brazilian black commission," Souza Dantas was not a "Brazilian *black*" but a "black *Brazilian*," and the event in Dakar was a stage for projecting a Brazilianness for which the possession of African qualities was inherent. By contrast, negritude was a movement of affirmation of *black* culture, peoples, and societies. Negritude could have white allies, but it existed specifically to extricate blackness from its subordination to whiteness. Henri Senghor sought to build momentum for negritude in Brazil, and to use the festival organized by his government in Dakar to give a platform to black Brazilians whose militancy echoed that of the negritude movement. He could not compel the Brazilian organizing commission to send artists who emphasized blackness rather than mixture.

Still, Senghor was able to give a voice to black Brazilian activists by arranging the publication of a "Letter to Dakar," written by Abdias do Nascimento on behalf of the Black Experimental Theater (Teatro Experimental Negro, or TEN). The letter was published in *L'Unité Africaine*, the weekly journal of Léopold Senghor's party. *L'Unité* serialized the letter into weekly segments, which sustained the critique for nearly a month. For most of May 1966 readers of *L'Unité* saw a systematic attack by Brazilian blacks against the idea of racial democracy, the Brazilian delegation to the festival, and Itamaraty itself. Abdias do Nascimento had been an activist against racial discrimination in Brazil since the 1930s. Nascimento's political and artistic activism aimed toward black mobilization, echoing the negritude movement.[54]

Over the course of a lifetime of militancy Nascimento's approach to the idea of racial democracy evolved. In the 1940s he treated it as an ideal that could be leveraged to combat racial discrimination. His newspaper, *Quilombo*, had a regular column entitled "Racial Democracy" which included guest essays by writers like Gilberto Freyre and Roger Bastide.[55]

But by 1966 Nascimento had become one of the most categorical critics of racial democracy, which he had come to see as a "myth" and a "hoax."[56] This was the tone that Nascimento struck in the "Letter to Dakar," which also vented Henri Senghor's frustrations with the Brazilian festival commission. Nascimento's TEN was one of the groups that Senghor fought to include in the Brazilian delegation. Although his effort failed, he gave Nascimento the means to criticize the character of the delegation and describe the system of values that reproduced racial discrimination in Brazil.

In *L'Unité* Nascimento wrote that after the abolition of slavery blacks in Brazil "were not accorded the basic rights of citizenship," and that whites maintained a system of values that inhibited blacks from asserting their negritude. In place of a clear racial consciousness, black Brazilians were forced to accept a values system that "keeps the Negro in his place, leaving him only the outlets of Samba and soccer. Blacks who contest the system are silenced by the condemnation that "that's a racist black man."[57] The composition of the Brazilian delegation was evidence of the project of Brazilian élites to "whiten" Brazilian blacks by compelling them to "integrate" culturally and socially into a society that confined them to subordinate roles and curtailed the expression of cultural or political blackness of the kind asserted by decolonization in Africa and the civil rights struggle in the United States. In this sense the representatives sent to Dakar, and the exclusion of the TEN from the delegation, were products of a foreign ministry that "has a bad attitude with regard to blacks."[58] The Brazilian presence at the festival only "collaborates with the maintenance of a wrongful racial democracy. It ridicules negritude."[59]

Ambassador Francisco Chermont Lisboa saw the letter as a "violent attack on what the authors see as the causes of the social situation of blacks in Brazil, wanting foreigners to believe that racial discrimination exists in Brazil and, in particular, in the Ministry of Foreign Relations, whose staff are accused of being imbued with racist ideals."[60] Lisboa wrote to Foreign Minister Juracy Magalhães that the letter received widespread attention because it appeared in *L'Unité*. Lisboa ascribed responsibility to Henri Senghor: "The letter is well written, in correct French, and expressing the ideas of *negritude* that are commonly invoked here. So without leaping to conclusions, I wonder if the Embassy of Senegal in Brazil didn't collaborate in writing it, or at least helping publish it." Lisboa found it "suspicious that the Black Experimental Theater could so easily reach an outlet like the official organ of the government party here."[61] Though

Henri Senghor could not challenge the dominance of the idea of racial democracy from within the Brazilian foreign ministry, he could nonetheless ease the task for those like Abdias do Nascimento who would attack it as outsiders.

Itamaraty spent lavishly to sustain the delegation, transporting beans and okra by air for the cooking of "traditional Afro-Brazilian" dishes.[62] A Brazilian sculpture won a prize. Officially, "mixed" Brazil prevailed over blackness. But Senghor undermined Itamaraty, facilitating the publication of Abdias do Nascimento's letter. A few months after the festival a telegram to Lisboa made clear how costly the experience had been for Itamaraty. Discussions had begun in Dakar about a second festival, to be held in a different country, and Lisboa was told, "it is not advisable to hold the next Festival in Brazil, both because of the expense involved, and because of the undesirable political consequences that it would bring. The countries of the 'negritude' wing would not agree with our inviting delegations from so-called 'Portuguese Africa,' and this type of controversy plays into the hands of demagogues."[63]

The Voyage of the Squadron

If the Castelo Branco government that came to power in 1964 was supportive of Portugal, the regime of his successor, General Artur Costa e Silva (1967–69), was even more so. As he toured Europe before taking office, Costa e Silva "affirmed that during his government, Brazil will defend Portugal's position at the United Nations at every opportunity."[64] Though planned a year earlier, Costa e Silva's remarks were followed by the voyage of a Brazilian naval squadron of two cruisers and two destroyers to Angola, where they participated in joint maneuvers with the Portuguese navy. That the naval squadron carried out exercises with the Portuguese off the coast of a colony then mired in war was a clear signal of Brazil's support for colonialism. Both Costa e Silva's remarks and the naval exercises mobilized vehement opposition by the governments of Senegal and other African countries.

In Rio, the Algerian, Ghanaian, and Senegalese ambassadors and the chargé d'affaires of the United Arab Republic sought a meeting with the Itamaraty chief of staff Pio Correia to protest Costa e Silva's remarks, the forthcoming voyage of the squadron, and rumors of Brazilian investments in Angola and Mozambique. Correia, a longtime ally of Portugal, dismissed their concerns. He responded that the movements for independence in Angola were not "legitimate" and added that Brazil's own experience with becoming independent showed the benefits of a "gradual maturing of the Portuguese African territories, and that one day the peoples of Portuguese Africa will be in a state to be able to validly decide their own destiny."[65] Frustrated by the outcome of the meetings, the Senegalese and Ghanaian ambassadors issued a press release repeating their concerns. Foreign Minister Juracy Magalhães reproached them for publicizing their criticism, which he called "proof of their own inexperience as diplomats." He added that "Brazil will not permit a repeat of the disagreeable communications."[66] *O Globo* echoed the criticism, calling the ambassadors "wretched diplomats" and chiding their "inexperience." The *Jornal do Brasil* stated that the ambassadors "demonstrated their total immaturity and total disrespect for diplomatic norms."[67]

Portugal's influence was accepted and even encouraged by its allies in the Brazilian foreign ministry. But when African diplomats questioned the Brazilian military for acting in tandem with Portuguese combat forces in Angola, they faced a different standard. The ambassadors found an ally in Rubem Braga, a writer who had been Quadros's ambassador to Tunisia (and Zora Seljan's first husband). Braga wrote in his column in *Diário de Notícias* that the squadron's voyage was "the perfect way to insult the young nations just barely freed from colonial exploitation," and suggested that "perhaps the Brazilian warships could escort a replica of a slave ship back to Brazil, to make an even more impressive show of solidarity with Portuguese colonialism."[68] Braga ridiculed the Navy's press release, which stated that the visit "strengthened Luso-Brazilian friendship." Braga remarked that "never has that friendship been so abundantly favored, sworn, proclaimed, toasted, promoted, agreed to, or registered."[69]

As most Brazilian embassies did each month, in February 1967 the embassy in Lisbon submitted its "Monthly Political Memorandum." This memo began with unusually cheerful language: "In February, Luso-Brazilian relations enjoyed one of the greatest moments of the auspicious new period inaugurated by the March 1964 Revolution." The great moment was the visit to Luanda of a Brazilian naval squadron. The memo was unambiguous: "It was a visit that had a political character in the sense that it clearly demonstrated Brazil's adherence to the Portuguese conception that Angola is an overseas province, that is, an integral part of its multi-continental territory. It also implied tacit support for the Portuguese government's policy of total and unrestricted combat against the liberationist terrorists acting in Angola."[70]

With the squadron docked in Luanda, the officers, crew, and two thousand accompanying marines engaged in symbolic acts such as parades and visits to monuments of prominent colonial figures shared by the histories of Brazil and Angola, like the Portuguese colonial governor of Rio de Janeiro Salvador de Sá, who in 1648 led the fleet that recaptured the colony from Holland. The governor general of Angola received a medal from the president of Brazil, the commanders of the Brazilian ships received Portuguese commendations, and the sailors received commemorative medallions.[71] Ambassador Ouro Preto traveled from Lisbon to greet the naval force. Through it all, Portuguese authorities were careful to make sure that "blacks or mulattoes with positions of responsibility, social prominence, or professional standing be present at all of the social events," to make sure that the image of Portuguese multiracial democracy was evident.[72] They were determined to avoid creating the kinds of images that the head of a delegation of Brazilian athletes carried back from Mozambique in 1959. The head of the delegation declared that "the racism of the Portuguese against blacks in their colonies is simply repugnant," and explained that "blacks and whites are separated in even the most basic things, like bus stops, park benches, movie theaters, restaurants and much more. The result: blacks have a mortal hatred of whites."[73]

By contrast, in 1967 the Brazilian squadron commander proclaimed in Luanda: "We are deeply shocked that a war is being waged against Portugal in her overseas territories . . . we are interested in all that happens in Angola . . . we will do everything we can for Portugal which is the victim of a great injustice." The Portuguese admiral welcomed the Brazilians, declaring, "A powerful Lusitanian-Brazilian naval force would ensure for our countries an indisputable position in the Central and South Atlantic Ocean, enabling us to call it '*mare nostrum*.'"[74] Portuguese shortwave radio broadcasts, received across much of Africa, reported on the presence of the fleet as evidence of "Brazil's political and military support for Portugal in Africa." The broadcasts invited a response from the representatives of Portuguese colonial independence movements, who "decried the Brazilian military maneuvers . . . intended to intimidate the Angolan patriots and demonstrate Brazil's complicity in Portuguese colonialism."[75] Brazil became a focus of the struggle.

Though the ambassadors of Senegal, Ghana, and Algeria could not stop the squadron, their protests made the event into a lightning rod both in Brazil and in Africa. The pro-Portuguese press attacked them, but their protest gained momentum in the anti-Portuguese *Diário de Notícias* and *Última Hora*. Meanwhile their protest resonated across Africa. In southern Africa the *Times of Zambia* quoted the ambassadors: "If an exchange of opinions with a friendly country on questions affecting our vital interests constituted interference in internal affairs . . . then the whole basis of the international system and international law would crumble."[76] In Nigeria the magazine *West Africa* reflected on the "lack of imagination on the part of a government of a country claiming to take the lead in establishing racial harmony." *West Africa* criticized the use of the term "inexperienced" to label the ambassadors and concluded: "African diplomats may have erred in issuing a joint communiqué to the newspapers. But the man who conceived this naval visit is living in another century."[77]

Perhaps the Brazilian naval visit to Luanda was, as Juracy Magalhães described it, one of the high points of his tenure as foreign minister, but it was also the high-water mark of Brazilian support for Portuguese colonialism. Despite persistent invitations by the Portuguese government, joint maneuvers would not be repeated. Joint naval exercises off the northeastern coast of Brazil already planned for 1968 were canceled, in part to dispel a swelling rumor that the Treaty of Friendship and Consultation of 1953 included secret agreements for Brazil to come to the aid of Portugal in Africa. In 1969 the Portuguese navy invited its Brazilian counterparts to participate in joint maneuvers off the coast of Portuguese Guinea, where the most intense struggle was taking place, and the invitation was again declined.

In 1969 Foreign Minister Mário Gibson Barboza sought to avoid the diplomatic costs of another naval exercise with the Portuguese by using the cold war language of communist containment to dissuade President Emílio Médici (1969–74). He suggested that the exercises (which the Brazilian navy had already agreed to) would create such a negative reaction among African countries fighting racism and colonialism that they might respond by "ceding naval bases to the Soviet Union."[78] The exercises were canceled.

African diplomatic unity against Portuguese colonialism elevated the costs of Brazilian ties to Portugal. Led by Henri Senghor, the small African diplomatic corps based in Rio de Janeiro made those costs clear. Though in later years the Brazilian government would be more cautious about the symbolic weight of its relationship with Portugal, the die had been cast and the Brazilian government had come to be seen in African countries as a backer of Portugal. During the decade after the military took power in Brazil, a rumor circulated freely in Africa and in Brazil that the Brazilian government was involved in secret negotiations with Portugal, South Africa, and Argentina to create an anticommunist South Atlantic military alliance akin to NATO. While South African and Portuguese authorities did occasionally broach the idea with their Brazilian and Argentine counterparts, I have found no evidence that either the Brazilian or the Argentine government ever considered the possibility. Leticia Pinheiro suggests that Brazilian writers discussed the idea but it never became policy, while Andrew Hurrell notes that interest within the Argentine navy never spread to the rest of its government.[79] Still, Brazilian actions and African reactions had created an environment in which such possibilities seemed plausible.

The public tone with regard to Africa and race relations during the first years of Brazil's dictatorship was captured in a popular novel published by Jorge Amado in 1969. In *Tent of Miracles*, a newspaper editor and a university professor in Salvador debate how to commemorate a mulatto amateur ethnographer and sage who had written books celebrating Brazilian racial mixture. The professor proposed holding a seminar that would compare Brazilian race relations favorably to those of the United States and South Africa: "It may turn out to be a real landmark in the history of Brazilian culture—the first really systematic, scientific debate on the problem of race, which is now more vital, more a burning issue than ever before. It is exploding all over the world, particularly in the United States, where black power is a new factor to be reckoned with, and in South Africa, where the legacy of Nazism appears to have aggravated the problem." The professor suggested that "if Brazil has contributed anything truly significant to world civilization, it is miscegenation—that is our gift to humanity's treasure house."[80]

The politically savvy editor saw the risks in this approach, and warned that the conference was a bad idea in the "present situation" (alluding to the dictatorship). The professor insisted: "On the contrary . . . the moment could hardly be more propitious, now that the racial struggle in the United States has almost reached a state of civil war, now that the new African nations are beginning to play an important role in world politics."[81] The editor reminded the professor of Brazil's "commitment" to the United States and tightening commercial relations to South Africa, including commercial flights soon to be inaugurated between Rio de Janeiro and Johannesburg. He proposed an alternative: an essay contest, the prize being an expenses-paid trip to Portugal. Not surprisingly, Amado's books were banned in Portugal and its colonies, placing them among an extensive list of prohibited texts ranging from the writings of Antonio Gramsci to anything about yoga.[82]

The Brazilian dictatorship found alignment with Portugal increasingly costly. In March 1967 the Portuguese ambassador had lunch with José Sette Câmara, Brazilian ambassador to the United Nations from 1964 to 1968 and subsequent publisher of the Rio de Janeiro daily *Jornal do Brasil*. Câmara told him that while the Brazilian government would continue to do everything in its power to help Portugal, the costs of this assistance were mounting. For instance, in November 1966 Brazil was elected to a rotating seat on the UN Security Council, but "if the election had taken place after the naval squadron's visit to Angola, there is no doubt whatsoever that Brazil would not have gotten the seat." The Portuguese ambassador responded with a terse question: "What is more important for Brazil: conserving the lusitanity of the Portuguese overseas provinces, or posts in the UN?"[83] This question was answered by Foreign Minister Juracy Magalhães. When he was told that Brazil had lost a vote for a seat on a UNESCO commission "because of the reaction of the Afro-Asiatics against that country's policies in relation to Portugal," Magalhães responded that "it was better to do what needed to be done than to have a UNESCO seat."[84]

From the early 1960s onward the Senegalese government seized upon the Brazilian interest in Africa to pursue its goal of completing African decolonization and in particular liberating the neighboring territory of Portuguese Guinea. Aware of the Brazilian authorities' sensitivities about racial identity, President Léopold Senghor and Ambassador Henri Senghor by turns praised Brazil's racial mixture and built a critique of its idea of racial democracy. Senegal led a growing number of African nations that expressed their hostility to Portugal's continuing attempts to dominate large parts of the continent.

Senegalese policy toward Brazil frequently faced both pedantic paternalism from white Brazilians about the nobility of the country's race relations and frequent suggestions that "young" countries like Senegal had "immature" foreign policies, unlike the "mature" and "elder" Portugal (symbolized by the aging dictator Salazar). But what Minister Magalhães and *O Globo* criticized as immature was really an exercise of activist diplomacy intended to constrain the military regime's instinctive embrace of Portugal and keep the door open to alternative policies. The Brazilian regime would ultimately pursue these policies in the 1970s, under the stewardship of Foreign Minister Mário Gibson Barboza. Gibson would continue to find Léopold Senghor "the most influential" African leader.[85] Together the two would attempt to mediate a negotiated end to Portugal's colonial wars.

6 Gibson Barboza's Trip

"Brazil [Re]discovers Africa"

"BRAZIL DISCOVERS AFRICA" was the title of a memorandum sent in 1972 by the United States ambassador in Brazil, William Rountree, to the State Department, relating the month-long visit by Foreign Minister Mário Gibson Barboza to nine West African countries. According to Rountree, "Brazil, which sees itself as both an emerging world power and a leader of the Third World, wants to strengthen its ties with Africa. In particular, the Brazilians sought to demonstrate with some success that their special cultural ties with Portugal should not unduly hamper closer economic and political relations with Black Africa."[1] Rountree captured the essence of the diplomatic opening toward Africa which Gibson Barboza painstakingly began to organize in early 1971, and which culminated in his trip to Africa. The trip and Gibson Barboza's new diplomacy toward Africa were part of a broader strategy to break the fealty to Portugal that had consolidated under military rule, while employing Brazil's racial and cultural connections to Africa to build economic partnerships and export markets that would support the industrial and consumer expansion of the early 1970s, known as the "economic miracle."

Gibson Barboza found the political continuity and autonomy that had eluded Afonso Arinos and San Tiago Dantas when they attempted similar diplomacy in the early 1960s. And unlike foreign ministers of the first years of the military regime, Gibson Barboza was more willing and able to free Itamaraty from the ideological and sentimental commitments of the military, whose anticommunism and lusophilia made them easy tools of the Portuguese. Finally, Gibson Barboza contended with Portugal's influence at a moment when it struggled under the weight of interminable colonial wars waged by a regime that each day seemed further lost in time. But in essence, Gibson Barboza still faced the same challenges that his predecessors failed to overcome.

In his memoir Gibson Barboza explained his sense of this challenge, noting that his attempt to develop a new relationship with Africa inevitably meant renegotiating Brazil's relationship with Portugal:

> When I became foreign minister, I immediately confronted the tremendous obstacle that the Portuguese colonial problem presented. In 1971, I formally proposed a new foreign policy line to President Médici. I explained that in a rapidly approaching future, as an Atlantic country, Brazil will have interests and responsibilities on the other side of the ocean that bathes our shores. It would be prudent to, within our abilities, increase the Brazilian presence in Atlantic Africa. These are not only the lands across the river, they are the place where the overwhelming majority of our black population originates. Institutions and customs from that region have framed our social comportment. We maintained such intense and constant contact during the Empire that even today there are Brazilian vestiges in neighborhoods in Accra, Lagos and across Togo and Benin, where families proudly keep Portuguese names and their status as descendants of Brazilians. It is with these countries that we dialogue over the maintenance of the prices of our tropical commodities . . .
>
> [Visiting West Africa] will allow us to express our views on international affairs and will help generate a better understanding that can reduce or eliminate the climate of mistrust, coldness and even veiled hostility toward Brazil that could take root in Africa because of the position we have traditionally taken on the problem of Portugal's territories. I am aware of the risks we are assuming with my visit to these African countries, because we will confront each of their grievances with Brazil. But I believe it is better to be frank and open with regard to the difficult question, rather be the silent subject of threats, as we are now.[2]

Médici authorized Gibson's trip, which symbolized the two means by which the Brazilian government would relate to African countries in the 1970s. Gibson justified strengthening relations by invoking Brazil's racial mixture and cultural proximity to Africa, and an increasingly refined understanding of local conditions within African countries. In the case of Gibson Barboza's visit this understanding was generated by an unprecedentedly intense year of planning trips by Itamaraty staff. If Brazilian diplomats still relied on a sentimental connection to Africa, they also increasingly relied on local knowledge. As with most of the diplomats who preceded and followed Gibson Barboza to Africa, the idea of Brazilian democratic racial and cultural mixture created a sense of comfort with being in Africa and confidence about the Brazilian mission there. This construction was vastly more meaningful for Brazilian diplomats than for the African counterparts who received them. African leaders and diplomats understood the Brazilian diplomats' desire to express their Africanness, and used it to either challenge or encourage the Brazilians. When Gibson Barboza arrived in Lagos, President Gowon received him with arms spread and an effusive "Welcome home!" The remark so struck Gibson Barboza that he placed it in his memoirs and repeated it in our interviews thirty years later. It even resonated in the halls of the Portuguese foreign ministry, which spied on Brazilian communications during the trip and fretted over Gibson Barboza's enthusiasm about the remark.[3]

Gibson Barboza

I first met Mário Gibson Barboza in 2003 at his beachfront apartment in Rio de Janeiro. With sweeping views of the South Atlantic that he regarded as Brazil's shared border with Africa, the apartment had modern décor punctuated with African art and artifacts received as gifts during his trip in 1972. In our first conversation Gibson Barboza engaged in a mediation of identity that is a familiar part of this book. He asked me to call him Gibson and spoke of his maternal grandfather, who had come from Scotland. He mentioned an affinity for the actor Sean Connery, whose demeanor he admittedly bore (a United States diplomat described him as "the image of the suave statesman, exuding competence and confidence").[4] But in the same way that he presented a Scottish identity when we first met (eschewing the equally plausible Portuguese in Mário and Barboza), Gibson Barboza also recounted in our interviews and his memoirs the Africanness of his identity that was carried on his trip, giving particular stress to the Nigerian president's "Welcome home!"[5]

When I asked Gibson Barboza how he became interested in Africa, his answer connected to the central arteries of this book. As a law student in Pernambuco in the 1930s, he frequented intellectual gatherings at Gilberto Freyre's home that he recalled as "true classrooms of sociology" where Brazil's "Africanism" was discussed. He and other students attending these gatherings would then go out and conduct research for *The Mansions and the Shanties* (1938). He attended the First Afro-Brazilian Congress, organized by Freyre in 1934. He sustained a lifelong friendship with Freyre which he relied on in preparing for his visit to Africa. He began his career as a diplomat during the Second World War, when he was sent to the United States. He was struck by racial segregation: "I knew that there was social discrimination in Brazil, but not the racial discrimination that I saw in the United States." In a sign of Freyre's influence, Gibson Barboza explained that Brazil did not have these problems, because "our Lusitanian, Catholic foundations are different from the Calvinist formation of the United States." But there were limits to Freyre's influence in his thinking: "The romantic vision of slavery Freyre presented did not correspond to reality . . . It corresponded more to Freyre's feelings." In 1960 Gibson Barboza returned to the United States, serving under Cyro Freitas Vale at the UN. Watching the UN's demographics change as sixteen newly independent African nations took seats was a turning point for Gibson Barboza, giving him the sense that Brazil was part of a palpably different world.[6] Asked about his role in shaping policy toward Africa, he replied:

> It was just that when I found myself with sufficient authority to define a line of foreign relations, I immediately turned to an approximation between Brazil and Africa. Perhaps it all had to do with my formative experiences in law school, with Gilberto Freyre, later my six years of life at the embassy in Washington, where I was revolted by the discrimination, all of that drew me toward Africa. I always thought, I still think, Brazil has a great debt toward Africa. In truth we were colonized by the labor of African slaves. Brazil is not an African country, it is a "melting pot" like the United States, but it has a strong current that is African. Even in terms of geography. It occurred to me to call Africa our eastern frontier . . . in my view the ocean connects us. Its is a means of communication . . . Most of Brazil's population practices a mixture of Christianity and African rites . . . All of this has always held my interest.[7]

Gibson Barboza's opening toward Africa was a consequence of the most repressive presidency of the Brazilian dictatorship, that of Emílio Garrastazu Médici in 1969–74. The political stability brought about when the faction of the officers behind Médici consolidated power, along with the increasing abrogation of civil liberties and the violent repression of dissent within Brazil, produced a political environment in which foreign policy could be conducted with greater consistency than it had been in over a decade. Between 1961 and 1964 the position of foreign minister changed hands six times. Between the coup and Médici's administration three foreign ministers each served slightly less than two years.

By contrast, Gibson Barboza was foreign minister for a full presidential term, and his tenure began an era of unequaled continuity in Brazilian foreign policymaking. His successor, Antonio Azeredo da Silveira, was Gibson Barboza's chief of staff for a period, and served for the full term of President General Ernesto Geisel (1974–79). Azeredo da Silveira was succeeded by his own chief of staff, Ramiro Saraíva Guerreiro, for the full presidency of General João Baptista Figueiredo (1979–85). All three foreign ministers were professional diplomats, unlike the majority of their predecessors. Gibson Barboza's diplomatic experience helped him to overcome internal divisions that had long been evident. Médici's governing style, which gave considerable autonomy to his ministers, also opened space for Gibson Barboza. The balance was that "of the four years and three months I was minister, at least a third of my time was dedicated to African problems: Brazil's entrance into Africa and the attempt to convince the Portuguese government to take action in favor of its colonies' independence."[8]

Brazil's Economic Miracle

The context that shaped Gibson Barboza's opening toward Africa was the "economic miracle," a period of extraordinary economic growth that coincided with Médici's presidency. Between 1969 and 1974 Brazil's gross domestic product grew at an annual rate of 11 percent, propelled by a combination of rapid industrialization, swelling consumer demand among a growing middle class concentrated in Brazil's southeastern cities, and a surge in exports. By 1972 Brazil's manufactured exports surpassed the value of its agricultural and mineral exports, and between 1967 and 1977 the Brazilian merchant marine's carrying capacity increased fivefold.[9] It seemed that Brazil was leaping into the developed world. Ambassador Rountree observed, "The Brazilians are extremely proud of their high rate of economic growth and believe that as leaders of the Third World they can assist others along the path they have come."[10] When Gibson Barboza traveled to Africa he signed agreements for technical cooperation in agriculture, the development of commercial markets, infrastructure engineering, housing, and education.

Portugal, its colonists, and its supporters in Brazil sought to cast the economic miracle as having turned Brazil into the economic locomotive of the "Luso-Brazilian community," and Portuguese authorities reversed the longtime practice of keeping Brazilian trade out of Angola and Mozambique. Now they sought to stimulate Brazilian commerce with the colonies to tie their rationales for colonialism to the logic of the miracle. *Província de Angola*, a newspaper in Luanda, published frequent accounts of Brazil's economic growth and the possibilities of tying Brazil's economy to Angola, with headlines like "Brazil Will Be the Japan of the 1970s" and "The Eyes of the World Are on Brazil."[11] By contrast, Gibson Barboza saw the miracle as a reason to break away from Portuguese fealty, which had begun to hamper Brazil's economic needs. And Africa seemed to be a potentially rich market for the export of the sorts of industrial consumer goods that Brazil was now producing for its domestic market.

The years of the economic miracle were also the period of greatest political repression. Gibson Barboza contended with a wave of kidnappings of foreign diplomats that revolutionary groups organized to break through the censored media and to secure the release of political prisoners. Beginning with the kidnapping of the United States ambassador in 1969, the ambassadors of Switzerland and Germany, as well as the consul of Japan in São Paulo, were kidnapped by revolutionary movements seeking to overthrow the dictatorship. Gibson Barboza opposed raiding the locations where kidnapped ambassadors were being held, arguing that the safety of foreign diplomats was the government's cardinal responsibility. At the same time, the climate of repression reached as far as Gibson Barboza's trip to Africa. The Brazilian air force, which provided the plane that flew the minister's delegation, refused to board a reporter from *O Estado de S. Paulo*, alleging that he and his wife engaged in "subversive activities" for which they had both previously been jailed.[12]

The violent tension between repression and subversion shifted the landscape of Brazilian foreign policy, especially with regard to Portugal. Until the end of 1970 the Brazilian foreign ministry and the foreign embassies in Brazil had remained in Rio de Janeiro although a striking new ministry palace had been erected in Brasília, even if the sites of embas-

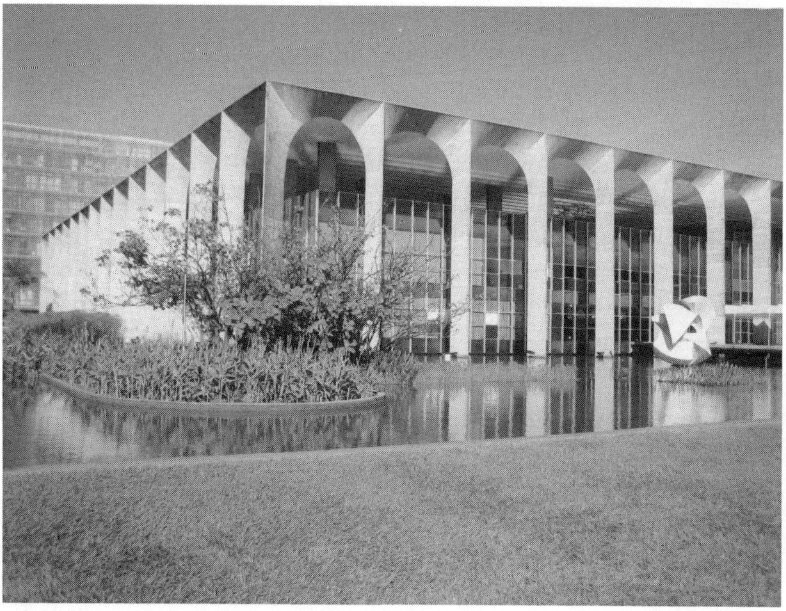

Itamaraty Palace, Brasília. Photo by author.

sies had already been plotted out. Both foreign and Brazilian diplomats shunned the sterile planned modernism of Brasília, which was no match for the bustle, restaurants, bookstores, nightlife, and beaches of Rio. Brazilian diplomats justified keeping Itamaraty in Rio because that was where the foreign embassies were, and the embassies justified remaining in Rio because that was where Itamaraty was. Gibson Barboza resolved to move the foreign ministry and the embassies to Brasília, which was after all the capital. He overcame resistance to the move by leveraging the wave of kidnappings, informing the embassies that the security staff that protected them from further kidnappings would move to Brasília at the end of 1970.[13]

Beginning in 1971 Brasília functioned as Brazil's diplomatic capital. The shift loosened the Portuguese lobby's grip on foreign policy. Brasília was nonetheless imprinted with Juscelino Kubitschek's lusophilic worldview, which was evident in the distribution of embassy sites. Three embassies were located immediately around the foreign ministry: those of the United States, Portugal, and the Papal Nunciate. Itamaraty and the Portuguese embassy were joined by Praça Portugal, a square with a murky pond and a modernist statue of Prince Henry the Navigator.

Gibson's Strategy

Gibson Barboza's strategy was to continue the course set by his predecessors of intensifying "Luso-Brazilian relations" while rekindling the relations with West Africa that had withered since the initial enthusiasm of Jânio Quadros's era. Then, from the vantage point of bilateral relations with Portugal and multilateral relations with West Africa, Gibson Barboza would try to mediate between the two factions. He relied on the assumption that Portugal could no longer sustain the social and economic costs of permanent wars across Africa and would soon have to recognize the inevitable independence of its colonies. When that recognition dawned, Gibson Barboza would have positioned Brazil to play the role of honest broker.

Ironically, the close relationship between Brazil and Portugal made Brazil more relevant to African countries. The trust between the Brazilian and Portuguese governments became an asset that West African countries would try to leverage. If Brazil could use the relationship with Portugal to ease decolonization, it would regain the African trust that had been shaken by years of diplomatic neglect. Rountree explained after Gibson Barboza's visit, "There were indications that both sides believe Brazil has a role to play as an intermediary between Portugal and Black Africa. The Africans strongly urged Brazil to use its special relationship to Portugal to convince the latter to accept gradual independence for its African territories."[14]

Gibson Barboza executed the strategy in three stages. First, he carried out a succession of high-profile diplomatic acts with Portugal, culminating in shared festivities of the 150th anniversary of Brazil's independence in 1972; the repatriation of the remains of Emperor Pedro I, the Portuguese monarch who proclaimed Brazilian independence in 1822; and the signing of an accord granting Portuguese in Brazil and Brazilians in Portugal virtually the same rights as full citizens. While doing so Gibson Barboza generally avoided showing support for Portuguese colonialism. Second, he staged the carefully orchestrated visit to nine West African countries, signing cultural and commercial accords, listening to the frustrations that African leaders felt toward Portugal and Brazil, and seeking to reintroduce Brazil as a culturally proximate partner. Third, he proposed to Premier Marcello Caetano and Foreign Minister Rui Patrício of Portugal that Brazil could host negotiations with African countries.

Gibson Barboza sustained the tone of "Luso-Brazilian approximation" that carried forward from the earlier years of the military regime, responding positively to the escalating contacts sought by Portuguese leaders. Premier Caetano visited Brazil in 1969 and 1972. On both occasions he was hailed in public commemorations by the Portuguese colony in Rio, which gave him ticker-tape parades. President Américo Thomaz attended the sesquicentenary commemorations, bearing the remains of Pedro I. Foreign Minister Rui Patrício visited several times. President Médici visited Portugal, as did Gibson Barboza on several occasions.

Only once did Gibson Barboza make a gesture of public support for the Portuguese position. At the end of Rui Patrício's visit to Brazil in September 1971 he issued a joint statement with Gibson Barboza in which they resolved to "totally reject the terrorist actions being carried out on several continents, condemning it as a step backward in civilization and a crime against humanity."[15] The repressive environment of the dictatorship under Médici helped make it politically feasible for Gibson Barboza to pursue an opening with Africa, but it also made it hard to differentiate between two right-wing authoritarian regimes engaged in the violent repression of armed resistance movements.

Despite Brazil's support of Portugal at the United Nations, Gibson Barboza tried to privately awaken his Portuguese counterparts to the futility of their efforts. Visiting Lisbon in 1970, he told Foreign Minister Rui Patrício and Premier Caetano: "Notwithstanding our votes at the U.N., with which we are trying to avoid embarrassing a brother country, we do not accept that the overseas territories are provinces of a unified state." He hoped that Salazar's replacement by Caetano would mean a change of course. But Caetano told him that he "had assumed responsibility over a wiped out country in which any proposed change aroused unease."[16] In a subtle sign of change, Gibson Barboza used the term "brother country," conveying equality, rather than the deferential "mother country."

Still, relations with Portugal remained as close as ever, driven by the desperation of the Portuguese regime, which made all manner of concessions to retain Brazil's support. When I asked Gibson Barboza why Caetano agreed to transfer the remains of Emperor Pedro I to Brazil, he succinctly responded, "because I asked." Brazil's first independent ruler, Pedro I abdicated and returned to Portugal, where he governed as Pedro IV. Though Brazilian governments had long sought the remains of the founder of their nation, Portuguese authorities refused to expatriate the remains of a monarch. But now the remains were delivered in a choreographed display of Luso-Brazilian fraternity. President Admiral Américo Thomaz of Portugal and an entourage, dressed in mourning, accompanied the remains on board an ocean liner from Lisbon to Rio de Janeiro, in what the *Financial Times* called "one of the oddest voyages undertaken by a modern head of state."[17] Thomaz toured Brazilian cities to display the remains, much as the victorious World Cup team had done in 1970 with its trophy. Finally, on 22 April 1972, 150 years after Pedro I rode to the Ypiranga River, raised his sword, and proclaimed "independence or death!," his remains were interred in a monument on the site, in a nationally televised ceremony headed by Presidents Thomaz and Médici. The *Financial Times* assessed the significance of the "symbolic journey," suggesting that it was a "step forward in Luso-Brazilian relations that could have an important bearing on Lisbon's African dilemma."[18]

Portuguese Obstruction

By the end of 1971 Ambassador Fragoso of Portugal understood that Gibson Barboza was preparing a new diplomatic push toward Africa that might culminate in a break in Brazilian support for colonialism. In particular, he detected efforts by Brazilian diplomats to prepare public opinion for a shift in policy, and he proposed a response to Foreign Minister Rui Patrício. Fragoso reasoned that although he had avoided sending Brazilian politicians to the colonies because of the cost, particularly given the weakened role of the Congress under military rule, he believed that the trips should be reinstated as part of a plan to buttress political opinion against Gibson Barboza.[19] He would mobilize friends in the press, "because our battle must continue on the front of public opinion." He proposed stationing additional military attachés in Brazil to cultivate the armed forces, and recommended binding businessmen to the colonies with economic enticements. Finally, he suggested "being more liberal with our policy of giving out decorations, which would certainly have a positive return with no expense."[20] These were the same means that worked so well at halting Brazilian policy between 1961 and 1971.

But Portuguese authorities also tried a new tactic to block Gibson Barboza: they sought out countervailing authorities in the Brazilian government with whom they might negotiate separate agreements. These agreements would be highly favorable to Brazil, but at the cost of harnessing the country to the last, violent days of Portuguese colonialism. The Portuguese government approached Finance Minister Antônio Delfim Netto with a proposal to open Angola and Mozambique to Brazilian exports, free of tariffs. Delfim Netto was credited with producing the Brazilian economic miracle, making him the most powerful minister of Médici's government. Access to captive colonial markets would be an easy way to improve Brazil's trade balance and propel the miracle. Portuguese authorities similarly lured the president of Petrobras, General Ernesto Geisel, with an offer to provide access to the Angolan oil fields. Most oil in Brazil was imported, and Petrobras struggled to meet the growing economy's demand for energy. Angola could be a close and abundant source of oil. At that same moment, the senior military in Brazil coalesced around General Geisel as President Médici's successor in 1974. The offers were made to the two people in Brazil other than the president who could eclipse Gibson Barboza's objectives.

Gibson Barboza was forced to face down both Delfim Netto and Geisel. Geisel was easily persuaded that the political cost of opening the export market was too high.[21] The confrontation with Delfim Netto was more difficult, because he saw both the economic advantages of exporting goods to Angola and Mozambique and the opportunity for extending his influence over Itamaraty. As Delfim Netto pursued these markets over the first months of 1972, Ambassador Fragoso confidently predicted Gibson Barboza's resignation. He wrote to Foreign Minister Rui Patrício, speculating on possible successors for Gibson Barboza and recounting Delfim Netto's professed certainty that Brazil would pursue the economic opening with Angola and Mozambique.[22]

According to Gibson Barboza, Delfim Netto "thought the way into Africa was through the economic exploitation of Portugal's colonial markets. I subscribed to the theory—which was proven correct—that this was totally insane."[23] For Gibson Barboza, Delfim Netto saw only the short-term economic benefits of the relationship: "His point of view was purely economic, seeing only the commercial advantages Portugal was offering, the trading posts, teaming up on oil exploration in Angola." But Gibson Barboza recognized the ultimate consequences of that relationship: it was "an attempt to draw us into war in Africa." He explained: "Behind the commercial advantages, arms would follow."[24] Gibson Barboza resolved Delfim Netto's encroachment by offering his resignation. With his resignation letter on Médici's desk, he explained the costs of doing business in

Portugal's colonies. The president shut down Delfim Netto's negotiations with Portugal.

Just as Gibson Barboza faced down Portugal's offers to Geisel and Delfim Netto, he also confronted the pro-Portuguese press. With his experience under Arinos and Dantas, he understood how effectively the Portuguese embassy and the Portugal lobby could constrain foreign policymaking. In his memoir he recalled choosing not to use one new tool in his favor: he could have employed national security laws to censor material in the press, but he felt that doing so would poison Itamaraty's relationships with journalists and undermine the coverage he sought of his trip to Africa. Instead he called a meeting with Ambassador Fragoso and demanded that he stop the media campaign against him. According to Gibson Barboza, the confrontation reached the point of his threatening to expel Fragoso and remove the Brazilian ambassador in Portugal: "The conversation was tough and disagreeable. But the fact is that the press campaign completely stopped from that moment on."[25]

In a sign of the effect that Gibson Barboza's conversation had, shortly afterward Fragoso wrote to Rui Patrício expressing concern that an ally of Portugal in the Brazilian Congress had arranged a forthcoming trip by a retired Portuguese officer who would speak to Congress, the National Intelligence Academy, the Joint Chiefs of Staff, the headquarters of the Third and Fourth Armies, and several universities. His themes would be "subversive warfare in Africa" and "common interests of Brazil and Portugal in the anti-subversive struggle."[26] Worried that it was too late to cancel the trip, Ambassador Fragoso sought to minimize its impact, asking Rui Patrício to intervene to keep the officer from discussing Brazil, speaking to the press, or making the university visits. Fragoso observed, "As you know, the Chancellor is very sensitive to anything that might look like our interference with his trip to Africa."[27]

The Flying Embassy

Over the course of 1971 and 1972 the Brazilian diplomats Paulo Tarso de Flecha Lima, André Teixeira Mesquita, and Rubens Ricupero traveled repeatedly to West Africa to prepare for Gibson Barboza's trip. Meanwhile, Alberto da Costa e Silva, whose experience with Africa reached back to Senegal's independence ceremonies and Negrão de Lima's fact-finding trip to Angola in 1961, worked in Gibson Barboza's cabinet. They laid the groundwork for the commercial, cultural, and technical accords to be signed during the visit. They also crafted the itinerary and assessed the needs that the foreign minister would have during what would be a month-long trip. They understood that the Brazilian embassies in West Africa were too precarious to provide much logistical support. Instead their plan was for the trip to support the embassies. The minister of the air force lent the foreign ministry his Vickers Viscount, which had earlier served as the presidential plane. It was equipped with passenger seats, an office space, and a cabin with a bed. The plane functioned as a fully self-sufficient flying embassy, carrying everything that would be necessary for the journey, from communications equipment to gifts. There was a symbolic benefit to the plane too. As Gibson Barboza told Médici, "The presence of the Brazilian military aircraft powerfully reinforced one of the main goals of the trip: showing our flag, affirming Brazilian interest in the African continent."[28]

The aircraft had space for the Brazilian delegation and also for a traveling press corps that would report on Gibson Barboza's progress.[29] What is more, along the way it would resupply the embassies with the basic office equipment that they lacked, from typewriters to telex machines.[30] A second air force Viscount made two separate trips from Brazil to deliver seventy-six cases of scotch and *cachaça*, along with cans of canapés and soft drinks to serve at receptions hosted by the Brazilian delegation.[31] The commission numbered thirty-five person all told: Gibson Barboza, eleven diplomats, six reporters, a four-person clerical staff, ten air force officers and crew members, and three members of a "Mixed Commission" that would prepare for Brazil's participation in the Festival of African Arts and Culture (FESTAC), to be held in Lagos.[32]

The FESTAC commission included the only black member of the delegation, the Bahian psychiatrist George Alakija.[33] Alakija was named chair of the commission after Foreign Minister Enahoro of Nigeria flatly told Gibson Barboza that the head of the delegation could not be white. The director of the Itamaraty Cultural Division, Rubens Ricupero, recalled that Enahoro told Gibson Barboza, "Look, don't take this the wrong way. We all listen to and respect it when you say that the reason why there are few blacks in positions of authority is a social class problem rather than a racial problem. But we want a Brazilian to be vice-president of FESTAC, and we insist that he be a black Brazilian, because if he is not, we are not going to buy it."[34] Gibson Barboza's successor, Azeredo da Silveira, explained to President Geisel that Alakija "is not a specialist in Afro-Brazilian issues, but a figurehead who is capable of appearing before Africans as a living example of the ties that have always existed between Brazil and Nigeria."[35]

Waldir Freitas published a commentary in the Salvador daily *A Tarde* reflecting on the scale of the preparations for Gibson Barboza's trip. He compared it favorably to the "failed" diplomacy of the early 1960s. In the decade since Quadros opened the first embassies, "Brazil's presence in Africa was sustained more by ideology and political speeches than by facts, while our embassies vegetated without capabilities for action, without supplies, and without conditions for working." By contrast, "now it seems we have matured." Freitas wrote that "Brazil's return to Africa at this moment happily lacks the spirit of adventure of the other one carried out in the 1960s. This time, everything was carefully planned. During an entire year, a large team addressed the smallest details. Specialists in Africa all across Brazil, myself included, were consulted. No effort was spared."[36] Freitas recognized Itamaraty's changed approach to African policy. A small detail made the difference: by centralizing policymaking and execution within the foreign ministry, now based in Brasília, and by touching all the bases in Brazil representing interest in Africa, Itamaraty overcame the regional rivalries and resentment between Rio de Janeiro and Salvador, and diminished the undue influence of the Portuguese ethnic "colony" on policymaking.

Among the traveling press pool was Luiz Barbosa, a reporter for the pro-Portugal *Jornal do Brasil*. Since before the trip Itamaraty staff had worked to draw Barbosa into a closer reading of the diplomatic opening toward Africa. In the words of Ambassador Fragoso, Barbosa was "especially indoctrinated in order to be part of the press team accompanying the Chancellor on his visit."[37] At the end of the trip, writing from Dakar, Luiz Barbosa described Brazil as "the successful brother" of African countries which shared the struggle for development. He wrote that "political leaders of the young African countries never lose sight of their interest in Brazil's solidarity on the colonial question." He also reflected on Gibson Barboza's stamina: "This was a rigorous test of Mr. Gibson Barboza's physical and mental capacity. He spent, on average, three days in each of nine countries. The flights, the heat of the airports (akin to a Rio summer), the study of documents on board, were followed by unmercifully intense agendas on the ground—meetings, visits, receptions, formal dinners, and press conferences. There was a need to be intelligent, articulate, coherent, and objective in all of his conversations, and all that in a foreign language."[38]

Luiz Barbosa reported on the growing impatience of African countries with regard to Portuguese colonialism, presenting what he cast as Portugal's two options: negotiating with independent Africa over its colonies, or continental war. Change in Portugal's colonial situation was imminent and inevitable. A Portuguese diplomat in Brasília reported to his foreign ministry that Barbosa "reflects the point of view of Itamaraty, which possibly is using the press to create a climate in favor of its intervention in this matter or signals a hardening of their position with regard to our problems."[39]

A Month in West Africa

Gibson Barboza arrived in Abidjan, Ivory Coast, on 25 October, beginning a trip that would take him to Ghana, Togo, Benin, Zaire, Gabon, Cameroon, Nigeria, and Senegal. The choice of these countries and the order of their visit were intended to convey messages to three separate audiences. He intended to define Brazil before African leaders; to present Africa as significant to the Brazilian public and to members of the Brazilian military; and to signal to Portuguese authorities the need for change. Rubens Ricupero recalled: "Gibson Barboza's desire was to be able to influence the Portuguese colonial situation . . . He avoided confronting the question directly because the climate in Brazil did not sustain that. It was the Médici government, which was perhaps the high point of the dictatorship from the point of view of strictness and repression. So the Chancellor thought it necessary to start with the more acceptable countries, those that were not suspected of being communist."[40]

Gibson Barboza was received with the honors of a head of state. Local newspapers reported extensively on the visit, usually on the front page. Describing the nature of his reception to President Médici, Gibson Barboza remarked that "Brazil's political importance to African countries only increased, really, because of our special relations with Portugal. Brazil does not appear in Africa as Mexico, Argentina or Australia would, as just one more vote to be won at the U.N., but as a country that, by virtue of its friendship with Portugal, could act as a pacifier in a moment of great crisis."[41]

Gibson Barboza began the trip in the Ivory Coast because he saw the Ivoirian independence leader and president Felix Houphouët-Boigny as a moderate and hoped to strike a positive tone to carry through the rest of the visits. The trip ended in Senegal, and in between the delegation would zigzag around West Africa, choosing its destination based on the tone with which each country addressed Portugal, seeking to avoid having a succession of nations pile on pressure.[42] Houphouët-Boigny would set a welcoming tone for Gibson Barboza to frame the more strident pressure on decolonization by other countries in the visit.

On the eve of Gibson Barboza's arrival, the Ivoirian daily *Fraternité Matin* published two reports on Brazil prepared by Itamaraty. One, "Brazil Is a Country of Africans of Every Color," described Brazil as a melting pot where African characteristics were shared by Germans, Jews, Poles, Japanese, Italians, and others. It also presented Brazil as an emerging industrial powerhouse and a partner for Africa. The second, "A Country of Football," leveraged the single thing that Africans most associated with Brazil, discussing the country's unrivaled level of play and three World Cup trophies.[43] Immediately before Gibson Barboza's arrival in the Ivory Coast and the other countries, five television documentaries and several recorded radio programs about Brazil were broadcast locally.[44]

Houphouët-Boigny arranged three days of commemorations in Abidjan and his native city of Yamoussoukro. Traveling between the cities, the Brazilian delegation was repeatedly stopped by crowds in towns, who cheered "Vive le Brésil!"[45] The Ivoirian president organized a state dinner followed by music and performances featuring a dance similar to the *frevo* of northeastern Brazil, which Gibson Barboza had learned growing up. Alberto da Costa e Silva asked Gibson Barboza for permission to join the dance, and the rest of the delegation soon followed.[46] The visit dominated the front page of *Fraternité Matin*, which even showed members of the Brazilian delegation dancing in a large circle of Ivoirians, alongside the caption: "What a beautiful sight, this image of fraternity between Ivoirians and Brazilians, dancing, smiling, hand in hand to the sound of the music. Brazilian Samba has captured the Ivoirians as much as the Agbassa has captured the Brazilians."[47] According to Gibson Barboza, the tone set by the Ivoirians and the Brazilians "echoed through the continent, through the 'jungle drums,' of newspaper accounts and phone conversations between members of the governments. This first stop helped give me the strength to face the difficulties I knew lay ahead in Ghana."[48]

The Ghanaian military regime struck a harsh tone against Portugal at the Organization for African Unity, which Gibson Barboza saw as an echo of Nkrumah's pan-Africanism. The account that Gibson Barboza offers in his memoir of his first meeting in Ghana expresses the way his perceived Brazilian Africanness gave him confidence in the face of what promised to be an especially hostile reaction to Brazil's ties with Portugal.

On arriving in Accra he was met by Foreign Minister Nathan Aferi. Gibson Barboza described his officious demeanor, constructing him as a British, imperial figure: "Walking with the erect, slightly forward posture of British officers, a baton under his arm . . . courteous but not effusive and speaking with a strong Oxford accent." Minister Aferi led the Brazilian delegation directly to a luncheon at a seaside hall. As they entered they passed a statue of Xangô, which made Gibson Barboza feel "at home." The lunch was a buffet of foods that Minister Aferi told the Brazilians they "surely don't know. I regret if you find it disagreeable, but it is typical of what we eat, and we do not want to pretend to be who we are not." Was this a swipe at the presentation of Brazilians as Africans? Gibson Barboza responded to what he saw as a challenge:

> I perceived this as the first among several tests I would face. Here I was. White. With a delegation of whites (only the Brazilian doctor who accompanied us was black), proclaiming that in Brazil there is no racial discrimination and that we pride ourselves on our African roots. Aferi must have thought: let's unmask these people.
>
> "It gives me great pleasure to try new foods," I responded. I approached the clay pots on the table, which held things that were familiar from my childhood in Pernambuco and my visits to Bahia . . . I thought, I even like *vatapá*, *caruru*, etc., but all of this palm oil just as I travel from one set of meetings and am about to go into an even harder set of meetings is really rough . . . I thought to myself, "Patience and courage! Let's play their game."
>
> After helping me to an ample plate, the minister escorted me to the main table and with undisguised sarcasm said, "Perhaps it is too spicy for you, sir." I tasted it, and it was truly hot. But I could not give in, so I resolved to accept the challenge and go on the offensive.
>
> He asked, "What do you think?"
>
> "I really don't like it."
>
> "I knew you could not handle so much spice."
>
> "No, it's not that. It's that it really isn't hot enough. In my country, we eat this much spicier."
>
> Aferi tasted it and said, "That really is quite spicy." Not for me, I responded, and asked, "Would you do me the favor of asking for some more spice?" All for Brazil, I thought! I put on my sunglasses because I knew I was

> about to start crying. They brought the peppers and Aferi himself served me, abundantly and without mercy. Since I was wearing my sunglasses, he did not see me start to tear up. I pretended I had a cold and wiped my eyes.
>
> "How is it?"
>
> "Now it's good."
>
> Speaking loudly to the whole room, Aferi announced: "The minister likes pepper. That's my man!" He patted my back and warmed up. "He really is one of us. He likes spice and eats our food." I responded: "This is normal for me. Every day, at home, I only eat this."[49]

After lunch Aferi prepared a toast, and Gibson Barboza seized the opportunity for his counterattack. The Ghanaian minister poured a splash of champagne in the ashtray in front of him, in a version of the traditional offering to one's ancestors. Instead of returning the gesture with a toast of his own, Gibson Barboza declared that he was "deeply disappointed" by Aferi's gesture, and said that "in Brazil we have done a better job than you at guarding the traditions of this noble country, of which we have such important influences." He explained that these influences had been preserved in their true form in Brazil, even as they devolved in Ghana. "It is not to the ancestors that we drink, but to Xangô." He stood up, carried his champagne glass to a corner, poured a splash on the floor, and said, "To Xangô!"[50] Gibson Barboza related that Aferi stood up, declared that it was a shame their traditions had so fallen, and instructed his chief of protocol that from then on, the toast would be done in the traditional way.

By Gibson Barboza's account, Aferi challenged his Africanness. Gibson Barboza responded with an exaggerated and admittedly false embrace of the highly spiced food that was intended to signal his authenticity. He carried the challenge a step further by representing Brazilians as more faithful to African traditions than their Ghanaian hosts were. The dynamic of the event was magnified by the structure of Gibson Barboza's recounting, which depicted Aferi as British and himself as being "at home" alongside Xangô. His account is structured in the classic manner of anecdotes that demonstrate the ability of the narrators to use their wiles (their *jeito*) to turn around a difficult situation. But the account also shows how the possessive Brazilian investment in Africanness was the means that Gibson Barboza used to overcome his own trepidation about the hostility he expected from Ghanaian leaders because of Brazilian policy.

After lunch the true challenge came. In his office Aferi accused Brazil of supplying weapons, running prison camps holding rebels from Portuguese Guinea, and negotiating a defense treaty with Portugal and South Africa. Gibson Barboza rebutted all these accusations, which Aferi admitted were provocations made to see how far the relationship between Brazil and Portugal actually went.[51] The Ghanaian press sustained Aferi's defiant tone. At the end of the Brazilian visit the *Ghanaian Times* published an editorial arguing, "Brazilians and Africans have a lot to gain from cooperation among them. It is a fact that Brazil is more of a manufacturing country than a primary products producer, and with closer connections with Africa, she can count on a wider market for her manufactured products. But in exchange of this, Africans would demand the support of the great influence of Brazil in our struggle to rid the continent of Portuguese colonialism [and] South African apartheid."[52]

The Accra *Daily Graphic* was even more hostile, criticizing race relations in Brazil and its ties with Portugal. As the Brazilians arrived in the Ivory Coast, the *Daily Graphic* published an editorial reminding readers that one of the first acts of the regime that came to power in 1964 was jailing the African nationalists in Brazil. The editorial declared, "To be frank, since 1964 the relationship between Brazil and Portugal has been such that one may be excused to suspect that Brazilian cooperation with Africa could be misused as a means of softening Africa's fight against Portugal."[53] Looking at "Racism in the World," another article explained that "Only money can move a black Brazilian from the bottom and then he is only tolerated! Every black Brazilian who is ACCEPTED socially is expected to marry a white so that in succeeding generations the African strain will disappear! Pelé seems to be following this example. Africa must not become so mesmerized . . . by having new Brazilian (Portuguese) friends that it overlooks how its kith and kin are being treated."[54]

The scale of Ghanaian mistrust of Brazil was evident in the repeated provocations made publicly and privately about the country's race relations. While Gibson Barboza felt that he prevailed in the food round, Minister Aferi must have enjoyed the suffering that he made him endure to prove his Africanness. Rubens Ricupero recalled that the Brazilian delegation saw the meetings in Ghana as an enormous success because there had been an expectation that the Ghanaian government would be particularly hostile. While Aferi was confrontational, the Brazilian delegation and its Ghanaian counterparts nonetheless signed a series of accords and what Ricupero regarded as a "bland" joint declaration. The Brazilian delegation celebrated when it returned to the hotel. Ricupero was the lone abstainer. The minister noticed this and questioned him. Ricupero lamented what he saw as a lost opportunity: "The declaration doesn't say anything and doesn't help our cause here. I think we should be more incisive, showing that we are willing to play a real role here . . . the way it comes off, it seems we are trying to avoid any real commitment or responsibility. We are avoiding leadership, and that keeps us from being able to play the role of an honest broker. I understand that to be honest brokers, we don't need to criticize Portugal harshly, but we can't do it in a way that buries the question."[55]

Ricupero recalled that Gibson Barboza took him to lunch to explain the pressures he was under from the military, from the cold war ideology of "defense of the West" that had been exploited by Portugal, and from newspapers and other allies of Portugal. The minister wanted to proceed cautiously. Ricupero disagreed, suggesting that the joint declarations could be "a kind of trial balloon by which the delegation could, at a distance from home, see how far it could go with the language."[56] When I interviewed him in 2006 Ricupero expressed broader unease with the Brazilian tone, for which he had been partly responsible as chief of the Itamaraty Cultural Division: "I sustained a critical line throughout the trip. I thought at the time that we were depending too much on symbolic elements—elements like the appeal to the past, to history, to ethnicity, to the Brazilians who returned and formed communities in Africa. All of this was true and remains true today, but it was ambivalent. It was all, after all, related to slavery. So it wasn't rightly a glorious past, a role that had been positive for Brazil, so much so that in some countries, this caused uncomfortable reactions. Not every country saw this cultural memory positively, especially those that were seeking to modernize and westernize. They found nothing appealing in that Brazilian discourse about candomblé and so on, because for them this was something about the past that they wanted to move on from."[57] Gibson Barboza's delegation continued through Benin, Togo, Zaire, Gabon, Cameroon, Nigeria, and Senegal. Togo and Benin were scheduled after Ghana specifically because they were steeped in the cultural tone that disturbed Ricupero. Both countries had little political weight or potential for trade with Brazil, but they had large communities descended from Brazilians.

In Togo and Benin, Gibson Barboza shared the experience of other Brazilians like Antonio Olinto, finding the landscape similar to the coast of Pernambuco and the colonial city of Olinda where he had grown up. He met with agudás, including a clan named "Barbosa." During the state dinner in Togo musicians and dancers performed a Bumba-meu-boi and the minister's aides joined the dance. The French ambassador to Togo, seated next to Gibson, told him: "You Brazilians are unbeatable here in Africa. I am preparing the visit of Prime Minister Georges Pompidou next month with all the care that I can. But we can't do what you do, we can't dance with them, we don't know how. The Brazilians have that African trace in them, it's impossible to compete with you on that."[58] It was precisely on this dichotomy that the Brazilian diplomats were competing. The French Ambassador contrasted "his" government with "them," the Togolese. Gibson Barboza's delegation placed itself on the other side of that boundary, defining themselves as part of the "them."

The visits to Cameroon and Zaire addressed the Brazilian goal of extending the limit of its territorial waters to two hundred miles from the coast, a goal shared by Cameroon, and the possibility of commercial exchange with Zaire. All the countries visited questioned the pattern of Brazil's commercial airline routes to Africa: the only existing routes connected Brazil to the white minority–rule cities of Johannesburg and Luanda.[59] Though Gibson Barboza spent three days in Douala, President Ahidjo refused to meet with him. The United States embassy in Cameroon attributed this to "The President's stance on Portuguese possessions in Africa, against which Brazil's relationship with Portugal may be viewed unfavorably."[60]

The visit to Nigeria combined the hostility shown by Ghanaian authorities and the warmth of Togo, Benin, and the Ivory Coast. Gibson Barboza was received by President Yakubu Gowon, who met with him for over an hour. The delegation visited the Brazilian Quarter in Lagos and met with agudás. In his memoir Gibson Barboza described being rattled by the way the elderly agudás lined up and each asked him for "your blessing, father." He recognized this as a vestige of the submission of slaves to masters. As each one bowed and said the same thing, the minister wrote, "I strangely found myself, embarrassed, allowing each to kiss his hand and saying 'God bless you, son.' "[61]

One of the steps Itamaraty timed for the trip was the reestablishment of direct shipping between Brazil and West Africa by the Lloide Brasileiro merchant marine. Lloide had developed routes at the direction of President Quadros, but they had become inactive. Itamaraty now sought to again break the "vicious circle in which the absence of commerce begets the absence of transportation, and the absence of transportation impedes commerce." Lloide timed the arrival of its cargo ship at the port in Lagos to coincide with Gibson Barboza's visit. The ship carried $1.5 million in goods ranging from refrigerators to cheap electrical shower heads that heated water.[62]

Nigerian hostility toward Portugal was rooted in more than general anti-colonialism: it also came from the Portuguese government's logistical and military support for the secessionist region of Biafra in its civil war against Nigeria.[63] Nigerian newspapers used the visit to criticize Brazilian relations with Portugal and race relations in a manner similar to that of their counterparts in Ghana. The newspaper aligned with the government, the *Daily Sketch*, published a harsh critique of racial democracy, describing Brazil as having "policies that create the worst social injustice in the world, and that blacks are the most affected." Since the coup of 1964, it added, "the government has not concerned itself with the plight of the blacks or others who are poor."[64] The article described Brazilian interest in a South African Atlantic defense pact. Meanwhile, on the eve of the visit a headline in the Lagos *Daily Times* asked, "Brazil aims at trade links with black African states—What of ties with Lisbon?"[65] The newspaper criticized the "unsurpassable hypocrisy" of a Brazilian abstention on a Portugal vote at the United Nations that took place during Gibson Barboza's trip. It warned: "Brazil must realize that by voting against recognition of liberation movements in Africa, she has seriously compromised the genuineness of her desire to maintain contact with African countries. It is not out of place to say that her desired rapport with African countries is designed to soften African opposition to Portugal's colonial policy."[66]

Gibson Barboza's trip ended in Senegal, "deliberately chosen as the last stage of the trip" because of Léopold Senghor's history of dialogue with Brazil.[67] Gibson Barboza and Senghor met over several days, discussing strategies for contending with Portugal. Senghor related secret talks with General António de Spínola, the military commander of Portuguese Guinea, where the PAIGC had seized most of the national territory and was moving toward a declaration of sovereignty. Spínola saw the futility of the war and embraced Senghor's proposal of a ceasefire and negotiated independence. When Spínola presented the idea to Caetano, he was removed from command.[68] Senghor and Gibson-Barboza shared a vision of how to proceed. Ricupero described the breakthrough: "Senghor concretely and for the first time proposed that Brazil mediate."[69] Gibson

Barboza would sponsor a meeting of Portuguese and African leaders. At the meeting, which would take place in Brasília, African leaders would propose a truce with Portugal, in return for a ceasefire in the colonies. This would give Portugal room to take steps toward granting autonomy to the colonies in a way that preserved cultural and economic ties to Portugal. The alternative was continental war against the Portuguese.

The tone of the Senegalese press coverage of Gibson Barboza's visit could not have been more different from that of the Ghanaian press. Newspapers in both countries echoed the tone of their political leaders, and the Dakar daily *Le Soleil* drew upon the gentle construction of Brazil as an example of the negritude and latinity expressed by Senghor. In an article entitled "The Black African in Brazilian Society," *Le Soleil* recognized but also minimized racial inequality, arguing that "though there is social distance between blacks and whites, it is largely psychological and based on class differences. The mixture between blacks and whites reduces the distance between the groups and has prevented the emergence of segregation, prejudice or discrimination based only on skin color."[70] The story was part of a page of reporting on Brazil during Gibson Barboza's meeting with Senghor and was paired with an article that recounted the experience of the Brazilian national football team in an "Independence Cup" against Portugal as part of the sesquicentenary celebrations and pondered what would become of Brazilian football after Pelé. If Pelé was a negative symbol of whitening in Ghanaian reporting, in Senegal he was a positive but fleeting symbol of Brazilian Africanness against a background framed by ties to Portugal.

Senghor reassured Gibson Barboza and the Brazilian public that he and other African leaders expected Portugal's colonies to remain culturally and linguistically Portuguese. He stressed that his government provided Portuguese-language teachers to work in the camps for Bissauan refugees.[71] He presented Gibson Barboza with a telegram from the PAIGC leader Amílcar Cabral appealing for Brazil's support. The message, which Gibson Barboza handed to Médici when he returned to Brazil, explained that Portuguese Guinea was "continuing the work of those who, after the historic Shout of Ypiranga, fought for independence, establishing the base upon which the great Brazilian nation of today was built."[72] Gibson Barboza endorsed the message by describing Amílcar Cabral to Médici as the Portuguese African independence leader who was most highly regarded by African statesmen.

Typically anti-Portuguese newspapers like *O Estado de S. Paulo* and the *Correio da Manhã* emphasized the challenge presented to Portuguese colonialism by Gibson Barboza's trip. The Portuguese exile and *O Estado de S. Paulo* columnist Miguel Urbano Rodrigues concluded that "for Brazil, the choice is clear: to support Portugal at the UN and to try to justify Portuguese colonialism means closing the doors to dialogue with Africa." The *Correio da Manhã* declared that "bitter times lie ahead for Portugal in Africa . . . if Portugal does not change its colonialist policy, and does not accept the independence of Angola, Mozambique and Guinea, it will confront a sharp new fact: armed conflict with numerous African countries." The Portuguese embassy saw a pattern of reporting intended to "create a public opinion favorable to a change of policy for Brazil with regard to Portugal."[73] The pro-Portuguese *Gazeta Mercantil* suggested that "the trip came at the right time" and that it was part of Brazil's mission of "attaining its destiny of grandeur."[74] Even the avidly pro-Portugal *O Jornal* described the trip as "victorious."[75]

The tone of the reporting, especially in the newspapers allied with Portugal, was evidence of the success of Gibson Barboza's trip, but it was a sign of something deeper. By 1972 Portugal's allies could only feel apprehension when they beheld the condition of Portugal and its colonies after a dozen years of war. It was possible in the early 1960s to imagine that Portuguese Africa was different and that decolonization was a passing phenomenon. It was possible to imagine in the late 1960s that an alliance between Portugal and Brazil would reignite a sixteenth-century domination of the South Atlantic as a "Lusitanian lake." By the early 1970s there was little reason for optimism about continued Portuguese dominion in Africa. Instead lusophiles could take greater comfort in Senghor's declaration that "Brazil is the heir of the great Lusitanian tradition, of those men who conquered the world for Christ . . . It is Brazil that continues that legacy."[76]

Gibson Barboza and his delegation were not the only Brazilians traveling in Africa in November 1972. The pop star Roberto Carlos performed a concert in Luanda just as Gibson Barboza was digesting his spicy lunch.[77] Was it a coincidence? Or did the show intentionally overlap with the diplomatic trip to signal to anxious colonists that Brazil was still on their side? The Portuguese government observed Barboza's trip with trepidation and avidly gathered information as the voyage unfolded. The Portuguese foreign ministry collected and analyzed Gibson Barboza's speeches and reviewed possibly every shred of reporting on it in Brazil, in Africa, and throughout the world. In fact, the most extensive sources available for understanding the trip are the records of the Portuguese foreign ministry.

In a sign of the capacity of the Portuguese foreign ministry to watch the Brazilian government, relying even on allies within Itamaraty itself to obtain confidential information, the chargé d'affaires at the embassy in Brasília forwarded to Lisbon internal communications sent by Gibson Barboza's delegation to Itamaraty. These included the telegram describing Gibson Barboza's enthusiasm about President Gowon's reception, of which a Portuguese diplomat wrote: "It is difficult for me to fully convey the emphatic tone of the account of Gibson's meeting with the chief of state, who welcomed him with the exact words 'Welcome Home!' and instead of meeting for fifteen minutes, spoke for an hour and a half, twice telling Gibson 'don't look at your watch.'"[78] A week later the chargé d'affaires in Brasília observed that "the mood at the heart of Itamaraty is euphoric over the success of the visit, and it seems that the foreign minister and his delegation were susceptible to the pressure put on them about Portuguese affairs by the Africans."[79] Ambassador Rountree detected a similar tone from the Brazilian delegation, who "are more than pleased with the overall results of their African venture."[80]

Sá Machado, the new Portuguese ambassador arriving in Brasília at the end of November 1972, suggested quickly preparing a trip to offer to the journalists who accompanied Gibson Barboza, along with some members of Congress, to limit the sweep of favorable opinions that Brazilian newspapers expressed about the trip. [81] Meanwhile, he also conveyed to Ambassador Rountree that "the Portuguese are especially miffed because Brazil seems to be catering to Black Africa during the year marking Brazil's 150th anniversary of independence when the Portuguese President and others have visited Brazil in a show of close friendship and cooperation between the two nations."[82] It was the kind of criticism that a Portuguese ambassador would have once addressed to the Brazilian foreign minister, or even the president.

Shuttle Diplomacy

Two months after his trip to Africa, Gibson Barboza met with Rui Patrício for four hours, pressing him to agree to talks with African leaders and warning of the possibility of war by African countries against the Portuguese.[83] Rui Patrício agreed to the talks, provided that they were discreet and were held with African heads of state rather than representatives of the Portuguese anticolonial movements. Gibson Barboza reflected optimistically on the opportunity, which, he told Médici, "opened a line of credit for us with the Africans." Suddenly, "rather than be burdened with a conflict over which it had no say, Brazilian diplomacy could for the first time exert influence to help find a peaceful solution for an armed conflict that had gone on for thirteen years."[84]

Over the course of the year Gibson Barboza worked with Portuguese, Senegalese, and Ivoirian counterparts on a framework for the talks. They agreed to limit the early dialogue to the question of Guiné-Bissau and not to formally include leaders of the independence movements. Gibson Barboza traveled repeatedly to Portugal and met with African leaders. But by the last months of 1973 it became clear that Caetano was delaying the summit. The Ivoirian diplomats who had helped develop the moderate stance in favor of talks with Portugal reversed course and advised Gibson Barboza that Brazil should abandon its role in the face of Portuguese bad faith. They warned that the Brazilian government risked creating the impression among African countries that it was helping the Portuguese to stall, undermining the gains realized by Gibson Barboza's trip.

The possibility of talks between Portugal and African countries finally disappeared when Marcello Caetano gave an interview to a pro-Portuguese journalist from *O Globo* in December 1973, declaring that Portugal did not want Brazil's mediation to find solutions for the Portuguese problem. It only wanted "Brazil to help explaining Portugal's position to Africa."[85] Ricupero recalled that this interview was followed by a crude remark by the Portuguese foreign minister, Rui Patrício, who dismissed the offer of mediation: "Look, we're going to solve this beating each other with our rods [*cacetes*]. Which ever one has the harder rod wins . . . This dialogue thing is nonsense. Whoever has the fatter rod wins."[86]

Though Gibson Barboza's trip was a watershed in Brazilian relations with Africa, it was only the first of several steps made especially difficult by the Portuguese regime's refusal to negotiate. Ricupero believed that "Portugal only wanted Brazil as a base of support, not as a broker. The judgment one is forced to make is that the strategy failed. It was wrong, but that doesn't mean it didn't have other merits. It had the merit of reconnecting a policy that was moribund, and created the basis for a more vigorous policy toward Africa, even toward Portuguese Africa, as we would see later with Azeredo da Silveira. It has those merits, but that was a secondary objective. The primary objective was not attained."[87]

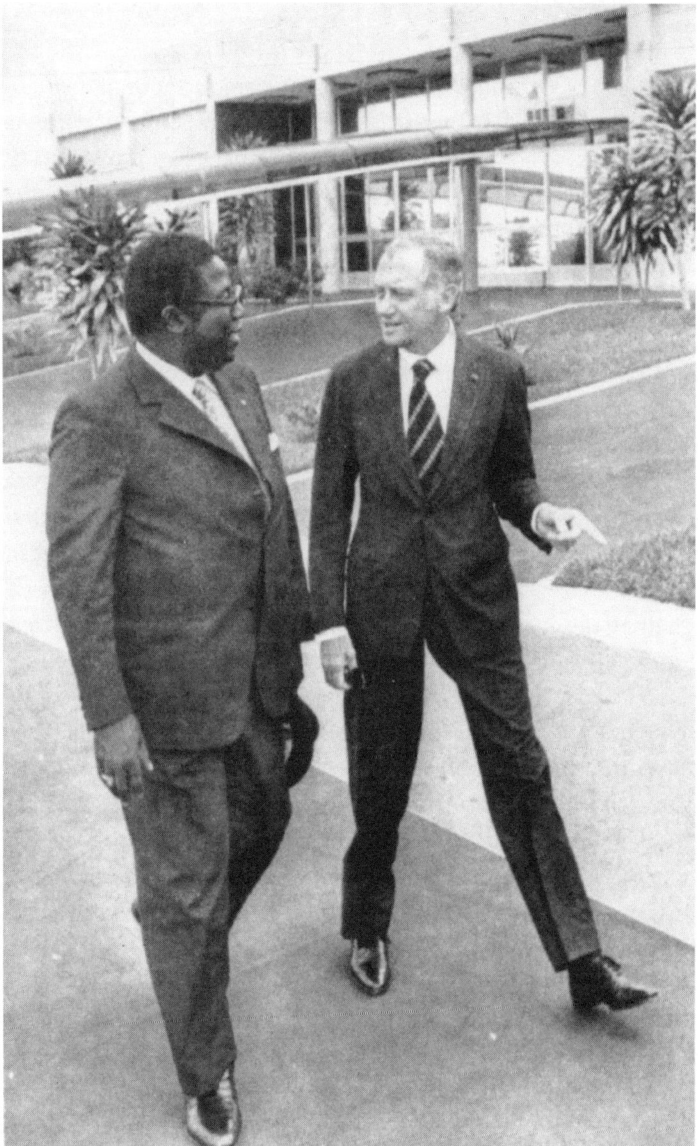

Gibson Barboza with Ivory Coast Foreign Minister Arsenne Usher Assouan, in Brasília, November 7, 1973. Última Hora/Folha Imagem.

The End

Caetano's letter and Gibson Barboza's reaction came as both of their administrations ended. Rather than leave Portugal's "impertinence" to his successor, Gibson Barboza submitted a forty-five-page letter to Médici (it was drafted by Alberto da Costa e Silva) calling on the National Security Council to authorize a break with Brazil's past support for Portugal. He outlined the costs of doing business with Portugal—costs understood within the context of Brazil's economic development and its need for sources of energy. The clearest drawback was Argentina's success at impeding Brazil's construction of the Itaipu hydroelectric dam on the Paraná River, the largest hydroelectric project of the twentieth century. The Argentine government fought the dam because of concerns about ceding control over a river that flowed through its territory to a rival country. (Theoretically, opening the dam could flood Argentina's agricultural heartland all the way to Buenos Aires). In 1973 Argentina secured a United Nations resolution requiring prior consent for the use of shared water resources, halting the dam project despite the Brazilian delegation's "determined and tireless efforts." Gibson Barboza attributed its success solely to a decision by African countries to collectively vote in favor of Argentina and "teach Brazil a lesson for its support of Portuguese colonialism."

For Gibson Barboza the dam rights could have been won by simply "voting once or twice in favor of resolutions against Portuguese colonialism." The Ethiopian ambassador had confided, Gibson Barboza told Médici, that though the vote went against his country's national interests, it "demonstrated to Brazil that it would pay a high price for not clearly and loudly dissociating itself from Portugal's policies." Worse, for all the costs that Brazil bore for supporting colonialism, the Portuguese chose to see Brazil as a "satellite," expecting constant fealty. Other than repatriation of the remains of a dead emperor, support of Portuguese colonial policy had brought no benefit to Brazil. In Gibson's words, Brazil had "mortgaged itself" to Portugal, and if that regime continued with its intransigence, Brazil would have to "dissociate itself."

The National Security Council approved the new policy, and redefined the relationship with Portugal as a burden, particularly within the "delicate sector of oil imports." The problem touched on crucial aspects of national security, including the possibility of "a reduction in the supply of Arab oil out of pressure from African states." Gibson Barboza explained:

> Arab countries have demanded the full solidarity of African countries in their struggle against Israel, prompting the breaking of diplomatic relations between African states and Tel Aviv. These countries broke with Israel en masse, despite the fact that in some cases the suspension of relations came at considerable cost and in spite of their excellent relations with Israel. All of the countries of the Non-Aligned Bloc have committed themselves to the struggle against Portugal and South Africa . . . If tensions become chronic or continue to escalate in the Middle East, we must anticipate that African states will collect on their support of the Arabs, asking oil producers to extend the boycott that they have applied to Portugal, to include countries they believe have supported the government in Lisbon, either directly or indirectly . . . Brazil's position in the face of the mass of countries in the developing world is rapidly changing.

Indeed the decision was forced by a convergence of international crises: the Arab oil embargo of 1973, the reemergence of the Non-Aligned Nations Movement as a political force, and the declining influence of the United States at the end of the Vietnam War and of Richard Nixon's presidency all created a climate that was particularly inhospitable to Portugal and its allies.

Médici and the National Security Council agreed to present Portugal with an ultimatum: grant independence or face Brazil's "unequivocal rejection of Portuguese colonial policy." Except that there was no time for cither the Brazilian or the Portuguese government to change course. Caetano's interview appeared on 28 December 1973. The National Security Council met just after the meeting of the Electoral College on 15 January used by the military to indirectly elect the next president. General Geisel would be inaugurated on 15 March. His new foreign minister, Antonio Azeredo da Silveira, attempted to execute the break engineered by Gibson Barboza, but on 25 April 1974 the Portuguese regime was overthrown.

7 Brazil and the Portuguese Revolution

ON 8 APRIL 1974 the diplomat Ramiro Saraiva Guerreiro flew into the Brasília airport from his post in Geneva and was met by Brazil's new foreign minister, Antonio Azeredo da Silveira. Riding into the city with Silveira, Saraíva Guerreiro learned of the foreign policy goals laid out by Ernesto Geisel: reestablish diplomatic relations with Communist China; develop "a more impartial position in the Arab-Israeli conflict," meaning one less favorable to Israel; and supporting Portuguese decolonization, "plainly and positively, regardless of the reaction of the Portuguese government or of its Brazilian admirers."[1] Geisel's goals were an abrupt departure from the right-wing cold war orthodoxy drawn by Brazil's military presidents since 1964. Silveira asked Saraíva Guerreiro to become his chief of staff. He agreed.

From 1974 to 1979 Saraíva Guerreiro helped Silveira to chart a new and often contradictory foreign policy for Brazil. From 1979 to 1985 he continued these policies as foreign minister to President João Baptista Figueiredo. The new foreign policy was called "responsible pragmatism." It was first and foremost a response to the challenges presented by the Arab oil embargo of 1973, which jarred the Brazilian economy. Between 1968 and 1972 Brazil imported through the Petrobras state monopoly an annual average of $276 million in oil. The cost of oil imports climbed to $710 million in 1973 and $2.8 billion in 1974, feeding a $4.5 billion trade deficit.[2] As a result, Brazilian foreign policy after 1974 sought to increase diplomatic relations with oil-exporting countries and their allies, and to distance Brazil from the United States and Israel. Responsible pragmatism also entailed pursuing markets for Brazilian exports to sustain the pace of economic growth attained during the "miracle" of the early 1970s.

José Flávio Sombra Saraiva suggests that actions like Brazil's recognition of Angolan independence under the MPLA were intended to "signal" autonomy from the United States in the "power play that tied this question to the Brazilian nuclear program, development of its arms industry and the pursuit of energy independence through huge hydroelectric projects." For Sombra Saraiva, "Brazil sought to develop a certain degree of autonomy in its international relations, and for that it was necessary to give signs of this effort. The Angolan question guaranteed a number of reflectors for Brazilian diplomacy."[3]

Within Africa responsible pragmatism meant expanding Brazil's presence. Only months after becoming foreign minister, Azeredo da Silveira gained President Geisel's approval for a plan to open a string of new embassies, and to have existing embassies cumulatively represent a growing number of African countries. Within two years Brazil would have a diplomatic presence in most of sub-Saharan Africa. Table 2 shows Azeredo da Silveira's expansion plan of 1974, highlighting existing embassies, new embassies to be created, and the expansion of cumulative representation arrangements.

Geisel and Silveira sought to change Brazilian ties to Portugal as part of the shift in foreign policy. They saw the ties with Portugal as a "mortgage" on Brazil's international relations: the empire of the past was a noose around the land of the future. Still, political events unfolded much more quickly in Portugal than in Brazil. On 25 April 1974 Portuguese army officers overthrew Caetano's regime. In its place an increasingly radical revolutionary government pursued decolonization, and the Brazilian government reversed course on decades of diplomatic, legal, and rhetorical accommodation to Portugal, seeking instead to separate itself from the new regime. Azeredo da Silveira and the Brazilian government suddenly found themselves in a difficult situation. Though no longer troubled by the ongoing Portuguese wars in Africa, the regime faced the creation of a socialist state in its once anticommunist ally, and a legacy in Africa of having done little to distance itself from Portugal during years of violent conflict. This chapter looks at the Brazilian government's perceived new foreign policymaking autonomy and the challenges that it faced from the

Table 2

Location of Embassy	Proposed Additional Countries to Be Served
Abidjan, Ivory Coast	Upper Volta, Liberia, Sierra Leone
Accra, Ghana (also serving Togo)	none
Dakar, Senegal (also serving Mali, Mauritania)	Gambia, Guinea
Kinshasa, Zaire	Burundi, Congo, Gabon, Rwanda
Lagos, Nigeria (also serving Dahomey [Benin])	Niger
Nairobi, Kenya (also serving Uganda, Tanzania, Zambia)	Malawi, Mauritius
Addis-Ababa, Ethiopia (new embassy)	Somalia, Sudan
Bissau, Guinea-Bissau (new embassy)	none
Yaounde, Cameroon (new embassy)	Chad, Central African Republic, Equatorial Guinea
Maputo, Mozambique (new embassy)	Botswana, Lesotho, Madagascar, Swaziland
Luanda, Angola (new embassy)	none

socialist revolution in Portugal and the Marxist revolutionary regimes in Portuguese Africa.

The Portuguese Revolution

On 4 March 1974, a few days before Geisel was sworn in as president, Premier Marcello Caetano spoke to the Portuguese National Assembly, calling for continued perseverance by invoking the ideal of "a multi-continental and multi-racial society."[4] For years this rhetoric had been far from the violent realities of guerrilla warfare that had consumed Portugal's African colonies and gradually worn down the metropolis and its armed forces. A Brazilian study put the Portuguese military toll of the war at 8,000 killed and 28,000 wounded. The material and human costs of the war were borne by a country that had an annual per capita income of $637 and a literacy rate of 70 percent, the lowest in Western Europe.[5] While Salazar's and Caetano's regimes succeeded in suppressing domestic dissent, the regime was less successful in arresting discontent within its overextended armed forces.

Brazilian diplomats in Portugal saw the mounting unrest. In February 1974, two months before the revolution, Ambassador Gama e Silva of Brazil wrote to Minister Azeredo da Silveira on the deteriorating mood in Portugal. He explained: "For the youth the perspective of three to four years of military service, two of which would be spent in Africa, receives little enthusiasm."[6] Gama e Silva presciently recognized the emergence of a youth radicalism in Portugal, pointing to the "growing divorce between the country of today, that does not know which way it is going, and the nation of the future, that knows where it does not want to be led, preferring the integration of Portugal into tomorrow's post-national Europe over colonialist adventures . . . [the future of the colonies] will be at the mercy of a generation that has ceased believing in the African mission of the nation."[7] His successor, Carlos Alberto da Fontoura, remarked a few months after the revolution that "the only solid things the regime still possessed were the machinery of repression and the system of press censorship."[8]

Discontent reached the highest levels of the Portuguese army. In 1972 the Portuguese military commander in Guiné-Bissau, António Spínola, attempted to negotiate a truce with the PAIGC and the establishment of political autonomy in Guiné-Bissau. Caetano removed him. Back in Portugal, Spínola published *Portugal and the Future* in February 1974, advocating a ceasefire in all the colonies, followed by plebiscites by which colonial populations could choose independence. *Portugal and the Future* was a mix of old and new ideas. Spínola recognized that the colonial wars could not be won: "Pretending to win a war of subversion through military means is to accept defeat from the outset," and not even the United States had achieved this in Vietnam.[9] Nonetheless, he still managed to imagine that "the Africans prefer to be Portuguese" and wished to remain tied to Portugal in some form of federation.[10] Spínola looked to Brazil as an example for the future because it preserved "our way of being, living and coexisting in the environment of authentic racial miscegenation that Gilberto Freyre has praised."[11] But he also recognized that metropolitan Portugal could never create "future Brazils," since Brazil was independent. Nor could Portugal "proclaim multiculturalism and at the same time claim that European Portuguese are the most fit to hold power."[12]

Caetano's regime, unwilling to respond to pressure on the wars from its senior military commanders, was even more aloof to pressures from the general officer corps. The scale of the wars outstripped the ability of Portugal's military academies to produce officers, so the ranks of captains and lieutenants were filled through field promotions and the drafting of university graduates. These junior officers bore both a distaste for the conflict and radical ideas about changing Portuguese society. These officers organized the Armed Forces Movement (MFA), commonly known as the "Captain's Movement." On 25 April 1974 officers of the "Captain's Movement" overthrew Caetano. The coup became known as the Carnation Revolution because of the flowers that cheering Portuguese placed in the barrels of the rebels' rifles.

After 25 April the Carnation Revolution unfolded along several lines. The MFA chose General Spínola as Portugal's provisional president. Though a critic of Caetano, Spínola had long ties to the regime. When the former colonial minister Sarmento Rodrigues wrote to Freyre about events in Portugal, he expressed optimism: "The leaders of the Provisional Government . . . are in many cases my friends, sometimes intimate friends, beginning with the President . . . I have seen them frequently and they have honored me by consulting me. They are good people with good intentions."[13] At the same time, the Carnation Revolution unleashed long-repressed social and ideological pressures. In the same letter to Freyre, Sarmento Rodrigues warned: "Clearly some people have gotten carried away, especially in their rhetoric. This is natural, because in a free country everyone wants their spoon in the bowl . . . But it creates serious dangers."[14] Workers and students formed radical organizations that at times were able to drive national events. Exiles like the socialist Mário Soares returned. The Portuguese Communist Party emerged from clandestinity. Leaders of the old regime—Marcelo Caetano, Américo Thomaz, and Rui Patrício, among others—took asylum in Brazil.

The different factions of the Carnation Revolution agreed to an immediate ceasefire in the African combat areas, speedy decolonization, an end to the PIDE, and the creation of a representative government. But the revolution tapped a deep desire for change, particularly among young Portuguese workers and soldiers. Ambassador Fontoura reflected on the speed of Portugal's transformation: "Everything is happening so quickly that, if you forget the local circumstances that produced the change, you could only explain it by accepting the marxist thesis of the acceleration of history."[15] The revolution quickly turned Portuguese politics from the most conservative to the most radical in Western Europe.

In the months after the Carnation Revolution, President Spínola was compelled by the MFA to set a course for decolonization rather than forming a federation. Finally, on 27 July 1974, on national television and radio, he announced recognition of "the right of peoples of the Portuguese overseas territories to self-determination, including the immediate recognition of their independence." Spínola proclaimed his certainty that "the leaders of the new countries will honor the sense of justice that comes from being multiracial countries of Portuguese expression," forming the "vast and unified spiritual community that Gilberto Freyre called 'the world the Portuguese created.' "[16] At the moment when the president of Portugal finally announced the end of colonialism, he grounded the change in the reassuring certainty that whatever came would unfold within the comforting familiarity of the Freyrean ideal.

In his newspaper column Gilberto Freyre quoted Spínola's reference to him and discussed "the practically new Brazils that are Guinea, Angola and Mozambique." Since they shared the Portuguese language, "that common language characterizes a Portuguese world unified by ways of life . . . One of these ways of life is the tendency to be a racial democracy in contrast to a world so divided by race hatred."[17] The idea that the Portuguese language itself was a bearer of culture that sustained miscegenation and racial equality perhaps tempered the immediate psychological impact of decolonization for Portuguese tied to the old regime, like Spínola. But Freyre and his lusotropicalism were anathema to the new generation of political leaders emerging in Portugal after 1974.

Mário Soares, first foreign minister of the new government and leader of the Portuguese Socialist Party, who would be twice prime minister and later president of Portugal, explained: "We have a real prejudice against Gilberto Freyre." For Soares *The World the Portuguese Created* is an admirable book. But the theory that Portuguese colonialism was unique was grist to the mill of the dictator Salazar's policies, to his resistance to inevitable decolonization."[18] Still, Gilberto Freyre's worldview gave meaning to both colonialism and decolonization. It even set the tone of a book about connections between Brazil and Portugal that was written jointly by Soares as former president of Portugal and Fernando Henrique Cardoso as president of Brazil. In the first paragraph of the introduction, Soares describes Brazil as "original, racially mixed, convivial and open . . . the jewel and greatest pride of the 'world the Portuguese created,' to use the title of Gilberto Freyre's celebrated book."[19]

Freyrean as it may have been, the change in government was a surprise and a challenge for Geisel's administration. It solved the problem of reconciling Brazil's African objectives with its sense of obligation to Portugal, but it robbed Geisel's government of any credit for deciding to change Brazilian policy, choking Itamaraty's momentum in building sympathy for Brazil either in Africa in general or in the Portuguese colonies in particular. Brazil was the first to recognize the government which took power on 25 April, responding within three hours to the notice delivered to Itamaraty by the Portuguese ambassador in Brasília.[20] But the Brazilian government was equally quick to distance itself from the new regime as it radicalized.

The regimes which had converged in ideology and symbolism during the previous decade became strangers. Portugal seemed to spiral into communism and chaos. The same radical leftists whom the Brazilian government strained to repress at home were governing Portugal. Could this radicalism spread to Brazil through the recently widened channels of migration that allowed Portuguese citizens to enter automatically? By contrast, to Portuguese who had liberated themselves from four decades of dictatorship, surveillance, censorship, colonialism, and war, Brazil symbolized everything they had left behind.

In an unfortunate coincidence, just before the Carnation Revolution Geisel named as his first ambassador to Portugal General Carlos Alberto da Fontoura, head of the National Intelligence Service (SNI). In reality Geisel was ridding himself of Fontoura, who had been a "powerful opponent" of his presidential nomination.[21] Geisel planned to send him abroad and appoint an ally, General João Baptista Figueiredo, to the sensitive job of SNI chief. Fontoura had not yet arrived in Lisbon when the revolution broke out. He instantly became a symbol of fascist authoritarianism. The new Portuguese foreign minister, the Socialist Mário Soares, called the Brazilian embassy in Lisbon to warn of "popular protests involving Portuguese, Brazilians and other foreigners, due to the arrival of Ambassador Carlos Alberto da Fontoura . . . Even if the Portuguese government used the army to cordon off the embassy and prevent demonstrations and violence for a time, say a week or a little more, it would not have the means to do this permanently . . . It would be preferable to name a different ambassador whose life would not be threatened and whose presence would not cause problems for the Portuguese government."[22] Soares sharpened this message by noting that Fontoura's presence would stand in the way of the "Brazilian mediation to help resolve the Portuguese situation in Africa," thus threatening the Brazilian government's goal of being present in the Portuguese colonies as they became independent.[23] Geisel tersely responded that if Portugal did not accept Fontoura, he would not send another ambassador for the remainder of his five-year term.[24] In his response to Soares, Silveira used softer language but kept Geisel's meaning: "Portugal's relationship with Africa is Portugal's problem."[25] Soares relented.

As Soares had warned, the protests were announced on the radio and in newspapers. Flyers signed by the "Autonomous Group of the Socialist Party" were handed out across Lisbon, reading: "Out Brazilian PIDE, Fontoura Fascist Assassin. Naming Carlos Fontoura, until now the director of the SNI (Brazilian PIDE), as the Brazilian dictatorship's ambassador, is a threat to the security of the Portuguese people. A known collaborator of the Portuguese fascist regime overthrown on April 25, we see in him an ally for the forces of reaction. We believe this alliance will create for Portugal the conditions that caused disaster in Chile. Come all to Pedro de Alcântara street Monday the 27th at 6pm for the march to the Brazilian Embassy. The CIA doesn't stop. Fontoura will collaborate with fascism. We do not want a new Chile."[26] Fontoura's presence rallied Portugal's fractious leftist movements, which held protests in front of the embassy. Fontoura responded in character by discreetly photographing the protesters and seeking to identify which of them might have been Brazilian students studying abroad.[27]

In the months after Fontoura's arrival Portuguese politics continued to radicalize. A junta of radical officers from the MFA functioned as a parallel government that checked Spínola's authority and helped drive Portuguese politics to the left. The Portuguese Communist Party, which had survived in clandestinity, brought structure to the new government, while even more radical youth and worker movements took to the streets. Spínola was forced to resign after five months in office. He found refuge in Brazil, where he attempted to organize a military force to invade Portugal and save it from communism. He had the support of at least part of the Brazilian intelligence services, which provided him with a false passport confiscated by Swiss authorities in 1975.[28]

After Spínola resigned, Portuguese politics radicalized. Kenneth Maxwell quotes the *New Yorker* reporter Janet Kramer's observation that "Portugal today is a place where Socialists are called Fascists, Marxists are called Moderates . . . where conservatives label the entire left Communist, [and] Communists label the rest of the left conservative."[29] The leftist MFA consolidated power in Costa Gomes's new government. Students and workers formed nongovernmental organizations and social service programs that promoted rural literacy and other social and cultural projects. The government expropriated large land holdings and nationalized businesses.

Revolutionary Portugal became a home abroad for hundreds of Brazilian exiles, many of whom had been forced to flee Chile after Pinochet's coup but were now welcomed by a new revolutionary society that spoke Portuguese. Portugal became a haven for persecuted politicians and military officers, opposition leaders, and exiled revolutionaries. Spies and informants from Brazilian military intelligence followed, keeping close watch on the Brazilian exile community.

The Portuguese Revolution in Brazil

As the Portuguese revolutionary government radicalized, the Brazilian intelligence agency SNI and the DOPS police worried that the Portuguese would spread subversion to Brazil. They thought that the Portuguese government was replacing career diplomats with radicals and communists who would "act on the Brazilian political processes" to radicalize the Portuguese colony and undermine the Brazilian government.[30] The intelligence services also suspected that other Portuguese government entities in Brazil, like tourism offices, were becoming centers of communist subversion.[31]

Businesses with operations in both Brazil and Portugal became sites of contestation and radicalization. One of the principal supermarket chains in Portugal was tied to a leading Brazilian chain, Pão de Açúcar. Workers at the Portuguese chain went on strike and seized stores. After the Portuguese government supported them and nationalized the chain, Itamaraty worked to restore control of Pão de Açúcar's Portuguese operation.[32] The Portuguese airline TAP was similarly seized by workers and nationalized. With offices and operations in Brazil, the new TAP was a security risk in the eyes of Brazilian intelligence services. Beyond the risk that TAP might send communist subversives to Brazil, there was a more practical challenge: the workers' commission at TAP ordered the firing of the airline's manager in Brazil, who refused to accept the legitimacy of the commission. Eventually the TAP manager was removed, to the alarm of the DOPS and the SNI, as they watched communists abroad firing Brazilian businessmen in Brazil.[33]

Meanwhile, tens of thousands of Portuguese moved to Brazil, fleeing either the politics of the new regime or the unemployment and economic turmoil that the country experienced as it socialized and decolonized. At the beginning of 1975, as the migratory flow to Brazil gained steam, Ambassador Fontoura wrote that "the social crisis caused by unemployment of proportions unknown in Portugal's recent history (210,000 people, or 7 percent of the labor force), has been caused both by the economic recession . . . and by the return of demobilized soldiers and of Portuguese from the colonies, afraid of the process of decolonization."[34] By the end of the year the number of unemployed had doubled.[35]

Between 1974 and 1976, 500,000 colonists returned to Portugal from Angola alone.[36] Meanwhile, probably tens of thousands of refugees from Portugal and its colonies moved to Brazil. The Brazilian government provided aid but sought to block the flow of refugees. One federal task force helped refugees to obtain identification and work documents and enroll in schools, while another one looked for discreet ways to use the law and to pressure airlines to stem the flow of refugees. An aid society, the Movement for Aiding Portuguese Emigrants (MAEP), was created in July 1975 by members of the Portuguese colony to help refugees find housing, health care, and jobs. The former ambassador Negrão de Lima was one of the society's leaders.

It is difficult to determine how many people fled to Brazil from Portugal and from the colonies during the revolution and decolonization. Because many traveled as tourists and stayed, while others remained for a few years and returned to Portugal, Brazilian census data provide little insight.[37] Ovídio de Melo recalled issuing up to five thousand family visas per month for emigrants to Brazil over the course of 1975, as Angola moved toward independence and civil war.[38] Meanwhile, data from Embratur, the Brazilian state tourism agency, show that the number of Portuguese entering Brazil as tourists nearly quadrupled between 1973 and 1975. Assuming that the economic turmoil in Portugal and its colonies must have dampened the rate of Portuguese tourism overseas, most of this increase in "tourists" would have consisted of emigrants or temporary emigrants. In 1972 and 1973 tourists from Portugal entered at an average rate of ten thousand a year. Between 1974 and 1976 they entered at a rate of thirty thousand a year. By this reading, perhaps as many as sixty thousand refugees entered Brazil under tourist visas during the Portuguese Revolution, in addition to the thousands who entered with immigrant visas.

As Brazilian policymakers contended with the implications of the exodus from Portugal and its colonies, the Brazilian diplomatic representative in Luanda during the transition to independence, Ovídio de Melo, faced the thousands of fleeing colonists who sought refuge in Brazil. Portuguese authorities in Angola, who in the first six months of 1975 had issued over twenty thousand passports, ran out of booklets to issue.[39] Ovídio de Melo suffered from insomnia, and started to paint the scenes which unfolded around him. He explained: "I painted a family packing its crate. The old, fat Portuguese woman was filling it with plates. Her husband carrying things into it, all very perturbed. But on top of the crate there are a black boy and a white boy playing . . . In other words, the children didn't have any racial animosity, only the adults. But it was impressive: the line of trucks with the possessions of the Portuguese, stretched in the end from the consulate, which was nowhere near the port, all the way to the port. The port was clogged with crates."[40] Despite the grim image of crates stretching across the city as hundreds of thousands of whites fled, Melo remained optimistic, representing children in his paintings as immune from the tensions that surrounded Angolan independence. This ambivalent optimism was evident at the consulate as well—Ovídio de Melo recalled that it was one of only two buildings in Luanda receiving a fresh coat of paint, even as steel plates were being affixed to the front windows to protect them from the frequent gunfire.[41]

Who went to Brazil? For Ovídio de Melo, some who sought Brazilian visas were former members of the PIDE who risked jail in Portugal. Others chose Brazil because of their disenchantment with the Portuguese system they had been a part of. The night guard at the consulate wouldn't return to Portugal: "I came here and was put to work chasing after blacks, shooting blacks, killing blacks . . . with the Carnation Revolution, I lost my house, my wife left me . . . I spent ten, twelve years of my life, running, fighting, arresting blacks, watching them get beaten. I can't forget that. The only thing I learned was to shoot. So if I go to Portugal, I am going to shoot."[42]

One of the Portuguese colonists entering on a tourist visa, a former soldier, was interviewed by the *Jornal do Brasil* after he returned to Angola as a mercenary fighting against the MPLA during the country's post-

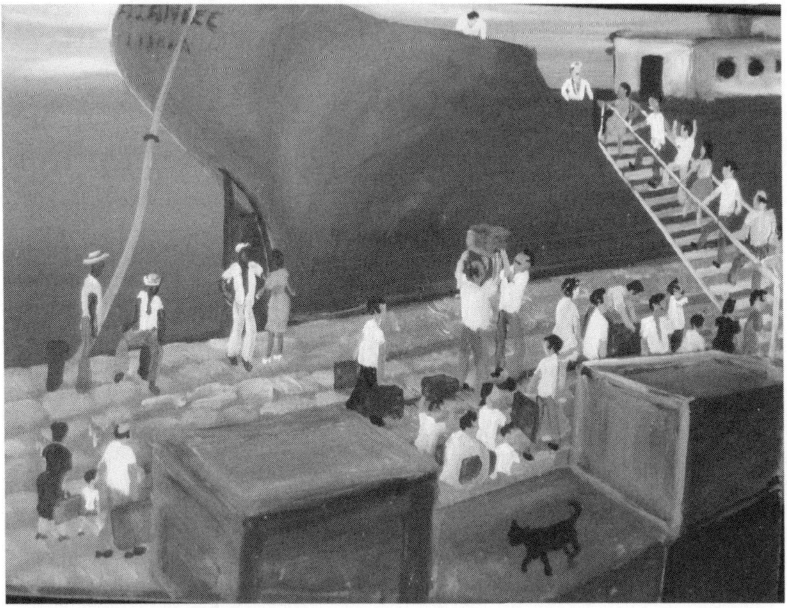

Portuguese colonists fleeing Angola, 1975. Image courtesy of Ovídio de Melo.

independence civil war. After being discharged from the military he "lived for two months in Rio as a tourist." The mercenary declared, "I love Brazil . . . money was a problem. Even while I was still on the plane, I was offered a job as a policeman, but I knew I would have trouble as a cop. I believe that when a cop confronts a bandit or a subversive or whatever, they are the enemy. I don't have patience with enemies, I am brutal when I am in action. When I lose control, zap, I tear off the head of one of those blacks. Imagine the complications that would bring me. If the Death Squads, which are a truly Brazilian organization, have so much trouble, imagine what would happen to a foreigner like me."[43]

As Portugal radicalized, and as the flow of Portuguese emigrants to Brazil and Brazilian exiles to Portugal continued, Geisel's government became alarmed about the risk of "subversion" spreading from the former ally. Geisel established a "Working Group on Portugal," consisting of members of the National Security Council, Brazil's intelligence service SNI, and the foreign ministry. The task force reported to President Geisel that Portuguese authorities were deliberately exploiting the agreements with Brazil as a means of dissipating the economic and refugee problems

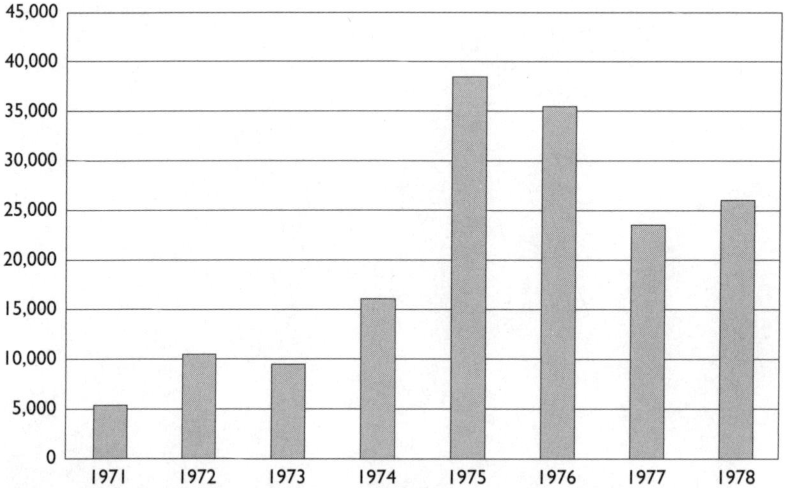

Entrance of Tourists from Portugal to Brazil, 1971–1978. Totals include tourists coming from the colonies until their respective independence in 1974–1975. Embratur, *Anuário Estatístico Embratur*, Brasília, 1973–1979, Table 1.1.10.

they were facing. They observed that "Portuguese emigration authorities know plainly well the practical effects of the Brazilian law allowing Portuguese tourists to arrive without visas. The mechanism is being used to promote hidden emigration, paying for tourist trips for anyone who can demonstrate having relatives in Brazil or a job offer. These are generally unskilled workers who are competing with Brazilians in the labor force."[44]

Examining the risks that subversion might spread from Portugal, the task force reported to Geisel on the "increasing control of political power by the most radical sectors of the military revolutionary movement," and raised the possibility that Portugal would become a communist country.[45] The group recommended informally "neutralizing" the accords by not ratifying anything new, charging for tourist visas, and developing a registration form for Portuguese tourists.[46] Geisel suspended the scholarship program for Portuguese students. Seeking to at least partially restore the scholarship program, Azeredo da Silveira suggested a new structure aimed at "reducing or eliminating the security risks" by having the Brazilian embassy in Lisbon screen candidates, and requiring them to register with the federal police in the city where they were studying. In addition, scholarships would be reduced in number and only awarded to students working in "technical subjects." Geisel agreed.[47]

But as large as the emigration pressure from Portugal was, it was dwarfed by the exodus of Portuguese colonists from Africa. Facing the prospects of unemployment and chaos in Portugal, many refugees emigrated to Brazil and South Africa. Geisel sought to stem this flow, both to avoid its demographic impact on Brazil and to avoid the impression that Brazil was benefiting from an Angolan brain drain. In October 1975 Silveira met with Geisel to discuss ways of blocking migration. He noted the political difficulties that would be created by imposing new visa restrictions and instead suggested that the government could discreetly approach Varig, requesting that it cease accepting charter flights from Angola, including the flights that were increasingly being booked by the Portuguese government. The air force could deny landing rights to foreign aircraft suspected of carrying refugees. Geisel recorded his response in the margin of the minutes of his briefing papers: "Completely agreed. Brazil is not a warehouse."[48]

Both Varig and the Brazilian air force discreetly agreed to the request. Varig "spontaneously" suspended even flights that had already been scheduled.[49] Over the ensuing months a task force with representatives from Itamaraty, the ministries of justice, agriculture, and labor, and the intelligence services looked at the broader challenge of massive Portuguese emigration to Brazil. They worried that most of the Portuguese refugees from Africa could wind up in Brazil, and suggested mechanisms for blocking immigration. For example, the task force proposed not admitting tourists entering with one-way tickets, as well as restricting immigration visas only to emigrants applying to go to Brazil through the European Intergovermental Committee for Migration.

The task force also suggested a return to the agricultural settlement policies of the 1930s, noting that "the ecology of certain areas of the north and center of the country are propitious to farming techniques that the Portuguese developed successfully in Africa and which are important to our national economy. It would be convenient to introduce to the Amazon human resources that have socio-cultural characteristics more similar to the Brazilian than those of other immigrants settled there since the 1930s."[50] This idea was not well received by Geisel. A few months earlier, nearly one thousand Portuguese Angolan farmers who had traveled with their equipment to South Africa sent two emissaries to Brazil, with the support of the Portuguese embassy. They contacted Itamaraty to inquire about the possibility of obtaining land and transportation to settle in Brazil. Their request was presented to Geisel, who responded by hand on the memorandum: "Prevent them coming as much as possible. They should go to Portugal!"[51]

Exiles in Portugal

In the months after the Carnation Revolution, Portugal became a haven for exiled Brazilians. The legal groundwork for their presence in Portugal had already been laid by the agreements between Brazil and Portugal under Salazar and Caetano. Portugal was a haven where the exiles could live in Portuguese, and it was a revolutionary society where they could openly express their views and participate in the process of social change. When Foreign Minister Silveira traveled to Portugal in December 1974, one of his briefing papers explained: "growing numbers of Brazilians opposed to the regime in their country or banished from it have settled in Portugal . . . Naturally, they follow leftist ideologies and have the support of important segments of the Portuguese political leadership."[52] The report gave the example of a professor expelled from the Federal University of Pernambuco who was now the rector of the University of Porto and was "recruiting Brazilian intellectuals and professors, some of whom passed through Chile and others through Algeria, to fill the vacuum caused by the purge of faculty tied to the deposed regime."[53]

Two exiled Brazilian revolutionaries, Maria do Carmo Brito (Lia) and Chizuo Osava (Mário Japa), followed a trajectory that carried them through revolutionary Portugal and on to Angola once the colony gained independence. Brito had been a leader of an armed guerrilla group called the Revolutionary Popular Vanguard (VPR) in Rio de Janeiro, within which she was known by the code name Lia. Osava, of Japanese descent, joined the VPR in São Paulo and was given the code name Mário Japa. Since then he has used the name Mário Osava. Both were captured by state security authorities and tortured until the VPR negotiated their release into exile in exchange for two diplomats whom they had kidnapped: the German ambassador in Rio de Janeiro and the Japanese consul in São Paulo.[54] Osava went into exile in Cuba and later Chile, and Brito went to Chile, where the two met, married, and collaborated with Salvador Allende's regime. After

Augusto Pinochet's coup in 1973 they fled to Panama and later Belgium. Eventually they went to Portugal and Angola, where they saw the opportunity to carry out the projects of revolutionary transformation they had sought for Brazil.

In late 1974, a few months after the Carnation Revolution, Osava and Brito traveled to Portugal. They went to work for a postrevolutionary government agency, the General Directorate for Permanent Education (DGEP), implementing the Paulo Freire method for developing adult literacy and raising critical consciousness.[55] For the Brazilian military regime Paulo Freire's pedagogy of liberation was an undesirable export, though it was one of the country's most successful ones. Revolutionary governments employed Freire's literacy program to build critical consciousness around ideals of social justice. It was especially popular with the radical regimes that held power over post-Salazarist Portugal and its former colonies, all of which developed Freirean educational projects. Brazilian ambassadors in these countries watched and reported on his consulting for these programs. When the DGEP implemented the Freire method in Portugal, Ambassador Fontoura wrote: "Everything indicates that, as was the case in Northeastern Brazil the 'Paulo Freire Method' will be used to 'conscientize' rural populations for the class struggle."[56]

I met Maria do Carmo Brito (Lia) and Mário Osava (Japa) at their apartment in Rio de Janeiro in 2006. We spoke about their experiences in Angola and Portugal as we sat near a large photograph of Ho Chi Minh. The two spoke excitedly about the postrevolutionary creativity they had experienced in Portugal and Angola. Osava recalled: "When Portugal opened up, it was a beautiful thing. There was popular mobilization on the streets, people were discussing everything, trying to do new things. For us, it was where things were happening that we had always dreamed about. We were leftists, militants, progressives, wanting to make revolution or at least improve the situation of the people. In Portugal, that was happening. That's why we went there. It was a creative moment. New things were happening in the theaters, in culture, these community initiatives, cooperatives, local development projects. It was a world of things. For us, it was a happy time, because we could see things happen that we wanted for Brazil, that we saw a little bit in Chile."[57] Just as Portugal became a refuge for many Brazilian exiles, it also became a center of espionage where the Brazilian government monitored, and potentially tried to execute, members of its exiled opposition. Portugal was also a tumultuous and politically unstable country, and a year after their arrival, Osava and Brito felt that the window of political innovation and social experimentation was closing. A series of power blackouts indicated, in their eyes, that the conservative opposition was signaling to the left to "stop playing around, we control this country."[58] As the moderate Portuguese Socialist Party consolidated control, the "political work" projects that Osava and Brito had been participating in were ended. "The process started to lose steam and the momentum shifted to the colonies, which were becoming independent that year, 1975. There were some contacts that were sort of an invitation, for us to go to Angola."[59] They had friends in the MPLA, who invited them to collaborate with the newly independent government. They packed their bags for Angola.

Many other Brazilian exiles would follow Osava's and Brito's path into Portugal, which until the Brazilian amnesty of 1979 was a socialist haven from which they could challenge the authoritarian regime in Brazil. This role became evident in the first months after the Carnation Revolution, when national Portuguese newspapers began carrying interviews with leaders of the Brazilian exile community like the former governors Miguel Arraes and Leonel Brizola. As governor of Pernambuco in the early 1960s, Arraes had sponsored Freire's adult literacy project. As governor of Rio Grande do Sul, Brizola had pressured his brother-in-law João Goulart to support the most radical demands of workers and peasants. Now the two found in the Portuguese press a new means of engaging in dialogue with the Brazilian government and communicating with other members of the political opposition.[60]

Spying in Portugal

The foreign ministry maintained an intelligence bureau, the Center for Foreign Information (Centro de Informações do Exterior, or CIEX), tied to the SNI. After 1974 the CIEX infiltrated the exile community in Portugal and maintained an elaborate system of information gathering. One informant kept tabs both on the Brazilians living in Portugal and on those who visited for meetings, like the exiled former congressman José Talarico, who shuttled between Uruguay, Algeria, and Europe, helping to organize the opposition into what would become the Brazilian Workers Party (PTB).[61] Another informant reported in 1978 on how Leonel Brizola and Miguel Arraes had made a trip to Portugal to "thank Mario Soares personally on behalf of the thousands of Brazilian exiles for the fraternal way in which they offered the hospitality of the mother country after the government of Uruguay cancelled their asylum."[62]

The CIEX also had the responsibility of debunking supposedly leaked documents ordering the assassination of Brazilian exiles in Portugal, and of refuting accusations published in a Venezuelan magazine that the directors of the Chilean and Brazilian intelligence services had agreed to collude in their operations. Documents published by the magazine *Cuestiones* apparently showed that Jaime Contreras, director of the Chilean National Intelligence Agency (DINA), and General João Baptista Figueiredo, head of the SNI, who would succeed Geisel as president, had agreed to exchange information and support each other's operations against subversives. If true, the report would be consistent with the project known as Operation Condor in which the intelligence agencies of South American dictatorships shared intelligence and engaged in repression.[63] The documents, supposedly leaked in Lisbon, circulated in Venezuela and made it into Brazilian political and press circles. They reportedly showed that the SNI had arranged for the DINA to "code 12" two exiles in Lisbon, the former admiral Cândido Aragão and the lawyer Carlos Sá. "Code 12" reportedly meant an assassination made to look like an accident.

Since the allegations surfaced in 1978, as the Brazilian dictatorship was liberalizing, members of the intelligence services were forced to hold a meeting with legislators and journalists to dispute the authenticity of the *Cuestiones* report and the documents. They argued that the ciphering of the documents "did not correspond to techniques known by Itamaraty" and that the documents signed by Figueiredo and the DINA chief Jaime Contreras "violate a 'golden rule' of information exchange employed by any reasonably professional intelligence service, which is that the (false) documents were signed and perfectly clear, while the exchange of correspondence between intelligence services on the contrary is done in a way that conceals the identity of the author and the recipient."[64] A general with the SNI "attributed this maneuver to the CIA." He offered two reasons: Brazil was negotiating an accord with Germany for nuclear reactors and technology to enrich fuel for them, and this was a way for the United States to sabotage the accord by showing the Brazilian government to be "irresponsible"; and it was an attempt to force a return to civilian rule by sinking the presidential aspirations of Figueiredo. The research here does not provide sufficient information to determine whether the Brazilian government really tried to code 12 Aragão and Sá, or whether the operations were part of a CIA plot against the military regime, or whether there is some alternative explanation. But what is clear from the episode, as well as from the documents detailing the surveillance and infiltration of the exile community in Portugal, is that the political climates of Brazil and Portugal became radically incompatible after 1974. The Brazilian government attempted to contain the new Portugal, which in turn saw Brazil as a symbol of what it had overcome. The conflict with Portugal finally ended in 1979 with the Brazilian government's amnesty, which allowed exiles to return.

Decolonization

The challenge of contending with leftist governments extended past Portugal to its former colonies, whose new governments were also revolutionary Marxist regimes. While the Brazilian government could have chosen not to establish diplomatic relations with them, that position would have been incompatible with its broader goals in Africa. The Brazilian government waited too long to break with Portuguese colonialism, and did not have time to act on the decision before the regime of Salazar and Caetano was overthrown.

The Brazilian government still followed Portugal's lead in waiting to recognize the government of Guiné-Bissau, the former Portuguese colony that declared its independence in September 1974. By the time the Brazilian government extended recognition, eighty other countries had already done so. In mid-1974 José Maria Pereira traveled to Guiné-Bissau as director of the academic Center for African and Oriental Studies (CEAO) to see firsthand the conditions faced by the first Portuguese colony to have gained independence. He met there with members of the PAIGC, one of whom told him, "Gilberto Freyre's idea of lusotropicalism killed more people than the G3 [assault rifle used by the Portuguese army]."[65] Guiné-Bissau's new leadership, which had seen Brazil's support for Portuguese colonialism, now saw the slowness of its government in extending recognition.

The next Portuguese colony to declare its independence was Mozambique. There the Marxist FRELIMO movement reserved special hostility toward Brazil for its failure to support Mozambique's years of struggle. As Mozambique's declaration of independence in July 1975 neared, Itamaraty sent a diplomat, Ovídio de Melo, to meet with the FRELIMO foreign minister Marcelino dos Santos to offer aid to the new government and arrange for Brazil's recognition of Mozambican independence. Marcelino dos Santos rejected the Brazilian offer:

> In 1963, in order to help the Brazilian people understand the drama of the war against colonialism, Frelimo opened an office in Rio. That diplomatic office of a not yet independent country correlated, in an inverse sense, to the formal diplomatic relationship we wanted to establish with a country whose independence was not yet complete. But with the 1964 military coup, the Frelimo office in Rio was raided by the police, its staff was imprisoned and worked-over. What is more, they were threatened with deportation to Portugal, where they would be thrown into the dungeons of the PIDE. This disastrous deportation only didn't happen because Senegalese President Leopold Senghor intervened in favor of Frelimo. . . . Brazil was also once a colony . . . it fought bravely for independence; it had Tiradentes and Tomás Antônio Gonzaga, who was exiled to Mozambique, it is a half-African country, because of its roots and its culture, and owes a lot to Africa. For this reason, Mozambique had always expected Brazil's support which, morally, would have mattered a great deal before Portugal, before the world. So Brazil's abstentions [at the UN] were never enough. A Brazilian vote in favor of Mozambique possibly could have stopped the Portuguese war machine, ended the war sooner and given us our independence.[66]

The government of newly independent Mozambique refused to accept the presence of a Brazilian delegation at its independence ceremonies. It refused Brazil's offers of aid. And it refused to establish diplomatic relations with Brazil. A year after the Carnation Revolution it was clear that the Brazilian government would have to find a way to act much more forcefully to bury its past complicity with Portuguese colonialism. That opportunity came in Angola.

8 The Special Representation in Angola, 1975

IN NOVEMBER 1975 Brazil's military regime faced growing protests over the violence used to silence opposition from the left. In São Paulo the military regime had just tortured and killed the journalist Vladimir Herzog. Meanwhile, across the Atlantic, Angola tumultuously reached independence, ending five centuries of Portuguese rule in Africa. Three movements which had fought Portugal since 1961 now moved into a civil war that pitted factions supported by the United States and South Africa against a Marxist movement, the MPLA, supported by Cuba and the Soviet Union. Among the rival factions the MPLA claimed the widest popular base and controlled the capital, Luanda. And on 11 November the Portuguese relinquished sovereignty over Angola, and the MPLA claimed to be its government.

On 10 November at 8:01 pm in Brasília, which was just after midnight in Angola, an Itamaraty spokesman read a statement declaring Brazil's recognition of the new MPLA government. The repressive regime responsible for Herzog's death became the only western government to recognize Angolan sovereignty under the MPLA. Following orders from President Geisel, Itamaraty took pains to be the first government to extend recognition. Indeed, despite the deteriorating conditions in Luanda as opposition movements fought in the outskirts of the city and a column of South African tanks advanced on it, Brazil maintained a permanent diplomatic presence alongside the MPLA. From the perspective of the cold war these actions are contradictory: an authoritarian regime that violently repressed even moderate opposition at home openly supported a revolutionary Marxist movement overseas. But the recognition of Angola responded to a different logic.

This chapter traces the logic that tied military Brazil to Angola under the MPLA. The Brazilian presence within the independence of Angola was complex. Angola held multiple meanings for Brazil; and Brazil held multiple meanings for Angola. For the Brazilian government Angola was the gateway to Africa: swift recognition of Angola could overcome the political damage that came from supporting Portugal, and thus could open diplomatic and commercial doors to other parts of Africa. Brazil believed that Angola would become a source of oil and an export market. Yet the Brazilian government was alone in seeing Angolan independence as a positive step toward a bright future. As Brazilian diplomats arrived, Portuguese colonists fled to the three countries that they believed best reflected their experiences and identity: Portugal, Brazil, and South Africa.[1]

For Portuguese colonists in Angola, Brazil symbolized a new start in a world similar to the one they knew was ending. For them Brazil was "safe." The police and the military maintained order just as they had done in colonial Angola, and just as in Angola an illusion of racial harmony protected white privilege. The political and cultural connections between Angola and Brazil were symbolized by the Brazilian Varig Airlines flight that carried Portuguese colonists to Brazil, part of a regular route between Rio de Janeiro and Johannesburg. Just as the meaning of Brazil was clear to those who left, it was clear to those who remained. For Angolans in the capital, Luanda, many of whom were members of the MPLA, Brazil symbolized the type of capitalist fascism they had fought against in their war for independence from Portugal. The major daily newspaper reported regularly on the human rights abuses of the Brazilian military dictatorship. For those who remained, Brazil wasn't "safe."

There was symmetry between the visions of Brazil of the departing colonists and the triumphant revolutionaries. Both groups equated Brazil with capitalism, military rule, and the imagination of racial democracy that was so comforting to whites in colonial societies: the idea that everyone shared an identity and that nonwhites were happy in their place. The Brazilian diplomatic mission to Angola on the eve of its independence was intended, by those who supported it, to break down that symmetry. Yet once South Africa invaded Angola in October, followed by Cuban troops who came to the aid of the MPLA, conservative elements of the Brazilian government, the military, and the press reacted against Geisel's foreign policy. Despite the new plaque on the door, the Brazilian consulate in Luanda did not become an embassy; Melo was removed and his replacement only held the rank of chargé d'affaires. Domestic political pressure, the military government's enduring need to defer to the United States on foreign policy, and the aversion to risk that characterized Itamaraty combined to guarantee that this act was the culmination of Brazilian diplomacy in Africa rather than a new beginning.

Angolan Independence

On 15 January 1975 Angola's three armed factions, Agostinho Neto's MPLA, Holden Roberto's FNLA, and Jonas Savimbi's UNITA, groups that had fought the Portuguese and each other since the early 1960s, signed the Alvor Accord. The accord set a date for independence from Portugal and established a coalition transition government. The three movements soon fought, making the transition government into a fiction. In July 1975 street combat led by the MPLA and gangs from the *mussesseques*, Luanda's slums, resulted in the successful expulsion of the other movements from Luanda, igniting a struggle by these groups to retake the capital in advance of independence, and Angola's civil war.

Not only did the major daily newspaper in Luanda chronicle the increasingly violent transition to independence in Angola, but its own publication history reflected the growing conflict. For half a century it was published as *A Provínica de Angola*, a reference to the fiction that Portugal possessed "overseas provinces" rather than colonies. In early 1975 Holden Roberto's FNLA bought the newspaper to influence public opinion while it was taking part in the coalition transition government. It went as far as hiring as an advisor a Brazilian journalist who worked for *O Globo*, Fernando Câmara Cascudo. Through his collaboration the newspaper adapted propaganda slogans used by the Brazilian military regime. Among the recycled slogans was a variation of one original to the United States: "Angola—Love it or leave it!" It had been reused in Brazil and now was adapted to a new environment. Anywhere it was used, "love it or leave it" belied a reality of social unrest.[2]

When the balance of power in Luanda shifted to the MPLA in July, the renamed *Jornal de Angola* shifted hands as well. The workers at *Jornal de*

Angola revolted against the newspaper's FNLA directors, whom they called "loyal followers of the fascist colonial regime of Salazar and Caetano."[3] They expelled the directors, seized the newspaper, and denounced its "fascist tendencies." Câmara Cascudo fled to FNLA territory near Zaire, and a week later a bomb destroyed the *Jornal de Angola* newsroom. Perhaps it was set by departing Portuguese, or by departing FNLA members, or both.[4] Among the new directors was Fernando Lima de Azevedo, who had been one of the Angolan student activists detained by the Brazilian military regime in 1964.[5]

The new *Jornal de Angola* altered the tone of its reporting on Brazil, now a symbol of what the MPLA stood against: right-wing terror and racism produced by international capitalism. One story and its positioning illustrate what Brazil now symbolized. Under the headline "'Death Squad' Strikes Again," the issue of 14 August reported on the actions of a "death squad" that meted out vigilante punishments in a poor neighborhood of Rio de Janeiro, torturing and killing dozens of people during the so-called Holy Week Massacre. There was a photo of a Klansman alongside the story, with a provocative caption: "This member of the Ku-Klux-Klan let himself be photographed cleaning a bayonet. The Grand Wizard of the organization declared that it is they who keep the United States afoot. Naturally, the objectives of the Ku-Klux-Klan are different from those of the Brazilian 'death squads.'"[6] The evident meaning: racist violence in the United States and the vigilantism of death squads that acted with immunity under Brazil's dictatorship were the same thing. Not all Angolans embraced this vision. Tens of thousands fled to Brazil, producing another type of newspaper coverage. On 30 August the *Jornal de Angola* published photos of the crates and cars piling up in the city's port. The crates bore destinations in large letters: Rio de Janeiro and Santos, Brazil; and Durban, South Africa.[7]

Someone who remained in Luanda, who went to the movies and read the newspaper, would have a sharp image of the Brazil awaiting those who fled. A reader looking at the photo of the crates destined for Rio and Santos would also see an ad on the opposite page for the theatrical release of Costa-Gavras's *State of Siege*, a film about repression and resistance in Uruguay, under a regime similar to Brazil's. Over the remainder of the year the *Jornal de Angola* highlighted threats to Brazilian bishops who spoke out in favor of human rights and protested the detention, torture, and execution of political prisoners and prison conditions for the poor. The death of Vladimir Herzog and bad prison conditions were both subjects of reports under the headline "Brazil Becomes an Inferno": "In fascist countries, the prisons are always full . . . That is how it is in Brazil, where the Geisel government offers the opium of soccer and samba with one hand while the other holds the horrific dog collar. It is becoming commonplace to die violently or to disappear in Brazil."[8]

Negotiating the Brazilian "Special Representation"

In December 1974, on vacation in Rio de Janeiro from his post as consul in London, Ovídio de Melo was approached by his childhood friend Ítalo Zappa, who was head of the Itamaraty Africa and Asia Department. Zappa enlisted him to take part in the project of building relationships with the liberation movements of the Portuguese colonies. Zappa wanted someone he trusted and with whom he had a personal relationship to help develop these new ties. He and Ovídio de Melo had entered the foreign service together and were known for their comparatively leftist sympathies, interest in third world movements, and orientation toward Africa.[9] The Itamaraty chief of staff and later foreign minister Ramiro Saraiva Guerreiro said of Ovídio de Melo, "They say he is a communist, but I don't know." He described Zappa as "a leftist, but not a communist like people said. He was of the French leftist type."[10]

In January 1975, just after the Alvor Accord was signed, Melo left for Africa. In Tanzania, he met with the FRELIMO foreign minister Marcelino dos Santos to propose creating a Brazilian special representation in Mozambique. He offered Brazilian aid and asked dos Santos to draw up a list of priorities. Marcelino dos Santos responded tersely. He suggested that the Brazilian government should just offer what it sent to its Northeast during times of drought: trucks, food, and medicine. Dos Santos was unreceptive because, as he later told Melo, "After fourteen years of war, watching Brazil support Portugal that whole time, Mozambicans were not accustomed to considering Brazil a friendly country."[11]

Melo had difficulty meeting with the MPLA leader Agostinho Neto, who was traveling across the continent meeting with supporters before returning to Angola. Eager to finally meet with him, Melo flew to Nairobi to sit next to him on a flight to Dar-es-Salaam. Melo discussed the Brazilian government's desire to establish the special representation. Neto was receptive and gave Melo the impression that he had a "broad and comprehensive vision of the situation of Angola and Brazil in the world, and of the intense cooperation that would be possible between two countries bound by a brotherhood of culture, ethnicity and mixture." Neto would receive the special representation, but Melo was not the first Latin American representative he had received in Dar-es-Salaam as he made the transition back to Angola. Neto also met with Cuban envoys, from whom he requested military training and aid.

From Nairobi Melo traveled to Angola, seeking out Jonas Savimbi, leader of UNITA, and Holden Roberto, leader of the FNLA. Savimbi had neither criticism nor praise for the Brazilian government's earlier policies or for its new direction, but agreed to the establishment of the special representation. Melo left the meeting with the impression that "Savimbi knew little or nothing about Brazil and had never considered cooperation between the two countries." To meet with Holden Roberto, Melo traveled to an FNLA compound in Kinshasa, Zaire. Roberto too agreed to the special representation. He "praised the new Brazilian policy, without giving any sign that he may have resented the earlier policy."[12]

While FRELIMO had closed its doors to the Brazilian government, the three groups vying for control of Angola embraced it. Why was there such a difference in their responses to Melo's entreaties? FRELIMO was a consolidated movement that faced no internal competition. The movement could turn its back on what little the Brazilian government had to offer, and the decision would hardly hurt. The MPLA, like the other Angolan movements, welcomed the Brazilian special representation because each of the movements was in such a precarious condition in the three-way competition for control of the country that none benefited from rebuffing a potential external ally to settle old scores. They could not afford to say no.

Representing Brazil in Angola

Optimistic, Ovídio de Melo unpacked his bags at the Hotel Trópico in Luanda on 22 March 1975, followed a week later by his aide Cyro Cardoso. He began looking for a building that would better serve as an embassy than the old consulate. Melo found himself in a unique position as a buyer in one of the world's great buyer's markets, though the foreign ministry did not in the end allocate money for a new building. Despite his optimism about the future, he still noticed that "it was plain to see that everything was deteriorating. The hotel I got to know in February was not the same in March."[13] Soon after, his wife Ivony de Melo arrived; sensing the growing instability of Luanda, she turned one of the consulate rooms into a pantry and began stockpiling cans and sacks of food. She explained that the supermarket "was completely crazy. People were practically attacking each other as they grabbed items. There was almost nothing on the shelves. It was general panic." Their supermarket was soon bombed.[14] At times the escalating violence hit the consulate directly. One night the façade of the consulate was machine-gunned. Soon after, the Varig Airline offices were blown up.[15]

Luanda was swept by violence. Embittered colonists sabotaged and destroyed what they could not carry away, and attacked institutions associated with Angolan independence. Angolans took revenge on the colonists. The rival independence factions, as well as armed gangs from the shantytowns surrounding Luanda, fought each other. The three-part transition government disintegrated, but Melo sought to maintain an image of impartiality, arranging aid to all three factions. The Brazilian government donated police uniforms, and a Brazilian air force cargo plane carried eighteen tons of medicine to Luanda. According to Melo, a week later a Brazilian consulate aide was having lunch at the Hotel Trópico when a member of the hotel staff approached her and asked to show her something. She took her to the rooms of the floor reserved for FNLA members and showed her that they were filled with the medicines donated from Brazil. The hotel staff person said: "You were very kind, sending these medicines to Angola . . . [but] these medicines are all going to be sold in drug stores in Kinshasa."[16]

The Battle of Luanda

The Brazilian freighter *Cabo Orange* was stuck. Amid the fighting in mid-July and the instability that followed the MPLA's seizing control of the city, the dock ceased to operate. The freighter waited to unload its cargo of medical equipment purchased by the transition government. From the ship's decks the crew watched the fighting over control of the city, and its radio operator wrote a samba about the destruction. The samba made it into Melo's hands and he remitted it to the foreign ministry. At the beginning of August, after nearly a month in port, the *Cabo Orange* returned to Brazil with its cargo undelivered.[17] In the samba, "The War in Angola," the radio operator invokes *umbanda* (Afro-Brazilian conjuring) to give him strength to endure the fighting in what had once been a sought-after port of call:

From the ship we hear
The machine guns firing
Along with the rifles
And the cannon's roar
At night you see clearly
The columns of fire soaring upward
On the streets the sad scene
Of those who are homeless
Men, women and children
Escaping from danger
Their belongings on their head
Those who see it are moved
Because it is serious here
Don't you think
That this is just loose talk
I will stay until the end
But I do not want to return

Because not content with the fighting
That kills their own brothers
They give proof
Of not being civilized
Because out of revenge they eat
The hearts of their dead
This is true
And it makes me uneasy
Because I thought this didn't happen
But photos of this
Are published in the newspaper
At the Loide office
There isn't even hope
Because of the number of people
Looking for passage
Abandoning Luanda
To go to other shores
I can't relate it all here
The agonies are too great
In this Luanda that in other times

Brought happiness to so many
And today only brings sadness
With its savagery.[18]

The *Cabo Orange* exemplified Brazilian defiance of the currents of Angolan turmoil as it idled with its undelivered medical supplies. Even the name of the ship was pregnant with meaning for the Brazilian mission in Angola: Cape Orange was a point in northern Brazil held by the Dutch in the seventeenth century as they vied with the Portuguese for control of the south Atlantic. The ship's presence in Angolan waters had little to do with the Angolan reality of exodus and everything to do with the imagination of a natural bridge between Brazil and Africa through Angola, a bridge once maintained by the Portuguese and the Dutch and now sought by Brazilians amid the growing violence. The quixotic voyage of the *Cabo Orange* was not wasted. The ship evacuated two dozen Brazilians resident in Angola as well as consulate staff.[19]

During the July fighting and for months afterward, the FNLA repeatedly fired mortars at the water pumping station on the outskirts of the city. Ovídio and Ivony de Melo lived off water that they stored in their bathtub and treated with iodine. Food was scarce, and they relied on sugar, manioc flour, rice, beans, and pasta sent by Itamaraty on the Varig flight that stopped twice weekly in Luanda to carry refugees.[20] By early August the MPLA controlled Luanda, and the FNLA and UNITA joined forces against them. On 3 August the first Cuban military advisors arrived, followed by hundreds of other Cubans who established training centers for MPLA troops.[21] The FNLA received training from Chinese advisors in Zaire and was backed by Zairean troops and arms. UNITA and the FNLA also began receiving arms from the South African Defense Forces (SADF) and would soon begin receiving SADF advisors. In August the SADF also occupied border regions. From late July, after the battle for Luanda, through the end of August the United States government directed over $25 million in aid to the FNLA and UNITA through Zaire.[22]

Two days after the first Cubans arrived, and unaware either of their presence or of the mounting covert aid to FNLA and UNITA, Ítalo Zappa visited Luanda. Arriving at the offices of the special representation, he was struck by the condition of its staff, which "looked beaten down and had lost weight," as well as the scene around the consulate.[23] Outside the consulate he witnessed "close to three thousand desperate people demanding visas."[24] Zappa wanted to remove Melo, who insisted on staying. Mirroring the optimism with which they faced their privations in 1975, Ivony de Melo cast their physical condition in a more positive light than Zappa had seen it: "It was great, we all went on a diet."[25] Zappa cabled Foreign Minister Silveira and recommended that the special representation be reduced to local staff. Noting Ovídio de Melo's objections and his desire to stay, he nonetheless argued that the special representation "now no longer serves any objective, because the constitutional circumstances that justified it [the Alvor Agreement] has now been surpassed. To the contrary, its continuing presence could be counterproductive should it be interpreted as support for one of the three movements, not equal distance from the three."[26]

Silveira sided with Ovídio de Melo about remaining, made emergency evacuation plans with the air force and navy, and arranged to send a security detail to the consulate. Showing his anxiety about the increasingly complex situation in Angola, Silveira concluded his telegram with the admonition "read and destroy this message, including its [telex] tape."[27] Silveira and Zappa maintained the mission but ordered Ovídio and Ivony de Melo as well as Cyro Cardoso back to Brazil for "consultations," both to hedge on conditions in Angola and to give them time to physically recover. When Ovídio and Ivony de Melo returned to Angola at the end of September, they flew on the Varig flight that still traced the route from Rio through Johannesburg to Luanda. They were the only passengers on the leg to Luanda.[28]

While Ovídio and Ivony de Melo were in Brazil, conditions in Luanda continued to deteriorate. Garbage service broke down and the vacant lot in front of the consulate became a dump. Dozens of trucks stopped each day and unloaded trash. The smell became unbearable. The trees were iridescent from the green flies that hovered around the garbage, flies which laid their eggs on the clothing that the consular staff hung out to dry, causing infections and abscesses on those who wore them.[29] Gil de Ouro Preto, a consulate aide who would later replacc Melo as head of the mission, hired what he called an "African commando group" of children to shovel the garbage over the precipice at the edge of the vacant lot. He eventually got the city council to send a bulldozer to push all the garbage over the edge of the cliff. He declared: "We've defeated the dump—irrevocable victory of Brazilian diplomacy in Angola. Victory over laziness, chaos, flies, parasites and stench."[30]

The DOPS Meets the MPLA

After Ovídio de Melo blocked an attempt by a group of forty former PIDE agents and their families to charter a flight to Brazil, he worried that the agents might react violently against the Brazilian consulate or the Varig Airlines office. Melo asked the Portuguese military commander in Luanda to post guards in front of both offices. The commander suggested that the presence of Portuguese guards would only make the buildings more of a target.[31] In turn, asking the MPLA, which controlled the city police, would make them targets for the FNLA and UNITA. Amid the rapidly rising violence Itamaraty sent three bodyguards whom Melo referred to in my interview as "DOPS agents," but they were sent by Itamaraty's CIEX. They had flown directly from Chile, where they had been stationed at the Brazilian embassy since the aftermath of Pinochet's coup in 1973.[32]

The security agents surveyed the consulate's and the city's situation, and their urgent order to Itamaraty for supplies reflected the precarious environment they found: four HK MP5 machine guns, with twenty clips for thirty rounds, along with six hundred 9 mm rounds; four Taurus .38 medium-barrel, 76 mm revolvers, with two hundred rounds of ammunition; a 12-gauge shotgun with one hundred rounds; ten tear gas grenades and five gas masks; and two walkie-talkies. They asked that the weapons be unmarked so that they could not be traced to the Brazilian police or military.[33] A CIEX agent, Jean Claude Guilbaud, brought the weaponry in two lead-lined cases. Ovídio de Melo recalled that Guilbaud was so traumatized by the chaos in Luanda that when he tried to leave, he "attacked the Varig agent at the airport. The agent told him there was no room on the flight and Guilbaud became infuriated and grabbed him by the neck. He wanted to strangle him." When Cyro Cardoso returned from dropping him off, Melo recalled his saying, "If all of our spies are like Guilbaud, we are going to have terrible problems."[34] Though the agents brought additional security, Ivony de Melo worried about finding enough food to feed them. On the other hand, their presence meant that members of the consular staff could now use their bullets as poker chips—instead of the beans she was hoarding—as they wiled away the nightly curfew.[35]

Melo issued new passports to the agents when he saw that they had come straight from Chile, with entry stamps dated 1973. He worried that Angolans, particularly the MPLA, would associate them with the reviled Pinochet regime. It was too late: MPLA-controlled radio denounced the "invasion of Angola by Brazilian . . . evildoers," declaring they "were the same ones who worked in Chile, in the service of the CIA."[36] The presence of this security detail, associated with repression in both Brazil and Chile, was incongruous with the political climate taking hold in Luanda, as the MPLA consolidated its hold on the city and began establishing the framework for a national government. The presence of the agents was mitigated by the Brazilian government's willingness to remain in Luanda despite the collapse of the transition government, the exodus of whites, and the shuttering of other foreign delegations and businesses.

The security agents alongside the nascent Marxist state foreshadowed the repercussions that the Brazilian government would face both domestically and abroad for its support of the MPLA. The decision to remain in Luanda, and its implied support for the MPLA, put the Brazilian government in an unusual position among western governments, some of which (the United States, France, South Africa, Zaire, and Zambia) were backing its foes. At the same time, Mozambican authorities had expelled the Brazilian consul when their country became independent in June 1975, signaling the importance to Brazil of success in Angola. The challenge presented by Mozambique was put succinctly by the former consul, who sent a memorandum to Silveira after he had been asked by FRELIMO to leave and close the consulate. He explained that FRELIMO "rightly or wrongly resents Brazil for the fact that they did not receive support of any kind during the nearly ten years of struggle against colonialism."[37]

FRELIMO was rumored to have invited exiled leaders of the Brazilian Communist Party to participate in the independence ceremonies. While this rumor was unfounded, the exiled former governor of Pernambuco Miguel Arraes did attend as a guest of the new Mozambican state. His relations with FRELIMO, as with the MPLA, had been formed in Algeria. A Brazilian reporter asked Prime Minister Joaquim Chissano about future relations with Brazil. He responded with three questions: "What has Brazil done for African liberation movements? What has Brazil done for FRELIMO? And what is it prepared to do for Mozambique?"[38] For the Brazilian foreign ministry, perhaps the answer to the last question could be found in Angola.

The MPLA's public denunciation of the Brazilian security agents reflected misgivings within the movement about relations with Brazil. While Agostinho Neto supported Brazil's presence, other members of the MPLA leadership shared the sentiments of FRELIMO. The MPLA leadership debated whether to invite a Brazilian delegation to the independence ceremonies. In the end the precarious position of the movement meant that the legitimacy conferred by the presence of a Brazilian delegation outweighed resentments, and the invitation was issued.[39]

The Invasion of Angola

On 20 October a South African military force consisting of black Angolans and white South African Defense Forces (SADF) troops invaded southern Angola. Their goal was to seize towns and cities controlled by the MPLA on a march to Luanda, joining forces with UNITA and the FNLA, backed by Zaire, to expel the MPLA before the transfer of sovereignty from Portugal on 11 November. By 3 November, reinforced by nearly a thousand South African troops, the invading force had advanced halfway to Luanda. Leveling the opposition and clashing with Cuban military trainers, the SADF forces were optimistic that they could seize Luanda and displace the MPLA before Angola became independent.[40]

As the South African army advanced, Geisel met with Silveira to decide what to do about Angolan independence. Silveira proposed recognizing the MPLA government and presented a report written by Zappa that advocated making a public display of recognition before any other country could do so, having Ovídio de Melo remain in Luanda as the Brazilian government's emissary to the independence ceremonies, and credentialing Melo as ambassador to the new government.[41] His proposal included a report prepared by the chief of staff secretary Saraiva Guerreiro, who weighed the advantages and disadvantages of recognizing a government that Brazil "would not desire."[42] Even Portugal kept its distance from the MPLA, and on 10 November it would withdraw, announcing vaguely that it extended sovereignty to the "people of Angola."

At the time that Geisel and Silveira met, they did not know of the South African invasion or of their fighting with Cuban instructors in Angola, and the Cuban government had not yet decided to send troops to repel the South Africans. Geisel and the Brazilian government knew of fighting in southern Angola but did not associate it with South Africa. They believed that the troops there were a "UNITA-FNLA force," although the FNLA was situated in and fighting in the north of Angola and UNITA was concentrated in its central plateau. The Cuban decision to send troops to combat the South African invasion became the decisive event of Angolan independence, both because the Cubans succeeded in repelling the South Africans, keeping the MPLA in power, and because of the reaction against Cuba by western countries. Indeed, the role of Cuban troops alongside a government supported by Brazil created a backlash against Geisel's government within Brazil, led by senior military officers. As they weighed their course of action before Angolan independence, what did Geisel and Silveira know about the Cuban presence in Angola?

When I asked Ovídio de Melo if he had been aware that there were Cuban troops fighting in Angola on the eve of independence, he denied knowing so at the time. He explained that the Cubans who were there were in the south, not in Luanda.[43] This is consistent with Piero Gleijeses's account of initial Cuban military trainers as having been dispersed to MPLA installations around the country, and the first airlifts of soldiers going straight to the battlefronts, not only in the south, against South Africa, but also northeast of the city of Luanda, where they fought FNLA and Zairean troops.[44] The available foreign ministry and presidential documents made no mention of Cubans in Angola before independence. And when the Brazilian ambassador in Washington, Araújo Castro, met with Walter Cutler, head of the State Department Africa Desk, on 4 November to talk about Angola, Cutler made no mention of Cubans.[45] Still, when Geisel was asked in 1994 if the presence of Cuban troops was already known, he replied, "It was already known, but we had other considerations."[46]

There is a seeming contradiction between on the one hand Geisel's assertion that he knew of the Cuban presence and on the other hand the documentary record and Ovídio de Melo's assertion that the Brazilian government did not know of Cuban troops in Angola. This contradiction is reconciled by Saraiva Guerreiro's recollection: "Ovídio de Melo . . . informed us correctly. He confirmed and told us about the growing presence of Soviet and Cuban military advisors in Luanda. Critics of our recognition say: 'You recognized the government when it was already handing itself over to Cuba.' That's not exactly true, but it was clear—I had no doubts about this—that in that situation, Cuba, the Soviet Union through Cuba, if you wish, were doing everything they could . . . Was there really any alternative? Was there any western government that would help these guys out when they were up against the wall? Would Brazil—which had multiple interests in Angola—send troops and so forth? . . . This was the president's opinion and he immediately authorized recognition."[47] By this account both Geisel and Melo were right: the government knew of

Cuban military advisors, who had been present since August, but not of the airlift of Cuban fighting forces nor of their clashes with South African forces. Saraiva Guerreiro also recognized that in the absence of western support for the MPLA (and a sober recognition that Brazil did not possess the military means to provide this support, as he also noted in his memorandum to Geisel), Brazilian interests in Angola were best defended by the Cuban and Soviet support given to the MPLA.

The Brazilian government's options were either to withdraw Melo and withhold recognition or recognize the MPLA government. It discarded the option of withdrawing, recognizing that doing so would make Brazil "irrelevant." It understood that the other former Portuguese colonies would recognize the MPLA government, that the MPLA had the best-organized armed forces, the greatest popular support, and the largest amount of territory, and that the MPLA was the closest thing that Angola had to a national government. They ignored the MPLA's Marxism: regardless of its ideology, the Angolan government would need diplomatic and commercial contacts with the West, and these could propel its relationship with Brazil. Finally, Itamaraty pragmatically recognized that the Brazilian government lacked the means—military or logistical—to change the balance of power in Angola. At the same time, Itamaraty was aware that Brazil would act alone among western countries, and that there would be a domestic backlash.[48]

Whose decision was it, in the end, to recognize the MPLA government? By insisting in remaining in Luanda despite adversity, Ovídio de Melo created and sustained the preconditions for the Brazilian government to recognize the MPLA. Though Ítalo Zappa worried about Melo's safety and once tried to have him sent back to Brazil, he saw Melo's presence as the key not only to Brazil's future in Angola but to its relations with all of Africa. Saraiva Guerreiro was a strong advocate for recognizing the MPLA government, going so far as to append his personal opinion to the memorandum on recognition that he submitted to Geisel and circulated to the Brazilian National Security Council. Saraiva Guerreiro's memo stressed the advantages of recognizing the MPLA government and concluded that since "Brazil does not intend to intervene to change the facts, both out of principle and because we lack the means . . . [recognition] seems to me, under the circumstances, the only possible option and has the fewest negative consequences."[49] Saraiva Guerreiro recalled that his note was based on his presumption that "the independence of the Portuguese territories could only be achieved by the communists" and that it made a particularly positive impression on the National Security Council. One member of the council told him: "They read your note very carefully and thought it was formidable."[50]

Though Silveira was, according to Saraiva Guerreiro, "really worried about the possible consequences," he too backed recognition. For Silveira, Brazil's late separation from Portugal and slow recognition of Guiné-Bissau weighed in favor of acting decisively in Angola. Yet a political action this incongruous would have been impossible without President Geisel's consent. Ruben Ricupero suggested that Geisel acted on Silveira's recommendation. He explained:

> My impression is that the greatest responsibility and credit goes to Ovídio, who was there. I think that in second place, it was Silveira's. Silveira was convinced by him. From what I knew of him, and for a time I was one of his chief negotiators . . . I don't think it had to do with Geisel, he wasn't one to make that kind of decision without a strong influence from Silveira. In the end, he was a military man. He was pragmatic for a military man, had been the president of Petrobras. My impression is that Ovídio would not have been enough, because he did not have the authority for that. In terms of the power, you could say it was Silveira, aided by Ovídio. I believe it was the President's decision, but if the minister had not presented that position, I doubt he would have taken it. I don't think that if Silveira had said, "Look, it doesn't matter whether or not we recognize the MPLA," Geisel would have said "OK, let's do it." For sure Silveira went and said, "My representative there gives the following arguments for why we have to bet on the MPLA." And they bet.[51]

The final decision was reached by President Geisel on 3 November. In the week between the decision and independence, at Silveira's request Ítalo Zappa asked Brazilian ambassadors throughout Europe, Africa, and the Americas to inquire of the governments to which they were posted what their positions on recognizing the MPLA government would be. Aside from the most radical African countries, such as Tanzania and the Democratic Republic of the Congo, and the other former Portuguese colonies, only Sweden seemed likely to recognize the MPLA government. Most countries would simply wait for the outcome of the fighting in Angola. They offered the first information, from Britain, that "South African mercenaries" were fighting in southern Angola, as well as information from

France that the MPLA received weapons from the Soviet Union and that the Zairean army was supplying and supporting the FNLA in the north. In Washington, Ambassador Araújo Castro met with the head of the State Department Africa Desk, Walter Cutler. Cutler gave him the impression that "time was running out for the MPLA."[52]

Geisel and Silveira understood that their policy ran contrary to the goals of the United States in Angola and in clear defiance of United States hopes for cooperation in defeating the MPLA. While it is not clear whether Brazilian authorities knew about United States support for South Africa, they knew that the United States supported the FNLA through Zaire. In fact, a United States official asked Geisel whether Brazil could send a contingent of "black sergeants" to support the FNLA.[53] The United States reasoned that the "black sergeants" could communicate in Portuguese in Angola and their color could keep their identity and intentions concealed, maintaining the clandestinity of United States intervention. Geisel tersely responded that the army had "Brazilian sergeants, and not black sergeants." What is more, Brazilian troops "could not be used to intervene in the internal affairs of other countries. This is something Brazil does not do."[54]

On 6 November Silveira and Geisel again discussed the Brazilian embassies' responses about other countries' intentions toward Angola.[55] They did not know that there were Cubans already fighting South Africans in Angola and that the first airlift of Cuban troops and supplies had begun. As they confirmed the plans to recognize the MPLA, they prepared for the domestic and international backlash. Saraiva Guerreiro calculated that they could expect "fierce criticism from the Brazilian press, which nonetheless will calm down as the Angolan situation unfolds."[56] They also expected a backlash from conservative officers. To prepare this constituency Silveira gave a speech to the Naval War College in Rio de Janeiro on 10 November, hours before announcing recognition. With the decision made and the announcement in place, Silveira presented his government's policy on Angola to officers from the three branches of the armed forces. Silveira appealed to his audience's nationalism: Brazil was becoming a nation that mattered and that could not shirk difficult decisions like the one presented by Angola.[57]

Silveira explained that Brazil had achieved a unique position by establishing agreements with the three movements in the transition government to maintain the special representation. He acknowledged that this position was complicated by the collapse of the power-sharing agreement, leaving the MPLA in Luanda. He conceded: "Clearly we would have preferred a thousand times over that the independence process in Angola had been peaceful and that the government installed in the largest Portuguese-speaking country in Africa were democratic and tied to us by other affinities beyond those of language," but "we cannot write other people's history."[58] He ridiculed the idea that Brazil could wage an "overseas military adventure" to impose a different outcome in Angola. "I can't comprehend how any of these ideas could be serious . . . Even if foreign intervention turns Angola into an African Vietnam, I do not believe that the MPLA can be dismissed . . . to break with the MPLA at the moment of independence is to alienate a party that will continue to play an important role in Angola under any circumstances."[59]

Silveira explained that Angola was economically unlikely to become a Soviet satellite, but that more importantly, it would be a mistake for Brazil to isolate Angola—to "Cubanize" it, in his words. "We cannot ignore Angola and for much better reasons than the ones that we have for not ignoring other governments of every shade of red." Instead, "Brazil can be a path for the MPLA to diversify its international connections beyond those with Eastern Europe and other African countries. Otherwise, Luanda would become more dependent on these countries, and not only for ideological reasons." What neither Silveira nor anyone else at the Navy War College knew that day was that the regime they were about to recognize was being propped up by Cuban troops engaging in combat against South African armored columns.

Angolan Independence

Two days before independence, Ovídio and Ivony de Melo checked into the Hotel Trópico as part of the international delegations that were to be present at the next day's independence festivities organized by the MPLA. The hotel remained eerily empty—even many African countries awaited the outcome of the fighting before extending recognition to the winning faction. The United States and British consuls had departed. The plane from Lisbon carrying Eastern European dignitaries had been diverted, supposedly because of the risk of landing through the celebratory machine-gun fire in Luanda. One of the few delegations to arrive was from Mozambique. Foreign Minister Marcelino dos Santos, who had rebuffed Melo a year earlier, encountered him and Ivony having lunch at the otherwise empty hotel restaurant. Melo recalled: "Marcelino saw me, came in my direction, and expressed satisfaction with the Brazilian decision, telling me that from then on Brazilian relations with Mozambique would be friendly."[60] This was the outcome hoped for by Silveira. When the Brazilian army chief of staff questioned Silveira in 1977 about the concrete results of supporting Marxist Angola, Silveira replied, "We had really negative stock in Africa, and this has now disappeared."[61]

Since Varig had ceased its flights, Cyro Cardoso returned from Brazil via Lisbon. He was on the plane of dignitaries that circled Luanda and turned back. Melo had sent the consulate driver to the airport, who returned in a panic. He heard gunfire and saw numerous military trucks at the airport, and assumed that this meant the South Africans had reached the city. Ovídio de Melo later learned that the plane had been diverted so that Cuban planes airlifting troops and equipment could land and be unloaded without notice. The trucks were taking the Cubans directly to the front.[62]

On Independence Day Ovídio and Ivony de Melo sat on the nearly empty dais for foreign diplomats watching the festivities. The MPLA police maintaining order around the parade wore uniforms donated by the Brazilian government. Meanwhile, twenty miles to the north Cuban and MPLA troops repelled FNLA and Zairean forces, and to the south Cubans fought off the advancing South African armored column. Among the few foreign dignitaries present on the dais with Ovídio and Ivony de Melo was the widow of the Guiné-Bissau independence leader Amílcar Cabral. When she saw that she was assigned a seat next to Ivony de Melo, she marched off in disgust, declaring, in a reference to Brazilians, "I hate those people!"[63] Ovídio de Melo painted the view from the dais, with its red carpet at the foreground. At the center of the canvas the deep red of the jerseys on the women's guard marching past contrasts with their bright yellow headscarves. Crowds line the street and sit atop gray rooftops, cheering. A single white photojournalist stands in the middle of the street, turning his camera to the dais. The painting depicts a great Angolan moment and the spectacle of being a solitary foreigner there to witness it, looking in at that festive moment surrounded by uncertainty.

As Melo recounted, for two days after Angolan independence the consulate's telex machine in Luanda sat silent. Melo imagined the reason: the government was paralyzed by the negative reaction to its recognition of the Marxist regime. After Secretary of State Henry Kissinger declared pub-

First Independence Day Parade in Luanda. Image courtesy of Ovídio de Melo.

licly that there were Cuban troops fighting alongside the MPLA in Angola, the telex machine finally came back to life, with a message headed by the question "Where are the Cubans?"[64] The consequences of Brazil's decision were about to be felt.

The decision was hard for many to digest, especially in the military. The *Estado de S. Paulo* dedicated four consecutive days of editorials to criticizing the decision. It took the recognition as a sign of the "Mexicanization" of Brazilian foreign policy, referring to the support that the Mexican government usually extended to radical revolutionaries in the Americas as a means of asserting its own revolutionary credentials.[65] Most provocatively, the *Estado de S. Paulo* suggested that any Brazilian journalist or intellectual who had the same ties with a Marxist state that the Brazilian government had just established "would wind up having problems with the DOPS."[66] This was only a week after the murder of Herzog.

As criticism mounted, Ovídio de Melo was told to "immobilize" himself.[67] While the plan had been to elevate the consulate to an embassy and promote Melo to ambassador, the orders never came. Instead Melo spent the last days of 1975 waiting to be withdrawn from his post as leaks to the press from the presidential palace blamed him for "inducing a Brazilian error."[68] Ovídio de Melo was removed "for health reasons" and replaced with a chargé d'affaires, Gil de Ouro Preto. He was at first rejected by the MPLA because he was confused with his relative, Carlos Silvestre de Ouro Preto, the Brazilian ambassador in Lisbon who had traveled to Angola in 1967 to meet the Brazilian naval squadron. Melo's last mission to Luanda was a return trip in January 1976 to reassure Angolan authorities that the new Ouro Preto was different from the old one.[69]

Meanwhile in Brazil, some senior officers were discomfited by what they saw as a violation of the spirit of the "1964 Revolution." The Army chief of staff, Sylvio Frota, confronted Geisel, presenting the president with the "bitter commentary" within the officer corps and declaring, "We do not understand how our revolutionary government, founded on anticommunism, could have been the first to recognize Agostinho Neto, propped up by Cuban troops."[70] In 1977 Frota attempted a coup against Geisel. He failed and was forced to retire. Even two years after the act of recognition, Frota remained resentful of the decision in Angola. In the letter he issued to the officer corps as he resigned after the failed coup Frota cited "the precipitous recognition of the communist government of Angola," as one of his motives for challenging Geisel.[71]

"Subversive" Brazilians in Independent Angola

In the years after independence Brazil was one of Angola's few western connections. Geisel and Silveira relished the prestige and stature that this brought. When Geisel met with French, British, or United States leaders one of the first topics of conversation was Angola. Silveira felt so confident about Brazil's position compared to that of the United States that he lectured Secretary of State Kissinger about "African idiosyncrasies and the behavior of leaders on that continent," and stressed the importance of being open to relations with the new regime.[72] When British and United States mercenaries were condemned to execution in Angola, the governments conveyed their requests for clemency through Brazil.[73] But behind this prestige, the combination of Angola's civil war and its Marxist regime made the new country less attractive to Brazil's citizens, businesses, and government, which delayed sending its first ambassador until March 1976. Decades of Brazilian hopes and Portuguese fears that Angola would be drawn to Brazil and become its gateway to Africa fell away. Beyond these challenges was an almost impenetrable incompatibility between the political systems of the two countries.

Exiles Mário Osava and Maria do Carmo Brito were among the few Brazilians drawn to Angola in the years following independence. While their experiences as Brazilians traveling independently to Angola cannot be generalized, it is interesting that despite the radicalism of their vision of Brazil and their project in Angola, the ways they thought about their identity as Brazilians fit surprisingly well with the mainstream patterns of thought identified by Freyre and promoted by the Brazilian state. From their exile in Portugal, Brito and Osava received an invitation from MPLA members in Lisbon to go to Angola. By their count they were among fifteen Brazilians who lived in post-independence Angola.[74] Why Angola? The former Portuguese colonies—Cabo Verde, Guiné-Bissau, Mozambique, and Angola—were all undergoing revolutionary social transformations. At first Brito wanted to go to Cabo Verde, because she "thought Capeverdians were the most similar to Brazilians."[75] But she and Osava reckoned that the Cabo Verde Islands and Guiné-Bissau were too impoverished to hold opportunities for them. Mozambique under the FRELIMO became the destination for many more Brazilian exiles, like the future governor of the state of Amapá, João Capiberibe, and the historian Daniel Aarão Reis. But Brito and Osava avoided going there for political reasons: they thought FRELIMO was extremist: "Mozambique had a terrible, Chinese-style puritanism."[76]

The affinity for Cabo Verde and the eventual decision to go to Angola were grounded in racial and ethnic identity. Brito adopted the framework of race mixture in the Portuguese world described by Freyre, explaining that in Angola "color consciousness is reflected in the language itself. There are classifications for every nuance of pigmentation. Each racial mixture has its own name, there are sixteen names. The Angolan automatically recognizes someone's origins."[77] For Osava this meant that "they calculated how mixed you were. We don't have a notion of that anymore. No one is worried about that; it's mulatto, and that's it."[78] In Angola, Brito, "white with brown hair and blue eyes," identified herself as "cabrita," for having "distant participation of black blood."[79]

Osava, of Japanese descent, and Brito, of Portuguese descent and self-described as racially mixed, felt an affinity for Cabo Verde and Angola because they perceived their societies to be racially mixed like Brazil's. Though they espoused a radical critique of Brazilian society and its inequalities, they made choices about how and where to continue their activism in exile based on their interpretation of the significance of race mixture. For Osava and Brito, Angola was revolutionary and miscegenated. They still worried about being the victims of racism but found that Angolans differentiated their accents from those of metropolitan Portuguese. There was no racism "because we were Brazilians," Brito recalled, "I was white, but Brazilian. All I had to do was open my mouth and my accent was not Portuguese. That solved any problem. The fear I had was about being discriminated against for being white, I am excessively white, even more than I should be, I think. But we did not encounter racism there, because we were Brazilians."[80]

In Luanda the two worked on MPLA projects. Brito was a teacher, traveling through the war-torn countryside, while Osava worked in party communications. They arrived in Angola in early 1976 and remained for almost two years. As Brazilians, not to mention exiles and revolutionaries, they were well regarded. Brito recalled that there was a "special sympathy" toward Brazilians, and that Brazil was especially visible through soccer.[81] This goodwill was essential, because there were few functioning stores and little merchandise, and the family had practically no money. They were given an apartment in a modern building that housed the families of government officials and Cuban advisors. And they were able to furnish it through gifts and loans from others.

Their building became the subject of an Angolan novel about a pig living on the veranda of a seventh-floor apartment. The novel, *I Would Like to Be a Wave*, by Manuel Rui, reflects on the expectations created by independence, the difficulties of daily life under civil war, and the surreality of the spirit of revolutionary liberation that took hold in Luanda. The novel opens with a man bringing a pig up the elevator of the building—he will fatten it up to feed to his family during carnival, but his two sons form a bond with the pig and conspire to save it from the knife. The pig develops "bourgeois tastes" because it is washed with Brazilian soap and fed with scraps from the Hotel Trópico ("food for ambassadors"). The pig "was one of the living creatures most benefitted by the revolution."[82]

Brito and Osava came to call Angola's situation "National Surrealism."[83] Brito taught for the Angolan Institute for the Study of Social Services (IESSA), which she loved for its "creative frenzy."[84] IESSA focused on the problem of war refugees and soon began working with the MPLA to educate groups of soldiers. Working with IESSA, Brito traveled out of the relatively safe capital to rural and conflict-riven areas throughout the interior, where she witnessed the costs of the war. As she traveled through the interior Brito not only faced the consequences of war but also contracted malaria. The malaria and the experiences merged in a dreamlike mix of images and memories.

The confused mix of revolutionary ideologies in Angola challenged Osava's worldview. Brito recalled that when she first met Osava in the early 1970s she had been intimidated by his "radical Stalinism." [85] Yet in Angola, Cuban and Soviet conceptions of Marxism and revolution combined with the expectations of social transformation brought about by the newly won national independence, with the mobilization of war, and with inexperience to produce sometimes bizarre results. Osava explained:

> In Angola, like in a lot of Africa, the party, the group that produced independence and took power, thought of itself as Marxist and began teaching Marxism to the population. So people were learning that there are these things called dialectics and metaphysics . . . So when the [attempted] coup happened [in 1978], the coup leaders would end their manifestos saying, "Down with metaphysics, viva dialectics." And on the streets, when someone asked you for a favor, say, "Could you give me a cigarette," and you replied, "I don't smoke," they would respond, "Comrade, you are not being dialectical." Or when you picked up a hitchhiker, which was very common because there was very little transportation, if you said, "I am going to such-and-such neighborhood," the person you were giving a ride to would say "No, that's not possible, I am going the other way." And he would come at you again with "the comrade is not being dialectical." . . . So this Marxist thing was just crazy, it was absurd, because you are talking about working-class ideology in a place where a working class practically didn't exist.[86]

After they were exiled from Brazil, Maria do Carmo Brito went to Chile and Mário Osava to Cuba, where he censored letters written by other Brazilian exiles. Brito's first experience with Osava was receiving letters redacted by him with the notice "Censored for not being organic." It was this dogmatism that fell away in Angola.[87]

A failed coup attempt against Neto prompted Brito and Osava to leave, just as the counterrevolutionary violence drove them out of Portugal and Pinochet's coup had driven them from Chile. They returned to Portugal in late 1977 and yearned to return to Brazil. Osava and Brito went to the embassy and their request was sent directly to President Geisel. Briefing Geisel on the requests by them and other exiles in Portugal, Foreign Minister Silveira reported that Brito had approached the Brazilian embassy in Lisbon indicating that she was willing to return "even if it meant being jailed," but that "unless the banishment is revoked, the citizens it applies to cannot return to Brazil."[88] Their request was rejected. A year later, in August 1979, the Brazilian government decreed amnesty both for opponents of the regime and for state agents of repression. Immediately after, Brito and Osava returned.

Their experiences in Angola prompted Brito and Osava to rethink Brazil and their militancy. Brito explained that "misery in Brazil is a kettle for brewing rebellion. I did not become politically active for theoretical reasons, it was for feeling deeply uncomfortable with violence, with hunger. Just that. It was never an attempt to make history. Misery disturbs me deeply, I still bear that today. The question of curable human suffering. But direct intervention for change, I think that has ended for many of us."[89] Osava's reflections were more theoretical:

> Angola, with all of its craziness, showed us that these Marxist ideas, this whole set of things, were completely . . . Returning here we saw that . . . [collecting his thoughts] Well, Angola, let's say, is at the extreme of social confusion, tremendously unequal, riddled with contradictions . . . But Brazil has a lot of this as well. It is not like in the books, where you see, theoretically, that the classes are neatly divided. These aren't well structured, logical systems. In Angola, we saw that there was none of that, that it was total confusion. We imagined that back in Brazil there was a certain order. Returning, I saw that here too there is a lot of that disorder. You can't really think in terms of categories . . . the working class here is very small. It is very far from a Europe, where you see two-thirds of the working age population has a formal, regular job. . . . We don't have that relationship with work in Brazil . . . work for me is fundamental to organization. The United States, developed countries, they are organized through work. The major part of the adult population has a relationship with work, so it is organized around that. We don't have that . . . here the informality is almost absolute.[90]

Both Brito and Osava described Angola as an extreme version of the problems they perceived in Brazil, problems of poverty and exclusion that they saw increasingly as rooted in Brazil's Portuguese influence. In our interview Brito explained that living in Brazil, Portugal, and Africa made her discover that "this country is more Portuguese than African or Indian, by its political structures, by the structure of its social relations. The cultural influence of Indians and blacks is enormous, but this does not reach into the system of social organization. The social organization side of Brazil is Portuguese, and backward Portuguese at that." Osava echoed this sentiment: "What we saw is that Brazilian culture has a lot of African influence to it, but there is very little in the dominant culture." For them Brazil's African influence was chiefly the capacity to survive poverty and exclusion through interpersonal relationships.[91] Osava's revolutionary Marxist ideology yielded to a critique of the cultural values system disseminated by the Portuguese.

Thirty years after Gilberto Freyre celebrated Portugal's creation of "future Brazils" as he traveled through Portugal and its African colonies, Osava and Brito fought against the Brazilian order that Freyre had defended. They agreed that Brazil inherited traits from Africans. And they agreed that Brazil and Angola shared a historical trajectory. But the content of that agreement meant something very different. If Angola was a "future Brazil," that was not because of its lusotropical splendor and model of development but rather its disorganization and misery. If Brazil was shaped by Portugal, that was because of the rigidity and exclusion in its institutions and class structure. They gave connections a different meaning.

As exiled Brazilians living in Portuguese Africa, Brito and Osava personified the multiple contradictions of Brazil's international posture in the late 1970s. On a personal level they reflected on the contradictions of their political ideologies in the face of Angolan realities. And by their presence they personified the irreconcilable gap between right-wing repression within Brazil and the government's foreign policy. These experiences were echoed in Mozambique. Though after the Brazilian recognition of Angola the government of Mozambique established diplomatic relations with Brazil, those relations were strained by the ideological gulf between the regimes. The political difficulties were assuaged by the naming of the former Itamaraty African Division head Ítalo Zappa as ambassador in 1977. Perceived as one of Brazil's most leftist diplomats, whom some called the "red ambassador," Zappa would be posted to countries where his political leanings would seemingly coincide with those of the regime. After his tenure in Mozambique he served as ambassador to Vietnam, China, and

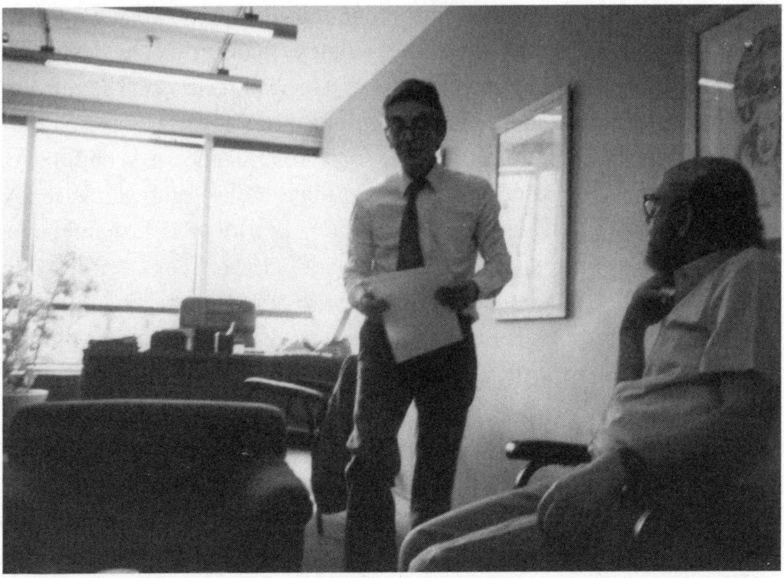

Ítalo Zappa with José Maria Pereira. Photo courtesy of José Maria Pereira.

Cuba. Zappa contended with the Mozambican government's support for Brazilian exiles like the Brazilian Communist Party leader Luis Carlos Prestes (whose daughter worked in Mozambique). In 1978 President Samora Machel sent Prestes "birthday wishes," published in the Maputo newspaper *Notícias*, in which he expressed solidarity with "the heroic brother peoples of Brazil, engaged in a difficult and courageous fight against a fascist dictatorship."[92]

Mozambican leaders felt an affinity toward members of Brazil's exiled opposition. Several hundred exiled Brazilians worked in Mozambique in activities ranging from agriculture to university teaching.[93] According to Osava, Mozambique was more attractive for Brazilian exiles than Angola because the FRELIMO's unified political and party structure brought a degree of order. The Mozambican government also had a policy of recruiting Brazilian exiles. By contrast, Osava and Brito arrived in Luanda without clear plans or work opportunities. Still, the Mozambican experience was also temporary for Brazilians, because "even though it took longer, the situation there still deteriorated into the same confusion, the same division, war and destruction."[94] Like Osava and Brito, the Brazilians in

Mozambique seemingly tempered their revolutionary fervor after living and working in a Marxist African society. After the amnesty of 1979 the Brazilian exiles in Mozambique requested passports and returned to Brazil. In a batch of a dozen passport applications consulted, only one of the Brazilians listed "political asylee" when asked to declare a motive for going to Mozambique. The others only listed their professions.[95]

Televising the Revolution

In the years after Angola's independence Brazil was one of its few western connections, so the few Brazilian citizens and businesses connected to Angola held conspicuous roles in the life of the new country, though their roles were limited. This presence was nonetheless sustained by a $50 million line of credit issued by the Bank of Brazil for Angolan purchases of Brazilian goods (such as the "bourgeois" soap used to clean the pig in Manuel Rui's novel); by the trade of oil, other goods, and services between the Angolan oil company Sonangol and Petrobras; and by Brazilian television programming broadcast by Angolan Popular Television (TPA). Angola shed much of the sentimental imagination it had held for Brazilians. Instead, Brazilian trade with Angola followed the same pattern as its trade with other African nations: it remained dependent on Itamaraty and Petrobras as intermediaries. Meanwhile, cultural exchange spurred by television programming replaced "lusotropicalism" with critiques of capitalism and third-world dependency similar to Osava's and Brito's diagnoses of Brazil and Angola.

Brazilian television programming, especially programming by Brazil's largest network, TV Globo, gained a lasting role not only in Angola but in the other new African countries whose colonial language had been Portuguese. In a deal in 1978 facilitated by Itamaraty, Angolan Popular Television bought syndication rights to the Globo Television soap opera *Gabriela*. The soap opera serialized the novel *Gabriela, Clove and Cinnamon* by the Bahian author Jorge Amado, whose works had been banned in Portugal and its colonies until 1974. *Gabriela* examined class conflicts caused by early-twentieth-century modernization in the cacao-growing region of Bahia. In Luanda *Gabriela* was such a hit that it sparked a series of letters to the editor published by the *Jornal de Angola* debating the revolutionary appropriateness of its broadcast time and subject matter. The debate opened with a letter addressed "to the comrades of the *Jornal de Angola*, to whom

I offer my Revolutionary Salutations." The reader was concerned that the schedule conflicted with weeknight classes and suggested that the program should be broadcast on Sunday evenings. The author complained that "because of this film, many worker-students are missing class . . . We do not want to miss required courses on Wednesdays because of *Gabriela*. Our country needs skilled workers, not *Gabriela*.[96] Another reader responded that the letter writer underestimated the educational value of having Angolans watch and discuss the soap opera. She asked:

> Has the comrade already forgotten our 500 years of suffering and Struggle? Watch the film and try to understand its political significance. You will see why people won't miss it.
>
> See the film as though you were watching colonialist habits, the way they treated us and tell me what side you were on back in the days of Salazar & Co.
>
> Or look at the colonial habits, the struggle for power, the class divisions, and understand why that happens. If you don't know, watch and see why you should skip a bender on Saturdays and see the film.[97]

Just as Africa served as a mirror for Brazilians, so too were Angolans using Brazilian television to interpret their society and its past.

But the transmission of Globo television programming in Angola also demonstrated the distance between the racial and political values of a South American military dictatorship and a newly liberated African nation. In 1979 Angolan Popular Television canceled its broadcasts of the Globo children's program *Sitio do Picapau Amarelo* because it only depicted black characters in subordinate positions.[98] But if TV Globo children's programming ran afoul of Angolan authorities for its characterization of blacks, other TV Globo children's programming designed to be shown in Angola generated anxieties with the Brazilian intelligence services. The programming, educational segments for elementary school children, was commissioned in 1979–80 by the Brazilian Ministry of Education and Culture (MEC) for transmission in Brazil. Under the agreement with the MEC Globo had the right to resell this programming abroad. The network took advantage of this right by developing programs that simultaneously met the reading and social studies goals demanded by the MEC agreement and included content that would make it appealing in Portuguese-speaking African countries that also purchased it. This content drew concern from the intelligence service of the Brazilian Air Force (CISA), which analyzed it for pedagogical approach and subversive content.

CISA also looked at the radicalism of the programming's creators. The director of the social studies modules, Kazumi Munakata, "was jailed in 1971 for militancy in the Press Sector of the Communist Workers Party, code name 'Oswaldo.' He entered the organization in 1968 when he was still in high school. In 1972, he was sentenced under the National Security Law."[99] The programming's pedagogy followed the Paulo Freire method for instilling critical thinking among students, conducting exercises like one that emphasized "raising social problems, especially: 'drought,' 'the responsibility and importance of the government.' Stressing the words 'hunger,' 'drought' and 'poverty.'"

The TV Globo program included lessons on Angola's struggle for liberation, including reading exercises that employed Agostinho Neto's poetry. Readings explored the African path to socialism, the PIDE and its torture methods, and the reconstruction of Angola through collective struggle. One reading exercise asked students to "draw analogies between the situations of Brazil and Angola, given the common colonial origins of these peoples." In another lesson students read a short story about an Angolan fisherman who gets extorted and threatened by encroaching Portuguese colonists. The students were then asked to draw parallels between the Angolan fisherman's experience and the experience of Brazilian indigenous peoples after the arrival of the Portuguese.

While the TV Globo network used the MEC programming to develop a product that it could sell in Portuguese-speaking Africa, the producers used the African market to develop content that had not been tolerated by the military regime's censors. The show even used the narrative of the struggle for African liberation to produce "reflections on the problem of racism," lesson plans that emphasized "generating data about blacks and indians (socially persecuted) and the creation by the dominators of stereotypes about their incapacity. Stress is given to the solidarity among blacks as a form of resistance."

This radical Brazilian-African programming by TV Globo and MEC was the product of a historical convergence. After its independence Angola became a market for the type of programming that TV Globo could produce, and TV Globo, Brazil's largest television network, produced programming like this by commission from federal ministries, especially the MEC. The air force intelligence report on the programming emphasized links between the programs and Minister of Education Eduardo Portella, who in 1961 had been one of the architects of Jânio Quadros's diplomatic engagement with Africa, and was the first director of IBEAA. Finally, the report captures a moment in the decline of the repressive apparatus of the military regime. The Brazilian air force still maintained an intelligence service so far-reaching that it monitored government-commissioned children's programming. But by 1981 it could do little more than complain about how much public money would be spent on this type of "subversion."

Geisel's decision to make Brazil the lone western nation to recognize the MPLA government in Angola framed a contradictory international presence for Brazil. On the one hand it was an anticommunist military dictatorship seeking to expand its political and economic influence abroad, suppress internal dissent, and carry out surveillance on Portuguese citizens in Brazil and Brazilian exiles in Portugal. On the other hand, the government pursued a course for political and economic autonomy from the United States and supported third world nations' struggles against poverty and exclusion. The *Estado de S. Paulo* was exactly right when it suggested that the Brazilian government was clutching the same objectives in one fist that it squashed with the other.

This approach was exemplified by the language used by Brazilian officials, their Angolan counterparts, and the press during a visit to Brazil in 1979 by the Angolan oil minister, Jorge de Morais. The trade mission aimed to increase the Brazilian credit line for exports to Angola from $50 million to $80 million, to purchase fourteen fishing vessels for the Angolan state fishing company, and to increase Brazilian participation in Angolan oil production engineering.[100] Morais and his Brazilian hosts emphasized cooperation despite their ideological differences, and the *Jornal do Brasil* (Rio de Janeiro) and the *Jornal de Angola* (Luanda) described the visit in identical terms, saying that it showed Brazil's "open alignment with the third world . . . [and was] historically tied to its true origins." During the minister's visit Itamaraty representatives emphasized Brazil's "desire to establish our political and economic independence," while the governor of Bahia, meeting with Minister Morais, expressed satisfaction that the Brazilian government had recognized Angola's independence "without waiting for permission from the United States."[101]

9 Miracle For Sale

Marketing Brazil in Nigeria

WHEN MÁRIO GIBSON BARBOZA arrived in Nigeria in November 1972, his visit coincided with the delivery of a shipment of electrical showerheads. The showerheads, common in Brazil, had an electrical coil that could heat water without the need for a heater tank. The showerheads sold well, since they could easily be installed in homes with electricity, and cost only $10. *Veja* reported that the showerheads were a "sensation," but they were unlikely to begin a significant increase in trade in Africa, since "the foreign trade of those countries continues to be solidly monopolized by companies based in the old metropolitan centers."[1] The showerheads foreshadowed the goods that the Brazilian government and businesses would sell in Africa and the rationales used to sell them. They were "tropical technology."

From the beginning of his six-year tenure as Brazilian ambassador to Nigeria, Geraldo de Heráclito Lima made the case that Brazilian goods like the showerheads were ideal for Nigeria. As he met with President Gowon of Nigeria during his credentialing ceremony, Heráclito Lima explained that Brazilian industrial products "are especially qualified for Nigeria because they have designs and specifications that are adapted to the tropical market." In particular, they were supposedly simpler and more rugged, more resistant to voltage fluctuations and humidity, and easier to repair. Gowon responded by offering examples of problems that Nigerians had experienced with European goods. At the end of the meeting the Brazilian ambassador prepared to leave in the Rolls-Royce that had brought him to the presidential palace, but the engine would not start after repeated attempts. Heráclito Lima watched anxiously as the president walked down the stairs of the palace to observe the scene. Making light of the problem, the Brazilian ambassador suggested: "It seems as if the car heard our conversation about the suitability of equipment to the tropics."[2]

Were Brazilian goods better suited to the tropics? Or was this a marketing gimmick? In some cases, as with the showerheads, there were goods made for Brazilian consumers that were cheaper and simpler. Other products, like the Mercedes-Benz passenger buses made in Brazil and exported to Nigeria, which had large, easy-to-open windows and rugged suspensions, were indeed adapted to hot weather and rough roads. But in general the experiences of consumers related in Nigerian newspapers did not reveal a particular tropical merit to Brazilian goods. To the contrary, they were often criticized as shoddy. Still, during the mid-1970s and early 1980s trade between Brazil and Nigeria flourished. The Brazilian government monopoly Petrobras purchased hundreds of millions of barrels of oil from Nigeria, which at prices elevated by the oil embargo of 1973 and boosted again by the second oil shock after the Iranian Revolution of 1979, spurred the Nigerian demand for consumer goods from Brazil.

The strength of trade between Brazil and Nigeria sustained other contacts. In 1977 the Brazilian airline Varig began Brazil's first direct service to a majority-ruled African country (Varig also flew to South Africa, and earlier aircraft with shorter range had stopped in Dakar to refuel on European routes). As oil revenue funded Nigerian development projects, hundreds of Brazilian engineers, technicians, and businessmen went to work on projects in Nigeria. When the Nigerian government built a new capital, Abuja, in the center of the country, it contracted with Novacap, the development company that had worked on Brasília, to aid in the urban planning of the city. The Nigerian oil boom also funded a reprise of the Senegalese Festival of African Arts and Culture. FESTAC, held in 1977, included a large Brazilian delegation which again stressed the cultural ties between West Africa and Brazil. The event became a stage for the exiled Brazilian activist Abdias do Nascimento, present as a member of the United States delegation, to challenge Brazil's image as a racial democracy and highlight the country's systematic inequalities. Nascimento had written the protest "Letter to Dakar" that criticized Brazilian race relations at the time of the first festival in Senegal, in 1966.

In the relationship between Brazil and Nigeria in the 1970s the spotlight was shared by two black Brazilians with different messages. While Abdias do Nascimento (traveling on refugee papers because the Brazilian government had seized his passport) exposed the contradictions of racial democracy, the soccer star Pelé traveled to Nigeria as a corporate spokesman, first promoting Pepsi-Cola from the United States and then appearing as the public face of Brazilian appliances and electronics being introduced to Nigeria by a division of Petrobras under the brand name Tama. Buoyed by oil exports, Nigeria again became a stage on which Brazilians projected reflections on the country's identity. But Brazil's commercial penetration of Nigeria was short-lived. Economic crises in Brazil and Nigeria dampened trade in the 1980s. Still, in the mid-1970s Nigeria reflected Brazilian desires to imagine the country as an emerging industrial giant, to believe that Brazil was a different sort of world power based on a "tropical civilization" that produced "tropical technology," and to suppress criticism of the narrative that Brazil was a racial democracy.

The Land of the Future in a Changing World

During the Geisel years Brazilian political leaders and diplomats perceived new international challenges, like the oil embargo, but also new options for meeting them. They felt the latitude to loosen historic political and economic subordination to what they saw was a declining United States. They perceived a wider array of policy options based on a growing domestic economy as well as a more flexible world system in which previously subordinate regions such as the Middle East, Africa, Latin America, and Southeast Asia could shape events. For Brazilian leaders the domestic possibilities were generated by stunning economic growth and by faith in state planning. Foreign Minister Silveira captured the sense of confidence about Brazilian economic growth when he spoke in 1978 at the National Intelligence Academy:

> In 1960, Brazil was a country with 60 million inhabitants, and only 45% of its population lived in cities. The gross national product was $14 billion and per capita income was almost $200. The electricity generating capacity was 5,000 megawatts, our steel mills produced 2.5 million tons of steel ingots and our nascent shipyards delivered ships with a total capacity of 25,000 gross tons. The production of vehicles in our newly created automobile industry was 130,000 units. In 1960, Brazilian exports were worth less than

> $3 billion, 90% of which were primary commodities, while manufactured exports were no more than 5% of the total.
>
> Today we are 115 million people, 60% of which are urban residents. The GNP is $160 billion and per capita income is almost $1,500. The electrical generating capacity is 23,000 megawatts, and the steel industry produces 11 million tons of steel ingots. Our shipyards deliver ships with a total capacity of 500,000 gross tons and the annual vehicle production is on the verge of reaching the million unit mark. Our exports total $24 billion and manufactured goods are a third of that. By its dimensions, the Brazilian economy is today already the ninth in the world in GNP.[3]

These numbers sufficed for Silveira to proclaim Brazil a "radically new country" which existed in a world "that has undergone profound transformation."[4]

Silveira's data were just one facet of the governing conceptions about the "radically new" Brazil. Growing state stewardship of the economy shaped the "economic miracle." Before being president of Brazil, Geisel had been president of Petrobras, Brazil's largest company. That the state owned Brazil's largest company was not unusual or accidental. Over the course of the 1970s state participation in the economy grew exponentially. State enterprise competed with private enterprise, a pattern that was part of the dominant political culture and had deep roots in military culture. As President Geisel explained, "If Brazil wants to become a modern country, without hunger and the host of other ills we suffer from, we have to develop. The main instrument for that is the federal government. The nation won't just develop spontaneously. It is necessary to have someone who can guide and propel, and that role falls to the government. This is an old idea that I hold, long espoused by the Army War College."[5] Though Geisel attributed to military culture his belief in using the state to spur industrialization and development, Elio Gaspari suggested that Ernesto Geisel's commitment to industrialization "went beyond that of his military generation."[6]

By the end of 1975, according to the planning minister Reis Veloso, the federal government owned half the capital in the largest 1,069 companies in Brazil, and three-quarters of the 100 largest companies. This made the federal government the largest business employer, the largest purchaser, and the largest vendor in Brazil.[7] The state presence in the economy was a product both of planners' confidence in their ability to control the market and of their attempt to resolve the basic contradiction of the Brazilian miracle: Brazilian economic growth was based on unsustainable imports of energy and capital. Planners developed Brazil's export economy in an unsuccessful attempt to offset heavy imports with exports.

Taken together, economic growth and state planning fail to capture the sense of euphoria, even infallibility that Brazilian policymakers of the Geisel years conveyed while witnessing Brazil's seeming emergence as a global power. Brazil's grandeur could be located most broadly in a Southern Hemisphere that was ascendant over a decadent North. In a narrower sense it could be located in Brasília, the modernist expression of poured concrete, less than twenty years old and still unfinished. Under Geisel, Brasília was the center of a world that Brazil was trying to make. As Silveira told the Congress in 1976, "In my understanding, the very concept of the West is not static."[8]

Something separated Brazil from other nations in the minds of Geisel and his colleagues: racial democracy. Indeed, in the opening of an address to the Brazilian Congress, Silveira cited racial democracy as the example of a changing West, proclaiming that "historically, the West has nourished itself from the experiences created by new countries . . . The patterns of racial coexistence developed in the New World, and above all in our country, represent a new factor that illustrates that process."[9] All of Geisel's initiatives for building autonomy from the United States and building relations with the third world were saturated with the rhetoric of racial democracy. Geisel and Silveira were not alone in this perception. The idea that Brazil was a new world model of economic development and racial democracy was shared among conservative Brazilians. Gilberto Freyre was a proponent of this image, writing in his newspaper column: "Some of the young republics of Africa and the Orient are still confused and insecure, so they are anti-European and even make negritude into a dangerous racist ideology. These and other nations can profitably draw from the Brazilian experience of more than a century of independence and for centuries of development . . . as a civilization that is ethnically democratic and because of that, metaracial in the tropics."[10] The preeminent considerations of Geisel's government were the challenge of importing energy, promoting exports, and maintaining order in an undemocratic regime. Still, the character that political leaders gave to the idea of Brazilian autonomy and grandeur in the 1970s was shaped by beliefs about race and its role in Brazilian identity.

In foreign affairs Geisel's government followed an even bolder course than that struck by Quadros and Goulart between 1961 and 1964, pursuing policies that were less encumbered by past commitments like the "Portuguese mortgage." These policies included the most aggressive push to expand trade that would occur between Brazil and Africa. Where in 1969 Brazil exported $15 million in goods to Africa and expanded this to $150 million by 1973, in 1977 exports reached $587 million in goods, nearly half of them manufactured.[11] As Silveira told an audience at the Army War College, Brazil's rapprochement with Africa "reignites a historical process whose natural course had been blocked by the persistence of colonialism . . . Brazil has determined to share the technological patrimony it has accumulated in its experience as a tropical country with these African nations . . . In doing so, we are presenting a non-hegemonic alternative to African countries in their struggle to overcome underdevelopment."[12]

Brazil, Inc.

For nearly a decade after the oil embargo of 1973 Nigeria's newfound wealth and population of eighty million made it a coveted market. The Nigerian economy was unprepared for the sudden wealth, so there was little domestic manufacturing capacity to meet the sudden demand for goods ranging from cars to appliances and even meat. Imports surged beyond the capacity of Nigeria's port infrastructure. In 1975 the Brazilian embassy in Lagos reported a constant backlog of seventy to ninety ships in Nigeria's principal port, a problem that would last for years and meant a costly wait of up to several months for ships to dock and unload.[13] Itamaraty, Brazilian companies, and the state-owned oil monopoly Petrobras avidly pursued the perceived opportunities in Nigeria. Petrobras was particularly active in developing trade with Nigeria, which was a potential means of alleviating the deepening deficits that it faced in paying for oil imports.

Between 1972 and 1976 Brazilian exports to Nigeria soared from $1 million to $86.7 million, of which 90 percent were manufactured goods.[14] Brazilian exports to Nigeria peaked at $770 million in 1981, when Nigeria became the "second largest market for [Brazilian] manufactures after the United States."[15] In addition to manufactured goods, Nigeria became a market for Brazilian technical and engineering services. In 1977 Silveira described Nigeria as "currently our most important market for exporting services. There are Brazilian companies there supervising telecommunications services, planning hydroelectric projects, building roads, railroads, etc."[16] By 1977 the embassy in Lagos counted six hundred Brazilians living and working in Nigeria.[17]

Doing business in Nigeria had considerable pitfalls. Brazilians faced endemic corruption, bottlenecks at the port, and unpredictable regulatory and market restrictions caused by the economic instability based on the volatile price of oil. In 1979 and 1982 the Nigerian government imposed sudden restrictions on imports that proved ruinous for export schemes developed by Interbras, a subsidiary of Petrobras which invested heavily in establishing markets in Nigeria for Brazilian meat, appliances, and consumer electronics. In addition, Brazilian exporters faced a tough market in which newspapers regularly published complaints about the quality of Brazilian goods and services. The Brazilian ambassador Heráclito Lima attributed the bad press to campaigns by European and United States companies seeking to keep Brazil out of the market, but whatever its origins, the press on Brazilian products was overwhelmingly negative, and Nigerian studies suggested that the country was a "dumping ground" for Brazilian goods.

One of the first Brazilian companies to establish a presence in Nigeria was Volkswagen of Brazil, a subsidiary of the German company. Volkswagen attempted to repeat the success of its pioneering assembly plant in Brazil, opened with fanfare during Kubitschek's presidency. In 1975 VW of Brazil became one of two companies to begin assembling cars in Nigeria under a Nigerian program to stimulate manufacturing. The cars were assembled from CKD ("completely knocked down") kits sent from Brazil. The first shipment of 1,370 CKD vehicles was reportedly "the largest shipment of Brazilian vehicles in history," with a value of $6 million.[18] The cars counted both as Brazilian exports and as Nigerian manufactures. The two companies benefited from import barriers established by the Nigerian government to stimulate the creation of a domestic car industry, giving them a captive market for the sale of small-engine cars. Ambassador Heráclito Lima described the imposition of these quotas to protect domestic assemblies as "very good for Brazil, at least for the short term, since all of the cars assembled in Nigeria originate in Brazil."[19]

Along with other manufacturers, Volkswagen saw its assembly in Kaduna, Nigeria, hampered by the bottleneck at the port of Lagos. Volkswagen and the Brazilian shipping line Lloide Brasileiro "took measures to give a higher priority to its ships" at the port. Rather than wait weeks or months in a line of seventy to ninety ships at the port, the Loide ships carrying the dismantled VWs waited on average forty-eight hours. These "measures" in turn sustained the shipping capacity that helped Mercedes-Benz of Brazil begin exporting buses and trucks to Nigeria. In 1975 alone 3,330 Mercedes and Marco Polo trucks and buses were shipped to Nigeria.[20] Volkswagen's Nigerian production and imports from Brazil grew quickly. From the first shipment in January 1975 through October, 4,463 assembled and 6,132 CKD Volkswagens, with a value of $21.2 million, were sent to Nigeria.[21]

Within a few years Volkswagen of Brazil held a major share of the Nigerian automotive market. By 1977 one in three cars sold in Nigeria was a VW whose parts originated in Brazil. The cars ranged from VW Beetles to vans and Passat sedans. These were all German designs with one exception, a hatchback designed in Brazil called the Brasília. The car used an air-cooled engine similar to the Beetle's and in Nigeria was marketed as the Igala. This was one example of "tropical technology": the vehicle was known for being simple and rugged, having been designed for a country that still largely relied on dirt roads.[22] Despite the vehicles' commercial success, they were not marketed as Brazilian. Advertising for the vehicles simply presented them as sporty and modern, and renamed the Brasília as Igala, the name of a Nigerian ethnic group, stripped a clear Brazilian identifier from the one model that could justly be credited as Brazilian.

Brazilian Beef

A delegation from the Nigerian ministry of agriculture visited Brazil in 1975 to study its cattle industry. The oil boom had both intensified rural-to-urban migration and increased consumers' demand for meat. The delegation proposed an audacious plan to export Brazilian beef to Nigeria. To bypass the bottleneck at the port in Lagos, the Nigerian Meat and Livestock Authority would pay to fly the beef to market and would subsidize its price for Nigerians through its "Feed the Nation" program.[23] In Brazil a partnership between a rancher who owned the meatpacking company Cotia and Braspetro, a division of Petrobras, organized to supply the beef. The deal became a gateway for Cotia to become a diversified exporter and for efforts by Braspetro and its successor, Interbras, to offset the costs of Petrobras's oil imports.

Braspetro's involvement was a financial failure that spurred debate about the appropriateness of having the Brazilian government involved in business and the economy under military rule. Braspetro was the division of Petrobras responsible for foreign oil purchases, which made its director, Carlos Santana, acutely aware of the impact of Brazilian oil consumption on the country's balance-of-payments deficit. Braspetro began seeking ways of diminishing Brazil's trade deficits with the countries from which it imported oil by engaging in joint engineering and oil exploration projects, sharing refining and oil byproduct processing activities, and engaging in commodities trades, which brought dollars into Petrobras's accounts. By 1976 these commercial activities became important enough for Petrobras to divide the operations. Braspetro returned to oil imports and a new subsidiary, Interbras, would carry on Petrobras's other growing and increasingly complex financial transactions.

Between 1976 and 1979 Interbras initiated a series of failed commercial projects in Nigeria. In 1984 the journalist J. Carlos Assis used these as examples of state overreaching in the marketplace in his book *The Republic's Mandarins*, a reference to the bureaucratic class of imperial China. The director of Interbras, Santana, published a rebuttal, *Interbras: Fiction and Reality*. Together the two books provide a rare window into Brazilian trade with Nigeria. For Assis, Interbras's failures were an example of Brazilian governmental incompetence and inappropriate competition with the private sector. For Santana they were evidence of Brazil's broadening commercial presence abroad and of the need for the state to aid Brazilian businesses and shield them from the growing pains of establishing an export presence in Africa.

Cotia had the capacity to supply the Nigerian market, but it did not have the financial or commercial infrastructure to export, especially at the levels entailed by the Nigerian deal. Interbras (still Braspetro at the beginning of the deal) lent Cotia the capital to increase production, established the banking channel for Cotia to receive payments, negotiated the airfreight on Varig cargo planes, and oversaw the early meat shipments. As a sign of the vicissitudes of trade between Brazil and Nigeria, when the first Varig Boeing 707 was being loaded in Rio de Janeiro, President Murtala Muhammad of Nigeria was assassinated in a failed coup. The Lagos airport was closed and martial law declared. The Brazilian embassy telegrammed Brasília to say that all the Brazilian workers were reported safe, and that Pelé, who was in Lagos for a promotional event for

Pepsi-Cola, was secure in his hotel. The meat deal was significant enough, however, that the Nigerian minister of agriculture made arrangements for the airport (now named after Muhammad) to reopen for the arrival of the Varig plane and its cargo of beef.[24] Nearly every day for the rest of the year, a Varig 707 loaded with thirty-five tons of beef took off from Rio de Janeiro or São Paulo. There were 288 shipments, worth $22.5 million, in the first year. Santana reported that this was the largest cargo contract Varig had signed until then, and suggested that it laid the groundwork for the airline to begin passenger service to Lagos in the following year.[25]

In 1977 both Cotia and Interbras acted to renew the deal, but now they acted separately. Cotia signed a direct deal with the Nigerian Meat and Livestock Authority and Varig, and continued exporting meat for the next two years. In total Cotia sold almost twenty thousand tons of beef in Nigeria.[26] Meanwhile Interbras used its capital and organization to develop a logistically complex deal under which a pool of Brazilian producers provided beef that was shipped frozen to the port of Abidjan, Ivory Coast, which did not have the delays of the port in Lagos. The meat would be cold-stored in Abidjan, and shipments of it would be flown a thousand miles by Air Afrique to Lagos, where it would be distributed by the Lagos State Butchers' Cooperative. As part of the arrangement Interbras shipped four trucks to the Butcher's Cooperative to move the meat from the airport in Lagos into its distribution network.

Assis criticized the deal as an example of the state competing with private enterprise, suggesting that Interbras attempted to take business from Cotia to ease Petrobras's balance-of-payments deficit. Santana defended the arrangement by arguing that it provided an opportunity for a broader number of Brazilian meat producers and enabled Brazil to dominate a foreign market that had a capacity beyond what Cotia could satisfy. Regardless, the Interbras project was a disaster. The beef arrived in Abidjan and the trucks were delivered to the Lagos Butchers' Cooperative. The first shipment of beef was flown to Lagos and received by the Butcher's Cooperative, but no payment was made. Another shipment was sent, and again no payment was received. Assis explained: "According to the plan, if the butchers did not make the payments, the next delivery would be suspended. Still, the meter on the cold storage in Abidjan kept ticking and the Air Afrique contract had heavy penalties for cancellations, so Interbras paid whether or not there was a shipment. Lacking an alternative, Interbras preferred to advance another shipment of meat and continue the de-

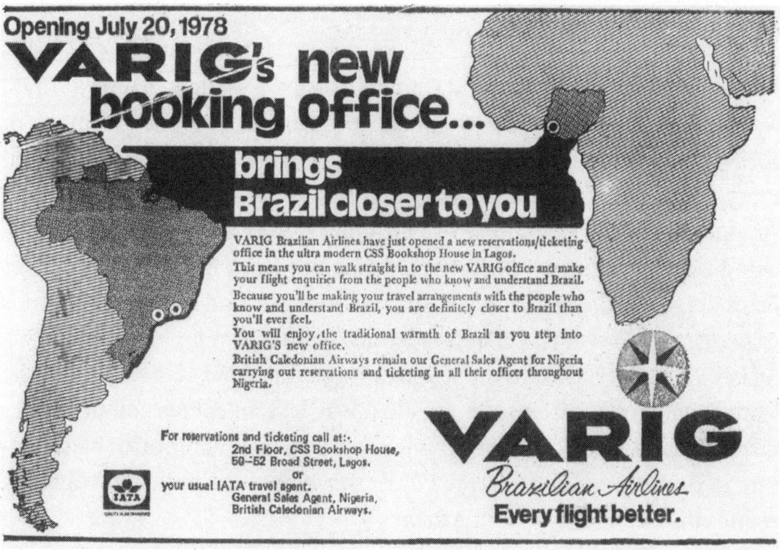

Varig advertisement emphasizing the proximity between Brazil and Nigeria.

liveries . . . [They] didn't pay again. Worse, the butchers absconded with the trucks." Soon after, the Nigerian government banned meat imports that did not have existing state licenses (which Cotia had and Interbras did not). Interbras sold the remaining stock of beef at a loss in Abidjan. Assis suggested that the scheme lost $3 million, while Santana estimated the loss at only $900,000, including the lost trucks.[27]

Cotia continued to thrive, contracting with the Nigerian government for projects that ranged from consulting for its ranching industry to setting up a network of cold-storage and meat processing facilities, which made the company a leading exporter of ceramic tile.[28] In 1977 it arranged for a pool of Brazilian pharmaceutical companies to ship medicine and supplies to Nigeria, "the first exports of Brazilian medicines to Africa."[29] By 1980 it had seven subsidiary companies operating in Nigeria. Alberto da Costa e Silva, then ambassador in Lagos, attended the inauguration of a Cotia soft drink plant, Drinco, which made soda from Brazilian guaraná concentrate. Costa e Silva remarked that the "sixty Brazilian workers [at Drinco], with their families, are imbued with a rare spirit of seriousness and a feeling that they are carrying out a pioneering effort of great interest to Brazil."[30]

Challenging Racial Democracy: FESTAC

The Festival of African Arts and Culture (FESTAC), held in Lagos in 1977, was an opportunity for the Nigerian government to evoke an image of African leadership sustained by oil profits. For the Brazilian government FESTAC was an opportunity to promote Brazil's Africanness and thus support the growing number of consumer goods and technical services being sold in Nigeria. The festival, which ran from mid-January to mid-February, drew thousands of artists, intellectuals, and activists to a series of performance events and an academic seminar that highlighted the African cultural presence in the world. Larger and more elaborate than the festival held in Dakar in 1966, FESTAC was less an expression of the negritude espoused by Léopold Senghor and more a celebration of black culture in the shadow of the Black Power movement overseas and Nigeria's economic ascendancy within Africa.

Unexpectedly, the Brazilian and Nigerian projects at FESTAC were reappropriated by exiled Brazilian intellectual Abdias do Nascimento. Stripped of his passport because of his militancy against Brazilian racial discrimination, Nascimento taught in the United States and at the time of the second FESTAC was a visiting professor at the University of Ife in Nigeria.[31] Excluded from the Brazilian delegation, which presented African culture as infusing a racially democratic Brazil, Nascimento attended the academic seminar at FESTAC to draw attention to discrimination in Brazil. Nascimento and the official Brazilian delegation clashed over the true nature of Brazilian society, debating whether racial democracy was a virtue or a fraud.

Nascimento approached the organizers of the seminar, seeking to present a paper that was subsequently published as the book *Brazil: Mixture or Massacre?* The paper challenged the dominant view that racial mixture was a means of racial integration, arguing that it was instead a means of "whitening" through which marginalization and intermarriage would gradually erase Brazil's black population. This argument increasingly found echoes in Brazil, where the regime suppressed studies of racial discrimination, and was consistent with the emerging scholarly consensus on Brazilian racial inequality and the "whitening" ideal. Nascimento's critique drew press attention in Lagos. Nigerian newspapers interviewed Nascimento and quoted his mimeographed paper. His protest led to an editorial in the leading Lagos newspaper, the *Daily Times*, cautioning that "wherever Africans and people of African descent live, be it in South

Africa or in Brazil, they must be accorded the respect and dignity due them as humans."[32]

Since Nascimento chose such a public forum to challenge Brazilian race relations, his participation in FESTAC spurred a campaign led by Itamaraty and supported by the Brazilian delegation to silence him and suppress his message. This campaign stretched from the Brazilian delegation and the embassy in Lagos to the halls of Itamaraty and even to President Geisel, who was briefed on Nascimento and the campaign against him. Brazilian diplomats kept Nascimento from formally participating in the FESTAC symposium. But persecuting him caused a backlash. Nascimento's cause was championed by the delegation from the United States and resonated in the press despite Brazilian efforts to have reporting on him censored.

A "black brother" within the embassy in Lagos shared with Nascimento copies of the classified diplomatic correspondence about him. Nascimento published a summary of these documents in a book on the confrontations at FESTAC entitled *Besieged in Lagos*. His account of persecution is so extreme that it almost seems implausible. Yet I was able to find the documents he summarized, and others beyond the ones he was given, at the Itamaraty archives and the papers of Foreign Minister Silveira. Together they confirm his account of the Brazilian government's efforts to silence him. But just as Nascimento was aided by informants, so too was the Brazilian government, which counted on information about Nascimento's intent to present the critical text at FESTAC from another Brazilian visiting professor at the University of Ife who was sponsored by Itamaraty.[33]

Ambassador Heráclito Lima first learned of Nascimento's presence in Nigeria in October 1976, when the Senegalese ambassador in Lagos commented to him that a Brazilian with travel documents from the United States had approached him for a visa to visit Senegal, where he hoped to meet with President Senghor. Standing together at the Nigerian independence day parade, the Senegalese ambassador asked Heráclito Lima "whether the Government of Brazil has something against Mr. Abdias do Nascimento." He sought information on "the refugee Nascimento." On vacation in Brazil, "checking with the competent authorities," Heráclito Lima "learned that it was a case of a man of color, agitator, member of the Integralist Party, and having a record as a member of the Communist Party."[34] Heráclito Lima took preventive measures. He ensured that the Brazilian delegation already had the maximum number of representatives (meaning that no other Brazilians could participate), and he informed the heads of the Brazilian delegation that "it was important for our foreign policy to maintain the image that Brazil is the only country in the world that has managed to build a multi-racial society without clash or conflict, a belief I hold personally and which is one of the great universal contributions of Brazil."[35]

Both in newspaper interviews, and from his seat in the audience of FESTAC events, Nascimento questioned the legitimacy of the Brazilian delegation. He argued that it was not representative of Brazilian society or of black Brazilians, and was a mouthpiece of the dictatorship, repeating the false doctrine that the country was a racial democracy.[36] At the sessions on African influences on Brazilian culture, Nascimento used the discussion periods, in the words of Ambassador Heráclito Lima, to "intervene violently and to theatrically condemn 'white minority domination' in Brazil." One delegate, Fernando Mourão, responded that the theme of the symposium was African cultural and linguistic influence in Brazil, and that this "scientific" discussion precluded "political" debates.[37]

Nascimento's objective was to compel the organizers of the academic symposium to acknowledge racial discrimination in Brazil in the symposium's final report, and to have the report call for an international commission to investigate race relations in Brazil.[38] As Brazilian delegates and diplomats labored to keep Nascimento's challenge out of the symposium's report and out of the press, members of the United States delegation rallied to keep him and his work visible. Delegates from the United States helped Nascimento distribute *Mixture or Massacre?*[39] At the closing ceremonies, the head of the delegation from the United States, Ron Karenga, "attacked the Brazilian delegation as part of the white majority that oppresses the blacks."[40]

African representatives seized upon the questions raised by Nascimento and included in the final report of the conference a recommendation for a commission to investigate race relations in Brazil. They rejected objections by the Brazilian delegation: if Brazil was truly a racial democracy, was there anything to fear?[41] The Brazilian government intensified its campaign to silence Nascimento. To placate the Brazilian diplomats, Minister of Education Ahmed Ali gave an interview to the *Daily Times* in which he described Nascimento's text as "outside of 'academic consideration' . . . [and] 'propaganda.'" What is more, the government also agreed to prevent Nascimento's text, or the resolution to investigate Brazilian race relations, from appearing in the final report of the symposium.[42]

Heráclito Lima worried about Nascimento's motives and the motives for his support from the delegation from the United States. He wrote to the foreign ministry: "I have the impression that black American groups are orchestrating a campaign . . . to use FESTAC to defame Brazil in the United States and world press, for the benefit of a domestic audience, making Brazil rather than the United States into the 'execrable' country that possesses 'a new form of apartheid.'"[43] He wrote a letter to the editor, submitted for review to Itamaraty.[44] In the letter, he described Nascimento as

> living for more than ten years in the USA, where he is, under the cover of giving lectures, working as a political activist, with dubious groups engaged in protest against racial segregation . . . Mr. Abdias do Nascimento's contradictions are so blatant that it would be innocuous to answer them. The backbone of his papers is the contention that the Brazilian melting pot, its miscegenation by intermarriage, the absence of separate quarters for African, Italian, German, Portuguese, Japanese descendants is a subtle way of destroying the black race; acts of racial integration which Mr. Abdias do Nascimento has the audacity to call "genocide," offending 90% of the Brazilian population—a happy result and example to the world—of a successful intermingling of all Brazilians, most of them with Indian, Black, European and Asiatic blood. The best way of judging Mr. Nascimento is to read his own papers. He himself is a living contradiction to his thesis, since he has married twice—a Brazilian white lady and now, at the age of 62, he persistently commits "genocide" by being wed to a 19 year old American blonde.[45]

Heráclito Lima went on to describe Nascimento as "a laughing stock" who "might be mentally unbalanced," and concluded: "The Brazilian Embassy is confident that no Nigerian will be taken for a ride, since Brazil is known all over the world and quoted by thousands of political and social scientists as a country able to build a multiracial civilization . . . nobody has ever heard of racial troubles or conflicts in Brazil."[46] Heráclito Lima held strategy meetings with the Brazilian academic delegates in his office, and in the end they dissuaded him from publishing the letter, to avoid fanning the controversy.

With a mind to silencing rather than challenging Nascimento, Heráclito Lima asked the representatives of Mendes Junior, a Brazilian construction company with business in Nigeria, to use their "public relations" to "block the interviews with Abdias in the newspapers."[47] At this point President Geisel learned of the confrontation in Lagos. Silveira briefed him on Nascimento's advocacy at the conference and on the arguments of

Mixture or Massacre? Silveira reported that he had instructed the diplomats in Nigeria to complain to the Nigerian foreign and education ministries. The education minister agreed to block Nascimento's actions, if necessary by appealing to the Nigerian president directly. Meanwhile, Ambassador Heráclito Lima's appeals to the minister of education bore fruit: "[I] received word from a mutual friend that Colonel [Minister] Ali wanted me to know that I could relax and that the Inspector General of the Police was going to investigate the terms under which Abdias do Nascimento was present in Nigeria."[48] Heráclito Lima concluded the affair by suggesting that the foreign ministry needed to more actively promote Brazilian race relations abroad, perhaps by putting together a magazine on racial and ethnic relations. To make the magazine seem legitimate, it should not only look at the black experience but also reflect on the "Syrian-Lebanese, the Italians, the Poles, the Germans, the Indians, the Portuguese and the Japanese."[49]

Paying Attention

Nascimento provided an alternative narrative about race relations that clashed with the official Brazilian message which fit an increasingly critical line of reporting about Brazil in the Nigerian press. Criticism ranged from discussion of racial inequality to complaints about the quality of Brazilian goods and services in the Nigerian market, and to questions about Brazil's motives in Africa and whether the "Brazilian miracle" was an appropriate model for Nigeria. An article in *New Nigerian*, a news magazine, captured these misgivings: "Approach with Caution: Nigeria-Brazil Relations." The article presented the Brazilian economic miracle as the outcome of western imperialism and authoritarian repression, asserting that "the recent rapprochement between the Nigerian ruling classes and the Brazilian dictatorship is terribly disturbing."[50]

As companies like Volkswagen took root, they were followed by Brazilian banks, which were in turn followed by Interbras. In 1977 Varig Airlines established passenger service between Lagos and Rio, with an inaugural flight that carried the Nigerian ministers of industry, housing, urban development, and agriculture to Rio.[51] By 1980 Varig would add a leg from Lagos to Luanda.[52] Brazilian consulting firms were involved in developing reforestation, cattle ranching, pig raising, cold storage, telecommunications, and the steel industry.[53]

The Brazilian presence caught the attention of Nigerian authorities. In 1976 the Nigerian foreign minister hosted a seminar at the Nigerian Institute of International Affairs on the "Nigeria-Angola-Brazil Axis." One of the presenters asked, "How best can Nigeria employ Brazil's new enthusiasm in this continent?" He recommended that Nigeria "resist attempts to sustain Brazil's economic interest without necessarily becoming a dumping ground for some Brazilian inferior manufactures. Our present stage of development—particularly our keen interest to improve telecommunication services and roads construction has invited some Brazilian construction firms . . . We must encourage Brazil's adventurism into areas where they can effectively compete with other foreign firms."[54] Another panelist agreed: "Nigeria should not for any reason be considered a dumping ground for Brazilian products."[55]

The *Daily Times* published an editorial on the proceedings of the conference, picking up concern by the panelists that Brazil was not truly an autonomous political and economic power but a kind of subimperialist agent of European and United States multinational companies (like Volkswagen). The *Daily Times* reminded readers of Brazil's past support of "fascist" Portugal's "genocidal colonial wars," and concluded that "it would be wishful thinking that . . . Brazil could be influenced to modify her domestic policies to become more liberal towards the black population of Brazil."[56]

Meanwhile criticism of Brazilian products mounted. There were complaints about the reliability of the Brazilian Volkswagens assembled in Nigeria, for example. In April and May 1978 the *Daily Times* published three articles on problems with Volkswagen vehicles assembled in Nigeria. One criticized the Igala for "frequent overheating because water is not used in the cooling system," adding that "engine parts are not as durable as in other cars." There were also complaints about faulty wiring and reports of the car catching fire.[57] Similarly, the Volkswagen Passat made one commentator "battle with one kind of problem or the other . . . Sometimes the heat gets so much I am tempted to park and leap out of the car . . . should we be paying so much for 'lemons'?"[58]

Some of this criticism was directed at Brazilian engineering firms responsible for expanding the Lagos telephone network. By March 1976 a group of Brazilian companies had secured a series of lucrative contracts. Hidroservice and Promon had contracts totaling $28 million to inspect communications equipment imported from Europe; Protec-Sobratel had a contract for $20.9 million to maintain the telephone system in Lagos; Graham Bell of Brazil was finalizing a contract for $20.8 million to upgrade telephone switching stations. Altogether, there were $120 million in contracts under way or under negotiation at the time.[59]

These contracts made Brazilian firms the target of Nigerians' frustration when they picked up their phones and didn't get a dial tone. The *Daily Times* published an editorial in February 1978 entitled "Dead Telephones," in which it related: "Two years ago, the P and T signed a contract with some foreign interests for the revamping of telephone services in the country. Despite the contract, our telephone services still remain as unreliable as before. Several people have questioned the slow pace at which the Brazilians are working and it is being argued that perhaps, if they were working faster, things could have improved as promised."[60] Heráclito Lima commented that Nigerians wrongly believed the Brazilians to be responsible for the poor telephone service in Lagos: "Few understand that the Brazilian companies are consultants: they do inspections to verify that the machines sent by the large foreign companies (ITT, Siemens, Marubeni, Westinghouse, etc) are manufactured according to Nigerian Government standards. What causes the poor public impression is the work of Protec-Sobratel and Graham Bell. The first is responsible for managing the old network in Lagos, and the other for laying the new network. 180 to 200 Brazilians work day and night to keep the telephones talking, and face every difficulty imaginable: lines that are restored only to have delivery trucks or regular cars crash into the poles, or restored lines that connect to aging, malfunctioning and overburdened switching stations. Or pirate lines that connect who knows how . . . All of this frustrates a public that just wants to have the phones work."[61]

When President Carter visited Nigeria in 1978 the *Daily Times* criticized the Brazilian telecommunications contractors, noting that during President Eisenhower's visit to Brasília in 1960 the United States government had sent a telephone exchange to support the Americans' communications: "By an irony or fate, another United States president plans to visit Nigeria. Lagos has no telephone system to boast of; and Brazilians have been hired to make the phones function."[62] Heráclito Lima believed the article was "part of a campaign organized against Brazilian firms that are working with the Nigerian ministry of communications, carried out by companies that are not having their commercial interests served."[63] Was there a campaign against Brazilian businesses? Heráclito Lima's judgment about Brazilian goods being driven from the market by foreign companies buying bad press was an opinion formed by someone who had used the "public relations" of Mendes Júnior to silence the press on Abdias do Nascimento.

Tama

Even Pelé became the subject of Nigerian press criticism when he arrived in Lagos in April 1978 for a twelve-day tour as a spokesperson for Tama. An editorial in the *Daily Times* declared Pelé's trip "purely a business affair" (which it was). Ambassador Heráclito Lima again saw the hand of competing companies behind the criticism: "As I have discovered, the news was inserted by European rivals who are worried about the volume of sales that has already taken place."[64] According to the *Daily Times*:

> From all accounts, the recent appearance in this country of soccer star Pelé was less than sporting. What most people here did not realize is that the overweight superstar was in Nigeria for business not pleasure, and thus gave the boot to Nigerians' expectations of a football fiesta. To be precise, King Pelé was here on a . . . promotional campaign for TAMA, a team of Brazilian exporters hastily grouped together by the economically hard-pressed regime of General Geisel of Brazil. This group represents firms of various industrial competences, so that one cannot guarantee that this TAMA product is as good or as bad as the next.
>
> The question to ask here is whether the Nigerian Standards Organization or the ministry of trade have tested these products to make sure that they are suited for the Nigerian market or any other market for that matter.
>
> The association of a Lebanese "Nigerian" with the promotion cannot be said to be entirely reassuring. As far as I can find out, the gentleman's business expertise consists in running gaming houses, night clubs and race horses. But if horse racing gives him a sporting edge to host Pelé, methinks it is just not cricket to flood the unsuspecting Nigerian market with untested products.
>
> Anyone for a leak-proof Brazilian battery?[65]

Tama was a project developed by Carlos Santana to develop export capabilities for Brazilian manufactured consumer goods. He reasoned that individual Brazilian manufacturers did not have the export experience, local distribution networks, or marketing resources to place their products abroad. He believed that Interbras could provide the umbrella for independent manufacturers to sell their goods to oil-exporting countries and

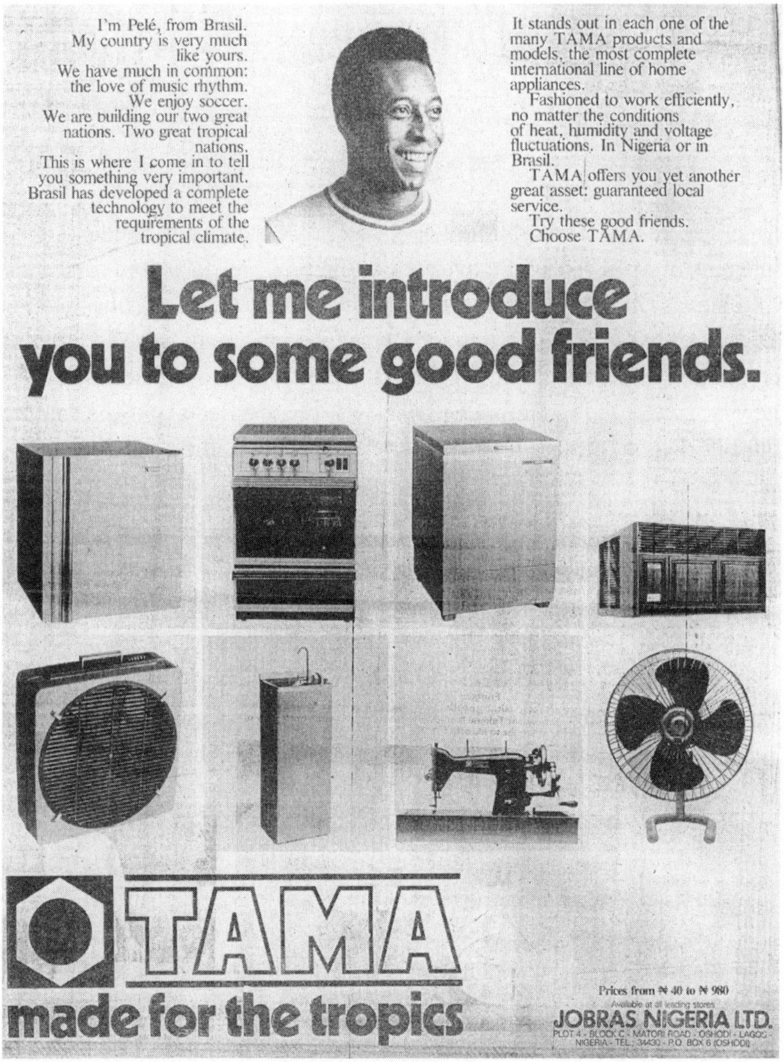

Pelé, in a Tama advertisement for "tropical technology."

to Africa in general. Interbras created the brand named Tama, defined a set of common specifications, and invited Brazilian manufacturers of refrigerators, fans, air conditioners, sewing machines, alarm clocks, and a dozen other goods to furnish them. Interbras would collect them at a port warehouse in São Paulo and ship them to Nigeria. In Nigeria, Interbras created an integrated distribution system, with a warehouse and repair center in Lagos, English-language literature, manuals, and technical documents, and distribution facilities across the country. It would arrange placement in Nigerian stores and handle the unified marketing of the entire Tama line.

Santana explained that "the idea was basically to look at consumer markets in the Third World, and its point of departure was that these products, in Brazil, incorporate modifications that make them more resistant to typical conditions of developing countries, like fluctuations in current, rough handling, climatic extremes (heat and humidity), and the deficiency of technical assistance."[66] Nigeria was a prime market for these goods because in 1976 it imported $36 million in appliances and $100 million in small electrical and electronic goods, and the number of homes in Nigeria with electricity was increasing at a rate of 18 percent a year. According to Santana, by 1976 "the Nigerian worker was the best paid in West Africa, and the country was going through a consumer boom. Everything was imported from everywhere."[67]

In early 1978, while goods began arriving at the port in Brazil, Interbras assembled a massive marketing campaign for Tama. It spent $1.2 million on advertising and marketing (one-quarter of which for Pelé). This bought 340 commercial spots on television and 2,070 on radio, as well as billboards in 400 locations in Lagos. A forty-five-minute infomercial about Brazil, assembled with TV Globo footage, was broadcast during prime time.[68] Full-page ads ran, sometimes daily, in newspapers across Nigeria. Unlike Volkswagens, which did not advertise their Brazilian origins, Tama was selling Brazil, from Pelé's image to the slogan "Tama—Made for the Tropics."[69] A sewing machine ad offered: "The tropical fashion machine," while ads for the full product line promised:

> Tama: home appliances for the tropics.
> The only international line of electronic home appliances specially tailored to meet the stress of tropical heat and humidity.
> A technology specially developed for this purpose.
> Tested at the source: a tropical country, Brazil.

> Tama is air conditioners, refrigerators, water coolers, sound equipment, electric irons, meat grinders, mixers, blenders, sewing machines.
> These and many other products, in many models.
> All of them manufactured to work beautifully in a hot, tropical climate like Nigeria's.
> Able to stand up against the most sudden changes in voltage.
> Carrying a warranty for local service.
> That is why you can depend on TAMA.[70]

Each of these ads featured Pelé wearing a football jersey reading, "Tama." He was the face of Brazilian "tropical technology."

For his part, Pelé performed admirably, as even Assis conceded, the criticism of the *Daily Times* notwithstanding. The Varig DC-10 that carried him and the Fluminense football team arrived to an eager crowd at Murtala Muhammad Airport (perhaps as a Varig cargo plane carrying tons of meat taxied in the distance). Pelé greeted the crowd and held a press conference, which was reported on the front page of the *Daily Times*. He and Fluminense played three exhibition games. The first filled National Stadium beyond its capacity of seventy thousand. Pelé thrilled the crowd by running onto the field in a Brazilian national team jersey, pulling it off to reveal the jersey of the Nigerian team, and playing with the Nigerians. For the match, Pelé was Nigerian.[71] The press reported that not even for FESTAC had there been such a crowd. The publicity paid off, and in the first months of sales Nigerians bought $2.2 million worth of Tama products.

The success was short-lived. As oil prices dropped in the months before the second oil shock, the Nigerian government imposed import restrictions barring almost all products sold under the Tama brand. Wayne Selcher explains: "The venture was thwarted after initial early success because of errors in marketing, choice of Nigerian partners, and the way the failure of a small number of products detracted from the image of the line as a whole. 'Tama' was also unable to adapt to the pressure to manufacture locally as import substitution policies were adopted in Nigeria stemming from the oil slump."[72] Interbras and its Nigerian distribution partner tried in vain to keep the market open by attempting to manufacture refrigerators in Nigeria.[73]

The approach belatedly proposed by Interbras was the model that had worked for Cotia, which exported meat while providing technical assistance on the production of an integrated cattle and meat-processing industry. In this sense Cotia was a better fit for the Nigerian market, since the government had development ideas that were similar to those carried out by the Brazilian government in its own economic planning. The Nigerian government welcomed imports as part of a process to develop national production capacity. Cotia understood this, adapting into a company that exported the materials used to make facilities in Nigeria to produce the very product it had exported. Interbras worked differently: it was a Brazilian development project that relied on Nigeria as a consumer, placing it at odds with Nigeria's own development plans.

In the end Interbras sold $6.7 million in appliances in Nigeria and lost $2.5 million on the venture.[74] J. Carlos Assis saw the Tama project as an example of corruption and incompetence. He pointed to goods delivered with the wrong plugs and voltage, and suggested that across its dealings Interbras's partners, from the shipping company to the Nigerian distributor, were taking advantage of the naïveté of the Brazilians. For his part, Santana argued that the experience launched a brand that continued to sell in nine other African countries, from Senegal to Angola. He reflected that "Petrobras is Brazil's biggest buyer," which gave it the latitude to support deals like the sale of 55,000 Tama refrigerators in Algeria in exchange for phosphates, the construction of a $1.3 billion railroad in Iraq, and the sale of soy and steel to Iran.[75] According to Santana, $32 million in Tama products were sold in twenty-seven countries between 1978 and 1985.[76]

Like Tama, the Brazilian export drive to Nigeria was short-lived. In the early 1980s it declined under the weight of indebtedness, economic turmoil, and political upheaval in both Nigeria and Brazil. High interest rates saddled both countries with onerous debt payments abroad, while slowing the world economy and depressing the price of oil, further hampering Nigeria's ability to import. At the time Selcher wrote: "In 1982, Brazil-Black Africa economic relations fell upon difficulties that will persist for at least a number of years. Progress has been blocked by the onset of more serious economic difficulties on both sides, mounting debts, international recession, and lower commodity prices. For example, Nigeria's oil prosperity and its development ambitions as the leading regional power have fallen into disarray since the world oil market collapse due to oversupply."[77] He added: "Most of the political and economic impetus in the relationship between Africa and Brazil was initiated by Brazil under the assumption that Africa represented a long-run growth market worth the high short-run costs and efforts." Santana, like Heráclito Lima and Silveira, believed that these costs were worth the long-term rewards, though the rewards did not materialize in the twentieth century.

Epilogue

IN THE WAKE OF A MASSACRE in the Nova Holanda favela in Rio de Janeiro in February 2000, police repeated a rumor that the perpetrators were Angolan refugees adapting guerrilla tactics into the drug trade. In a city besieged by spiraling violence, the image of veteran African combatants, armed with AK-47 assault rifles, bringing tactics with names like "suicide trolley" and "Soviet attack" to the predominantly black drug gangs resonated with racialized foreboding in Rio's newspapers.[1] The state military police launched an investigation into Angolan participation in gang warfare; 850 police entered the favela complex to question and create records of the Angolans living there, but the police admitted finding no evidence that Angolans had been involved in the violence. The Angolan refugees gathered in protest outside the police station where the investigation was being coordinated. They complained that the rumors and the investigation increased the prejudice they experienced. One explained: "[I'm a] refugee, Angolan, black, I live in a favela. Does anybody think that makes it easy for me to get a job? And on top of that I am now a mercenary? Because of this story, two of my colleagues have lost their jobs."[2]

While Brazil's leaders held hope in 1975 that newly independent Angola would become its commercial and political gateway into Africa, the Angolan civil war that lasted until 2003 eroded much of that potential. Instead Brazilian relations with Angola were shaped by the war. In the 1990s a company of Brazilian army engineers took part in a United

Nations peacekeeping mission, clearing minefields.[3] Brazil became home to Angolan war refugees. Of the 2,700 refugees in Brazil in 2001, the majority were Angolan, followed in number by Liberians.[4] By 2007 there were 1,750 Angolan refugees in Brazil, along with other Angolans living there illegally.[5] Angolan refugees received modest assistance (a monthly stipend of less than $100 from the Catholic Archdiocese of Rio de Janeiro) and congregated in poor neighborhoods in the city center or in favelas. Even when the secretary of public safety in Rio de Janeiro acknowledged that Angolans had not been involved in the massacre, he insisted that "though there is no proven involvement [in drug gangs] now, it is absolutely certain that over time there will be."[6]

The unfounded rumor and investigation drew national attention that included an editorial critical of the police in the newspaper *Folha de S. Paulo*, declaring that "the truculent action resulted in mistreatment and humiliation for the Angolans living in the favela and caused a diplomatic incident. The Angolan Consulate in Rio de Janeiro now demands a just apology. The police action was also a demonstration of racism, a lack of compassion, and a disregard for the rule of law."[7] The editorial concluded that "at a moment in which we see the return of the ghost of xenophobia in wealthy and developed Europe . . . this is an excellent opportunity for Brazil to show its virtues—which truly exist in this area—and demonstrate itself on the world stage as a nation in which intolerance, one of the plagues of the century, does not rule."[8] Curiously, the editorial characterized the episode as both an act of racism and an example for the world that Brazil was immune to racism. Africa—or in this case a group of African refugees—was yet again a stage on which a benign national self-image was projected, even in the face of acknowledged racial discrimination.

At the beginning of the twenty-first century "Africa" remained an abstraction for Brazilians, as it had been for decades, and a stage upon which questions about Brazilian race relations and national identity were interpreted. The period between 1960 and 1980 was a kind of golden age for Brazilian relations with African countries. It began with the enthusiasm generated by the decolonization of Africa and the sense of change and possibility that it brought. This enthusiasm translated into substantive but short-lived political and economic connections in the mid-1970s that declined abruptly with the Brazilian debt crisis in the 1980s. In an example of this decline, in 2008 an Itamaraty briefing paper on Brazilian relations with Africa followed a three-page description of relations during the 1970s with a single sentence on the 1980s and 1990s: "the relationship with Africa decelerated due to the effects of the second oil crisis, the Brazilian [debt] moratorium and the Asiatic crisis."[9]

Decline and Contradiction

In 1982, as President General João Baptista Figueiredo of Brazil prepared to visit President Ronald Reagan, *Veja* reported that "the *terceiromundismo* [third-worldism] and the Africanist policies of Itamaraty have frequently translated in the day-to-day of Brazilian diplomatic action into anti-Americanism . . . This might not have been significant in times of economic prosperity, but with Brazil needing ever more international resources and good commercial relations with the countries where the money is, these disagreements have become problematic. Several Brazilian ministers have even suggested that there is not a problem between Brazil and the United States, there is a problem between Itamaraty diplomats and the United States."[10]

For a decade Brazil's military dictatorship had worked to build economic and political autonomy from the United States by developing ties with African countries. But Figueiredo's trip to Washington came at a moment when the Brazilian government risked defaulting on the largest foreign debt in the developing world, and at the cusp of a crisis that devastated its economy and wrecked its currency for the next decade. The crisis, a combined result of the second oil shock of the late 1970s, government spending, and a vertiginous rise in interest rates, called into question the rhetoric of Brazil's emergence as a world power autonomous of the United States. As *Veja* suggested, "Itamaraty emphasized differences with the developed world and privileged relations with the Third World in general and African countries in particular." This now caused conflicts in its relations with the countries through which Brazil's "vital economic arteries flow."[11]

The article in *Veja* marked the end of an age that can be measured in trade and diplomats. Brazilian trade with Africa peaked in 1984, at 7.9 percent of exports. By 1990 exports to Africa declined to 3 percent.[12] Trade withered under the weight of the debt crisis on both Brazil and Africa, where the capacity to import was cut in half between 1979 and 1991.[13] These exports had been supported by lines of credit which the Brazilian government could no longer provide and African governments could no longer repay. Part of Africa's debt burden consisted of defaulted loans from Brazil. Another way to measure the decline in relations is by looking at the number of Brazilian diplomats posted to African nations, which shrank from thirty-four to twenty-four between 1983 and 1993, even as the number of diplomats posted abroad increased from 362 to 418.[14]

The era was also characterized by a persistent contradiction that was invoked by a naval officer who questioned Foreign Minister Silveira after an address to the Naval War College. The officer asked: "Isn't there a conflict between Brazil's internal and foreign policies with regard to combatting communism?"[15] This contradiction was lived by leftist Brazilian exiles who moved to Angola and Mozambique to participate in nation-building projects within the two Marxist countries supported by the Brazilian dictatorship that had persecuted and in some cases sought to kill them for their political beliefs.

The contradiction extended into Brazil as well, where relations with Angola created an opening for the types of political and critical dialogues that had been suppressed under military rule. The expansion of Brazil's external influence was tempered by pressure against the systematic violation of human rights by the Brazilian police and segments of the military. The regime's repression reached all segments of society. Hundreds were killed, thousands were tortured, and tens of thousands were jailed by a regime that employed the rhetoric of democracy as it governed arbitrarily and ruled through fear. The bureaucratization of the dictatorship and its rhetoric could be seen even in small details, like a hand stamp that sat on the desks of intelligence agents, who officiously pounded its message onto the streams of paper that passed before them: "The 1964 Revolution is irreversible and will consolidate democracy in Brazil."[16]

In 1975 Geisel created a task force to find ways to limit the damage that human rights violations were having on Brazil's international image and foreign relations. The task force reported that "the replacement of regimes that had earlier absorbed much of the international criticism (like Greece and Portugal), as well as the end of colonialism, help free up energy for addressing human rights."[17] But with the end of colonialism, Brazil could also count on new allies as it blocked human rights pressure. In 1976 Brazilian diplomats at the United Nations Human Rights Commission succeeded in shelving a report on abuses in Brazil after winning the votes of Nigeria, Rwanda, Sierra Leone, Tanzania, and Upper Volta. In the following year an attempt by "developed countries" to reopen the question by a UN subcommission failed, "thanks in large part to the support again received by developing countries," including Ghana.[18]

After 1977 President Carter's administration fulfilled a campaign pledge to promote human rights in countries like Brazil. Geisel's government saw Carter's criticism of Brazilian human rights violations as an effort to reassert influence over Brazil, and it responded by depicting the United States as a nation in decline. When Secretary of State Cyrus Vance visited Brazil in 1977, one of the briefing documents prepared at Itamaraty stated that "the diversification of Brazilian foreign policy responds to true national interests, apart from our relationship with the United States, which has shown itself incapable of renewal."[19] In fact, as Itamaraty presented the question, "the U.S. Government does not seem fully aware of the new weight of Brazil in the international system . . . Brazil is arriving at an international *status* that is different from mere formal independence. It will take time for all of the segments of Brazilian society, not to mention other nations, adapt to this new reality."[20]

In 1977 First Lady Rosalynn Carter visited Brazil and pressured Geisel on human rights. According to Elio Gaspari, Geisel was indignant about being lectured by the wife of a president. When Carter inveighed against Brazil's human rights record Geisel responded: "The fact that better than any other reflects the profound Brazilian respect for human rights is the absence of racial and religious prejudice. Brazil is really perhaps an example to the world, with its multi-racial society coexisting in harmony. We have legislation that has been in place for many years, and which severely punishes any racist tendencies. We are a free country that respects freedom." Carter acknowledged there were still problems in this area in the United States but contended that the country had done much in recent years to remedy them. The terse exchange ended their meeting.[21]

1st Lady Carter & President clash

Pressure from the United States pushed Brazil away. In 1977, when the U.S. Congress began reviewing human rights conditions as precondition for renewing military agreements with foreign countries, Geisel's government canceled the Military Assistance Agreement that had been in place between the two countries since 1957. Gradually the Brazilian government ended other United States government programs, for example expelling the Peace Corps. Another United States entity expelled was the Inter-American Foundation (IAF). The IAF annually spent $3.5 million funding social and cultural projects in Brazil, some of which were in communities of descendants of runaway slaves or were otherwise concerned with race relations. The IAF was expelled "for creating racial tensions in Brazil by mobilizing groups of black Brazilians" and "supporting activities that are foreign to Brazilian culture, altering the climate of racial tolerance that exists here."[22] The expulsion of the IAF fit the pattern of Brazilian government hostility to United States aid projects in Brazil in response to pressure on human rights. But it also fit a pattern of defending racial democracy from foreign and domestic criticism.

In 1978 the Brazilian tourism agency Embratur sought Itamaraty's support for an event being organized in Brazil by a United States travel agency, called the First World Festival of the African Diaspora. The festival combined academic, cultural, and artistic activities and brought African Americans to Salvador and Rio de Janeiro to experience black Brazilian culture. The festival became a subject of discussion between Geisel and Silveira, who sought the authority to block government support for the event. Embratur supported the festival because it opened the doors to "capturing the potential of black tourists from the United States." But Silveira argued that an event about the "African diaspora" was problematic: "That denomination indicates that the Festival is inspired by a vision of the black problem that is incompatible with the traditions of Brazilian society and the position of the Brazilian government. In fact, we do not accept that the idea of a 'diaspora' is applicable to Brazilians of the black race. Diaspora is a concept that in its true sense belongs to a cultural and religious tradition that is totally different." He highlighted the differences between Brazil and the United States: "Our society is organized not only against discrimination, but also in favor of racial integration." Silveira opposed the event not only because it was incompatible with Brazilian culture but also out of concern that "during the Festival, criticisms [might be] made against the Brazilian racial situation, from the point of view of black cultural 'emancipation.'"[23]

That the concept of the "African diaspora" was incompatible with Brazilian society is curious but meaningful. Though Brazilian diplomats in Africa had lauded Brazil's connections to the continent, the term "African diaspora" implied a connection between peoples of African descent across countries of the Americas, suggesting that they shared an experience transcending national boundaries. Here lay Silveira's critique, since he and other Brazilian diplomats, intellectuals, and even Geisel, when he refused the United States request for "black sergeants," insisted that Africans were racially and culturally integrated in Brazilian society. In this sense there were no blacks in Brazil who were not first Brazilians, and there were no Brazilians who were not black. This criticism mirrored the one made by Gilberto Freyre in 1963, when he declared that "'Africanists' . . . pretend even to create in Brazil a figure that does not sociologically exist:

the black Brazilian. A black that is substantially black and only adjectively Brazilian."[24]

Change and Continuity

In the context of Brazil's redemocratization after 1985, both race relations and the basis for relations with Africa changed. Though during the 1960s and 1970s there had been little political mobilization or engagement in policy toward Africa on the part of black Brazilians, by the end of the dictatorship a black political movement gained momentum in challenging racial inequality and pressuring for changes in public policy, including foreign relations. In the late 1970s black Brazilian activists coalesced around challenges to the military regime's defense of racial democracy, and became advocates for a broader social and political redemocratization. While the energies of these activists were at first directed toward Brazilian challenges, by the 1990s growing black political consciousness became more expansive in asserting connections between their struggle for racial equality and the Brazilian relationship with Africa.[25]

After the 1970s the meaning of a common refrain, "Brazil owes a debt to Africa," changed from an expression of gratitude into a recognition of the cost of the slave trade to Africans, as well as the impact of slavery and subsequent discrimination on the descendants of Africans in Brazil. One diplomat, Rubens Ricupero, captured that changing tone in 1986 when he appeared before the Congressional Committee on Foreign Relations and said that relations with Africa "demand a transformation of Brazil itself. So long as our society continues divided by intolerable imbalance in wealth and income . . . it will be hard for us to really face that debt . . . we have to be conscious of the need to transform Brazilian society, so that government and society give the black population the conditions to realize itself."[26] In 2006 he reflected on that discussion, recalling: "We really needed to change Brazil before doing anything with Africa. I am still convinced of that today . . . Brazil cannot pay its debt to Africa, because it is unpayable . . . what we must do is begin to pay that debt here, to the descendants of Africa. That was, and remains, the contradiction inherent in our policies."[27]

In the 1990s black militancy, a growing recognition of racial inequality, and changes in Brazil's political leadership combined to change public policy with regard to race. The idea of racial democracy was replaced by an understanding that Brazil was profoundly unequal and that the state had a mandate to remedy the inequality. The conflict between the past rhetoric of racial democracy and contemporary black political mobilization against racial inequality was inadvertently highlighted by Nelson Mandela when he visited Brazil shortly after being released from prison. Mandela shocked black Brazilian activists, for whom his fight against apartheid had been an inspiration, when he declared his intention to make South Africa into a country that resembled Brazil in its race relations. One activist captured the reaction: "Many of us turned up our noses at this because we were just at the beginning of demolishing the perverse myth of racial democracy, which for many years paralyzed us, preventing a more honest recognition of race relations and, above all, punishing blacks."[28]

President Fernando Henrique Cardoso (1994–2002) became Brazil's first national leader to recognize the existence of racial inequality and to enact policies intended to promote integration. Much like earlier affirmations of racial democracy, the new initiatives about racial integration within Brazil were often projected against an African backdrop. For instance, in 2000 President Cardoso took advantage of a visit by President Thabo Mbeki of South Africa to describe himself as having "a foot in the kitchen" (a colloquial expression referring to sexual mixture between his white family and its black servants) and to affirm that "the Brazilian state still has a lot to do in order to ensure that the black majority of the population has full access to the process of democratization of rights and social guarantees . . . repairing the damage done by centuries of oppression, prejudice and discrimination is an obligation of the State."[29] Consistent with this pattern, Cardoso's administration used the UN World Conference against Racism in Durban, South Africa, in 2001 as the setting for introducing racial quota and affirmative action policies in public sector hiring and university admissions.

The new policies included a scholarship program for black candidates to the Itamaraty training academy, the Rio Branco Institute. When the scholarship program was created in 2002 President Cardoso criticized Itamaraty's "notable lack of diversity" and called the diplomatic corps "monochromatic."[30] By the beginning of the administration of Luis Inácio "Lula" da Silva in 2003, the Brazilian federal government and many municipal and state governments were introducing quota and affirmative action programs. They also established cabinet positions to confront questions of race relations, like SEPPIR, the Special Presidential Secretariat for the Promotion of Racial Equality.

In 2003 the Brazilian Congress passed a law requiring public and private schools to teach the "history of Africa and Africans, the black struggle in Brazil, black Brazilian culture and the role of blacks in social, economic and political aspects of the history of Brazil."[31] Just as all but the most stereotyped and romantic representations of slavery and race relations had been omitted from Brazilian education, teaching about Africa had been almost nonexistent. Africa had been characterized merely as a space from which Brazil's slaves had originated and upon which European colonialism had been practiced, just as black Brazilians had been represented as peoples upon whom white Brazilians acted. At least on paper, the new law marked a change.

Implementing the law proved difficult. Though MEC and SEPPIR had provided curricular training to 44,000 teachers by 2008, they recognized that the law had had little effect and were preparing to relaunch the curriculum. One of the MEC technicians responsible for the curriculum acknowledged: "Only a few public schools where teachers were interested adopted the law. The private schools haven't even raised the idea. . . . Black children still don't recognize themselves in the schools because there is nothing there for them to identify with."[32] I witnessed this myself when visiting a public high school in 2006, where a banner with images of black Brazilians hung in the computer lab. An instructor presented the banner as the only thing the school had done with the law, and said it was only there because visiting politicians liked having their picture taken under it. Even if the law had accomplished little, its presence was a sign of Brazil's changing landscape of race relations, one which recognized inequality as a defining national characteristic and the state as an instrument to remedy it.

Amid this change Brazilian relations with Africa reemerged during Lula da Silva's presidency. Between 2003 and 2009 President Lula da Silva made eight trips to African nations, including visits to Angola, Mozambique, Nigeria, São Tomé, and South Africa. These trips began early in his presidency, as he sought to claim a role as a world leader of poor peoples and nations. Lula's objectives and the role of Africa in his political project not only echoed the Independent Foreign Policy but rekindled the foreign policy approach developed by the military regime in the 1970s. While traveling to Africa, Lula would declare that "the 19th Century was Europe's, the 20th Century of the United States, and the 21st Century must be for Brazil and for African nations."[33] Domestic political change reprised foreign policies from the past.

By defining Brazil as a leader among poor nations, Lula's government sought support for attaining a permanent seat on the United Nations Security Council (a perennial goal of Brazilian foreign policy), as well as leverage in world trade negotiations. In part, Lula also cultivated an image as a leader in Africa to offset disappointment among some political supporters over the conservative economic policies and limited reforms carried out by his government. Finally, the renewed initiative toward Africa aimed to rebuild the export markets that had deteriorated in preceding decades. During his visits Lula announced the cancellation of debts to Brazil held by the governments of Nigeria and Mozambique and the renegotiation of debts held by Angola and Ghana.[34] In his first trip to Angola in 2003 he spoke of the need to repay "the political, moral and historical debt of Brazil toward Africa" and promised to end tariffs for imports to Brazil from poor countries, beginning with Angola.[35]

The renewed architecture of Brazil's relations with Africa relied upon frequent trips by the president, a return of Brazilian state entities to projects in African countries, and intensified commercial exports and business investment. The expansion of operations of two state agencies in 2008 characterizes this relationship. EMBRAPA, an institute which develops agricultural methods and technologies, such as specialized varieties of sugarcane for biofuel production, opened an office in Accra, Ghana, to disseminate Brazilian "tropical technology" in agriculture to African nations. The Oswaldo Cruz Foundation, which engages in biomedical and social scientific research and produces generic medicines, opened an office in Maputo, Mozambique, and was building a pharmaceutical factory that would produce generic medications, including anti-retroviral drugs.[36]

As in the 1970s, where government led, business followed. Between 1997 and 2007 the combined value of imports and exports increased from $3.5 billion to between $15 and $20 billion, amid what the *Folha de S. Paulo* called "Africa fever."[37] Trade reflected the sale of high-value industrial goods like Embraer passenger jets, consumer goods like Ellus jeans and fast food sold through Bob's franchises, as well as Globo television programming.[38] Beyond the sale of goods, companies that had provided construction, engineering, and technical services since the 1970s, including

Petrobras, brought a growing number of Brazilian engineers and technicians to countries across Africa.[39] The president of Vale do Rio Doce mining explained: "Africa is characterized by unstable government, armed conflict and other forms of violence, problems with sanitation and immense poverty. But it is also one of the few natural frontiers still open to the expansion of business opportunities in sectors like oil, gas and mining."[40] Among the means by which the Brazilian government sought to expand this market was the signing of an orthographic agreement among Portuguese-speaking countries in 2007. Standardizing language between Brazil, Portugal, Angola, Mozambique, Guiné-Bissau, and São Tomé and Principe increased the marketability of Brazilian printed and television media, especially schoolbooks and educational programming. These educational connections included scholarships for students from Portuguese-speaking Africa, especially Angola, to study in Brazil.[41]

This book was researched and written at a moment when the golden age of relations with Africa was being rekindled. Did this mean that the connections cultivated in the 1960s and 1970s were finally bearing fruit? Was it just another cycle of domestic politics and international economic opportunity? There is one difference, as well as one similarity, between past and present that may hold the answer to these questions. The difference is the degree of social and political mobilization in favor of racial integration in Brazil at the time this book was written, which reflects a quick and almost unimaginable change in the ways Brazilians imagine their society, the nature of race relations, and the role of the state. The similarity lies in the nature of public policy execution—even if popular pressure has resulted in a federal law mandating the teaching of African and black Brazilian themes, this pressure has been so far incapable of turning a law into a practice. Along these lines, Brazilian foreign policy toward Africa in the early twenty-first century still seemed disconnected: restricted to symbolism about race relations in Brazil and about Brazil's aspiring role in the world and trade.

In May 2005 I made my first trip to the Itamaraty archives in Brasília. On my first day there, I spoke to the archivists about my research and one suggested: "You know, today is the Day of Africa. There is going to be an event in the auditorium." I had never heard of the Day of Africa, but seized on the invitation. The event epitomized the abstraction which Africa meant in Brazil. There were almost no Brazilians present other than the event staff and the secretary of SEPPIR, Matilde Ribeiro, who presided. Several African diplomats posted to Brasília spoke. The audience consisted of several hundred adolescent soccer players, rounded up from the Community of Portuguese Speaking Countries Junior Football Cup. Whisked from the field and still in their uniforms, the young athletes from Brazil, Portugal, Angola, Mozambique, and the other former Portuguese colonies did their best to stay awake and respectful until the Nigerian ambassador spoke. The restless adolescents could not help laughing at his halting Portuguese.

From the Angolan "mercenary" refugees in Rio de Janeiro to the teenagers at the Day of Africa, the connections between Brazil and Africa endured. But the patterns of the past still reflect on the present, and Africa remained an abstraction in Brazil, a canvas on which Brazilian national aspirations and racial values were rendered. This canvas is significant because of the perception that all Brazilians share an African heritage. This connection was invoked by President Fernando Henrique Cardoso when, standing next to President Mbeki, he described his "foot in the kitchen." On the other hand, the connection was invoked for President Lula da Silva on his second trip to Africa, in an exchange captured by a reporter from *Folha de S. Paulo* who was traveling with him: "President Lula spoke yesterday with Brazilians who live in Cabo Verde . . . During that visit, a couple spoke about how Lula had changed. 'Lula is looking white,' commented the Brazilian Wilson Alexandre. 'But he is white,' replied the Caboverdian Leni. 'No. He is Brazil's first black president,' the Brazilian retorted. 'Well, he whitened, then,' said Leni. After a few seconds in silence, Alexandre concluded: 'He doesn't get sun anymore. It must be the air conditioning in his office.'"[42] Cardoso's "foot in the kitchen" and Lula's "air conditioning" are different yet the same. They are different in that Cardoso, once a professor of sociology and from a wealthy family, could invoke remote black ancestry in a political exercise as president, while Lula, once a metalworker and from a poor family, had his racial identity ascribed, and gained his "diploma of whiteness" by becoming president. Yet the two exercises in Brazilian racial identity are the same: both took place with Africa as their context.

Notes

Abbreviations

AAS Antonio Azeredo da Silveira Collection
AHI Arquivo Histórico do Itamaraty, Brasília and Rio de Janeiro
AHU Arquivo Histórico Ultramarino, Lisbon
AN Arquivo Nacional, Rio de Janeiro
ANTT Arquivo Nacional Torre do Tombo, Lisbon
APERJ Arquivo Público do Estado de Rio de Janeiro
BL British Library Newspaper Collection
CPDOC/FGV Centro de Pesquisa e Documentação Histórica, Fundação Getúlio Vargas
DOPS Departamento de Ordem Política e Social Collection
EG Ernesto Geisel Collection
FGF Fundação Gilberto Freyre
FPV Fundação Pierre Verger
JM Juracy Magalhães Collection
MNE Ministério dos Negócios Estraneiros, Lisbon
NARA U.S. National Archives and Records Administration
NL Francisco Negrão de Lima Collection
OA Osvaldo Aranha Collection
PIDE Polícia Internacional de Defesa de Estado, Lisbon
VG Videoteca Global / TV Globo

Introduction

1. Interview with Ovídio and Ivony de Melo, 25 July 2006.
2. Ibid.
3. This idea is owed to Leo Spitzer, whose *Hotel Bolivia* suggests an approach to reading these experiences based on the conceptual and methodological

insights developed to examine memory in the Jewish refugee experience in Bolivia. Spitzer, *Hotel Bolívia.*

4. Dzidzienyo, "The African Connection and the Afro-Brazilian Condition," 138.
5. U.S. Embassy in Brasília to Department of State, "Itamaraty's Role in Formulation of Brazilian Foreign Policy," 5 September 1970, Pol 1 Braz, RG 59, box 2129, NARA.
6. Arinos gave as an example his travel to Algeria and Israel, opposite sides of "the racial curtain," noting that it was widely known among the people with whom he interacted that he had written "Brazil's anti-racist law."Arinos de Melo Franco, *Evolução da crise brasileira*, 241.
7. Interview with Mário Gibson Barboza, 18 April 2006.
8. "Conferéncia pronunciada por Sua Exceléncia o Senhor Embaixador Antonio F. Azeredo da Silveira, ministro de estado das relações exteriores, na Escola Superior de Guerra, em 7 de julho de 1975," AAS mre ag 1975.05.27, Azeredo da Silveira Archive, CPDOC/FGV.
9. Gleijeses, *Conflicting Missions*; Moore, *Castro, the Blacks and Africa.*
10. Garcia, *Cronologia das relações internacionais do Brasil*, 49; Magalhães, *Breve história das relações diplomáticas entre Brasil e Portugal*, 32.
11. Amos and Ayesu, "Sou brasileiro," 36.
12. Gilberto Freyre, "Africa," *Correio da Manhã*, 19 February 1941, Artigos de Jornal de Gilberto Freyre, AJ-2, 1941–1944, FGF.
13. Gaines, *African Americans in Ghana*; Wright, *Black Power.*
14. Khadiagala and Lyons, eds., "Foreign Policy Making in Africa," *African Foreign Policies*, 3. Their analysis echoes that of Stephen Wright, ed., in *African Foreign Policies.*
15. Dzidzienyo, "África e diáspora," 213.
16. Bezerra de Menezes, *O Brasil e o mundo ásio-africano*, 17.
17. Ibid.
18. Ibid., 25.
19. Ibid., 313.
20. Ibid., 317.
21. Ibid., 329–30.
22. Ibid., 85, 93–94.
23. Ibid., 7.
24. Ibid., 57.
25. Ibid., 104.
26. Arinos de Melo Franco, *Evolução da crise brasileira*, 256.

Chapter 1: Brazil in the Lusotropical World

1. Oliveira Lima's argument about racial mixture and the absence of racial prejudice in Brazil, *O Movimento da independência, 1821–1822* (São Paulo: Melhoramentos, 1922), 30, was offered as evidence of "ethnic democratization" in 1941 in the first issue of *Cultura Política*, the intellectual journal of Getúlio Vargas's Estado Novo, to assert that "Brazilian nationalism does

not sustain racial prejudice." "A igualdade de raças no Brasil: suas raízes históricas," *Cultura Política* 1 (March 1941), 202.

2. Freyre, *Casa-grande e senzala*, 367.
3. Needell, "Identity, Race, Gender, and Modernity in the Origins of Gilberto Freyre's Oeuvre," 70.
4. Pallares-Burke, *Gilberto Freyre*; Luiz Costa Lima, introd. to Benzaquen de Araújo, *Guerra e paz*, 9.
5. Luncheon invitation, 11 October 1973, "Artigos de Jornal Sobre Gilberto Freyre," n. 39, 1973, FGF.
6. Boxer, *The Portuguese Seaborne Empire*.
7. *Brasil: 500 anos de povoamento*. Rio de Janeiro: IBGE, 2000, http://www.ibge.gov.br/brasil500/index2.html (accessed 26 February 2008).
8. Manoel Sarmento Rodrigues to Gilberto Freyre, 25 October 1954, CR Port., p. 7, FGF.
9. Costa Pinto, *O fim do império português*, 86.
10. Iñiguez, *Sueños paralelos*, 304.
11. *Instruções para a elaboração das estatísticas ultramarinas*, série 2, no. 1. Lisbon: Instituto Nacional de Estatística, 1949, http://inenetw02.ine.pt (accessed 26 February 2008).
12. Ball, *The Past Has Another Pattern*, 277; Rodrigues, *Salazar-Kennedy*, 300.
13. Needell, "Identity, Race, Gender, and Modernity in the Origins of Gilberto Freyre's Oeuvre," 51.
14. Ibid., 75.
15. Freyre, *O mundo que o português criou*, 58.
16. Ibid., 48.
17. Ibid., 51.
18. Ibid., 46, 58.
19. Gilberto Freyre to Manoel Sarmento Rodrigues, 4 July 1951, copy of Arquivo Mário Soares document AMS 4292.001 im. 13, FGF.
20. Cited in Castelo, *"O modo português de estar no mundo,"* 89.
21. "Declarações de Gilberto Freyre ao chegar ao Brasil," *Novidades* (Lisbon), 18 February 1952, Artigos de Jornal Sobre Gilberto Freyre, n. 15, 1952, FGF.
22. Freyre, *Aventura e rotina*, 41.
23. Alberto Costa e Silva, preface to *Aventura e rotina*, 19.
24. Freyre, *Aventura e rotina*, 270.
25. Ibid.
26. Alberto Costa e Silva, preface to *Aventura e rotina*, 20.
27. Manoel Sarmento Rodrigues to Gilberto Freyre, 16 September 1952, CR Port., p. 6, FGF.
28. Gilberto Freyre to Sarmento Rodrigues, 7 September 1954, copy of Arquivo Mário Soares document AMS 4292.001 im. 7, FGF.
29. Manoel Sarmento Rodrigues to Gilberto Freyre, 25 October 1954, CR Port., p. 7, FGF.
30. Andrade, "O mito lusotropical," 46–47.
31. Interview by Jerry Dávila, 2006. While this person formally consented to the

interview and its use in this book, my judgment in this case is to withhold his name.

32. Freyre, *Casa-grande e senzala*, 424.
33. Interview with Fernando Mourão, 16 August 2006.
34. Gérard, *European-Language Writing in Sub-Saharan Africa*, 398.
35. Interview with Fernando Mourão, 16 August 2006.
36. Interview with José Maria Pereira, 27 May 2006.
37. Ibid.
38. Rodrigues, *Brazil and Africa*, 294.
39. Interview with José Maria Pereira, 27 May 2006.
40. Vianna Moog, *Revista Época*, 11 November 1972, SR 110, Recortes de Imprensa II, 1971/Ago-1972/Dez MU/GM/GNP/110/C1, AHU.
41. Paulo, "*Aqui também é Portugal*," 184, 221.
42. Interview with Antônio Gomes da Costa, 1 September 2006.
43. Morais, *Chatô*, 586.
44. Interview with Alberto Costa e Silva, 14 December 2005.
45. Interview with Antônio Gomes da Costa, 1 September 2006.
46. "Em vastos territórios espalhados pelos continentes, Portugal ergeu obras de engenharia social jamais conseguidas por qualquer outro povo," *Diário da Manhã* (Lisbon), 11 April 1952, Artigos de Jornal Sobre Gilberto Freyre, n. 15, 1952, FGF.
47. Gilberto Freyre to Sarmento Rodrigues, 7 September 1954, copy of Arquivo Mário Soares document AMS 4292.001 im. 7, FGF.
48. Rodrigues, *Brazil and Africa*, 297–98.
49. Pinheiro, "Brasil, Portugal e descolonização africana," 101.
50. Ibid.
51. Rodrigues, *Brazil and Africa*, 296; Pinheiro, "Brasil, Portugal e descolonização africana," 106.
52. Marcelo Mathias to Portuguese Ministry of Foreign Affairs, 9 November 1961, PROC 922 PAA 283, Diversos, MNE; "The Reaction in Brazil over the Indian Aggression against Goa," *Portugal News*, Portuguese legation in Bangkok, 10 January 1962, SR 185, Comemorações Henriquianas, 1961 Proc. 15.00 e 15.081 MU/GM/GNP/185/Pt. 1, AHU.
53. Pedro Calmon to Negrão de Lima, 20 June 1960, Francisco Negrão de Lima Archive, NL ad po 1960.06.07, CPDOC/FGV; Documentos tratando da criação do Instituto Luso-Brasileiro de Astronáutica, Brasília, NL ad po 1960.05.26, CPDOC/FGV.
54. Interview with Alberto Costa e Silva, 14 December 2005.
55. Letter from Portuguese embassy in Rio de Janeiro to Ministry of Foreign Affairs, 21 November 1956, Proc 902, 1 PAA 155; "Questão racial: Preconceitos paciais nas Províncias Ultramarinas Portuguesas (excursão do clube de regatas 'Vasco da Gama' à África Portuguesa)," MNE.
56. Ibid.
57. Ibid.
58. "Prêtos podem jogar em Portugal," *Tribuna da Imprensa*, 23 November 1956, Proc 902, 1 PAA 155; "Questão racial: Preconceitos raciais nas Províncias

Ultramarinas Portuguesas (excursão do clube de regatas 'Vasco da Gama' à África Portuguesa)," MNE.

59. Ibid.
60. Telegram 70 from Portuguese embassy in Rio de Janeiro to Ministry of Foreign Affairs, 14 March 1963, Proc. 922 PAA 282 1963/6, MNE; "Visita do clube de regatas Vasco da Gama," 3 June 1963, dispatch 101, embassy in Lagos to foreign ministry, AHI.
61. "As armas que estão em Cuba são as mesmas que cercam os territórios da África Portuguesa," *Diário de Notícias* (Lisbon), 3 May 1963, Proc. 922, PAA 282 1963/66, MNE.
62. Interview with João Clemente Baena Soares, 30 June 2006.
63. Ibid.
64. Ibid.
65. Ibid.; Magalhães, *Breve história das relações diplomáticas entre Brasil e Portugal*, 94.
66. Interview with João Clemente Baena Soares, 30 June 2006.
67. Ibid.
68. Ibid.
69. Ibid.
70. Ibid.
71. Ibid.
72. "Saudação do embaixador Negrão de Lima ao desembarcar em Portugal," Negrão de Lima Archive, NL ad po 1959.12.04, CPDOC/FGV.
73. Francisco Negrão de Lima to Augusto de Lima Junior, 15 July 1960. Negrão de Lima Archive, NL ad po 1960.06.07, CPDOC/FGV.
74. "Manifesto: 'Brasileiros': Distribuidos aos milhares na doca e nos arranha-céus," Frente Católica pro-Libertação de Portugal, Lisboa, 3 July 1959, "Manoel Maria Sarmento Rodrigues," PIDE/DGS, SC SR 5671 u.i. 2421, ANTT.
75. PIDE report on the measures for the arrival of Sarmento Rodrigues, 26 June 1959, "Manoel Maria Sarmento Rodrigues," PIDE/DGS, SC SR 5671 u.i. 242, ANTT.
76. "Escola de guerra proíbe perguntas sobre Salazar," *Tribuna da Imprensa*, 9 June 1959, "Manoel Maria Sarmento Rodrigues," PIDE/DGS, SC SR 5671 u.i. 242, ANTT.
77. "Um dia e uma comunidade," *Diário de Notícias*, 10 June 1959, "Manoel Maria Sarmento Rodrigues," PIDE/DGS, SC SR 5671 u.i. 2421, ANTT.
78. Selcher, *The Afro-Asian Dimension of Brazilian Foreign Policy*, 18–19.
79. Interview with Candido Mendes de Almeida, 24 November 2004.
80. Quadros, "Brazil's New Foreign Policy," 19.
81. Ibid., 21.
82. Ibid., 25.
83. Ibid., 24.
84. Lesser, *Welcoming the Undesirables*, 66.
85. Arinos de Melo Franco, *Evolução da crise brasileira*, 241.
86. Dávila and Morgan, "Since *Black into White*," 409–23.

87. "Entrevista concedida ao Diário Popular, de Lisboa, sobre as relações luso-brasileiras," Juracy Magalhães Archive, JM pi Magalhães, J. 1966.08.24/3, CPDOC/FGV.
88. Gibson Barboza to Médici, 22 January 1974. Azeredo da Silveira Archive, AAS mre rb 1974.05.23, CPDOC/FGV.

Chapter 2: Africa and the Independent Foreign Policy

1. Thanks to Uri Rosenheck for finding the album.
2. Howes, "Damata, Gasparino," 100.
3. Mário Vieira de Mello to Foreign Ministry, dispatch 116, "Situação Política de Gana," 19 June 1968, AHI.
4. Interview with Candido Mendes de Almeida, 24 November 2006.
5. Foreign Ministry to embassy in Accra, telegram 90, "Vinda ao Brasil do Embaixador R. Souza Dantas," 7 November 1961, AHI; Foreign Ministry to embassy in Accra, telegram 34, "Fornecimento de café do IBC para consumo das missões diplomáticas e repartições consulares," 29 May 1962, AHI.
6. "Jornalistas na diplomacia," *Correio da Manhã*, 25 April 1961, 2.
7. José Honório Rodrigues, "O racismo às avessas do presidente Jânio Quadros," *O Jornal*, 2 March 1961, p. 4; Souza Dantas, *África difícil*, 51.
8. Corrêa do Lago to Foreign Ministry, telegram 94, "Problemas africanos: Conversa com o senhor ministro de estado em Dacar," 11 April 1961, AHI.
9. Corrêa do Lago to Foreign Ministry, telegram 9, "Política brasileira na África Ocidental," 8 February 1961, AHI.
10. Wright, *Black Power*.
11. Souza Dantas, *África difícil*, 14.
12. Wright, *Black Power*; Gaines, *African Americans in Ghana*.
13. Souza Dantas, *África difícil*, 35–36.
14. Ibid., 39.
15. Ibid., 55.
16. Ibid., 40.
17. The remark was also cited by Sombra Saraíva, *O lugar da África*, 90; interview with João Clemente Baena Soares, 30 June 2006.
18. Interview with Candido Mendes de Almeida, 24 November 2006.
19. Souza Dantas, *África difícil*, 37.
20. Ibid., 55.
21. Ibid., 31.
22. Ibid., 36.
23. Ibid., 95.
24. Ibid., 21.
25. Ibid.
26. Foreign Ministry to embassy in Accra, telegram 36, "Fornecimento de café do IBC para consumo das missões diplomáticas e repartições consulares," 8 June 1961, AHI.

27. Foreign Ministry to embassy in Accra, telegram 34, "Fornecimento de café do IBC para consumo das missões diplomáticas e repartições consulares," 29 May 1962, AHI.
28. Mário Vieira de Mello to Foreign Ministry, telegram 11, "Situação da Ebaixada em Acra," 21 March 1968, AHI.
29. Mário Vieira de Mello to Foreign Ministry, dispatch 43, "Relações comerciais Brasil e Gana," 22 April 1969, AHI.
30. Interview with Maria Yedda Linhares, 22 May 2008.
31. Moraes, "Entrevista com Maria Yedda Linhares," 225.
32. Interview with Maria Yedda Linhares, 22 May 2008.
33. Moraes, "Entrevista com Maria Yedda Linhares," 230.
34. Interview with Maria Yedda Linhares, 22 May 2008.
35. Ibid.
36. Ibid.
37. Foreign Ministry to embassy in Accra, telegram 5, "Exposição fotográfica itinerante 'Brasília e outras cidades brasileiras,'" 19 February 1963, AHI.
38. Teles dos Santos, *O poder da cultura e a cultura no poder*, 22, 67.
39. Ibid., 28.
40. Hollanda, *Pierre Verger*.
41. Matory, "The 'Cult of Nations' and the Ritualization of their Purity," 200.
42. Matory, "The English Professors of Brazil," 73.
43. Fry, "Gallus Africanus est," 43.
44. Dantas, *Vovó nagô e papai branco*; Motta, "L'invention de l'Afrique dans le candomblé du Brésil," 65–85; Matory, "The English Professors of Brazil," 78–79.
45. Interview with Waldir Freitas de Oliveira, 2 August 2006.
46. Ibid.
47. Interview with Antonio Olinto, 26 May 2006.
48. Seljan, *No Brasil ainda tem gente da minha cor?*, 27.
49. Zora Seljan Braga to Pierre Verger, n.d. (probably 1955), Correspondência, FPV.
50. Ibid.
51. Ibid.
52. Interview with Antonio Olinto, 26 May 2006.
53. Ibid.
54. Ibid.
55. Interview with Antonio Olinto, 14 June 2006.
56. Ibid.
57. Vivaldo Costa Lima to Pierre Verger, 2 November 1961, Pasta correspondência com Vivaldo Costa Lima, FPV.
58. Pierre Verger to Vivaldo Costa Lima (Ogundeyi), 25 November 1961, Pasta correspondência com Vivaldo Costa Lima, FPV.
59. Interview with Antonio Olinto, 26 May 2006.
60. Vivaldo Costa Lima to Pierre Verger, n.d. (probably 3 June 1967), Pasta correspondência com Vivaldo Costa Lima, FPV.

61. Pierre Verger to Vivaldo Costa Lima, 25 November 1961; Pierre Verger to Vivaldo Costa Lima, 17 April 1965; Vivaldo Costa Lima to Pierre Verger, n.d. (probably 3 June 1967), all in Pasta correspondência com Vivaldo Costa Lima, FPV.
62. Souza Dantas, *África difícil*, 77.
63. "Jovens africanos tiveram na Bahia seu primeiro contacto com o Brasil," *África e Ásia*, April–May 1962, 1.
64. Interview with Waldir Freitas de Oliveira, 2 August 2006.
65. Interview with Maria Yedda Linhares, 22 May 2008.
66. Ibid.

Chapter 3: "The Lovers of the African Race"

1. "Envoy Falls 3 Floors to His Death," *Sunday Times*, 15 September 1963; "Recortes de jornal: falecimento do secretário Antonio Carlos da Souza Tavares," 28 September 1963, dispatch 153, embassy in Lagos to Foreign Ministry, AHI; Ebenezer Curtis, "Tribute to Carlos Tavares," *Nigerian Morning Post*, 20 September 1963, 11, BL.
2. "Chegada e posse do Ministro Luiz de Souza Bandeira," 22 January 1963, telegram 8, embassy in Lagos to Foreign Ministry, AHI.
3. "Transporte do corpo do Embaixador Luiz de Souza Bandeira," 10 February 1963, telegram 29, embassy in Lagos to Foreign Ministry, AHI.
4. José Osvaldo Meira Penna to Minister Vasco Leitão da Cunha, 5 March 1965, "A Lei de Parkinson e a embaixada em Lagos," dispatch 63, embassy in Lagos to Foreign Ministry, AHI.
5. Ibid.
6. Interview with José Osvaldo Meira Penna, 11 June 2006.
7. José Osvaldo Meira Penna to Minister Vasco Leitão da Cunha, 5 March 1965, "A Lei de Parkinson e a embaixada em Lagos," dispatch 63, embassy in Lagos to Foreign Ministry, AHI.
8. Curtin, "'The White Man's Grave,'" 94.
9. Cited in Dantas, *Vovô nagô e papai branco*, 150.
10. "Un pays d'africains de toutes les couleurs," *Fraternité Matin*, 23 October 1972, 9.
11. Lesser, *A Discontented Diaspora*.
12. Costa e Silva, *Um rio chamado Atlântico*, 240.
13. Interview with Alberto Costa e Silva, 17 June 2004.
14. Ibid.
15. Costa e Silva, *Das mãos do oleiro*, 83.
16. Ibid., 45.
17. Ibid., 180.
18. Olinto, *Brasileiros na África*, 259.
19. Seljan, *No Brasil, ainda tem gente da minha cor?*, 26; interview with Antonio Olinto, 26 May 2006.
20. Olinto, *Brasileiros na África*, 271.
21. Interview with Antonio Olinto, 26 May 2006.

22. Olinto, *Brasileiros na África*, 207.
23. Interview with José Osvaldo Meira Penna, 11 July 2006.
24. "Mudança de residência Embaixada," 13 February 1963, telegram 31, embassy in Lagos to Foreign Ministry, AHI.
25. "Visita ao Ministro dos Negócios Estrangeiros," 3 September 1962, dispatch 1, embassy in Lagos to Foreign Ministry, AHI.
26. Seljan, *No Brasil, ainda tem gente da minha cor?*, 26.
27. Olinto, *Brasileiros na África*, 55.
28. "Programa de trabalho da secretaria geral adjunta para a África e Oriente próximo," 1 March 1968, dispatch 35, embassy in Lagos to Foreign Ministry, AHI.
29. *Banco do Brasil, Carteira de Comercio Exterior, CACEX: Séries estatísticas, 1974* (Rio de Janeiro: Carteira de Comercio Exterior, 1974), 30–33.
30. "Good Jim Quits," *Daily Times*, 10 January 1963; "Remessa de recortes de jornal: James Meredith," 10 January 1963, dispatch 6, embassy in Lagos to Foreign Ministry, AHI.
31. Ibid.
32. "Influência da cultura brasileira no Daomé," 28 January 1963, dispatch 18, embassy in Lagos to Foreign Ministry, AHI.
33. Olinto, *Brasileiros na África*, 192.
34. Ibid., 180.
35. Ibid., 189.
36. Zora Seljan, "Brazilian Artists," *Lagos This Week*, 19–25 May 1963, 8.
37. "Exposição de artistas brasileiros contemporâneos," 3 June 1963, dispatch 99, embassy in Lagos to Foreign Ministry, AHI.
38. Zora Seljan, "Brazilian Artists," *Lagos This Week*, 19–25 May 1963; "Exposição de artistas brasileiros contemporâneos," 3 June 1963, dispatch 99, embassy in Lagos to Foreign Ministry, AHI.
39. "Brazilian Arts Exhibition Opened," *Independent*, 25 May–1 June 1963; "Exposição de artistas brasileiros contemporâneos," 3 June 1963, dispatch 99, embassy in Lagos to Foreign Ministry, AHI.
40. "Brazilian Arts Exhibition Opened," *Independent*, 25 May–1 June 1963; Zora Seljan, "Brazilian Artists," *Lagos This Week*, 19–25 May 1963; "Exposição de artistas brasileiros contemporâneos," 3 June 1963, dispatch 99, embassy in Lagos to Foreign Ministry, AHI.
41. John Rover, "Culture: Brazilians Took This from Us," *Sunday Times*, 5 May 1963; dispatch 78, Antônio Tavares to Hermes Lima, 3 June 1963, "Exposição de artistas brasileiros"; dispatch 78, embassy in Lagos to Foreign Ministry, AHI.
42. "Visita do Clube de Regatas Vasco da Gama," 3 June 1963, dispatch 101, embassy in Lagos to Foreign Ministry, AHI.
43. "At Home," *Daily Times*, 24 May 1963; "Vasco Can Be Licked," *West African Pilot*, 24 May 1963; "Visita do clube de regatas Vasco da Gama," 3 June 1963, dispatch 101, embassy in Lagos to Foreign Ministry, AHI.
44. "Soccer Massacre: 'Green Eagles' Beaten 6–0," *Sunday Times*, 26 May 1963; Babington Bakre, "'Green Eagles' Thrashed 6–0: It's Slaughter at KGV Sta-

dium," *Sunday Express*, 26 May 1963; "Visita do clube de regatas Vasco da Gama," 3 June 1963, dispatch 101, embassy in Lagos to Foreign Ministry, AHI.

45. "Oferecimento de contrato para técnico brasileiro de futebol," 21 May 1963, telegram 43, Foreign Ministry to embassy in Lagos, AHI; "Pedido de treinador de futebol," 16 October 1967, telegram 22, Foreign Ministry to embassy in Accra, AHI.
46. Olinto, *Brasileiros na África*, 120.
47. Ebenezer Curtis, "Tribute to Carlos Tavares," *Nigerian Morning Post*, 20 September 1963, 11, BL.
48. Ebenezer Curtis, "Brazil Celebrates Her 141st Anniversary," *Morning Post*, 7 September 1963, BL.
49. "Brazil's Links with Nigeria," *Lagos This Week*, 1–7 September 1963; "Recortes de jornal sobre o Brasil," 8 November 1963, dispatch 190, embassy in Lagos to Foreign Ministry, AHI.
50. Brazilian embassy in Lagos to Foreign Ministry, "Falecimento do secretário A.C. de Souza Tavares: Remessa de relatório," Secret Dispatch 165, 25 October 1963, AHI.
51. "First-Ever Lady Envoy," *Daily Times*, 17 January 1964; "Recortes de jornais com notícias sôbre o Brasil," 24 January 1964, dispatch 23, embassy in Lagos to Foreign Ministry, AHI.
52. Meira Penna to Itamaraty, 8 February 1965, "Estado de saúde do Conselheiro Paulo Rio Branco Nabuco de Gouvêa," telegram 16, embassy in Lagos to Foreign Ministry, AHI; interview with Antonio Olinto, 26 May 2006.
53. "Remessa de Credenciais," 26 August 1971, telegram 45, Foreign Ministry to embassy in Lagos, AHI.
54. Ebenezer Curtis, "Tribute to Carlos Tavares," *Nigerian Morning Post*, 20 September 1963, 11, BL.
55. Arthur Omorodion, "The Late Mr. A. C. de Souza Taveres," *Daily Telegraph*, 10 October 1963, 3, BL.
56. Arthur Omorodion, "Afro-Brazilian Relationship," *West African Pilot*, 25 October 1963, BL.
57. Funk, "In the Battle for Emergent Independence: Calypsos of Decolonization," http://anthurium.miami.edu/volume_3/issue_2/funk-inthebattle.htm.
58. Arthur Omorodion, "Afro-Brazilian Relationship," *West African Pilot*, 25 October 1963, BL.
59. Interview with Antonio Olinto, 26 May 2006. Quadros named the black journalist and presidential aide Raymundo Souza Dantas ambassador to Ghana in 1961.
60. Interview with Antonio Olinto, 14 June 2006.
61. Ibid.
62. Ibid.
63. Interview with Adyel Silva, 4 July 2008.
64. "Olympic Champ Turns Diplomat," *Morning Post*, 5 March 1964; "Recortes

de jornais com notícias sôbre o Brasil," 17 March 1964, dispatch 62, embassy in Lagos to Foreign Ministry, AHI.

65. "Da-Silva Showing Them How," *Morning Post*, 27 April 1964; "Recortes de jornais com notícias sôbre o Brasil," 6 May 1964, dispatch 95, embassy in Lagos to Foreign Ministry, AHI.
66. "Relatório annual do adido cultural em Lagos," 19 March 1965, dispatch 68, embassy in Lagos to Foreign Ministry, AHI.
67. Ibid.
68. Ibid.
69. "Relatório sôbre a divulgação de música brasileira no exterior," 20 August 1964, dispatch 150, embassy in Lagos to Foreign Ministry, AHI.
70. "Our Lady of Brazil," *West African Pilot*, 7 January 1964; "Recortes de jornais com notícias sôbre o Brasil," 24 January 1964, dispatch 23, embassy in Lagos to Foreign Ministry, AHI.
71. Meira Penna to Foreign Minister Araújo Castro, 15 January 1964; "Entrega de credenciais," dispatch 12, embassy in Lagos to Foreign Ministry, AHI.
72. Ibid.; "Brazil 'a Laboratory of Inter-racial Cooperation,' Envoy Told," *West African Pilot*, 14 January 1964, 1; dispatch 12, embassy in Lagos to Foreign Ministry, AHI.
73. Interview with José Osvaldo Meira Penna, 11 June 2006.
74. José Osvaldo Meira Penna, "Visita oficial à região ocidental da Nigéria," 26 May 1964, dispatch 106, embassy in Lagos to Foreign Ministry, AHI.
75. Interview with Antonio Pitanga, 30 May 2008.
76. Ibid.
77. Ibid.
78. "Viagem de ator brasileiro com apresentação de filmes 'Ganga Zumba,'" 13 November 1964, dispatch 188, embassy in Lagos to Foreign Ministry, AHI.
79. Ibid.
80. Ibid.
81. Ibid.
82. Ibid.
83. Ibid.
84. Interview with Antonio Pitanga, 30 May 2008.
85. Ibid.
86. "Antonio's Thriller!," *Sunday Post*, 22 November 1964; "Apresentação de filme brasileiro em Lagos: Viagem do ator Antonio Luiz Sampaio," 26 November 1964, dispatch 202, embassy in Lagos to Foreign Ministry, AHI.
87. "Viagem de ator brasileiro com apresentação de filmes 'Ganga Zumba,'" 13 November 1964, dispatch 188, embassy in Lagos to Foreign Ministry, AHI.
88. Interview with Antonio Pitanga, 30 May 2008.
89. "Viagem de ator brasileiro com apresentação de filmes 'Ganga Zumba,'" 13 November 1964, dispatch 188, embassy in Lagos to Foreign Ministry, AHI.

90. "A lei de Parkinson e a embaixada em Lagos," 5 March 1965, dispatch 63, embassy in Lagos to Foreign Ministry, AHI.
91. Ibid.
92. Ibid.
93. "Acontecimentos políticos no Brasil: Repercussões na Nigéria," 12 May 1964, dispatch 99, embassy in Lagos to Foreign Ministry, AHI.
94. Ibid.
95. Interview with José Maria Pereira, 27 May 2006.
96. "Programa de trabalho da secretaria geral adjunta para a África e Oriente próximo," 1 March 1968, dispatch 35, embassy in Lagos to Foreign Ministry, AHI.
97. Ibid.
98. "O Brasil na rádio nigeriana: Programa de Natal," 5 January 1966, dispatch 6, embassy in Lagos to Foreign Ministry, AHI.
99. Adhemar Ferreira da Silva, "Relatório de viagem," 3 January 1966, dispatch 1, embassy in Lagos to Foreign Ministry, AHI.

Chapter 4: War in Angola, Crisis in Brazil

1. Cited in Arinos Filho, *Diplomacia Independente*, 204.
2. Ibid., 202.
3. Lesser, *Welcoming the Undesirables*, 133.
4. Costa Pinto, *O fim do império português*, 41.
5. Ibid., 43–44.
6. Rodrigues, *Brazil and Africa*, 371.
7. Arinos de Melo Franco, *Planalto*, 194.
8. Rodrigues, *Salazar-Kennedy*, 89–96.
9. Noer, *Cold War and Black Liberation*, 89.
10. Rodrigues, *Salazar-Kennedy*, 145.
11. "1742 (XVI): The Situation in Angola," General Assembly, Sixteenth Session, *Resolutions Adopted without Reference to a Committee*, 67, http://daccessdds.un.org/doc/RESOLUTION/GEN/NR0/167/95/IMG/NR016795.pdf?OpenElement, accessed 5 March 2008.
12. Letter from the director do gabiente dos negócios políticos do Ministério dos Negócios Estrangeiros to the director da Polícia Internacional e de Defesa do Estado (PIDE), 11 March 1963, SR 024, Estados Unidos da América, 1959/JUL/23–1967/MAR/09, H.5.1.1 MU/GM/GNP/024, AHU.
13. Ibid.
14. Letter from the director geral dos negócios políticos e da administração interna do gabinete dos negócios políticos do Ministério do Ultramar, 22 January 1963, SR 024, Estados Unidos da América, 1959/JUL/23–1967/MAR/09 H.5.1.1 MU/GM/GNP/024, AHU.
15. Noer, *Cold War and Black Liberation*, 74–75.
16. "U.S. Backing Red Plot in Africa," *Shreveport Journal*, 21 November 1962, SR 024, Estados Unidos da América, 1959/JUL/23–1967/MAR/09 H.5.1.1 MU/GM/GNP/024, AHU; letter from the director geral dos negócios políticos

e da administração interna do Minstério dos Negócios Estrangeiros to gabinete dos negócios políticos do Ministério do Ultramar, 22 January 1963, SR 024, Estados Unidos da América, 1959/JUL/23–1967/MAR/09 H.5.1.1 MU/GM/GNP/024, AHU.

17. "The Pan-African Peril," *News and Courier*, 23 November 1962, SR 024, Estados Unidos da América, 1959/JUL/23–1967/MAR/09 H.5.1.1 MU/GM/GNP/024, AHU.
18. Thomas Noer, "Segregationists and White Rule," *Window on Freedom*, ed. Plummer, 142.
19. Unsigned memorandum received 31 August 1963, SR 024, Estados Unidos da América, 1959/JUL/23–1967/MAR/09, H.5.1.1 MU/GM/GNP/024, AHU.
20. Arinos de Melo Franco, *Planalto*, 145.
21. Ibid., 148.
22. Ibid.
23. Leitão da Cunha, *Diplomacia em alto-mar*, 230.
24. Arinos Filho, *Diplomacia independente*, 211.
25. Ibid., 212.
26. Ibid.
27. Gibson Barboza, *Na diplomacia, o traço todo da vida*, 343–44.
28. Brazilian embassy in Lagos to Foreign Ministry, "Falecimento do secretário A.C. de Souza Tavares: Remessa de relatório," Secret Dispatch 165, 25 October 1963, AHI.
29. Interview with Alberto Costa e Silva, 17 July 2004.
30. Manuel Brás, chefe do posto da PIDE em Nova Lisboa, "Visita do senhor embaixador do Brasil, Dr. Negrão de Lima, a esta cidade nos dias 29 e 30 do mês findo," 3 June 1961, IDE/DGS, Del A Dinf 11.32.D/4u.i. 1862, ANTT.
31. Ibid.
32. "Eu gostava de ser negro: Eu sou sincero," *Picada de Marimbondo* (1961), cited in *European-Language Writing in Sub-Saharan Africa*, ed. Gérard, 301.
33. Celestino Alexandre Pires, chefe da PIDE de Sá Bandeira, 5 June 1961, "Brasil," PIDE/DGS, Del A Dinf 11.32.D/4u.i. 1862, ANTT.
34. Carlos Casaca Velez, chefe da PIDE em Lobito, "Visita do excelentíssimo embaixador do Brasil em Lisboa a Lobito e Benguela," 6 June 1961, "Brasil," PIDE/DGS, Del A Dinf 11.32.D/4u.i. 1862, ANTT.
35. Ibid.
36. Dáskalos, *Um testemunho para a história de Angola*, 88–89.
37. Interview with Alberto Costa e Silva, 17 July 2004.
38. Dáskalos, *Um testemunho para a história de Angola*, 95.
39. Subdirector da PIDE Luanda, "Informação muito secreta: Posição assumida por certos sectores brasileros em relação à política ultramarina de Portugal," 18 May 1963, "Brasil," PIDE/DGS, Del A Dinf 11.32.D/4u.i. 1862, ANTT.
40. Ibid.
41. Brazilian embassy in Lisbon to Foreign Ministry, "Conduta do cônsul do Brasil em Luanda," telegram 157, 26 August 1962, AHI.

42. Francisco Negrão de Lima to Afonso Arinos de Melo Franco, "Angola," dispatch 226, 20 June 1961, AHI.
43. Carta ao embaixador Francisco Negrão de Lima, 15 April 1963; José Paulo Silva Graça to Negrão de Lima, 20 November 1963, both in Negrão de Lima Archive, NL ad po 1960.08.26, FGV/CPDOC.
44. Francisco Negrão de Lima to Jânio Quadros, 14 July 1961, Negrão de Lima Archive, NL ad po 1960.08.26, FGV/CPDOC.
45. Ambassador Ramos to Ministry of Foreign Affairs, 21 September 1961, PROC 922 PAA 283: Diversos, MNE.
46. Ibid.
47. "Atitude do Dr. Francisco Negrão de Lima, embaixador em Lisboa, 18 May 1962, PROC 922 PAA 283: Diversos, MNE.
48. Memorandum of conversation between Franco Nogueira and Negrão de Lima, 22 August 1962, PROC 922 PAA 283: Diversos, MNE.
49. Ibid.
50. Freyre, "Brasil na face das Áfricas negras e mestiças," 56.
51. Ibid.
52. Boxer, *Race Relations in the Portuguese Colonial Empire*, 1.
53. Ibid., 40.
54. Gilberto Freyre, "'Minorias Africanas' no Brasil?," *Correio da Manhã*, 2 April 1941, Artigos de Jornal de Gilberto Freyre, AJ-2, 1941–1944, FGF.
55. Boxer, *Race Relations in the Portuguese Colonial Empire*, 120, 122.
56. Alden, "Charles R. Boxer," 945.
57. Gilberto Freyre, "Mais sobre o caso do Major Boxer," *O Cruzeiro*, 23 January 1965, Artigos de Jornal de Gilberto Freyre, AJ-13, 1963–1964, FGF.
58. Rodrigues, *Brazil and Africa*, 332.
59. Marcelo Mathias to Colonial Ministry, 27 June 1963. Proc. 922 PAA 283: Diversos, MNE.
60. Cited in Gaspari, *A ditadura escancarada*, 296.
61. Ramos to Portuguese Ministry of Foreign Affairs, 12 June 1963, PROC 922 PAA 282, Pasta 1963–1966, "Atitude de vários países relativamente à política e administração ultramarina portuguesa," MNE.
62. Rodrigues, *Brazil and Africa*, 318.
63. Campos Alves, consulate in São Paulo, to Portuguese Ministry of Foreign Affairs, 27 June 1962, PROC 922 PAA 282, Pasta 1961–1962, "Atitude dos vários países relativamente à política e administração ultramarina portuguesa," MNE.
64. "Entrevista com o chefe do Integralismo, Dr. Plínio Salgado," *A Crítica*, 26 June 1961, PROC 922 PAA 283: Diversos, MNE.
65. Ramos to Portuguese Ministry of Foreign Affairs, 2 October 1961, "Palestras e entrevistas do deputado Prof. Eurípides Cardoso de Meneses sobre o ultramar portugués," PROC 922 PAA 283: Diversos, MNE.
66. Ramos to Portuguese Ministry of Foreign Affairs, 6 October 1961, "Palestras e entrevistas do deputado Prof. Eurípides Cardoso de Meneses sobre o ultramar português," PROC 922 PAA 283: Diversos, MNE.
67. Ibid.

68. Ibid.
69. Coelho Lopes to Portuguese Ministry of Foreign Affairs, 31 October 1961, "Palestras e entrevistas do deputado Prof. Eurípides Cardoso de Meneses sobre o ultramar portugués," PROC 922 PAA 283: Diversos, MNE.
70. Interview with José Maria Nunes Pereira, 27 May 2006.
71. "Atitude favorável a Portugal no caso de Angola, do ex-candidato à presidência da República, Dr. Adhemar de Barros," PROC 922 PAA 283: Diversos, MNE.
72. "Atitude de Roberto de Oliveira Campos, indigitado embaixador do Brasil nos Estados Unidos," PROC 922 PAA 283: Diversos, MNE.
73. Telegram from Portuguese embassy in Rio de Janeiro to Ministry of Foreign Affairs, 12 October 1961, PROC 922 PAA 282: Diversos, MNE.
74. Ambassador João de Deus Bataglia Ramos to Portuguese Ministry of Foreign Affairs, 18 March 1963, PROC 922 PAA 282: Goulart, MNE.
75. Goulart, *Mensagem ao Congresso Nacional*, 161.
76. Rodrigues, *Brazil and Africa*, 334.
77. Ramos to Portuguese Ministry of Foreign Affairs, 17 March 1963, PROC 922 PAA 282, Pasta 1963–1964, "Atitude do Brasil quanto ao problema de Angola," MNE.
78. Ramos to Portuguese Ministry of Foreign Affairs, 18 March 1963, PROC 922 PAA 282, Pasta 1963–1964, "Atitude do Brasil quanto ao problema de Angola," MNE.
79. Ramos to Portuguese Ministry of Foreign Affairs, 16 March 1963, PROC 922 PAA 282, Pasta 1963–1964, "Atitude do Brasil quanto ao problema de Angola," MNE.
80. Ramos to Portuguese Ministry of Foreign Affairs, 18 March 1963, PROC 922 PAA 282, Pasta 1963–1964, "Atitude do Brasil quanto ao problema de Angola," MNE.
81. Ramos to Portuguese Ministry of Foreign Affairs, 12 February 1966, PROC 922, PAA 282 Castelo Branco, MNE.
82. Pio Correia, *O mundo em que vivi*, 683.

Chapter 5: *Latinité* or *Fraternité*?

1. Dzidzienyo, "The African Connection and the Afro-Brazilian Condition," 136.
2. Interview with José Manuel Gonçalves, 14 June 2008.
3. Interview with José Maria Pereira, 22 May 2008.
4. Interview with Waldir Freitas de Oliveira, 2 August 2006.
5. Interview with Candido Mendes, 24 November 2006.
6. "Relatório Geral," ministério de negócios estrangeiros to PIDE director general, 12 June 1962, "Movimento Afro-Brasileiro de Libertação de angola: MABLA," PIDE/DGS, SC/SR 435/61/ui. 3054, ANTT.
7. Interview with José Manuel Gonçalves, 14 June 2008; interview with José Maria Pereira, 27 May 2006.
8. "Relatório Geral," 12 June 1962, Movimento Afro-Brasileiro de Libertação de Angola, MABLA-PIDE/DGS, SC/SR 435/61/ui. 3054, ANTT.

9. Brazilian embassy in Lisbon to Foreign Ministry, "Asilo político: Duarte Vilhena Coutinho Ferreri Feio Gusmão," dispatch 293, 5 July 1960, \AHI.
10. Interview with José Maria Pereira, 27 May 2006.
11. "Relatório Geral," 12 June 1962, Movimento Afro-Brasileiro de Libertação de Angola, MABLA-PIDE/DGS, SC/SR 435/61/ui. 3054, ANTT.
12. Interview with José Maria Pereira, 27 May 2006.
13. Interview with Fernando Mourão, 16 August 2006.
14. "Fascismo sôbre patins," *Portugal Democrático*, November 1961, 2; Movimento Afro-Brasileiro de Libertação de Angola, MABLA-PIDE/DGS, SC/SR 435/61/ui. 3054, ANTT.
15. "Conferência proferida pelos dois estudantes angolanos Paulo Matoso e José Manuel Gonçalges, refugiados no Brasil. Local: Associação dos Universitários de Santo André," Movimento Afro-Brasileiro de Libertação de Angola, MABLA-PIDE/DGS, SC/SR 435/61/ui. 3054, ANTT.
16. Arinos de Melo Franco, *Planalto*, 69.
17. Interview with Fernando Mourão, 16 August 2006.
18. "Informação," 11 October 1960, "Polícia Brasileira," PIDE/DGS, SC Cl(2) 565u.i. 7023.
19. Letter from Silvio da Costa Mortágua, inspetor da D.G.S., to Alcides Cintra Bueno Filho, DOPS, São Paulo, 30 January 1973, "Polícia Brasileira," PIDE/DGS, SC Cl(2) 565u.i. 7023.
20. Brazilian embassy in Dakar to Foreign Ministry, "Informação sôbre Senhor Fidelis Cabral, representante do PAIGC no Brasil," telegram 10, 2 June 1964, AHI.
21. Brazilian embassy in Dakar to Foreign Ministry, "Prisão de dois nacionalistas angolenses no Brasil: Noticiário do *Le Monde*," telegram 11, 8 May 1964; Brazilian Foreign Ministry to embassy in Dakar, "Política do Brasil com relação à África: Prisão de nacionalistas angolanos," telegram 16, 12 May 1964; Brazilian Foreign Ministry to embassy in Dakar, "Prisão de nacionalistas angolanos," telegram 20, 22 May 1964, AHI.
22. Interview with José Maria Pereira, 27 May 2006.
23. Interview with José Manuel Gonçalves, 14 June 2008.
24. Ibid.
25. Ibid.
26. Leitão da Cunha, *Diplomacia em alto mar*, 231.
27. Ramos to Portuguese Ministry of Foreign Affairs, 5 December 1961, PROC 922 PAA 283: Atitude do Brasil, MNE.
28. Dávila, *Diploma of Whiteness*, 227.
29. Interview with João Clemente Baena Soares, 30 June 2006.
30. Leitão da Cunha, *Diplomacia em alto mar*, 276.
31. Ibid., 277.
32. Ibid., 278.
33. "Nós somos por Portugal," *Diário de Notícias*, 12 June 1964; "Visita de Carlos Lacerda: Visitas Presidenciais," SR 110, Recortes de Imprensa 1964 JUN MU/GM/GNP/110/Mc. 1, AHU.

34. "Chegou ontem a Lisboa, o governador do estado brasileiro de Guanabara que ontem mesmo foi recebido pelo chefe do estado," *Primeiro de Janeiro*, 13 June 1964; "Visita de Carlos Lacerda: Visitas Presidenciais," SR 110, Recortes de Imprensa 1964 JUN MU/GM/GNP/110/Mc. 1, AHU.
35. "Chegou ontem a Lisboa, o governador do Estado brasileiro de Guanabara que ontem mesmo foi recebido pelo Chefe do Estado," *Primeiro de Janeiro*, 13 June 1964; "Visita de Carlos Lacerda: Visitas Presidenciais," SR 110, Recortes de Imprensa 1964 JUN MU/GM/GNP/110/Mc. 1, AHU.
36. "Emorou mais de duas horas o encontro de Carlos Lacerda com o Prof. Oliveira Salazar," *Diário da Manhã*, 16 June 1964.
37. "O Sr. Carlos Lacerda, falando na TV e pela rádio, explicou a génese da Revolução Brasileira e disse aprovar tudo o que se destine a manter íntegra a nação portuguesa," *O Século*, 14 June 1964; "Visita de Carlos Lacerda: Visitas Presidenciais," SR 110, Recortes de Imprensa 1964 JUN MU/GM/GNP/110/Mc. 1, AHU.
38. Brazilian Foreign Ministry to Carlos Silvestre de Ouro Preto, secret dispatch, 3 June 1966, AHI.
39. Ibid.
40. Brazilian embassy in Lisbon to Foreign Ministry, "Comunidade Luso-Brasileira: Penetração comercial e cultural do Brasil no ultramar," secret telegram 210, 12 June 1967, AHI.
41. Brazilian Foreign Ministry to embassy in Dakar, "Visita do Presidente da República do Senegal ao Brasil," telegram 11, 4 April 1962, AHI.
42. Brazilian embassy in Dakar to Foreign Ministry, "Visita ao Brasil: Presidente Senghor, do Senegal," telegram 6, 2 March 1964.
43. "Senghor homenageia no Rio o soldado desconhecido e recebe título em Salvador," *O Globo*, 22 September 1964, 14.
44. "Ribeiro da Costa a Senghor, V. Exca é um ser de exeção a quem me enobrece conhecer," *O Globo*, 26 September 1964, 6.
45. "Senghor prega união luso-afro-brasileira," *O Globo*, 21 September 1964, 1.
46. "A herança da latinidade é o mais precioso laço a unir Brasil e Senegal," *O Globo*, 23 September 1964, 6.
47. "Carregando sôbre os ombros a esperança do mundo," *O Estado de S. Paulo*, 25 September 1964, 3.
48. "Senghor fará palestra hoje," *O Estado de S. Paulo*, 26 September 1964, 36.
49. "Senghor seguiu para Trinidad," *O Estado de S. Paulo*, 29 September 1964, 1.
50. Interview with José Maria Pereira, 22 May 2008.
51. Brazilian Foreign Ministry to embassy in Dakar, "Festival de artes negras," telegram 67, 10 September 1965, AHI; "Autorização de saque, I festival mundial de artes negras em Dakar," telegrams 25 and 26, 28 February 1966, AHI; "I festival mundial de artes negras em Dacar," telegram 28, 1 March 1966, AHI; "I festival mundial de artes negras," telegram 32, 4 March 1966, AHI; "I festival mundial de artes negras," telegram 48, 17 March 1966, AHI.

52. Interview with Waldir Freitas de Oliveira, 2 August 2006.
53. Brazilian Foreign Ministry to embassy in Dakar, "I festival de artes negras, Dakar," telegram 41, 26 January 1966, AHI.
54. Macedo, "Abdias do Nascimento," 76–77.
55. Guimarães, "Racial Democracy," 127.
56. Ibid., 129.
57. "Du théâtre expérimental noir de Rio-De-Janeiro au Festival Mondial des Arts Nègres," *L'Unité Africaine*, 5 May 1966, 7.
58. "Du théâtre expérimental noir de Rio-De-Janeiro au Festival Mondial des Arts Nègres," *L'Unité Africaine*, 12 May 1966, 12.
59. "Du théâtre expérimental noir de Rio-De-Janeiro au Festival Mondial des Arts Nègres," *L'Unité Africaine*, 19 May 1966, 12.
60. Francisco Chermont de Lisboa to Juracy Magalhães, "Carta-aberta do Teatro Experimental do Negro atacando a organização social brasileira," secret dispatch 110, 27 May 1966, AHI.
61. Ibid.
62. Brazilian embassy in Dakar to Foreign Ministry, "I Festival Mundial de Artes Negras," telegram 36, 13 April 1966, AHI.
63. Brazilian Foreign Ministry to embassy in Dakar, "Festival de Arte Negra," Unnumbered telegram, 17 January 1967, AHI.
64. Portuguese embassy in Rio de Janeiro to Ministry of Foreign Affairs, 4 February 1967, Proc 922, PAA 282, Costa e Silva, MNE.
65. Brazilian Foreign Ministry to embassies in Accra, Dakar, and Lagos, "Comunicado conjunto de embaixadores de países africanos," telegram 5, 12 January 1967, AHI.
66. Ibid.
67. Portuguese embassy in Rio de Janeiro to Ministry of Foreign Affairs, 11 January 1967, Proc 922, PAA 282, incidente, MNE.
68. Rubem Braga, "Feliz 1967," *Diário de Notícias*, 28 December 1966; Portuguese embassy in Rio de Janeiro to Ministry of Foreign Affairs, 11 January 1967, both in Proc 922, PAA 282, incidente, MNE.
69. Rubem Braga, "Feliz 1967," *Diário de Notícias*, 28 December 1966, 336.63, PEA 155, Processo Geral, MNE.
70. Brazilian embassy in Lisbon to Foreign Ministry, "Relatório Político mensal: Fevereiro de 1967," dispatch 229, 17 March 1967, AHI.
71. Portuguese Ministry of Foreign Affairs to embassy in Rio de Janeiro, 30 March 1967, Proc 922, PAA 282, 1967, MNE.
72. Portuguese embassy in Rio de Janeiro, 18 January 1967, 336.63, PEA 155, Processo Geral, MNE.
73. "Racismo na colonia de Portugal na África," *Diário Popular* (São Paulo), 13 April 1959.
74. "Brazil Looks at (Portuguese) Africa," *Africa Confidential*, Brazilian embassy in Lagos to Foreign Ministry, "O Brasil e a África portuguésa: Comentário da imprensa," dispatch 77, 18 April 1967, AHI.
75. Brazilian embassy in Dakar to Foreign Ministry, "Visita de fôrça-tarefa da marinha brasileira a Luanda: Comentário na imprensa senegalesa," telegram 17, 14 February 1967, AHI.

76. "Diplomats Angered by Newspaper Criticism," *Times of Zambia*, Portuguese consulate in Salisbury to Ministry of Foreign Afairs, 27 January 1967, Proc 922, PAA 282, incidente, MNE.
77. Brazilian embassy in Lagos to Foreign Ministry, "O Brasil e a política portuguêsa na África," dispatch 36, 28 January 1967, AHI.
78. Gibson Barboza to Médici, 22 January 1974, AAS mre rb 1974.05.23, CPDOC/FGV.
79. Pinheiro, "'Ao vencedor, as batatas,'" 89; Hurrell, "The Politics of South Atlantic Security," 181–82.
80. Amado, *Tent of Miracles*, 137.
81. Ibid., 139–40.
82. SR 100/Publicações proibidas em Portugal, 1963/AGO/14-1966/DEZ/27, Y.7 MU/GM/GNP/100, Pt. 1, AHU.
83. Portuguese embassy in Rio de Janeiro to Ministry of Foreign Affairs, telegram, 31 March 1967, Proc 922, PAA 282, Costa e Silva, MNE.
84. Portuguese Ministry of Foreign Affairs to delegation at the United Nations, 10 January 1967, Proc 922, PAA 282, Incidente, MNE.
85. Interview with Mário Gibson Barboza, 18 April 2006.

Chapter 6: Gibson Barboza's Trip

1. United States embassy in Brasília to Department of State, "Brazil Discovers Africa," 28 December 1972, Pol. 7 Braz, xr Pol, Afr-Braz, box 2131, NARA.
2. Gibson Barboza to Médici, "Ação diplomática brasileira na África atlântica," secret memorandum, 16 December 1971, AAS mre rb 1974.10.00, CPDOC/FGV; Gibson Barboza, *Na diplomacia, o traço todo da vida*, 346–48.
3. Portuguese embassy in Brasília to Ministry of Foreign Affairs, 17 November 1972, Proc 922, PAA 284, pt. 2, MNE.
4. United States consulate in Recife to Department of State, "Minister of Foreign Relations Speaks on Brazil's Foreign Policy," 14 January 1973, Pol. 1 Braz, RG 59, box 2129, NARA.
5. Interview with Mário Gibson Barboza, Rio de Janeiro, 5 August 2003; Gibson Barboza, *Na diplomacia, o traço todo da vida*, 398.
6. Interview with Mário Gibson Barboza, Rio de Janeiro, 5 August 2003.
7. Ibid.
8. Ibid.
9. Hurrell, "The Politics of South Atlantic Security," 184–85.
10. United States embassy in Brasília to Department of State, "Brazil Discovers Africa," 28 December 1972, Pol. 7 Braz, xr Pol, Afr-Braz, box 2131, NARA.
11. "O Brasil será o Japão da década de 70," *Província de Angola*, 6 April 1972, 16; "As ateções do mundo voltadas para o Brasil," *Província de Angola*, 13 June 1972, 1; "Portugal pode possibilitar ao Brasil talvez o maior mercado do mundo," *Província de Angola*, 17 June 1972, 11.
12. Portuguese consulate in São Paulo to Ministry of Foreign Affairs, 31 October 1972, PAA 922, Proc 284, pt. 1, MNE.
13. Interview with Mário Gibson Barboza, Rio de Janeiro, 5 August 2003.

14. United States embassy in Brasília to Department of State, "Brazil Discovers Africa," 28 December 1972, Pol. 7 Braz, xr Pol, Afr-Braz, box 2131, NARA.
15. Gibson Barboza and Rui Patrício, "Declaração Conjunta," 10 September 1971, AAS mre rb 1964.05.23, CPDOC/FGV.
16. Gibson Barboza to Médici, 22 January 1974, AAS mre rb 1974.05.23.
17. "A Symbolic Journey," *Financial Times*, 21 April 1972, Proc 922, PAA 282, cx. 282, MNE.
18. Ibid.
19. Portuguese embassy in Rio de Janeiro to Ministry of Foreign Affairs, 31 January 1972, Proc 922, PAA 282, Brasil Geral, MNE.
20. Portuguese embassy in Rio de Janeiro to Ministry of Foreign Relations, 9 October 1971, Proc 922, PAA 292, MNE.
21. Gibson Barboza, *Na diplomacia, o traço todo da vida*, 355.
22. Portuguese embassy in Rio de Janeiro to Ministry of Foreign Affairs, 13 March 1972, Proc 922, PAA 282, Relações Econômicas, MNE.
23. Interview with Mário Gibson Barboza, Rio de Janeiro, 5 August 2003.
24. Ibid.
25. Gibson Barboza, *Na diplomacia, o traço todo da vida*, 352.
26. Portuguese embassy in Rio de Janeiro to Ministry of Foreign Affairs, 31 January 1972, Proc 922, PAA 282, Brasil Geral, MNE.
27. Portuguese embassy in Brasília to Ministry of Foreign Affairs, 26 July 1972, Proc 922, PAA 282, Brasil Geral, MNE.
28. Gibson Barboza to Médici, "Exposição de motivos ao presidente da república: Ação diplomática brasileira na África atlântica," secret memorandum, 29 December 1972, AHI.
29. Gibson Barboza, *Na diplomacia, o traço todo da vida*, 400.
30. Interview with Rubens Ricupero, 26 July 2006.
31. Brazilian embassy in Dakar to Foreign Ministry, "Visita do ministro de estado," 4 October 1972, AHI.
32. Brazilian embassy in Senegal to Foreign Ministry, "Visita do ministro de estado," 26 September 1972, AHI.
33. Brazilian embassy in Senegal to Foreign Ministry, "Visita do ministro de estado," 26 September 1972, AHI; Gibson Barboza, *Na diplomacia, o traço todo da vida*, 406.
34. Interview with Rubens Ricupero, 26 July 2006.
35. "Festival de Artes Negras e Africanas, Janeiro e Fevereiro de 1977," 7 October 1976, EG pr 1974.03.18, f-1980, CPDOC/FGV.
36. Waldir Freitas de Oliveira, "Brasil e África: A viagem do ministro," *A Tarde*, 17 November 1972; Portuguese consulate in Salvador to Ministry of Foreign Affairs, 28 November 1972, Proc 922, PAA 284, pt. 3, MNE.
37. Portuguese embassy in Brasília to Ministry of Foreign Affairs, 4 December 1972, Proc 922, PEA 284, pt. 3, MNE.
38. "Brasil um imão bem sucedido," *Jornal do Brasil*, 22 November 1972; Portuguese embassy in Rio de Janeiro to Ministry of Foreign Affairs, 24 November 1972, Proc 922, PAA 284, pt. 3, MNE.

39. Portuguese embassy in Brasília to Ministry of Foreign Affairs, 4 December 1972, MNE.
40. Interview with Rubens Ricupero, 26 July 2006.
41. Gibson Barboza to Médici, "Exposição de motivos ao presidente da república: Ação diplomática brasileira na África atlântica," secret memorandum, 29 December 1972, AHI.
42. Gibson Barboza, *Na diplomacia, o traço todo da vida*, 400.
43. *Fraternité Matin*, 22 October 1972, 9; 23 October 1972, 9.
44. Gibson Barboza to Médici, "Exposição de motivos ao presidente da república: Ação diplomática brasileira na África atlântica," secret memorandum, 29 December 1972, AHI.
45. Gibson Barboza, *Na diplomacia, o traço todo da vida*, 402.
46. Costa e Silva, *O vício da África e outros vícios*, 404.
47. *Fraternité Matin*, 30 October 1972, 1.
48. Gibson Barboza, *Na diplomacia, o traço todo da vida*, 405.
49. Ibid., 406–8.
50. Ibid., 409.
51. Ibid.
52. "An Example of Mutual Co-operation," *Ghanaian Times*, 3 November 1972, 2.
53. "Brazil and Africa," *Daily Graphic*, 31 October 1972, 2.
54. "Racism in the World," *Daily Graphic*, 21 November 1972, 5.
55. Interview with Rubens Ricupero, 26 July 2006.
56. Ibid.
57. Ibid.
58. Gibson Barboza, *Na diplomacia, o traço todo da vida*, 415.
59. Gibson Barboza to Médici, "Exposição de motivos ao presidente da república: Ação diplomática brasileira na África atlântica," secret memorandum, 29 December 1972, AHI.
60. United States embassy in Douala to Department of State, "Visit of Brazilian Foreign Minister to Cameroon, November 11–15," 21 November 1972, Pol. 7 Braz, xr Pol, Afr-Braz, box 2131, NARA.
61. Gibson Barboza, *Na diplomacia, o traço todo da vida*, 431–32.
62. Gibson Barboza to Médici, "Exposição de motivos ao presidente da república: Ação diplomática brasileira na África atlântica," secret memorandum, 29 December 1972, AHI; "De volta da África," *Veja*, 29 November 1972; Portuguese consulate in São Paulo to Ministry of Foreign Affairs, 29 November 1972; Proc 922, PAA 284, pt. 3, MNE.
63. Gibson Barboza, *Na diplomacia, o traço todo da vida*, 432.
64. "Jornal governista da Nigéria faz ataque ao Brasil," *O Estado de S. Paulo*, 19 November 1972; Portuguese consulate in São Paulo to Ministry of Foreign Affairs, 23 November 1982, Proc 922, PAA 284, pt. 3, MNE.
65. *Daily Times*, 19 October 1972, 10.
66. "The UN Vote on Liberation Movements," *Daily Times*, 22 November 1972, 3.
67. Gibson Barboza, *Na diplomacia, o traço todo da vida*, 434.
68. Gibson Barboza to Médici, "Exposição de motivos ao presidente da

república: Ação diplomática brasileira na África atlântica," secret memorandum, 29 December 1972, AHI.

69. Interview with Rubens Ricupero, 26 July 2006.
70. "Le noir africain dans la société brésilienne," *Le Soleil*, 20 November 1972, 2.
71. Gibson Barboza, *Na diplomacia, o traço todo da vida*, 437.
72. Gibson Barboza to Médici, "Política externa brasileira, áfrica: Guinea-Bissau," 27 November 1972, AAS mre rb 1974.10.00, CPDOC/FGV.
73. Portuguese embassy in Brasília to Ministry of Foreign Affairs, 29 November 1972, Proc 922, PAA 284, pt. 3, MNE.
74. "Gibson chega e despacha com Médici," *Gazeta Mercantil*, 23 November 1972; Portuguese consulate in São Paulo to Ministry of Foreign Affairs, 23 November 1972, Proc 922, PAA 284, pt. 3, MNE.
75. "Presença da África no mundo," *O Jornal*, 14 November 1972; Portuguese embassy in Brasília to Ministry of Foreign Affairs, 17 November 1972, Proc 922, PAA 284, pt. 2, MNE.
76. "O fim da viagem do Ministro," *Jornal da Tarde*, 22 November 1972; Portuguese consulate in São Paulo to Ministry of Foreign Affairs, 23 November 1972, Proc 922, PAA 284, pt. 3, MNE.
77. Advertisement, "O maior ídolo da canção brasileira: Roberto Carlos—e o Conjunto R.C. 7—no palco do Cinema Avis," *Província de Angola*, 1 November 1972, 3.
78. Portuguese embassy in Brasília to Ministry of Foreign Affairs, 17 November 1972, Proc 922, PAA 284, pt. 2, MNE.
79. Portuguese embassy in Brasília to Ministry of Foreign Affairs, 24 November 1972, Proc 922, PAA 284, pt. 3, MNE.
80. United States embassy in Brasília to Department of State, "Brazil Discovers Africa," 28 December 1972, Pol. 7 Braz, xr Pol, Afr-Braz, box 2131, NARA.
81. Portuguese embassy in Brasília to Ministry of Foreign Affairs, 28 November 1972, PROC 922, PAA 284, pt. 2, MNE.
82. United States embassy in Brasília to Department of State, "Brazil Discovers Africa," 28 December 1972, Pol. 7 Braz, xr Pol, Afr-Braz, box 2131, NARA.
83. Gibson Barboza to Médici, "Política externa do Brasil na África: Territórios ultramarinos portuguêses," 23 February 1973, AAS mre rb 1974.10.00, CPDOC/FGV.
84. Gibson Barboza to Médici, 22 January 1974, AAS mre rb 1974.05.23, CPDOC/FGV.
85. Ibid.
86. Interview with Rubens Ricupero, 26 July 2008.
87. Ibid.

Chapter 7: Brazil and the Portuguese Revolution

1. Interview with Ramiro Saraíva Guerreiro, 22 August 2006.
2. "Brazil," *Financial Times Survey*, 23 September 1975, cited in R. A. Tokuta, "Nigeria and Brazil: Problems and Prospects," paper presented at the con-

ference "Nigeria-Angola-Brazil Axis," Nigerian Institute of International Affairs, Lagos, April 1976; Brazilian embassy in Lagos to Foreign Ministry, 7 May 1976, AHI.

3. Sombra Saraíva, *O lugar da África*, 181.
4. Cel. Eng. Qema. João Tarcizio Cartaxo Arruda, *Portugal: Evolução Política* (Brasília: Trabalho de Estágio, 1983), 63; Azeredo da Silveira Archive, AAS ep 1983.05.25, CPDOC/FGV.
5. Cel. Eng. Qema. João Tarcizio Cartaxo Arruda, *Portugal: Evolução Política* (Brasília: Trabalho de Estágio, 1983); Azeredo da Silveira Archive, AAS ep 1983.05.25, CPDOC/FGV.
6. Brazilian embassy in Lisbon to Foreign Ministry, "XIII aniversário da rebelião nacionalista em Angola: Postura portuguesa com referência às Províncias Ultramarinas," dispatch 70, 28 February 1974, AHI.
7. Ibid.
8. Brazilian embassy in Lisbon to Foreign Ministry, "Situação política em Portugal: Análise perspectiva," dispatch 252, 5 June 1974, AHI.
9. Spínola, *Portugal e o futuro*, 47.
10. Ibid., 126.
11. Ibid., 117.
12. Ibid., 125.
13. Manoel Sarmento Rodrigues to Gilberto Freyre, 6 June 1974, GF/CR Port., 21, FGF.
14. Ibid.
15. Brazilian embassy in Lisbon to Foreign Ministry, "Situação política em Portugal: Análise perspectiva," dispatch 252, 5 June 1974, AHI.
16. Fontoura to Foreign Ministry, "Política ultramarina de Portugal," 27 July 1974, Azeredo da Silveira Archive, AAS mre/d 1974.04.23, CPDOC/FGV.
17. Gilberto Freyre, "Em torno de uma mensagem do presidente Spínola," *Diário de Pernambuco*, 18 August 1974, Artigos de jornal de Gilberto Freyre, AJ-18, 1972–1974, FGF.
18. Cardoso and Soares, *O mundo em Português*, 143.
19. Ibid., 9.
20. Cervo and Magalhães, *Depois das caravelas*, 252.
21. Skidmore, *The Politics of Military Rule in Brazil.*
22. Telegram from embassy in Lisbon to foreign minister, "Designação do embaixador Fontoura para Lisboa," 23 May 1975, Azeredo da Silveira Archive, AAS mre/rb 1974.05.23, CPDOC/FGV.
23. Ibid.
24. Gaspari, *A ditadura derrotada*, 372; telegram from the Foreign Ministry to embassy in Lisbon, "Relações Brasil-Portugal: Designação do embaixador Fontoura," 23 May 1975, Azeredo da Silveira Archive, AAS mre/rb 1974 .05.23, CPDOC/FGV.
25. Telegram from Foreign Ministry to embassy in Lisbon, "Relações Brasil-Portugal: Designação do embaixador Fontoura," 23 May 1975, Azeredo da Silveira Archive, AAS mre/rb 1974.05.23, CPDOC/FGV.

26. Telegram from embassy in Lisbon to Foreign Ministry, "Manifestação contra a Embaixada em Lisboa," 27 May 1974, Azeredo da Silveira Archive, AAS mre/rb 1974.05.23, CPDOC/FGV.
27. Ibid.
28. "General Spínola: Passaporte," 18 March 1976, EG pr 1974.03.18, f-1712, CPDOC/FGV.
29. Cited in Maxwell, *The Making of Portuguese Democracy*, 107.
30. EME, "Diplomatas portugueses na embaixada em Brasília," 3 July 1975, DOPS dossier 226: Portugal, DOPS/APERJ.
31. SNI, "Infiltração comunista portuguesa," 14 August 1975, DOPS dossier 226: Portugal, DOPS/APERJ.
32. "Política de defesa de investimentos privados brasileiros," 3 April 1975, EG pr 1974.03.18 f-1207, CPDOC/FGV.
33. SNI, "Atividades de portugueses no Brasil," 9 May 1975, DOPS dossier 226: Portugal, DOPS/APERJ.
34. Brazilian embassy in Portugal to Foreign Ministry, "Desemprego em Portugal: Emigração," telegram 70, 1 January 1975, AHI.
35. Maxwell, *The Making of Portuguese Democracy*, 142.
36. Ibid.
37. Between 1970 and 1980 the Portuguese-born population in Brazil (including the colonies) decreased from 410,216 to 398,616, but given that immigration dwindled in the 1950s, the reduction in population through the rate of mortality statistically conceals the influx of Portuguese immigrants to Brazil in the 1970s. "Estrangeiros, por sexo e situação do domicílio, segundo o país de nascimento," *Censo demográfico do Brasil, VIII recenceamento geral*, 1970, 20; "Naturalizados brasileiros e estrangeiros, por sexo, segundo o país de nascimento," *Censo demográfico do Brasil*, 1980, 52.
38. Ovídio de Melo, 12 June 1975, "Êxodo de portugueses de Angola," dispatch 22, special representation in Luanda to Foreign Ministry, AHI.
39. Ibid.
40. Interview with Ovídio and Ivony de Melo, 25 July 2006.
41. Melo, "*O reconhecimento de Angola pelo Brasil em 1975*," 57.
42. Interview with Ovídio and Ivony de Melo, 25 July 2006.
43. Orlando Senna, "Cortar Cabeças, uma profissão como as outras," *Jornal do Brasil*, AAS mre rb 1974.08.19, CPDOC/FGV.
44. "Imigração portuguesa: Proposta de diretrizes para seu tratamento global," 25 December 1975, EG pr 1974.03.18, f-1339, CPDOC/FGV.
45. Informação para o senhor presidente da república, relatório do grupo de trabalho Sobre Portugal" (214), 6 August 1975, AAS mre d 1974.03.26, vol. 5, CPDOC/FGV.
46. Ibid.
47. Informação para o senhor presidente da república, "Programa de estudantes-convênio com Portugal: Número de vagas" (043), 7 February 1975, AAS mre d 1974.03.26, vol. 5, CPDOC/FGV.
48. Informação para o senhor presidente da república, "Posição brasileira em relação ao problema migratório portugués," 2 October 1975, Azeredo da Silveira Archive, AAS mre/d 1974.03.26, CPDOC/FGV.

49. Informação para o senhor ministro de estado, "Deslocados de Angola: Entendimentos com o Ministério da Aeronáutica e Varig," Armido Branco Mendes Cadaxa, 7 October 1975, Azeredo da Silveira Archive, AAS mre/rb 1974.08.19, CPDOC/FGV.
50. Informação para o senhor presidente da república, "Imigração portuguesa: Proposta de diretrizes para seu tratamento global," 24 December 1975, Azeredo da Silveira Archive, AAS mre/d 1974.03.26, vol. 12, CPDOC/FGV.
51. "Imigração portuguesa: Exame da possibilidade de encaminhamento para o setor agrícola," 19 September 1975, Ernesto Geisel Archive, EG pr 1974.03.18, folder 4 (f. 1416), CPDOC/FGV.
52. "Visita de Azeredo da Silveira à Portugal, dezembro de 1974," AAS mre rb 1974.05.23, CPDOC/FGV.
53. Ibid.
54. Vianna, *Uma tempestade como a sua memória*; Lesser, *A Discontented Diaspora*.
55. Vianna, *Uma tempestade como a sua memória*, 147.
56. Brazilian embassy in Lisbon to Foreign Ministry, "Utilização do Método Paulo Freire," telegram 114, 14 January 1975, AHI.
57. Interview with Maria do Carmo Brito and Mário Osava, 25 May 2006.
58. Vianna, *Uma tempestade como a sua memória*, 148.
59. Interview with Maria do Carmo Brito and Mário Osava, 25 May 2006.
60. Brazilian embassy in Lisbon to Foreign Ministry, "Imagem do Brasil na imprensa de Portugal: Entrevistas de Miguel Arraes," dispatch 635, 5 December 1974, AHI.
61. CIEX/SEDOC, "Informe Interno 249: José Gomes Talarico," 9 August 1976, AAS mre/ag 1974.03.25, CPDOC/FGV.
62. CIEX/SEDOC, "Viagem de Brizzola [*sic*] a Portugal," 23 January 1978, AAS mre/ag 1974.03.25, CPDOC/FGV.
63. Dinges, *The Condor Years*.
64. Octavio Goulart to Azeredo da Silveira, "Suposta correspondência entre SNI e a Embaixada em Lisboa: Noticiário da imprensa brasileira," 8 May 1978, AAS mre/ag 1974.03.25, CPDOC/FGV.
65. Interview with José Maria Pereira, 23 June 2009.
66. Melo, "*O Reconhecimento de Angola pelo Brasil em 1975*," 37.

Chapter 8: The Special Representation in Angola, 1975

1. Hodges, *Angola*, 10.
2. Melo, "*O Reconhecimento de Angola pelo Brasil em 1975*," 46.
3. "Comunicado dos trabalhadores do *Jornal de Angola*," *Jornal de Angola*, 18 July 1975, 1.
4. Ibid.; "Comunicado do MPLA em denúncia do nosso jornal," *Jornal de Angola*, 18 July 1972, 2; "Deflagrou um engenho explosivo nas instalações do nosso jornal," *Jornal de Angola*, 24 July 1975, 1.
5. Interview with José Manuel Gonçalves, 14 June 2008; embassy in Luanda to Foreign Ministry, "Solicitação de assistencia a jornal angolano," telegram 162, 25 March 1976, AHI.
6. "'Esquadrão da morte' volta a actuar," *Jornal de Angola*, 14 August 1975, 10.

7. "Angola está a ficar mais pobre," *Jornal de Angola*, 30 August 1975, 5.
8. "O Brasil tornou-se um inferno," *Jornal de Angola*, 8 November 1975, 8.
9. Gaspari, *A ditadura encurralada*, 137, 139.
10. Interview with Ramiro Saraíva Guerreiro, 22 August 2006.
11. Melo, "*O Reconhecimento de Angola pelo Brasil em 1975*," 35.
12. Ibid., 29, 34.
13. Ibid., 47.
14. Interview with Ovídio and Ivony de Melo, 25 July 2006.
15. Ibid.
16. Ibid.
17. Ovídio de Melo, 2 August 1975, "'Cabo Orange,'" telegram 269, special representation in Luanda to Foreign Ministry, AHI.
18. Ovídio de Melo, 24 July 1975, "Impresão de um marujo brasileiro a respeito dos conflitos em Luanda," dispatch 187, special representation in Luanda to Foreign Ministry, AHI.
19. Ovídio de Melo, 1 August 1975, "Evacuação de brasileiros em Luanda," telegram 267, special representation in Luanda to Foreign Ministry, AHI.
20. "Envio de víveres para a representação Especial em Luanda," 4 August 1975, telegram 236, Foreign Ministry to special representation in Luanda, AHI.
21. Gleijesess, *Conflicting Missions*, 255–56.
22. Ibid., 293–95.
23. Melo, "*O Reconhecimento de Angola pelo Brasil em 1975*," 54.
24. Telegram from Ítalo Zappa to Azeredo da Silveira, 5 August 1975, AAS mre/rb 1974.08.19, CPDOC/FGV.
25. Interview with Ovídio and Ivony de Melo, 25 July 2006.
26. Telegram from Ítalo Zappa to Azeredo da Silveira, 5 August 1975, AAS mre/rb 1974.08.19, CPDOC/FGV.
27. Ibid.
28. Interview with Ovídio and Ivony de Melo, 25 July 2006.
29. Ibid.
30. Gil de Ouro Preto, 5 September 1975, "Percalços da vida diplomática: A derrota da lixeira," dispatch 212, special representation in Luanda to Foreign Ministry, AHI.
31. Ovídio de Melo to Foreign Ministry, "Expulsão de membros da PIDE," secret telegram 116, 30 May 1975, AHI.
32. Interview with Ovídio and Ivony de Melo, 25 July 2006; Ovídio de Melo to Foreign Ministry, "Agentes Federais," secret telelegram 146, 12 June 1975, AHI.
33. Ovídio de Melo to Foreign Ministry, "Agentes Federais," secret telelegram 146, 12 June 1975, AHI.
34. Interview with Ovídio and Ivony de Melo, 25 July 2006.
35. Ibid.
36. Ovídio de Melo to Foreign Ministry, "Situação interna de Angola," telegram 150, 17 June 1975, AHI.

37. O. L. de Berenguer Cesar, cônsul geral, "Relações Brasil-Moçambique: Informação para o senhor ministro de estado," 8 July 1975, Azeredo da Silveira Archive, AAS mre/d 1974.04.23, CPDOC/FGV.
38. Ibid.
39. Ovídio de Melo to Foreign Ministry, "Reconhecimento de Angola," telegram 474, 6 November 1975, AHI.
40. Gleijeses, *Conflicting Missions*, 301–3.
41. "Reconhecimento do Governo de Angola," Informação para o senhor presidente da república, 3 November 1975, Azeredo da Silveira Archive, AAS mre/d 1974.03.26, CPDOC/FGV; Saraíva Guerreiro, *Lembranças de um empregado do Itamaraty*, 189.
42. Ramiro Saraíva Guerreiro to Azeredo da Silveira, 3 November 1975, Azeredo da Silveira Archive, AAS mre/d 1974.03.26, CPDOC/FGV.
43. Interview with Ovídio and Ivony de Melo, 25 July 2006.
44. Gleijeses, *Conflicting Missions*, 308.
45. Brazilian embassy in Washington to Foreign Ministry, telegram 4377, 5 November 1975, Azeredo da Silveira Archive, AAS mre/rb 1974.08.19, CPDOC/FGV.
46. D'Araujo and Castro, eds., *Ernesto Geisel*, 344.
47. Interview with Ramiro Saraíva Guerreiro, 22 August 2006.
48. Ramiro Saraíva Guerreiro to Azeredo da Silveira, 3 November 1975, AAS mre/d 1974.03.26, CPDOC/FGV.
49. Ibid.
50. Interview with Ramiro Saraíva Guerreiro, 22 August 2006.
51. Interview with Rubens Ricupero, 26 July 2006.
52. Telegram from Divisão de África to embassies in the Americas, Europe, and Africa, "Reconhecumento de Angola," 4 November 1975; Brazilian embassy in London to Foreign Ministry, telegram 1651, 5 November 1975, Azeredo da Silveira Archive, AAS mre/rb 1974.08.19, CPDOC/FGV; Brazilian embassy in Paris to Foreign Ministry, telegram 983, 5 November 1975, Azeredo da Silveira Archive, AAS mre/rb 1974.08.19, CPDOC/FGV; Brazilian embassy in Stockholm to Foreign Ministry, telegram 375, 5 November 1975, Azeredo da Silveira Archive, AAS mre/rb 1974.08.19, CPDOC/FGV; Brazilian embassy in Washington to Foreign Ministry, telegram 4377, 5 November 1975, Azeredo da Silveira Archive, AAS mre/rb 1974.08.19, CPDOC/FGV.
53. Gaspari, *A ditadura encurralada*, 142.
54. "Resumo das conversações mantidas durante os encontros entre o Presidente Ernesto Geisel e o Presidente Antonio Ramalho Eanes, de Portugal, no Palácio do Planalto, em 22 e 23 de maio de 1978," prepared by Gilberto Coutinho Paranhos Velloso, Azeredo da Silveira Archive, AAS mre/d 1974.04.23, pasta XXXV, CPDOC/FGV.
55. Telegram from Azeredo da Silveira to Ramiro Saraíva Guerreiro, 6 November 1975, Azeredo da Silveira Archive, AAS mre/rb 1974.08.19, CPDOC/FGV.

56. Saraíva Guerreiro, *Lembranças de um empregado do Itamaraty*, 189–90.
57. "Conferência pronunciada por Sua Excelência o Senhor Ministro de Estado das Relações Exteriores, Embaixador Antonio F. Azeredo da Silveira, na Escola de Guerra Naval," 10 November 1975, Azeredo da Silveira Archive, AAS mre/ag 1974.05.27, CPDOC/FGV.
58. Ibid.
59. Ibid.
60. Melo, "*O Reconhecimento de Angola pelo Brasil em 1975*," 61.
61. "Respostas do Chanceler Azeredo da Silveira às perguntas que lhe foram formuladas após sua exposição sobre política exterior aos membros do Estado Maior das Forças Armadas," Azeredo da Silveira Archive, AAS mre/ag 1977.11.25, CPDOC/FGV.
62. Melo, "*O reconhecimento de Angola pelo Brasil em 1975*," 66.
63. Gaspari, *A ditadura encurralhada*, 150.
64. Melo, *O reconhecimento de Angola pelo Brasil em 1975*, 64.
65. "Mexicanização da diplomacia," *O Estado de São Paulo*, 12 November 1975, 3.
66. "Dize-me com quem andas e . . . ," *O Estado de São Paulo*, 13 November 1975, 3.
67. Melo, "*O reconhecimento de Angola pelo Brasil em 1975*," 67.
68. Ovídio de Melo to Foreign Ministry, "Chamado telefonico de jornalista," telegram 586, 24 December 1975, AHI.
69. Ovídio de Melo to Foreign Ministry, "Encarregatura de negócios," telegram 595, 29 December 1975, AHI; interview with Ovídio and Ivony de Melo, 25 July 2006.
70. Frota, *Ideais traídos*, 190.
71. Ibid., 547.
72. "Notas da reunião de trabalho com o Secretário de Estado Henry Kissinger, no Palácio Itamaraty," 19 February 1976, EG pr 1974.03.18, f-0614, CPDOC/FGV; "Notas sobre as conversações entre o Presidente Ernesto Geisel e o Presidente Carter," 29 March 1978, EG pr 1974.03.18, f-0614, CPDOC/FGV; "Notas sobre as conversações entre o Presidente Ernesto Geisel e o Presidente V. Giscard d'Estaing, no Palácio do Elysée," 24–25 April 1976, EG pr 1974.03.18, f-0614, CPDOC/FGV; "Reunião amliada entre o Senhor Presidente da República e o Primeiro Ministro James Callagham," 6 May 1976, EG pr 1974.03.18, f-0614, CPDOC/FGV.
73. Brazilian embassy in Luanda to Foreign Ministry, "Política: Brasil: Angola e Estados Unidos: Condenação de mercenários," 2 July 1976, AAS mre rb 1976.01.01, CPDOC/FGV.
74. Interview with Maria do Carmo Brito and Mário Osava, 25 May 2006.
75. Vianna, *Uma tempestade como a sua memória*, 149.
76. Ibid.
77. Ibid., 159.
78. Interview with Maria do Carmo Brito and Mário Osava, 25 May 2006.
79. Vianna, *Uma tempestade como a sua memória*, 159.
80. Interview with Maria do Carmo Brito and Mário Osava, 25 May 2006.
81. Ibid.
82. Rui, *Quem me dera ser onda*, 2.

83. Interview with Maria do Carmo Brito and Mário Osava, 25 May 2006.
84. Vianna, *Uma tempestade como a sua memória*, 154.
85. Ibid., 126.
86. Interview with Maria do Carmo Brito and Mário Osava, 25 May 2006.
87. Ibid.
88. "Brasileiros exilados no exterior: Possibilidade de regresso," Informação para o Senhor Presidente da República, 2 August 1978, Azeredo da Silveira Archive, AAS mre/d 1974.03.26, vol. 34, CPDOC/FGV.
89. Interview with Maria do Carmo Brito and Mário Osava, 25 May 2006.
90. Ibid.
91. Ibid.
92. Brazilian embassy in Maputo to Foreign Ministry, "Mensagem de Samora Machel a Luis Carlos Prestes," 4 January 1978, AAS mre rb 1974.08.19, CPDOC/FGV.
93. Interview with Mário Osava and Maria do Carmo Brito, 25 May 2006.
94. Ibid.
95. Brazilian embassy in Maputo to Foreign Ministry, passport request forms, 22 May–9 August 1979, AHI.
96. Rodolpho Godoy de Souza Dantas, "Gabriela: Recortes do jornal de Angola," 11 May 1978, embassy in Luanda to Foreign Ministry, AHI.
97. Rodolpho Godoy de Souza Dantas, "Gabriela: Recortes do jornal de Angola," 11 May 1978, embassy in Luanda to Foreign Ministry, AHI.
98. Dzidzienyo, "The African Connection and the Afro-Brazilian Condition," 145; Skidmore, "Race and Class in Brazil," 15.
99. Centro de Informações da Aeronáutica,"Programação de ensino supletivo 1o gráu: Rede Globo/MEC," 13 May 1981, DGIE dossier 306: Departamento Geral de Investigações Especiais Collection, DOPS/APERJ.
100. Rodolfo Souza Dantas, "Visita do Ministro dos Petróleos de Angola ao Brasil," telegram 197, 4 May 1979; "Visita do ministro dos petróleos de Angola ao Brasil: Recortes de imprensa," telegram 200, 6 May 1979, embassy in Luanda to Foreign Ministry, AHI.
101. Rodolfo Godoy Souza Dantas, "Relações Brasil-Angola: Visita do Ministro dos Petróleos: Noticia na imprensa local," telegram 218, 11 May 1979, embassy in Luanda to Foreign Ministry, AHI.

Chapter 9: Miracle for Sale

1. "De volta da África," *Veja*, 29 November 1972; Portuguese consulate in São Paulo to Ministry of Foreign Affairs, 29 November 1972, Proc 922, PAA 284, pt. 3, MNE.
2. Brazilian embassy in Lagos to Foreign Ministry, "Apresentação de credenciais do embaixador do Brasil em Lagos," dispatch 155, 26 October 1973, AHI.
3. "Conferência pronunciada pelo ministro de estado das relações exteriores, embaixador Antonio F. Azeredo da Silveira, na Escola Nacional de Informações, ESNI, Brasília," 12 June 1978, Azeredo da Silveira Archive, AAS mre/ag 1974.05.27, CPDOC/FGV.

4. Ibid.
5. D'Araujo and Castro, eds., *Ernesto Geisel*, 287.
6. Gaspari, *A ditadura derrotada*, 16.
7. "A palavra que falta," *O Estado de São Paulo*, 14 November 1975, 3.
8. "Pronunciamento do Senhor Embaixador Antonio F. Azeredo da Silveira, Ministro de Estado das Relações Exteriores, perante as Comissões de Relações Exteriores do Senado Federal e da C,mara dos Deputados, em reunião conjunta," 11 August 1976, Azeredo da Silveira Archive, AAS mre/ag 1974.01.16, CPDOC/FGV.
9. Ibid.
10. Gilberto Freyre, "O Brasil como um novo tipo de civilização," *Jornal do Comércio*, 4 April 1976, Artigos de Jornal de Gilberto Freyre, AJ-19, 1975–76, FGF.
11. "Conferência pronunciada pelo Embaixador Antonio F. Azeredo da Silveira, Ministro de Estado das Relações Exteriores, na Escola Superior de Guerra," 20 September 1978, Azeredo da Silveira Archive, AAS mre/ag 1974.05.27, CPDOC/FGV.
12. Ibid.
13. Brazilian embassy in Lagos to Foreign Ministry, "Relações Brasil-Nigéria: Problemas de navegação," telegram 139, 24 April 1975, AHI.
14. Informação para o senhor presidente da república, "Relações econômicas e comerciais Brasil-Nigéria," 21 June 1977, AAS mre d 1974.03.26, CPDOC/FGV.
15. *Banco do Brasil, Carteira de Comercio Exterior, CACEX: Séries estatísticas, 1981.* (Rio de Janeiro: Carteira de Comercio Exterior, 1981); Selcher, "Uncertain Partners," 11.
16. Informação para o senhor presidente da república, "Relações econômicas e comerciais Brasil-Nigéria," 21 June 1977, AAS mre d 1974.03.26, CPDOC/FGV.
17. Brazilian embassy in Lagos to Foreign Ministry, "Colonias estrangeiras na Nigéria," telegram 376, 11 August 1977, AHI.
18. Brazilian embassy in Lagos to Foreign Ministry, "Visita à Volkswagen da Nigéria," telegram 101, 7 March 1975, AHI.
19. Brazilian embassy in Lagos to Foreign Ministry, "Medidas de Proteção para a Volkswagen e a Peugeot," telegram 111, 3 April 1975, AHI.
20. Brazilian embassy in Lagos to Foreign Ministry, "Relações Brasil-Nigéria: Problemas de navegação," telegram 139, 24 April 1975, AHI.
21. Informação para o senhor presidente da república, "Missão Comercial à África," 3 March 1976, AAS mre d 1974.03.26, vol. 14, CPDOC/FGV.
22. Brazilian embassy in Lagos to Foreign Ministry, "Volkswagen da Nigéria: Mercado de automóveis," telegram 107, 5 April 1978, AHI.
23. Santana, *Interbras, ficção e realidade*, 98.
24. Informação para o senhor presidente da república, "Situação na Nigéria," 17 February 1976, AAS mre d 1974.03.26, CPDOC/FGV.
25. Santana, *Interbras, ficção e realidade*, 99, 105.
26. Ibid., 118.

27. Ibid., 105; Assis, *Os mandarins da república*, 66–68.
28. Brazilian embassy in Lagos to Foreign Ministry, "Estabelecimento de fazendas integradas: Frigorífico Cotia," telegram 178, 5 April 1977, AHI.
29. Brazilian Foreign Ministry to embassy in Lagos, "Promoção comercial Brasil-Nigéria: Exportação de remédios: Cotia," telegram 373, 12 July 1977, AHI.
30. Brazilian embassy in Lagos to Foreign Ministry, "Promoção cultural: Nigéria: Inauguração da Fábrica 'LIK,'" telegram 220, 4 April 1980, AHI.
31. Brazilian embassy in Lagos to Foreign Ministry, "II FESTAC," telegram 37, 20 January 1977, AHI.
32. Brazilian embassy in Lagos to Foreign Ministry, "Editorial na imprensa local: Critica ao Brasil," telegram 8, 6 January 1977, AHI.
33. Brazilian embassy in Lagos to Foreign Ministry, "II FESTAC," telegram 37, 20 January 1977, AHI; Nascimento, *Sitiado em Lagos*.
34. Brazilian embassy in Lagos to Foreign Ministry, "A atuação do Senhor Abdias do Nascimento no 'Colóquio' do II FESTAC," dispatch 27, 6 February 1977, AHI.
35. Ibid.
36. Brazilian embassy in Lagos to Foreign Ministry, "FESTAC: Imprensa: Entevistade Abdias do Nascimento," telegram 45, 24 January 1977; Brazilian embassy in Lagos to Foreign Ministry, "A atuação do Senhor Abdias do Nascimento no 'Colóquio' do II FESTAC," dispatch 27, 6 February 1977, AHI.
37. Brazilian embassy in Lagos to Foreign Ministry, "II FESTAC," telegram 40, 31 January 1977, AHI.
38. Brazilian embassy in Lagos to Foreign Ministry, "FESTAC: Imprensa: Entevista de Abdias do Nascimento," telegram 45, 27 January 1977, AHI.
39. Informação para o senhor presidente da república,"II Festival Mundial de Artes Negras: Acusações de racismo ao Brasil," 3 February 1977, AAS mre d 1974.03.26, vol. 23, CPDOC/FGV.
40. Brazilian embassy in Lagos to Foreign Ministry, "FESTAC: Participação de Abdias do Nascimento: Ataque à delegação brasileira," telegram 61, 24 January 1977, AHI.
41. Brazilian embassy in Lagos to Foreign Ministry, "A atuação do Senhor Abdias do Nascimento no 'Colóquio' do II FESTAC," dispatch 27, 6 February 1977; Brazilian embassy in Lagos to Foreign Ministry, "II FESTAC," telegram 51, 28 January 1977, AHI.
42. Brazilian Foreign Ministry to embassy in Lagos, "II FESTAC: Monografia de Abdias do Nascimento," telegram 74, 31 January 1977, AHI.
43. Brazilian embassy in Lagos to Foreign Ministry, "FESTAC," telegram 51, 27 January 1977, AHI.
44. Brazilian embassy in Lagos to Foreign Ministry, "A atuação do Senhor Abdias do Nascimento no 'Colóquio' do II FESTAC," dispatch 27, 6 February 1977, AHI.
45. Brazilian embassy in Lagos to Foreign Ministry, "FESTAC," telegram 51, 27 January 1977, AHI.
46. Ibid.

47. Brazilian embassy in Lagos to Foreign Ministry, "FESTAC: Participação de Abdias do Nascimento: Imagem do Brasil," telegram 58, 1 February 1977, AHI.
48. Ibid.
49. Ibid.
50. Femi Abubakar, "Approach with Caution: Nigeria-Brazil Relations," *New Nigerian*, 26 July 1977, 5; Brazilian embassy in Lagos to Foreign Ministry, "Imagem do Brasil no exterior: Artigo na imprensa nigeriana," dispatch 146, 28 July 1977, AHI.
51. Brazilian Foreign Ministry to embassy in Lagos, "Voo inaugural da Varig Lagos–Rio de Janeiro," telegram 338, 23 June 1977, AHI.
52. Brazilian embassy in Lagos to Foreign Ministry, "Transportes Aéreos: Brasil-Nigéria: Linha da Varig," telegram 444, 25 June 1980, AHI.
53. Informação para o senhor presidente da república, "Relações econômicas e comerciais Brasil-Nigéria," 21 June 1977, AAS mre d 1974.03.26, CPDOC/FGV.
54. R. A. Tokuta, "Nigeria and Brazil: Problems and Prospects," paper presented at the conference "Nigeria-Angola-Brazil Axis," Nigerian Institute of International Affairs, Lagos, April 1976, Brazilian embassy in Lagos to Foreign Ministry, 7 May 1976, AHI.
55. A. Odutola, "Expanding Diplomatic Relations between Nigeria and Brazil," paper presented at the conference "Nigeria-Angola-Brazil Axis," Nigerian Institute of International Affairs, Lagos, April 1976, Brazilian embassy in Lagos to Foreign Ministry, 7 May 1976, AHI.
56. Cited in Forrest, "Brazil and Africa," 14–15.
57. "Consumers Assess Igala," *Daily Times*, 11 April 1978, 16; "Are Igala Cars Defective?," *Daily Times*, 11 April 1978, 17.
58. "My Experience with the Passat," *Daily Times*, 2 May 1978, 12.
59. Informação para o senhor presidente da república, "Missão comercial à África," 3 March 1976, AAS mre d 1974.03.26, vol. 14, CPDOC/FGV.
60. "Dead Telephones," *Daily Times*, 17 February 1978, 3.
61. Brazilian embassy in Lagos to Foreign Ministry, "Nigéria: Telecomunicações: Comentários desfavoráveis às empresas brasileiras: Remessa de recorte," dispatch 46, 24 February 1978, AHI.
62. Brazilian embassy in Lagos to Foreign Ministry, "Nigéria: Telecomunicações: Campanha contra as firmas brasileiras estabelecidas em Lagos: Artigo na imprensa local," telegram 11, 25 January 1978, AHI.
63. Ibid.
64. Brazilian embassy in Lagos to Foreign Ministry, "Artigo na imprensa local sobre 'Pelé': Remessa de recorte," dispatch 130, 31 May 1978, AHI.
65. Ibid.
66. Santana, *Interbras, ficção e realidade*, 123.
67. Ibid., 124–25.
68. Ibid., 134; Brazilian embassy in Lagos to Foreign Ministry, "Programa de lançamento pela Interbras de produtos de eletrodomésitcos na Nigéria: Participação de Pelé," telegram 139, 24 April 1978, AHI.

69. *Daily Times*, 16 May 1978, 8.
70. Ibid.
71. Brazilian embassy in Lagos to Foreign Ministry, "Programa de lançamento pela Interbras de produtos de eletrodomésitcos na Nigéria: Participação de Pelé," telegram 139, 24 April 1978, AHI.
72. Selcher, "Uncertain Partners," 14.
73. Brazilian embassy in Lagos to Foreign Ministry, "Promoção comercial Brasil-Nigéria: Licenças de importação: Interbras/Jobrás," telegram 1329, 30 April 1979, AHI.
74. Santana, *Interbras, ficção e realidade*," 138.
75. Ibid., 175–76.
76. Ibid., 139.
77. Selcher, "Uncertain Partners," 20.

Epilogue

1. Soares, *Meu casaco de general*, 435; "PF ajudará a investigar atuação de angolanos na chacina no Rio," *Folha de S. Paulo*, 7 February 2000, IV-4.
2. Feranda da Escóssia, "Investigação de angolanos intimida favela," *Folha de S. Paulo*, 9 February 2000, III-5.
3. Carlos Eduardo Lins da Silva, "Angola pede que brasileiros fiquem," *Folha de S. Paulo*, 8 June 1997, I-19.
4. "Brasil diminui acolhida a refugiados," *Folha de S. Paulo*, 23 May 1997, I-18; "Brasil retoma plano para receber famílias afegãs," *Folha de S. Paulo*, 21 November 2001, A-14.
5. Adriana Marcolini, "Crescimento faz angolanos retornarem," *Folha de S. Paulo*, 13 May 2007, A-16; Feranda da Escóssia, "Investigação de angolanos intimida favela," *Folha de S. Paulo*, 9 February 2000, I-2.
6. "Exercício de Imaginação," *Folha de S. Paulo*, 12 Feburary 2000, I-2.
7. Ibid.
8. Ibid.
9. MFAN, "Brasil e áfrica," 3 June 2008, AHI.
10. "Guerreiro: polírica africanista em questão," *Veja*, 3 November 1982, 116, AAS ep 1982.10.13, CPDOC/FGV.
11. Ibid.
12. Ribeiro, "Crise e castigo," 51.
13. Ibid., 53.
14. Sombra Saraiva, *O lugar da África*, 218.
15. "Conferência pronunciada pelo senhor ministro de estado das relações exteriores na Escola de Guerra Naval, Rio de Janeiro," 9 November 1976, AAS mre ag 1974.05.27, CPDOC/FGV.
16. Fico, *Como eles agiam*, 99.
17. Relatório do Grupo de Trabalho Interministerial sobre Direitos Humanos, 22 December 1975, AAS mre ag 1974.03.25, CPDOC/FGV.
18. Posição do Brasil no tratamento internacional a questão dos direitos humanos, n.d., AAS mre ag 1974.03.25, CPDOC/FGV.

19. "Visita do Secretário Vance: As relações com os Estados Unidos (direitos humanos e questão nuclear)," AAS mre be 1977.01.27, CPDOC/FGV.
20. "Política externa brasileira: Características gerais e alguns aspectos regionais," AAS mre be 1977.01.27, CPDOC/FGV.
21. Audiência concedida por Sua Excelência o Presidente Ernesto Geisel à Senhora Carter, 7 June 1977, EG pr 1974.03.18, f-0177, CPDOC/FGV.
22. "Roteiro para conversações presidenciais," AAS mre 1976.00.00, CPDOC/FGV.
23. Informação para o senhor presidente da república, "Festival de Arte e Cultura Afro-Americana no Brasil," 19 June 1978, AAS mre d 1974.03.26, vol. 34, CPDOC/FGV.
24. Gilberto Freyre, "'Africanologistas' excesso de glorificação da negritude," *O Cruzeiro*, 21 December 1963, Artigos de Jornal de Gilberto Freyre, AJ-13, 1963–1964, FGF.
25. Alberti and Pereira, "Qual África?"; Alberto, "When Rio was *Black*." See also Mitchell, "Blacks and the *abertura democrática*"; González, "The Unified Black Movement"; and Skidmore, "Race and Class in Brazil."
26. Camara dos Deputados, Brasil, *Anais do Simpósio relações Brasil-África: uma nova perspectiva* (Brasília: Centro de Coordenação de Publicações, 1986), 108.
27. Interview with Rubens Ricupero, 26 July 2006.
28. Dulce Maria Pereira, "Mandela é referéncia para afro-brasileiros," *Folha de S. Paulo*, 30 May 1999, I-25; Penna Filho, "África do Sul e Brasil," 71.
29. Daniela Nahass, "FHC se define novamente como mestiço," *Folha de S. Paulo*, 14 December 2000, A-13.
30. "FHC elogia bolsas a negros e critica diplomacia do país," *Folha de S. Paulo*, 22 November 2002, A-10.
31. Law 10.639, 9 de janeiro de 2003, Altera a Lei no. 9.394 de 20 de dezembro de 1996, que estabelece as diretrizes e bases da educação nacional, para incluir no currúculo oficial da Rede de Ensino a obrigatoriedade da temática "História e Cultura Afro-Brasileira," e dá outras providências.
32. Cíntia Acayaba, "África Esquecida: Colégios ignoram lei que obriga ensino da cultura afro," *Folha de S. Paulo*, 27 October 2008, C-5; Eduardo Scolese, "Movimento negro cobra de secretaria 'efeitos práticos,'" *Folha de S. Paulo*, 31 January 2008, A-6.
33. Scolese and Nossa, *Viagens com o presidente*, 107.
34. "País perdoou menos dívidas que o anunciado," *Folha de S. Paulo*, 25 December 2008, A-6.
35. Eliane Cantanhêde, "Lula anuncia 'imposto zero' para os produtos Angolanos," *Folha de S. Paulo*, 4 November 2003, A-4.
36. MFAN, "Brasil e África," 3 June 2008, 14, 18, AHI.
37. Janaina Lage, "Comércio dobra, e empresas vivenciam 'febre da África,'" *Folha de S. Paulo*, 16 September 2007; MFAN, "Brasil e África," 3 June 2008, B-13, AHI.
38. "Prateleiras africanas incluem de comida a livros brasileiros," *Folha de S. Paulo*, 16 September 2007, B-18.

39. "Falta de infra-estrutura abre espaço a construtoras do país," *Folha de S. Paulo*, 16 September 2007, B-18; "Brasileiros buscam salário alto e desafios," *Folha de S. Paulo*, 16 September 2007, B-18.
40. "Petrobras e Vale entram em corrida por reservas," *Folha de S. Paulo*, 16 September 2007, B-18.
41. MFAN, "Brasil e África," 3 June 2008, p. 14, AHI.
42. "Lula conversa sobre futebol com brasileiros," *Folha de S. Paulo*, 30 July 2004, A-8.

Bibliography

Newspapers

Afrique Nouvelle, Dakar, Senegal
Correio Braziliense, Brasília
Correio da Manhã, Rio de Janeiro
Daily Graphic, Accra, Ghana
Daily Telegraph, Lagos, Nigeria
Daily Times, Lagos, Nigeria
Diário Carioca, Rio de Janeiro
Diário da Manhã, Lisbon
Diário de Luanda, Luanda, Angola
Diário de Notícias, Lisbon
Diário de Pernambuco, Recife
Diário Popular, Lisbon
Diário Popular, São Paulo
Estado de S. Paulo, São Paulo
Evening News, Accra, Ghana
Financial Times, London
Folha de S. Paulo, São Paulo
Fraternité Matin, Abidjan, Ivory Coast
Gazeta Mercantil, São Paulo
Ghanaian Times, Accra
O Globo, Rio de Janeiro
Independent, Lagos, Nigeria
O Jornal, Rio de Janeiro
Jornal da Tarde, Rio de Janeiro
Jornal de Angola (also *Província de Angola*), Luanda
Jornal do Brasil, Rio de Janeiro

Jornal do Comércio, Rio de Janeiro
New York Times
Nigerian Morning Post, Lagos
Notícias, Maputo, Mozambique
Portugal Democrático, São Paulo
Pretoria News
Le Soleil, Accra, Ghana
Spark, Accra, Ghana
Star, Johannesburg
Sunday Times, Lagos, Nigeria
A Tarde, Salvador
Times of Zambia, Lusaka
Tribuna da Imprensa, Rio de Janeiro
Última Hora, Rio de Janeiro
A Voz de Portugal, Rio de Janeiro
West African Pilot, Lagos, Nigeria

Books and Articles

Abegunrin, Olayiwola. *Nigerian Foreign Policy under Military Rule, 1966–1999*. Westport: Praeger, 2003.

Alberti, Verena, and Amilcar Araujo Pereira. "Entrevista com José Maria Nunes Pereira." *Estudos Históricos* 39 (2007), 121–56.

———. "Qual África? Significados da África para o movimento negro no Brasil." *Estudos Históricos* 39 (2007), 25–56.

Alberto, Paulina. "When Rio Was *Black*: Soul Music, National Culture, and the Politics of Racial Comparison in 1970s Brazil." *Hispanic American Historical Review* 89, no 1 (2009), 3–39.

Alden, Dauril. "Charles R. Boxer, 1904–2000." *Hispanic American Historical Review* 80, no. 4 (2000), 945–49.

Alencastre, Amílcar. *Brasil, África e o futuro*. Rio de Janeiro: Laemmert, 1969.

Alencastro, Luiz Felipe de. *O trato dos viventes: Formação do Brasil no Atlântico Sul*. São Paulo: Nacional, 2000.

Almeida, Paulo Roberto de. *Formação da diplomacia econômica no Brasil: As relações econômicas internacionais no império*. São Paulo: SENAC, 2001.

Amado, Jorge. *Tent of Miracles*. New York: Avon, 1988 [1971].

Amos, Alcione Meira, and Ebenezer Ayesu. "Sou brasileiro: história dos *tabom* afro-brasileiros em Acra, Ghana." *Afro-Ásia* 33 (2005), 35–66.

Andrade, Mário de. "O mito lusotropical." *Isto É*, 19 March 1980, 46–47 [reprint].

Arinos, Afonso, Candido Mendes, and Fernando B. de Ávila. *Senghor em diálogo*. Rio de Janeiro: Instituto Brasileiro de Estudos Afro-Asiáticos, 1965.

Arinos de Melo Franco, Afonso. *Evolução da crise Brasileira*. São Paulo: Nacional, 1965.

———. *Planalto: Memórias*. Rio de Janeiro: José Olympio, 1968.

Arinos Filho, Afonso. *Atrás do espelho*. Rio de Janeiro: Record, 1994.

———. *Diplomacia independente: Um legado de Afonso Arinos*. São Paulo: Paz e Terra, 2001.

Assis, J. Carlos de. *Os mandarins da república: Anatomia dos escândalos na administração pública, 1968–1984*. 7th edn. São Paulo: Paz e Terra, 1984.

Azevedo, Fernando de. *Brazilian Culture: An Introduction to the Study of Culture in Brazil*. New York: Macmillan, 1950.

Azevedo, Thales de. *As elites de cor numa cidade Brasileira: Um estudo de ascenção social*. Rio de Janeiro: Nacional, 1955.

Badji, Honore. "A política externa do Senegal e as relações com o Brasil: Da independência ao final da década de oitenta." M.A. thesis, University of Brasília, 2000.

Ball, George W. *The Past Has Another Pattern: Memoirs*. New York: W. W. Norton, 1982.

Bastos, Cristina, Miguel Vale de Almeida, and Bela Feldman-Bianco, eds. *Trânsitos coloniais: Diálogos críticos luso-brasileiros*. Lisbon: Instituto de Ciências Sociais, 2002.

Bastos, João Pereira. *Angola e Brasil: duas terras lusíadas do Atlântico*. Lourenço Marques: Minerva, 1964.

Bender, Jeremy. *Angola under the Portuguese*. Berkeley: University of California Press, 1978.

Benzaquen de Araújo, Ricardo. *Guerra e paz: Casa-grande e senzala e a obra de Gilberto Freyre nos anos 30*. 2nd edn. São Paulo: Editora 34, 2005.

Bezerra de Menezes, Adolpho Justo. *O Brasil e o mundo Ásio-Africano*. Rio de Janeiro: GRD, 1960.

———. *Ásia, África e a política independente do Brasil*. Rio de Janeiro: Zahar, 1961.

Birmingham, David. *The Decolonization of Africa*. Athens: Ohio University Press, 1995.

———. *Portugal and Africa*. Athens: Ohio University Press, 1999.

———. *A Concise History of Portugal*. 2nd edn. Cambridge: Cambridge University Press, 2003.

Borstelmann, Thomas. *The Cold War and the Color Line: American Race Relations in the Global Arena*. Cambridge: Harvard University Press, 2001.

Boxer, Charles. *Race Relations in the Portuguese Colonial Empire, 1415–1825*. Oxford: Oxford University Press, 1963.

———. *The Portuguese Seaborne Empire, 1415–1825*. New York: Alfred A. Knopf, 1969.

"Brasil e as colônias portuguêsas na África, O." *Política Externa Independente* 1, no. 3 (1966), 191–202.

"Brasil e o mundo Africano, O." *Política Externa Independente* 1, no. 3 (1966), 3–7.

Cardoso, Fernando Henrique, and Mário Soares. *O mundo em Português*. São Paulo: Paz e Terra, 1998.

Carvalho, Delgado de. *África: Geografia social, econômica e política*. Rio de Janeiro: IBGE, 1963.

Carvalho, José Jorge de. *Inclusão étnica e racial no Brasil*. São Paulo: Attar, 2006.

Castelo, Cláudia. *"O modo português de estar no mundo": O luso-tropicalismo e a ideologica colonial portuguesa (1933–1961)*. Porto: Afrontamento, 1999.

Castro, Celso, and Maria Celina D'Araujo, eds. *Dossiê Geisel*. Rio de Janeiro: FGV, 2002.

Castro Gomes, Angela de. *O Brasil de JK*. 2nd edn. Rio de Janeiro: FGV, 2002.

Cervo, Amado Luiz, and Clodoaldo Bueno. *História da política exterior do Brasil*. 3rd edn. Brasília: UNB, 2008.

Cervo, Amado Luiz, and José Calvert de Magalhães. *Depois das caravelas: As relações entre Portugal e o Brasil, 1808–2000*. Lisbon: Instituto Camões, 2000.

Chilcote, Ronald, ed. *Protest and Resistance in Angola and Brazil: Comparative Studies*. Los Angeles: UCLA, 1972.

Comitini, Carlos. *África arde*. Rio de Janeiro: Codecri, 1980.

Condé, Cláudia de Moraes Sarrmento. *Antonio Olinto: O operário da palavra*. 2nd edn. Rio de Janeiro: Univercidade, 2005.

Costa e Silva, Alberto. *O vício da África e outros vícios*. Lisbon: Sá de Costa, 1989.

———. *Um rio chamado Atlântico: A África no Brasil e o Brasil na África*. Rio de Janeiro: UFRJ, 2003.

———. *Das mãos do oleiro: Aproximações*. Rio de Janeiro: Nova Fronteira, 2005.

Costa Pinto, Antonio. *O fim do império português: A cena internacional, a guerra colonial e a descolonização, 1961–1975*. Lisbon: Livros Horizonte, 2001.

Curtin, P. D. "'The White Man's Grave:' Image and Reality, 1750–1850." *Journal of British Studies* 1, no. 1 (1961), 94–110.

Curto, José C., and Renée Soulodre-La France, eds. *Africa and the Americas: Interconnections during the Slave Trade*. Trenton: Africa World, 2005.

D'Adesky, Jacques Edgard. "Brasil-África: Convergência para uma cooperação privilegiada." *Estudos Afro-Asiáticos* 4 (1980), 5–19.

———. "Penetração Brasileira na áfrica Austral: Perspectivas políticas e entraves economicos." *Estudos Afro-Asiáticos* 10 (1984), 95–106.

———. "Pluralismo étnico e multiculturalismo." *Afro-Ásia* 19–20 (2001), 165–82.

Dantas, Beatriz Gois. *Vovó nagô e papai branco: Usos e abusos da África no Brasil*. Rio de Janeiro: Graal, 1988.

D'Araujo, Maria Celina, and Celso Castro, eds. *Ernesto Geisel*. Rio de Janeiro: FGV, 1997.

D'Araujo, Maria Celina, Celso Castro, Carolina Von der Weid, and Dora Rocha. *João Clemente Baena Soares: Sem medo da diplomacia*. Rio de Janeiro: FGV, 2006.

Dáskalos, Sócrates. *Um testemunho para a história de Angola: Do huambo ao huambo*. Lisbon: Vega, 2000.

Davidson, Basil. "Africa's Modern Slavery." *Harper's*, July 1954, 56–64.

Dávila, Jerry. *Diploma of Whiteness: Race and Social Policy in Brazil, 1917–1945*. Durham: Duke University Press, 2003.

———. "O comparativo e o transnacional nos estudos dos Estados Unidos e do Brasil." *Transit Circle: Revista brasileira de estudos americanos* 4 (2005).

Dávila, Jerry, and Zachary Morgan. "Since *Black into White*: Thomas Skidmore on Brazilian Race Relations." *Americas* 64, no. 3 (2008), 409–23.

Dinges, John. *The Condor Years: How Pinochet and His Allies Brought Terrorism to Three Continents*. New York: New Press, 2005.
Dudziak, Mary K. *Cold War Civil Rights: Race and the Image of American Democracy*. Princeton: Princeton University Press, 2000.
Dulles, John W. F. *Castello branco: O presidente reformador*. Brasilia: UNB, 1983.
Dunn, Christopher. *Brutality Garden: Tropicália and the Emergence of a Brazilian Counterculture*. Chapel Hill: University of North Carolina Press, 2001.
Dzidzienyo, Anani. "A África vista do Brasil." *Afro-Ásia* 10–11 (1970), 79–98.
———. "Brazil's View of Africa: 1." *West Africa*, 1972.
———. "Brazil's View of Africa: 2." *West Africa*, 1972.
———. "African (Yoruba) Culture and the Political Kingdom in Latin America." Paper presented at the Conference on Yoruba Civilisation, University of Ife, Nigeria, 1976.
———. "Activity and Inactivity in the Politics of Afro-Latin America." *SECOLAS Annals* 9 (1978).
———. "The African Connection and the Afro-Brazilian Condition." *Race, Class and Power in Brazil*, ed. Pierre-Michel Fontaine. Los Angeles: CAAS, 1985.
———. "Brazil." *International Handbook on Race and Race Relations*, ed. Jay A. Sigler. Westport: Greenwood, 1987.
———. "Abdias do Nascimento as Metaphor." *The Afro-Brazilian Mind: Contemporary Afro-Brazilian Literary and Cultural Criticism*, ed. Niyi Afolabi, Márcio Barbosa, and Esmeralda Ribeiro, 35–44. Trenton: Africa World Press, 2007.
———. "Uma perspectiva Africana continental." *Vivaldo da Costa Lima: Intérprete do Afro-Brasil*, ed. Jéfferson Bacelar and Cláudio Pereira. Salvador: Edufba, 2007.
———. "África e diáspora: Lentes contemporâneas, vistas brasileiras e afro-brasileiras." *A matriz africana no mundo*, ed. Elisa Larkin Nascimento. São Paulo: Selo Negro, 2008.
Ferreira, Manuel Ennes. "Performance económica em situação de guerra: O caso de Angola (1975–1992)." *África* 16–17, no. 1 (1993–94), 135–56.
Fico, Carlos. *Inventando o otimismo: Ditadura, propaganda e imaginário social no Brasil*. Rio de Janeiro: FGV, 1997.
———. *Como eles agiam: Os subterrâneos da ditadura militar*. Rio de Janeiro: Record, 2001.
Figuereido, Antônio de. "A questão racial em Angola e Moçambique." *Politica Externa Independente* 1, no. 3 (1966), 40–56.
Flecha de Lima, Paulo Tarso. "Diplomacia e comércio: Notas sobre a política externa brasileira nos anos 70." *Sessenta anos de política externa brasileira*, ed. José Augusto Guilhon Albuquerque, 219–37. São Paulo: Editora de Cultura, 1996.
Forrest, Tom. "Brazil and Africa: Geopolitics, Trade and Technology in the South Atlantic." *African Affairs* 81, no. 322 (1982), 3–20.
Freyre, Gilberto. *Casa-grande e senzala: Formação da familia brasileira sob o regimen de economia patriarchal*. Rio de Janeiro: Maia e Schmidt, 1933.

———. *Sobrados e mucambos: Decadencia do patriarchado rural no Brasil*. São Paulo: Nacional, 1936.

———. *O mundo que o português criou*. Rio de Janeiro: José Olympio, 1940.

———. *Um brasileiro em terras portuguêsas: Introdução a uma possível luso-tropicologia, acompanhada de conferências e discursos proferidos em Portugal e em terras lusitanas e ex-lusitanas da Ásia, África e do Atlântico*. Rio de Janeiro: José Olympio, 1953.

———. *New World in the Tropics: The Culture of Modern Brazil*. New York: Alfred A. Knopf, 1959.

———. *The Portuguese and the Tropics: Suggestions Inspired by the Portuguese Methods of Integrating Autochthonous Peoples and Cultures Differing from the European in a New, or Luso-Tropical Complex of Civilization*. Lisbon: Executive Committee for the Commemoration of the Vth Centenary of the Death of Prince Henry the Navigator, 1961.

———. *Portuguese Integration in the Tropics*. Lisbon: Executive Committee for the Commemoration of the Vth Centenary of the Death of Prince Henry the Navigator, 1961.

———. "Brasil na face das Áfricas negras e mestiças." *Portugal na África: Revista de cultura missionária* 23 (1966).

———. *Uma cultura ameaçada: A luso-brasileira*. Recife: Gabinete Português de Leitura de Pernambuco, 1989.

———. *Aventura e rotina: Sugestões de uma viagem à procura de constantes portuguesas de caráter e ação*. Rio de Janeiro: Topbooks, 2001.

Frota, Sylvio. *Ideais traídos*. Rio de Janeiro: Zahar, 2006.

Fry, Peter. "Gallus Africanus est, ou como Roger Bastide se tornou Africano no Brasil." *Revisitando a terra de contrastes: A atualidade da obra de Roger Bastide*, ed. Olga R. de Moraes von Simon. São Paulo: USP/FFLCH, 1986.

———. "Duas estórias e uma parábola: Uma experiência de cooperação Brasil-África." *O Brasil na virada do século: O debate dos cientistas sociais*, ed. Glaucia Villas Bôas and Marco Antônio Gonçalves. Rio de Janeiro: Relume Dumará, 1995.

———. *A persistência da raça*. Rio de Janeiro: Civilização Brasileira, 2005.

———, ed. *Moçambique: Ensaios*. Rio de Janeiro: UFRJ, 2001.

Funk, Ray. "In the Battle for Emergent Independence: Calypsos of Decolonization." *Anthurium: A Caribbean Studies Journal* 3, no. 2 (2005).

Gaines, Kevin K. *African Americans in Ghana*. Chapel Hill: University of North Carolina Press, 2006.

Galvão, Henrique. *Angola (para uma nova política)*. Lisbon: Livraria Popular Francisco Franco, 1937.

Garcia, Eugênio Vargas. *Cronologia das relações internacionais do Brasil*. Rio de Janeiro: Contraponto, 2005.

Gaspari, Elio. *A ditadura escancarada*. São Paulo: Nacional, 2002.

———. *A ditadura derrotada*. São Paulo: Companhia Editora das Letras, 2003.

———. *A ditadura encurralada*. São Paulo: Companhia Editora das Letras, 2004.

———. *A ditadura envergonhada*. São Paulo: Companhia Editora das Letras, 2004.

Gérard, A. S., ed. *European-Language Writing in Sub-Saharan Africa*. Budapest: John Benjamins, 1986.

Gibson Barboza, Mário. *Na diplomacia, o traço todo da vida*. 2nd edn. Rio de Janeiro: Francisco Alves, 2002.

Gilroy, Paul. *The Black Atlantic: Modernity and Double Consciousness*. Cambridge: Harvard University Press, 1993.

Gleijeses, Piero. *Conflicting Missions: Havana, Washington and Africa, 1959–1976*. Chapel Hill: University of North Carolina Press, 2002.

Gomes da Costa, Antonio. *O homem português e o Brasil*. Rio de Janeiro: Nordica, 1998.

———. *A brasilidade dos portugueses*. Rio de Janeiro: Nordica, 2002.

Gonçalves, Williams da Silva. "O realismo da fraternidade: As relações Brasil-Portugal no governo Kubitschek." Ph.D. diss., University of São Paulo, 1994.

Gonzalez, Lélia. "The Unified Black Movement: A New Stage in Black Political Mobilization." *Race, Class and Power in Brazil*, ed. Pierre-Michel Fontaine. Los Angeles: CAAS, 1985.

Goulart, João. *Mensagem ao Congresso Nacional, remetida pelo presidente da república na abertura da sessão legislativa de 1963*. Brasília: Imprensa Nacional, 1963.

Green, James. *Beyond Carnival: Male Homosexuality in Twentieth-Century Brazil*. Chicago: University of Chicago Press, 2001.

Guerra, Jacinto. *JK: Triunfo e exílio: Um estadista brasileiro em Portugal*. Brasília: Thesaurus, 2005.

Guimarães, Antonio Sérgio. "Racial Democracy." *Imagining Brazil*, ed. Jesse Souza and Valter Sinder. New York: Lexington, 2005.

———. *Preconceito racial: Modos, temas e tempos*. São Paulo: Cortez, 2008.

Guimarães, Edson. "Progresso técnico e exportações de manufaturados nos países em desenvolvimento: O caso brasileiro." *Estudos Afro-Asiáticos* 11 (1985), 109–17.

Gusmão, Neusa Maria Mendes de. *Os filhos da África em Portugal: Antropologia, multiculturalidade e educação*. Belo Horizonte: Autêntica, 2005.

Harris, Marvin. "Raça, conflito e reforma em Moçambique." *Política Externa Independente* 1, no. 3 (1966), 8–39.

Hernandez, Leila Leite. *A África na sala de aula: Visita à história contemporânea*. São Paulo: Selo Negro, 2005.

Hodges, Tony. *Angola: From Afro-Stalinism to Petro-Diamond Capitalism*. Bloomington: Indiana University Press, 2001.

Hollanda, Luiz Buarque de. *Pierre Verger: A Messenger between Two Worlds*. Synapse, 1998 [documentary film].

Hollinger, David A. "Amalgamation and Hypodescent: The Question of Ethnoracial Mixture in the History of the United States." *American Historical Review* 108, no. 5 (2003), 1363–90.

Howes, Robert. "Damata, Gasparino." *Who's Who in Contemporary Gay and Lesbian History: From World War II to the Present Day*, ed. Robert Aldrich. New York: Routledge, 2001.

Hurrell, Andrew. "The Politics of South Atlantic Security: A Survey of Proposals for a South Atlantic Treaty Organization." *International Affairs* 59, no. 2 (1983), 179–83.

"Igualdade de raças no Brasil, A: Suas raízes históricas." *Cultura Política* 1, no. 1 (1941).

Iñiguez, Carlos Pinheiro. *Sueños paralelos: Gilberto Freyre y el lusotropicalismo: Identidad, cultura y política en Brasil y Portugal*. Buenos Aires: Latinoamericano, 1999.

Isfahani-Hammond, Alexandra. *White Negritude: Race, Writing and Brazilian Cultural Identity*. New York: Palgrave Macmillan, 2007.

Khadiagala, Gilbert M., and Terrence Lyons, eds. *African Foreign Policies: Power and Process*. Boulder: Lynne Rienner, 2001.

Kissinger, Henry. *Years of Renewal*. New York: Simon and Schuster, 1999.

Krenn, Michael L., ed. *The African American Voice in U.S. Foreign Policy since World War II*. New York: Garland, 1998.

Lacerda, Carlos. *Depoimento*. Rio de Janeiro: Nova Fronteira, 1977.

Lafer, Celso. "O Brasil e o mundo." *Brasil: Um século de transformações*, ed. Paulo Sérgio Pinheiro, Jorge Wilheim, and Ignacy Sachs. São Paulo: Companhia das Letras, 2003.

Latham, Michael. *Modernization as Ideology: American Social Science and Nation Building in the Kennedy Era*. Chapel Hill: University of North Carolina Press, 2000.

Le Bouler, Jean-Pierre. *Pierre Fatumbi Verger: Um homem livre*. Salvador: Fundação Pierre Verger, 2002.

Lechini, Gladys Teresita. "A política exterior Argentina para África no marco referencial da política africana do Brasil: O caso da África do Sul na década de 1990." M.A. thesis, University of São Paulo, 2002.

Leitão da Cunha, Vasco. *Diplomacia em alto-mar: Depoimento ao CPDOC*. Rio de Janeiro: FGV, 1994.

Lesser, Jeffrey. *Welcoming the Undesirables: Brazil and the Jewish Question*. Berkeley: University of California Press, 1995.

———. *Negotiating National Identity: Immigrants, Minorities and the Struggle for Ethnicity in Brazil*. Durham: Duke University Press, 1999.

———. *A Discontented Diaspora: Japanese Brazilians and the Meanings of Ethnic Militancy, 1960–1980*. Durham: Duke University Press, 2007.

Lima, Vivaldo da Costa. *A família de santo nos candomblés Jejes-Nagôs da Bahia: Um estudo de relações intergrupais*. Salvador: Corrupio, 2003.

Lindsay, Lisa. "To Return to the Bosom of Their Fatherland": Brazilian Immigrants in Nineteenth-Century Lagos." *Slavery and Abolition* 15, no. 1 (1994), 22–50.

Lins, Álvaro. *Missão em Portugal*. Rio de Janeiro: Civilização Brasileira, 1960.

Macedo, Márcio José de. "Abdias do Nascimento: Trajetória de um negro revoltado (1914–1968)." M.A. thesis, University of São Paulo, 2005.

Madureira, Fernando Pinto. "As relações Brasil-África no contexto da política externa brasileira." Ph.D. diss., University of São Paulo, 1997.

Magalhães, José Calvet de. *Breve história das relações diplomáticas entre Brasil e Portugal*. São Paulo: Paz e Terra, 1999.

Magalhães, Juracy. *Minha experiência diplomática*. Rio de Janeiro: José Olympio, 1971.
Maio, Marcos Chor, and Ricardo Ventura Santos, eds. *Raça, ciência e sociedade*. Rio de Janeiro: FIOCRUZ, 1996.
Martins, José Abílio Lomba. "Guiné-Bissau da década de 50 à actualidade." *Africana* 10, no. 5 (1992), 81–143.
———. "África, comércio e desenvolvimento, I parte: O comércio mundial." *Africana* 12, no. 7 (1993), 113–64.
———. "Sistemas de colonização e conceitos de desenvolvimento, parte II: O debate sobre o desenvolvimento, os novos conceitos e os economistas." *Africana* 20, no. 13 (1999), 13–149.
Marx, Anthony. *Making Race and Nation: A Comparison of the United States, South Africa and Brazil*. New York: Cambridge University Press, 1998.
Matory, J. Lorand. "The English Professors of Brazil: On the Diasporic Roots of the Yoruba Nation." *Comparative Studies in Society and History* 41, no. 1 (1999), 72–103.
———. "The 'Cult of Nations' and the Ritualization of Their Purity." *South Atlantic Quarterly* 100, no. 1 (2001), 171–205.
———. *Black Atlantic Religion: Tradition, Transnationalism, and Matriarchy in the Afro-Brazilian Candomblé*. Princeton: Princeton University Press, 2005.
Maxwell, Kenneth. *The Making of Portuguese Democracy*. Cambridge: Cambridge University Press, 1995.
Meira Mattos, Carlos de. *A geopolítica e as projeções do poder*. Rio de Janeiro: José Olympio, 1977.
Meira Penna, José Osvaldo. *Política externa: Segurança e desenvolvimento*. Rio de Janeiro: Agir, 1967.
Melo, Ovídio de Andrade. *O reconhecimento de Angola pelo Brasil em 1975*. Unpublished memoir, n.d.
Melo Filho, Murilo. *O milagre brasileiro*. Rio de Janeiro: Bloch, 1972.
Meriwether, James H. *Proudly We Can Be Africans: Black Americans and Africa, 1935–1961*. Chapel Hill: University of North Carolina Press, 2002.
Mitchell, Michael. "Blacks and the *abertura democrática*." *Race, Class and Power in Brazil*, ed. Pierre-Michel Fontaine. Los Angeles: CAAS, 1985.
Monteiro, John M. "Raças de gigantes: Mestiçagem e mitografia no Brasil e na Índia Portuguesa." *Trânsitos coloniais: Diálogos críticos luso-brasileiros*, ed. Cristina Bastos, Miguel Vale de Almeida, and Bela Feldman-Bianco, 227–50. Lisbon: Instituto de Ciências Sociais, 2002.
Moore, Carlos. *Castro, the Blacks and Africa*. Los Angeles, CAAS, 1988.
Moraes, Marieta de. "Entrevista com Maria Yedda Linhares." *Estudos Históricos* 5, no. 10 (1992), 216–36.
Morais, Fernando. *Chatô: O rei do Brasil*. São Paulo: Círculo do Livro, 1994.
Morais, Vamberto. "Zimbabwe ou Rodésia?" *Política Externa Independente* 1, no. 3 (1966), 57–63.
Motta, Roberto. "L'invention de L'Afrique dans le candomblé du Brésil." *Storia, antropologia e scienze del linguaggio* 9, nos. 2–3 (1994), 65–85.
Mourão, Fernando Augusto Albuquerque. "O século XIX como fator de decifração das relações Brasil-África." *Studia* 52 (1994), 181–93.

Munteal, Oswaldo, Jaqueline Ventapane, and Adriano de Freixo. *O Brasil de João Goulart: um projeto de nação*. Rio de Janeiro: PUC-Rio, 2006.

Nascimento, Abdias do. *Sitiado em Lagos: Autodefesa de um negro acossado pelo racismo*. Rio de Janeiro: Nova Fronteira, 1981.

———. *O Brasil na mira do pan-africanismo*. 2nd edn. Salvador: EDUFBA/CEAO, 2002.

Needell, Jeffrey. "Identity, Race, Gender, and Modernity in the Origins of Gilberto Freyre's Oeuvre." *American Historical Review* (1995), 51–77.

Nina Rodrigues, Raymundo. *Os africanos no Brasil* São Paulo: Companhia Editora Nacional, 1935.

Noer, Thomas. *Cold War and Black Liberation: The United States and White Rule in Africa, 1948–1968*. Columbia: University of Missouri Press, 1985.

Nórton de Matos, José Mendes Ribeiro. "A minha concepção do império português." *Boletim da Sociedade Luso-Africana*, no. 6 (1933), 3–12.

Nunes, António Pires. *Angola, 1966–1974: Vitória militar no leste*. Lisbon: Tribuna da História, 2002.

Olinto, Antonio. *Brasileiros na África*. Rio de Janeiro: GRD, 1964.

———. *The Water House*. New York: Carroll and Graf, 1985.

Oliveira, Henrique Altemani de. "Política externa brasileira e relações Brasil-África." Ph.D. diss., University of São Paulo, 1987.

Oliveira Lima, Manoel. *O movimento da independência, 1821–1822*. São Paulo: Melhoramentos, 1922.

Ortiz, José M. *Angola: Un abril como giron*. Havana: Política, 1979.

Paim, Rodrigo de Souza. "A política externa brasileira para a República de Angola." *Relaçıes internacionais no mundo atual* 5, no. 5 (2005), 25–48.

Pallares-Burke, Maria Lúcia. *Gilberto Freyre: Um vitoriano vos trópicos*. São Paulo: UNESP, 2005.

Paulo, Heloisa. *"Aqui também é Portugal": A colónia portuguesa do Brasil e o salazarismo*. Coimbra: Quarteto, 2000.

Peixoto, Maria do Carmo de Lacerda, and Antônia Vitoria Aranha, eds. *Universidade pública e inclusão social: Experiência e imaginação*. Belo Horizonte: UFMG, 2008.

Penna Filho, Pio. "África do Sul e Brasil: Diplomacia e comércio (1918–2000)." *Revista brasileira de política internacional* 44, no. 1 (2001), 69–93.

———. "O Itamaraty nos anos de chumbo: O Centro de Informações do Exterior (CIEX) e a repressão no Cone Sul." *Revista Brasileira de Política Internacional* 52 , no. 2 (2009), 43–62.

Penna Filho, Pio, and Antônio Carlos Moraes Lessa. "O Itamaraty e a África: as origens da política africana do Brasil." *Estudos Históricos* 39 (2007), 57–82.

Pereira, José Maria Nunes. "Os estudos Africanos no Brasil e as relações com a África: Um estudo de caso: O CEAA, 1973–1986." M.A. thesis, University of São Paulo, 1991.

Peres, Damião. *Albino Souza Cruz: Uma vida, uma obra, um exemplo*. Lisbon: do Minho, 1961.

Petrus, Maria Regina. "Emigrar de Angola e imigrar no Brasil." M.A. thesis, Federal University of Rio de Janeiro, 2001.

Pinheiro, Letícia. "Brasil, Portugal e descolonização africana (1946–60)." *Contexto Internacional* 9 (1989), 91–111.

———. "'Ao vencedor, as batatas': o reconhecimento da independência de Angola." *Estudos Históricos* 39 (2007), 83–120.

Pinheiro, Paulo Sérgio, Jorge Wilheim, and Ignacy Sachs, eds. *Brasil: Um século de transformações*. São Paulo: Companhia das Letras, 2003.

Pio Correia, Manuel. *O mundo em que vivi*. Rio de Janeiro: Expressão e Cultura, 1995.

Plummer, Brenda Gayle, ed. *Window on Freedom: Race, Civil Rights and Foreign Affairs, 1945–1988*. Chapel Hill: University of North Carolina Press, 2003.

Presidência da República. *Metas e bases para a ação de govêrno*. Brasilia: I.B.G.E., 1970.

Quadros, Jânio. "Brazil's New Foreign Policy." *Foreign Affairs* 40, no. 1 (1961), 19–27.

Quintais, Luís. *As guerras coloniais portuguesas e a invenção da história*. Lisbon: Ciências Sociais, 2000.

Ribeiro, Claudio Oliveira. "Crise e castigo: As relações Brasil-África no governo sarney." *Revista Brasileira de Política Internacional* 51, no. 2 (2008), 39–59.

Rodrigues, José Honório. *Brazil and Africa*. Berkeley: University of California Press, 1965.

Rodrigues, Luís Nuno. *Salazar-Kennedy: A crise de uma aliança*. Lisbon: Noticias Editorial, 2002.

Romo, Anadelia. "Rethinking Race and Culture in Brazil's First Afro-Brazilian Congress of 1934." *Journal of Latin American Studies* 39 (2007), 31–54.

Rui, Manuel. *Quem me dera ser onda*. Lisbon: Cotivia, 1991.

Sansone, Livio, Elisée Soumonni, and Boubacar Barry, eds. *Africa, Brazil and the Construction of Trans Atlantic Black Identities*. Trenton: Africa World Press, 2008.

Santana, Carlos. *Interbras, ficção e realidade: Resposta a "Os mandarins da república."* Rio de Janeiro: Interbras, 1984.

San Tiago Dantas, Francisco Clementino. *Política externa independente*. Rio de Janeiro: Civilização Brasileira, 1962.

Saraíva Guerreiro, Ramiro. *Lembranças de um empregado do Itamaraty*. São Paulo: Siciliano, 1992.

Schopen, Lynn, Hanna Newcombe, Chris Young, and James Wert, eds. *Nations on Record: United Nations General Assembly Roll-Call Votes (1946–1973)*. Oakville-Dundas: Canadian Peace Research Institute, 1975.

Scolese, Eduardo, and Leonencio Nossa. *Viagens com o presidente: Dois repórteres no encalço de lula do planalto ao exterior*, ed. Leonencio Nossa. Rio de Janeiro: Record, 2006.

Scott, James C. *Seeing like a State: How Certain Schemes to Improve the Human Condition Have Failed*. New Haven: Yale University Press, 1998.

Selcher, Wayne. *The Afro-Asian Dimension of Brazilian Foreign Policy*. Gainesville: University of Florida Press, 1974.

———. "Brazil in the International System, 1982–March 1983: The Supremacy of the International System." *Latin American and Caribbean Contemporary Record* 11 (1984), 85–98.

———. "Dilemas políticos nas relações Brasil-África." *Estudos Afro-Asiáticos* 10 (1984), 55–72.

———. "Uncertain Partners: South-South Trade between Brazil and Black Africa." *Managing International Development* 1, no. 1 (1984), 7–23.

Seljan, Zora. *No Brasil ainda tem gente da minha cor?* 2nd edn. Salvador: Prefeitura da Cidade de Salvador, 1978.

Simpósio relações Brasil-África: Uma nova perspectiva, ed. Câmara dos Deputados. Brasília: Câmara dos Deputados, 1986.

Sita Gomes, José Manuel. "Estudantes na terra dos outros: A experiência dos universitários angolanos da Universidade Federal De Minas Gerais, Brasil." M.A. thesis, Federal University of Minas Gerais, 2002.

Skidmore, Thomas E. *Politics in Brazil, 1930–1964: An Experiment in Democracy*. Oxford: Oxford University Press, 1967.

———. "Race and Class in Brazil: Historical Perspectives." *Race, Class and Power in Brazil*, ed. Pierre-Michel Fontaine. Los Angeles: CAAS, 1985.

———. *The Politics of Military Rule in Brazil, 1964–1985*. New York: Oxford University Press, 1988.

———. *Black into White: Race and Nationality in Brazilian Thought*. 2nd edn. Durham: Duke University Press, 1993.

———. "Racial Mixture and Affirmative Action: The Cases of Brazil and the United States." *American Historical Review* 108, no. 3 (2003), 1391–96.

———. "Raízes de Gilberto Freyre." *Gilberto Freyre em quatro tempos*, ed. Ethel Volfzon, Claude Lepine Kosminsky, and Cláudio Arêas Peixoto. São Paulo: UNESP, 2003.

Soares, Luiz Eduardo. *Meu casaco de general: Quinhentos dias no front da segurança pública do Rio de Janeiro*. São Paulo: Companhia das Letras, 2000.

Sombra Saraíva, José Flávio. *O lugar da África: A dimensão atlântica da política externa brasileira (de 1946 a nossos dias)*. Brasilia: UNB, 1996.

———. "A África e o Brasil: Encontros e encruzilhadas." *Ciências e Letras* 21–22 (1998), 115–72.

———. "Política exterior do Governo Lula: O desafio Africano." *Revista Brasileira de Política Internacional* 45, no. 2 (2002), 5–25.

Souto Maior, Luiz Augusto. "A diplomacia econômica brasileira no pós-guerra (1964–1990)." *Sessenta anos de política externa brasileira*, ed. José Augusto Guilhon Albuquerque, 267–96. São Paulo: Editora de Cultura, 1996.

Souza Dantas, Raymundo. *África difícil (missão condenada: diário)*. Rio de Janeiro: Nova Fronteira, 1965.

Soyinka, Wole. *Myth, Literature and the African World*. Cambridge: Cambridge University Press, 1976.

Spektor, Matias. *Kissinger e o Brasil*. Rio de Janeiro: Zahar, 2009.

Spínola, António de. *Portugal e o futuro*. Rio de Janeiro: Nova Fronteira, 1974.

Spitzer, Leo. *Lives in between*. Studies in Comparative World History. Cambridge: Cambridge University Press, 1989.

———. *Hotel Bolivia: Culture and Memory in a Refuge from Nazism*. New York: Hill and Wang, 1998.

Stepan, Alfred, ed. *Authoritarianism in Brazil*. New Haven: Yale University Press, 1974.

Stockwell, John. *In Search of Enemies: A CIA Story*. New York: W. W. Norton, 1978.

Stoler, Ann Laura. *Carnal Knowledge and Imperial Power: Race and the Intimate in Colonial Rule*. Berkeley: University of California Press, 2002.

Taylor, Diana. *The Archive and the Repertoire*. Durham: Duke University Press, 2003.

Teixeira, Moema de Poli. *Negros na universidade: Identidade e trajetórias de ascenção social no Rio de Janeiro*. Rio de Janeiro: Pallas, 2003.

Teles dos Santos, Jocélio. *O poder da cultura e a cultura no poder: A disputa simbólica da herança cultural negra o Brasil*. Salvador: EDUFBA, 2005.

Telles, Edward. *Race in Another America: The Significance of Skin Color in Brazil*. Princeton: Princeton University Press, 2004.

Thomaz, Omar Ribeiro. *Ecos to Atlântico Sul: Representações sobre o terceiro império português*. Rio de Janeiro: UFRJ, 2002.

———. "Tigres de Papel: Gilberto Freyre, Portugal e os países Africanos de língua oficial Portuguesa." *Trânsito Coloniais: Diálogos críticos luso-brasileiros*, ed. Cristina Bastos, Miguel Vale de Almeida, and Bela Feldman-Bianco, 39–64. Lisbon: Instituto de Ciências Sociais, 2002.

Toscano, Daniella Maria Barandier. "A influência do sistema Petrobras sobre a ação externa do governo de Ernesto Geisel." M.A. thesis, University of Brasília, 2004.

Verger, Pierre. *Verger-Bastide: Dimensões de uma amizade*. Rio de Janeiro: Bertrand Brasil, 2002.

———. *Pierre Verger, repórter fotográfico*. Rio de Janeiro: Bertrand Brasil, 2004.

Vianna, Martha. *Uma tempestade como a sua memória: A história de Lia, Maria do Carmo Brito*. Rio de Janeiro: Record, 2003.

Vieira, Sérgio. "Vectores da política externa da Frente de Libertação de Moçambique." *Estudos Moçambicanos* 7 (1990), 31–55.

"Voz Do Senegal, A." *Política Externa Independente* 1, no. 3 (1966): 172–90.

Wiedmann, Luiz Felippe da S., ed. *Brasil: Realidade e desenvolvimento*. Biblioteca do Exército. São Paulo: Editora e Sugestões Literárias, 1972.

Wright, Richard. *Black Power: A Record of Reactions in a Land of Pathos*. New York: Harper and Brothers, 1954.

Wright, Stephen, ed. *African Foreign Policies*. Boulder: Westview, 1999.

Yergin, Daniel. *The Prize: The Epic Quest for Oil, Money and Power*. New York: Free Press, 1991.

Young, Cynthia. *Soul Power: Culture, Radicalism, and the Making of a U.S. Third World Left*. Durham: Duke University Press, 2006.

Index

JERRY DÁVILA

IS A PROFESSOR OF HISTORY

AND LATIN AMERICAN STUDIES AT

THE UNIVERSITY OF NORTH CAROLINA,

CHARLOTTE.

Library of Congress Cataloging-in-Publication Data

Dávila, Jerry, 1970–
Hotel Trópico : Brazil and the challenge of African
decolonization, 1950–1980 / Jerry Dávila.
p. cm.
Includes bibliographical references and index.
ISBN 978-0-8223-4867-2 (cloth : alk. paper)
ISBN 978-0-8223-4855-9 (pbk. : alk. paper)
1. Brazil—Foreign relations—Africa. 2. Africa—Foreign
relations—Brazil. 3. Brazil—Relations—Africa. 4. Africa
—Relations—Brazil. 5. Africa, Portuguese-speaking—
History—20th century. I. Title.
F2523.5.A4D38 2010 327.8106—dc22

2010016650